WHAT EVE

6

MW01490870

BOOK PRICE - $15.00 - POSTAGE PAID

This is the 64th Revised Edition of the book "WHAT EVERY VETERAN SHOULD KNOW," a service officer's guide since 1937. This year, the book has been completely revised and reorganized in an effort to make it easier for the user to quickly find relevant information.

Monthly supplements are available from the publisher, which provide updates to the information contained in this book. A one-year subscription to the supplement service is $27.00

The material herein covers veterans' benefits, rights, privileges and services over which the Veterans Administration has jurisdiction. All references to "VAR" pertain to Veterans Administration Regulations. Revised and new laws passed by the 106th Congress as of November 30, 2000, are incorporated in this text.

This reference book will enable veterans, service officers, and others interested in veterans' benefits to familiarize themselves with the scope of U.S. Federal benefits, services, entitlements, and the best ways to help veterans and their dependents to obtain benefits rightly due.

This guide was prepared solely for convenient reference purposes, and does not have the effect of law. Although diligent effort has been made to ensure its accuracy, in the event of any conflict between this book and any regulation, the latter is, of course, controlling.

You will find a Table of Contents, listing the main subject headings. There is also a complete index arranged in the back of the book for your convenience.

Veterans and the dependents of deceased veterans are advised to contact their local veterans organization service officers, or the nearest Veterans Administration Office, for help in completing any valid claim.

Veterans Information Service
P.O. Box 111
East Moline, Illinois 61244-0111
Telephone and Fax: (309) 757-7760
E-mail: vis111@home.com

SEND FOR YOUR **FREE** SAMPLE COPY OF THE ***MONTHLY SUPPLEMENT,*** DESIGNED TO KEEP THIS BOOK UP-TO-DATE.

★★★★★★★★★★

ONE-YEAR SUPPLEMENT SERVICE: $27.00

"WHAT EVERY VETERAN SHOULD KNOW"

★★★★★★★★★★

Veterans Information Service
P.O. Box 111
East Moline, Illinois 61244-0111

Phone and Fax: (309) 757-7760
E-mail: vis111@home.com

★★★★★★★★★★

A NOTE TO THE READER:

If you have been a reader of our publication in the past, you may notice that the format of this year's book is quite different from previous editions. The 2001 edition has been organized topically, while past editions have been organized alphabetically. This new format has been designed to make it easier for you to find all of the information you need on a certain topic in one location, rather than having to refer to several different areas of the book.

However, if you do not find the information you want, you may find the detailed index in the back of the book helpful, as many subjects have subdivisions.

Extensive research was done when preparing the 2001 edition to eliminate certain information that was no longer appropriate, and to add additional information to bring the book completely up-to-date.

We hope you enjoy this revised edition. Any comments or suggestions for future improvements are welcome.

© 2001
What Every Veteran Should Know
Library of Congress Cataloging in Serials
ISSN 1532-8112
ISBN 0-9670331-2-8

All rights reserved. Printed in the United States of America. No part of this publication may be reproduced, stored in a retrieval system, or transmitted in any form or by any means, electronic, mechanical, photocopying, recording, or otherwise, without the written permission of the publisher.

Publisher: Veterans Information Service
P.O. Box 111
East Moline, IL 61244-0111

TABLE OF CONTENTS

i

★★

★★

★★

★★★

★★

★★★

★★★

★★

★★★

★★★

★★

★★

★★

★★

★★

CHAPTER 1

PERIODS OF WAR

Indian Wars:
The period January 1, 1817 through December 31, 1898. Service must have been rendered with the United States military forces against Indian tribes or nations.

Spanish-American War:
The period April 21, 1898 through July 4, 1902. In the case of a veteran who served with the United States military forces engaged in hostilities in the Moro Province the ending date is July 15, 1903.

Mexican Border Period:
The period May 9, 1916 through April 5, 1917, in the case of a veteran who during such period served in Mexico, on the borders thereof, or in the waters adjacent thereto.

World War I:
The period April 6, 1917, through November 11, 1918. In the case of a veteran who served with the United States military forces in Russia, the ending date is April 1, 1920. Service after November 11, 1918 and before July 2, 1921 is considered World War I for compensation or pension purposes, if the veteran served in the active military, naval, or air service after April 5, 1917 and before November 12, 1918.

World War II:
The period December 7, 1941through December 31, 1946. If the veteran was in service on December 31, 1946, continuous service before July 26, 1947 is considered World War II service.

Korean Conflict:
The period June 27, 1950 through January 31, 1955.

Vietnam Era:
The period August 5, 1964 (February 28, 1961 for Veterans who served "in country" before August 5, 1964), and ending May 7, 1975.

Persian Gulf War:
The period August 2, 1990 through a date to be set by law or Presidential Proclamation.

Future Dates:
The period beginning on the date of any future declaration of war by the Congress, and ending on a date prescribed by Presidential Proclamation or concurrent resolution of the Congress. (Title U.S.C. 101)

★★★

CHAPTER 2

DISABILITY COMPENSATION
FOR SERVICE-CONNECTED DISABILITIES
TITLE 38, CHAPTER 11

BENEFIT DESCRIPTION

In grateful recognition of their dedication and sacrifice, the United States, through the Veterans Administration has provided its former servicemen and women with compensation and pension programs designed to assist disabled veterans and their dependents. The disability compensation program provides financial assistance to veterans with service-connected disabilities to compensate them for the loss of, or reduction in earning power resulting from comparable injuries and disease in civil life.

Disability compensation payments vary in amount, depending on the impairment of earning capacity suffered by the veteran. The degree is assessed in multiples of 10, from 10 percent to 100 percent, with special statutory rates for such disabilities as blindness and loss of use of limbs.

The VA shall adopt and apply a schedule of ratings in reductions in earning capacity from specific injuries or combination of injuries. The rating shall be based, as far as practicable, upon the average impairments of earning capacity resulting from such injuries in civil occupations. The Administrator shall from time to time readjust this schedule or ratings in accordance with experience.

If a veteran is evaluated as having a service-connected disability of 30 percent or more, the veteran is entitled to additional allowances for his or her dependents.

WAR TIME DISABILITY COMPENSATION

Eligibility

A veteran may be entitled to VA disability compensation for any medical condition or injury that was incurred in, or aggravated by his or her military service. The veteran must have been discharged or released under conditions other than dishonorable from the period of service in which the injury or disease was incurred or aggravated.

No compensation shall be paid if the disability is a result of the person's own willful misconduct or abuse of alcohol or drugs.

There is no time limit for applying for VA disability compensation. However, veterans are encouraged to apply within one year of release from active duty. If a claim is filed within this period, entitlement may be established retroactively to the date of separation from service. If a claim is filed beyond one year of release from active duty, the effective date of eligibility for benefits will be based upon the date of the claim, not the date of separation.

★★

Other Benefits Or Payments That May Affect VA Disability Compensation

By law, receipt of certain types of military pay may affect an individual's eligibility for VA Disability Compensation. Following are the categories of pay that may affect eligibility:

Military Retired Pay

The receipt of military retired pay affects the payment of VA disability compensation. If a veteran receives military retirement benefits, he or she must sign a waiver of retired pay in order to receive the full amount of VA disability compensation. Until a waiver is signed and takes effect, VA disability compensation will be adjusted or withheld, depending on the amount of military retired pay being received. (While this is a choice that must be made individually, one important consideration is that VA benefits are reportable for Federal tax purposes, but are not taxable. Veterans should check with the Internal Revenue Service for more tax information.)

Military Disability Severance Pay

The receipt of military disability severance pay and VA disability compensation for the same medical condition or disability is prohibited. If payment of both types is made, VA disability compensation will be withheld on a monthly basis until the total amount of military severance pay has been recovered.

Special Separation Benefit (SSB)

If a veteran has received special separation benefits, VA disability compensation will be withheld in full until the amount of the SSB has been recovered.

Voluntary Separation Incentive (VSI)

If a veteran has received a voluntary separation incentive, his or her annual VSI payment will be reduced by an amount equal to the amount of VA disability compensation for the same period.

Selected Reserve and National Guard

VA disability compensation is not payable to veterans while serving full-time on active duty in the Selected Reserve or National Guard. Additionally, if a veteran is an active member of the Selected Reserve or National Guard, VA disability compensation will be withheld at the rate of one day of pay for each drill period served.

★★

Benefit Rates For Service-Connected Disability Compensation

The first chart shows the basic monthly benefit payable. However, depending on the disability rating of the veteran, there are additional allowances for a spouse, children, children over age 18 & attending school, and parents. The additional charts show these rates in detail.

Basic Rates of Disability Compensation – Rates Effective December 1, 2000:		
Title 38, USC 1114 subsection:	**Disability Rating**	**Monthly Benefit:**
(a)	10 percent	$ 101.00
(b)	20 percent	194.00
(c)	30 percent	298.00
(d)	40 percent	427.00
(e)	50 percent	609.00
(f)	60 percent	769.00
(g)	70 percent	969.00
(h)	80 percent	1125.00
(i)	90 percent	1266.00
(j)	100 percent	2107.00

Detailed Rates of Disability Compensation – Rates Effective December 1, 2000:										
DEPEN-DENT STATUS	**DISABILITY RATING**									
	10%	20%	30%	40%	50%	60%	70%	80%	90%	100%
Veteran Alone	$101	$194	$298	$427	$609	$769	$969	$1125	$1266	$2107
Veteran & Spouse	101	194	334	475	669	841	1053	1221	1374	2228
Veteran & Spouse & 1 Child	101	194	360	510	713	893	1114	1291	1453	2315
Veteran & No Spouse & 1 Child	101	194	322	459	650	818	1026	1190	1339	2189

★★★

Detailed Rates of Disability Compensation –
(Continued from previous page)
Rates Effective December 1, 2000:

DEPEN-DENT STATUS	DISABILITY RATING									
Veteran & Spouse & No Children & 1 Parent	101	194	363	514	718	899	1121	1299	1462	2326
Veteran & Spouse & 1 Child & 1 Parent	101	194	389	549	762	951	1182	1369	1541	2413
Veteran & Spouse & No Children & 2 Parents	101	194	392	553	767	957	1189	1377	1550	2424
Veteran & Spouse & 1 Child & 2 Parents	101	194	418	588	811	1009	1250	1447	1629	2511
Veteran & No Spouse & No Children & 1 Parent	101	194	327	466	658	827	1037	1203	1354	2205
Veteran & No Spouse & 1 Child & 1 Parent	101	194	351	498	699	876	1094	1268	1427	2287
Veteran & No Spouse & No Children & 2 Parents	101	194	356	505	707	885	1105	1281	1442	2303
Veteran & No Spouse & 1 Child & 2 Parents	101	194	380	537	748	934	1162	1346	1515	2385

ADDITIONAL AMOUNT PAYABLE FOR SPOUSE REQUIRING AID & ATTENDANCE
(Rates Effective December 1, 2000)

Disability Rating	30%	40%	50%	60%	70%	80%	90%	100%
Monthly Benefit	$32	$43	$54	$65	$76	$87	$98	$108

ADDITIONAL AMOUNT PAYABLE FOR EACH ADDITIONAL CHLD UNDER AGE 18
(Rates Effective December 1, 2000)

Disability Rating	30%	40%	50%	60%	70%	80%	90%	100%
Monthly Benefit	$18	$25	$31	$37	$44	$50	$56	$63

ADDITIONAL AMOUNT PAYABLE FOR EACH ADDITIONAL CHLD OVER AGE 18 ATTENDING SCHOOL *(Rates Effective December 1, 2000)*								
Disability Rating	30%	40%	50%	60%	70%	80%	90%	100%
Monthly Benefit	$57	$76	$96	$115	$134	$153	$172	$192

Notes:
Rates for Children over age 18 attending school are shown separately in the above chart. All other entries in the above charts reflect rates for children under age 18, or helpless.

All references in the preceding charts to parents refer to parents who have been determined to be dependent by the Secretary of Veterans Affairs.

Higher Statutory Awards for Certain Multiple Disabilities

Title 38, USC 1114 subsection (k)
If a veteran, as the result of a service-connected disability, has suffered the anatomical loss or loss of use of one or more creative organs, or one foot, or one hand, or both buttocks, or blindness of one eye, having only light perception, or has suffered complete organic aphonia with constant inability to communicate by speech, or deafness of both ears, having absence of air and bone conduction, the rate of compensation shall be **$78** per month for each such loss or loss of use.

This additional amount is independent of any other disability compensation provided in subsections (a) through (j) of the above table, or subsection (s) described below; however, in no event may the total amount exceed **$2,621** per month.

In the event the veteran has suffered one or more of the disabilities previously specified in this subsection, in addition to the requirement for any of the rates specified in subsections (l) through (n), described below, the rate of compensation shall be increased by **$78** per month for each such loss or loss of use, but in no event may exceed **$3,677** per month.

Title 38, USC 1114 subsection (l)
If the veteran, as the result of a service-connected disability, has suffered the anatomical loss or loss of use of both feet, or of one hand and one foot, or is blind in both eyes, with 5/200 visual acuity or less, or is permanently bedridden or so helpless as to be in need of regular aid and attendance, the monthly compensation shall be **$2,621**.

Title 38, USC 1114 subsection (m)
If the veteran, as the result of a service-connected disability, has suffered the anatomical loss or loss of use of both hands, or of both legs at a level, or with complications, preventing natural knee action with prostheses in place, or of one arm and one leg at levels, or with complications ,preventing natural elbow and knee action with prostheses in place, or has suffered blindness in both eyes, having only light perception, or has suffered blindness in both eyes, rendering

★★★

such veteran so helpless as to be in need of regular aid and attendance, the monthly compensation shall be **$2,891.**

Title 38, USC 1114 subsection (n)
If the veteran, as the result of a service-connected disability, has suffered the anatomical loss or loss of use of both arms at levels, or with complications, preventing natural elbow action with prostheses in place, has suffered the anatomical loss of both legs so near the hip as to prevent the use of prosthetic appliances, or has suffered the anatomical loss of one arm and one leg so near the shoulder and hip as to prevent the use of prosthetic appliances, or has suffered the anatomical loss of both eyes, or has suffered blindness without light perception in both eyes, the monthly compensation shall be **$3,290.**

Title 38, USC 1114 subsection (o)
If the veteran, as the result of a service-connected disability, has suffered disability under conditions which would entitle such veteran to two or more of the rates provided in one or more subsections (l) through (n) of this section, no condition being considered twice in the determination, or if the veteran has suffered bilateral deafness (and the hearing impairment in either one or both ears is service connected) rated at 60% or more disabling, and the veteran has also suffered service-connected total blindness with 5/200 visual acuity or less, or if the veteran has suffered service-connected total deafness in one ear or bilateral deafness (and the hearing impairment in either one or both ears is service connected) rated at 40% or more disabling, and the veteran has also suffered service-connected blindness having only light perception or less, or if the veterans has suffered the anatomical loss of both arms so near the shoulder as to prevent the use of prosthetic appliances, the monthly compensation shall be **$3,677.**

Title 38, USC 1114 subsection (p)
In the event a veteran's service-connected disabilities exceed the requirements for any of the rates previously prescribed in this section, the Secretary of Veterans Affairs may allow the next higher rate, or an intermediate rate, but in no event in excess of **$3,677.**

In the event a veteran has suffered service-connected blindness with 5/200 visual acuity or less, and (1) has also suffered bilateral deafness (and the hearing impairment in either one or both ears is service connected) rated at no less than 30% disabling, the Secretary of Veterans Affairs shall allow the next higher rate, or (2) has also suffered service-connected total deafness in one ear or service-connected anatomical loss or loss of use of one hand or one foot, the Secretary shall allow the next intermediate rate, but in no event in excess of **$3,677.**

In the event a veteran has suffered service-connected blindness, having only light perception or less, and has also suffered bilateral deafness (and the hearing impairment in either one or both ears is service-connected) rated at 10 or 20% disabling, the Secretary shall allow the next intermediate rate, but in no event in excess of **$3,677.**

In the event a veteran has suffered the anatomical loss or loss of use, or a combination of anatomical loss and loss of use, of three extremities, the Secretary shall allow the next higher rate or intermediate rate, but in no event in excess of **$3,677.**

★★

Any intermediate rate under this subsection shall be established at the arithmetic mean, rounded down to the nearest dollar, between the two rates concerned.

Title 38, USC 1114 subsection (q)
This subsection was repealed by Public Law 90-493.

Title 38, USC 1114 subsection (r)
If a veteran is entitled to compensation under (o) of this section, at the maximum rate authorized under (p) of this section, or at the intermediate rate authorized between the rates authorized under subsections (n) and (o) of this section and at the rate authorized under subsection (k) of this section, is in need of regular aid and attendance, then, in addition to such compensation:

- The veteran shall be paid a monthly aid and attendance allowance at the rate of **$5,255**; or

- If the veteran, in addition to such need for regular aid and attendance, is in need of a higher level of care, such veteran shall be paid a monthly aid and attendance allowance at the rate of $6,027, in lieu of the allowance authorized in the previous paragraph. (Need for a higher level of care shall be considered to be need for personal health-care services provided on a daily basis in the veteran's home by a person who is licensed to provide such services or who provides such services under the regular supervision of a licensed health-care professional. The existence of the need for such care shall be determined by a physician employed by the VA, or in areas where no such physician is available, by a physician carrying out such function under contract or fee arrangement based on an examination by such physician).

Title 38, USC 1114 subsection (s)
If a veteran has a service-connected disability rated as total, and:

Has additional service-connected disability or disabilities independently ratable at 60% or more; or
By reason of such veteran's service-connected disability or disabilities, is permanently housebound, then the monthly compensation shall be **$2,359**.

For the purposes of this subsection, the requirement of "permanently housebound" will be considered to have been met when the veteran is substantially confined to such veteran's house (ward or clinical areas, if institutionalized) or immediate premised due to a service-connected disability or disabilities which it is reasonable certain will remain throughout such veteran's lifetime.

Title 38, USC 1114 subsection (t)
This subsection was repealed by Public Law 99-576.

★★★

Additional Compensation For Dependents (38 USC 1115)

Any veteran entitled to compensation under 38 USC 1114, and whose disability is rated not less than 30%, shall be entitled to additional compensation for dependents in the following monthly amounts:

If and while the veteran is rated totally disabled and:

1.	Has a spouse but no child living:	$121.00
2.	Has a spouse and one child living:	208.00
	(plus for each additional living child under age 18):	63.00
3.	Has no spouse, but one child living:	82.00
4.	(plus for each additional living child under age 18):	63.00
5.	Has a mother or father, either or both dependent upon him for support - for each parent so dependent:	98.00
6.	For a spouse who is a patient in a nursing home, or who is so helpless or blind as to require the regular aid and attendance of another person:	108.00 for a totally disabled veteran, and proportionate amounts for partially disabled veterans.
7.	For each child who is between the ages of 18-23, and who is pursuing a course of instruction at an approved educational institution:	192.00 for a totally disabled veteran, and proportionate amounts for partially disabled veterans.

NEW BENEFITS FOR SEVERELY DISABLED LENGTH OF SERVICE MILITARY RETIREES

Section 658 of the National Defense Authorization Act for Fiscal Year 1999, Public Law 106-65, dated October 5, 1999, (Title 10 U.S.C.1413) provided a "special compensation" for severely disabled length of service retirees of the Uniformed Services. This benefit is administered by the Department of Defense (DoD). This benefit is not paid by VA.

Eligibility

In order to be eligible to receive this special compensation veterans must meet the following criteria:

- They must have completed at least 20 years of uniformed service that are creditable for purposes of computing the amount of retired pay; and

- They must have retired for reasons other than disability; and

- They must have received a disability rating of at least 70% from VA within four years after leaving uniformed service.

★★★

DoD determines who is entitled to this payment based on data provided by the Department of Veterans Affairs (VA). The eligible retiree is entitled to this monthly benefit on or after October 1, 1999.

Amount Of "Special Compensation"

The amount of Special Compensation is determined according to the current disability rating (for the month of entitlement) as reported by the VA to DoD:

- $100 for a disability rating of 70 or 80 percent;
- $200 for a disability rating of 90 percent, and
- $300 for a disability rating of 100 percent or (IU).

Payments of the "Special Compensation" should have begun in early 2000. All payments should have been made retroactively to October 1, 1999.

Taxation of "Special Compensation"

Special Compensation paid under 10 USC 1413 is taxable income within the meaning of section 61 of the Internal Revenue Code.

Adjustment To Individual VA Awards

There will be no adjustment of VA awards. Special Compensation paid under 10 USC 1413 is provided under chapter 71, title 10, USC, "Computation of Retired Pay." However, it is NOT RETIRED PAY. It is to be paid from funds appropriated for pay and allowances of the recipient member's branch of service. Eligible retirees in receipt of VA disability compensation may receive this special compensation in addition to their VA disability compensation.

PRESUMPTIONS

Presumption Of Sound Condition

Every veteran will be assumed to have been in sound medical condition when examined, accepted, and enrolled for service, except any defects, infirmities, or disorders noted at the time of the examination, acceptance, and enrollment, or if there is clear and unmistakable evidence showing that the injury or disease did exist before acceptance and enrollment, and the injury or disease was not aggravated by such service.

Chronic Diseases:
- Anemia, primary
- Arteriosclerosis
- Arthritis
- Atrophy, progressive muscular
- Brain hemorrhage
- Brain thrombosis
- Bronchiectasis
- Calculi of the kidney, bladder, or gallbladder
- Cardiovascular-renal disease, including hypertension
- Cirrhosis of the liver
- Coccidiodomycosis

- Diabetes mellitus
- Encephalitis lethargica residuals
- Endocarditis
- Endocrinopathies
- Epilepsies
- Hansen's disease
- Hodgkin's disease
- Leukemia
- Lupus erythematosus, systemic
- Myasthenia gravis
- Myelitis
- Myocarditis
- Nephritis
- Organic diseases of the nervous system
- Osteitis deformans (Paget's disease)
- Osteomalacia
- Palsy, bulbar
- Paralysis agitans
- Psychoses
- Purpura idiopathic, hemorrhagic
- Raynaud's disease
- Sarcoidosis
- Scleroderma
- Sclerosis, amyotrohpic lateral
- Sclerosis, multiple
- Syringomyelia
- Thromboangiitis obilterans (Buerger's disease)
- Tuberculosis, active
- Tumors, malignant, or of the brain or spinal cord or peripheral nerves
- Ulcers, peptil (gastric or duodenal)
- Other chronic diseases the Secretary of Veterans Affairs may add to this list.

Tropical Diseases:
- Amebiasis
- Blackwater fever
- Cholera
- Dracontiasis
- Dysentery
- Filiariasis
- Hansen's disease
- Leishmaniasis, including kala-azar
- Loiasis
- Malaria
- Onchocerciasis
- Oroya fever
- Pinta
- Plague
- Schistosomiasis
- Yaws
- Yellow fever
- Other tropical diseases the Secretary of Veterans Affairs may add to this list.

★★

Presumptions Of Service-Connection Relating To Certain Diseases And Disabilities

In the case of any veteran who served for 90 days or more during a period of war, any of the following shall be considered to have been incurred in, or aggravated by such service, notwithstanding there is no record of evidence of such disease during the period of service:

- A chronic disease becoming manifest to a degree of 10% or more within one year from the date of separation from such service.

- A tropical disease, and the resultant disorders or disease originating because of therapy, administered in connection with such diseases, or as a preventative thereof, becoming manifest to a degree of 10% or more within one year from the date of separation from such service. Additionally, if it is shown to exist at a time when standard and accepted treatises indicate that the incubation period thereof commenced during active service, it shall be deemed to have incurred during such service.

- Active tuberculosis disease developing a 10% degree of disability or more within 3 years from the date of separation from such service.

- Multiple sclerosis developing a 10% degree of disability or more within seven years from the date of separation from such service.

- Hansen's disease developing a 10% degree of disability or more within three years from the date of separation from such service.

Presumptions Of Service-Connection Relating To Certain Diseases And Disabilities For Former Prisoners Of War

In the case of any veteran who is a former prisoner of war, and who was detained or interned for not less than thirty days, any of the following which became manifest to a degree of 10% or more after active military, naval or air service, shall be considered to have been incurred in or aggravated by such service, notwithstanding that there is no record of such disease during the period of service:

- Avitaminosis
- Beriberi (including beriberi heart disease)
- Chronic dysentery
- Helminthiasis
- Malnutrition (including optic atrophy associated with malnutrition)
- Pellagra
- Any other nutritional deficiency
- Psychosis
- Any of the anxiety states
- Dysthymic disorder (or depressive neurosis)
- Organic residuals of frostbite, if the VA determines the veteran was interned in climatic conditions consistent with the occurrence of frostbite
- Post-traumatic osteoarthritis
- Peripheral neuropathy, except where directly related to infectious causes
- Irritable bowel syndrome
- Peptic ulcer disease

★★★

Presumptions Relating To Certain Diseases Associated With Exposure To Radiation

VA may pay compensation for radiogenic diseases under two programs specific to radiation-exposed veterans and their survivors:

Statutory List

Veterans who participated in nuclear tests by the U.S. or its allies, who served with the U.S. occupation forces in Hiroshima or Nagasaki, Japan, between August 1945 and July 1946, or who were similarly exposed to ionizing radiation while a prisoner of war in Japan, are eligible for compensation for cancers specified in legislation.

The 15 types of cancer covered by these laws are:

- All forms of leukemia except chronic lymphocytic leukemia;
- Cancer of the thyroid,
- Cancer of the breast,
- Cancer of the pharynx,
- Cancer of the esophagus,
- Cancer of the stomach,
- Cancer of the small intestine,
- Cancer of the pancreas,
- Cancer of the bile ducts,
- Cancer of the gall bladder,
- Cancer of the salivary gland,
- Cancer of the urinary tract,
- Lymphomas (except Hodgkin's disease),
- Multiple myeloma,
- Primary liver cancer.

Regulatory List

Disability compensation claims of veterans who were exposed to radiation in service and who develop a disease within specified time periods not specified in the statutory list are governed by regulation. Under the regulations, various additional factors must be considered in determining service-connection, including amount of radiation exposure, duration of exposure, and elapsed time between exposure and onset of the disease. VA regulations identify all cancers as potentially radiogenic, as well as certain other non-malignant conditions: posterior subcapsular cataracts; non-malignant thyroid nodular disease; parathyroid adenoma; and tumors of the brain and central nervous system.

A final rule that expanded the regulatory list from more than a dozen specific cancers to add "any other cancer" (any malignancy) was published Sept. 24, 1998. The rulemaking began following a 1995 review of the radiogenicity of cancer generally by the Veterans Advisory Committee on Environmental Hazards. It concluded that, on the basis of current scientific knowledge, exposure to ionizing radiation can be a contributing factor in the development of any malignancy. VA also will consider evidence that diseases other than those specified in regulation may be caused by radiation exposure.

★★

Presumptions Of Service-Connection For Diseases Associated With Exposure To Certain Herbicide Agents

A disease specified below, becoming manifest in a veteran, who, during active military, naval, or air service, served in the Republic of Vietnam during the period beginning on January 9, 1962, and ending on May 7, 1975 shall be considered to have been incurred in or aggravated by such service, notwithstanding that there is no record of evidence of such disease during the period of such service.

The diseases referred to above are:

- Non-Hodgkin's lymphoma becoming manifest to a degree of disability of 10% or more.

- Each soft-tissue sarcoma becoming manifest to a degree of disability of 10% ore more other than osteosarcoma, chondrosarcoma, Kaposi's sarcoma, or mesothelioma.

- Chloracne or another acne form disease consistent with chloracne becoming manifest to a degree of disability of 10% or more within one year after the last date on which the veteran performed active military, naval, or air service in the Republic of Vietnam during the period beginning on January 9, 1962, and ending on May 7, 1975.

- Hodgkin's disease becoming manifest to a degree of disability of 10% ore more.

- Porphyria cutanea tarda becoming manifest to a degree of disability of 10% ore more within a year after the last date on which the veteran performed active military, naval, or air service in the Republic of Vietnam during the period beginning on January 9, 1962, and ending on May 7, 1975.

- Respiratory cancers (cancer of the lung, bronchus, larynx, or trachea) becoming manifest to a degree of 10% or more within 30 years after the last date on which the veteran performed active military, naval, or air service in the Republic of Vietnam during the period beginning on January 9, 1962, and ending on May 7, 1975.

- Multiple myeloma becoming manifest to a degree of disability of 10% or more.

- Acute and subacute peripheral neuropathy.

- Prostate cancer.

- On November 9, 2000, VA issued a News Release stating that Diabetes Mellitus (Type-II, adult onset diabetes) is being added to the list of presumptive diseases associated with herbicide exposure. As of the writing of this book, the VA is still writing the final rules for implementing this change. Interested veterans should contact the VA for the latest information.

- Each additional disease (if any) that the Secretary of the VA determines warrants a presumption of service-connection by reason of having positive association with exposure to an herbicide agent, becomes manifest within the period (if any) prescribed in such regulations in a veteran who, during active military, naval, or air service, served in the Republic of Vietnam during the period beginning on January 9, 1962 and ending on May 7, 1975, and while so serving was exposed to that herbicide agent.

Veterans having a disease referred to above, shall be presumed to have been exposed during such service to an herbicide agent containing dioxin or 2,4-dichlorophenoxyacetic acid, and may be presumed to have been exposed during such service to any other chemical compound in an herbicide agent, unless there is affirmative evidence to establish that the veteran was not exposed to any such agent during that service.

If the Secretary of the VA later determines that a previously established presumption of service-connection for one of the above diseases is no longer warranted, all veterans currently awarded compensation on the basis of the presumption shall continue to be entitled to receive compensation. Additionally, all survivors of any such veterans who were awarded dependency and indemnity compensation shall continue to be entitled to receive dependency and indemnity compensation on that basis.

Presumptions Of Service-Connection For Illnesses Associated With Service In The Persian Gulf During The Persian Gulf War

The VA may pay compensation to any Persian Gulf veteran suffering from a chronic disability resulting from an undiagnosed illness (or combination of undiagnosed illnesses) that:

- Became manifest during service on active duty in the Armed Forces in the Southwest Asia theater of operations during the Persian Gulf War; or

- Became manifest to a degree of 10% or more within the presumptive period prescribed below.

Presumptive Period

The Secretary of the VA shall prescribe by regulation the period of time following service in the Southwest Asia theater, or operations during the Persian Gulf War, which the Secretary determines is appropriate for presumption of service-connection. These determinations of such periods of time shall be made following a review of any available credible medical or scientific evidence, and the historical treatment afforded disabilities for which manifestation periods have been established, and shall take into account other pertinent circumstances regarding the experiences of the Persian Gulf War.

If the Secretary of the VA later determines that a previously established presumption of service-connection for an undiagnosed illness is no longer warranted, all veterans currently awarded compensation on the basis of the presumption shall continue to be entitled to receive compensation. Additionally, all survivors of any such veterans who were awarded dependency and indemnity compensation shall continue to be entitled to receive dependency and indemnity compensation on that basis.

Any diagnosed or undiagnosed illness becoming manifest within the prescribed period (if any) that the Secretary of the VA determines to warrant a presumption of service-connection (by reason of having a positive association with exposure to a biological, chemical, or other toxic agent, environmental or wartime hazard, or preventive medicine or vaccine known or presumed to be associated with service in the Armed Forces in the Southwest Asia theater of operations during the Persian Gulf War) shall be considered to have been incurred in or aggravated by service, notwithstanding that there is no record of evidence of such illness during the period of such service.

★★★

For purposes of this subsection, a veteran who served on active duty in the Southwest Asia theater of operations during the Persian Gulf War, and has an illness described in the previous paragraph, shall be presumed to have been exposed by reason of such service to the agent, hazard, or medicine or vaccine associated with the illness in the regulations prescribed under this section, unless there is conclusive evidence to establish that the veteran was not exposed to the agent, hazard, medicine or vaccine by reason of such service.

Presumptions Rebuttable

If there is affirmative evidence to the contrary, or evidence to establish that an intercurrent injury or disease which is a recognized cause of any of the diseases or disabilities mentioned in the above sections, has been suffered between the date of separation from service and the onset of any such diseases or disabilities, or if the disability is due to the veteran's own willful misconduct, payment of compensation shall not be made.

Special Provisions Relating To Claims Based Upon Effects Of Tobacco Products

Effective July 22, 1998, a veteran's death or disability will not be considered to have resulted from personal injury suffered, or disease contracted in the line of duty if the injury or disease is attributable to the use of tobacco products by the veteran during the veteran's service.

PEACETIME DISABILITY COMPENSATION

Basic Entitlement

A veteran may be entitled to VA disability compensation for any medical condition or injury that was incurred in, or aggravated by his or her military service, during any period other than a period of war. The veteran must have been discharged or released under conditions other than dishonorable from the period of service in which the injury or disease was incurred or aggravated.

No compensation shall be paid if the disability is a result of the person's own willful misconduct or abuse of alcohol or drugs.

Presumption of Sound Condition

Every person employed in the active military, naval, or air service during any period other than a period of war, for 6 months or more, will be assumed to have been in sound medical condition when examined, accepted, and enrolled for service, except any defects, infirmities, or disorders noted at the time of the examination, acceptance, and enrollment, or if there is clear and unmistakable evidence showing that the injury or disease did exist before acceptance and enrollment, and the injury or disease was not aggravated by such service.

Presumptions Relating to Certain Diseases

If a veteran who served in the active military, naval, or air service after December 31, 1946, during any period other than a period of war, for 6 months

★★

or more, contracts any of the following, it shall be considered to have been incurred in, or aggravated by such service, notwithstanding there is no record of evidence of such disease during the period of service:

- A chronic disease becoming manifest to a degree of 10% or more within one year from the date of separation from such service.

- A tropical disease, and the resultant disorders or disease originating because of therapy, administered in connection with such diseases, or as a preventative thereof, becoming manifest to a degree of 10% or more within one year from the date of separation from such service. Additionally, if it is shown to exist at a time when standard and accepted treatises indicate that the incubation period thereof commenced during active service, it shall be deemed to have incurred during such service.

- Active tuberculosis disease developing a 10% degree of disability or more within 3 years from the date of separation from such service.

- Multiple sclerosis developing a 10% degree of disability or more within seven years from the date of separation from such service.

- Hansen's disease developing a 10% degree of disability or more within three years from the date of separation from such service.

In the case of any veteran who served for 90 days or more during a period of war, service-connection will not be granted in any case where the disease or disorder is shown by clear and unmistakable evidence to have had its inception before or after active military, naval, or air service.

Presumptions Rebuttable

If there is affirmative evidence to the contrary, or evidence to establish that an intercurrent injury or disease which is a recognized cause of any of the diseases or disabilities mentioned in the above sections, has been suffered between the date of separation from service and the onset of any such diseases or disabilities, or if the disability is due to the veteran's own willful misconduct, payment of compensation shall not be made.

Rates Of Peacetime Disability Compensation

The compensation payable shall be the same as the compensation payable for Wartime Disability Compensation. (Please refer to the charts beginning on page 4 of this book.)

Additional Compensation For Dependents

Any veteran entitled to peacetime disability compensation, and whose disability is rated as 30% or greater, will be entitled to additional monthly compensation for dependents in the same amounts payable for Wartime Disability Compensation. Please refer to the charts beginning on page 4.

GENERAL DISABILITY COMPENSATION PROVISIONS

Cost-Of-Living Adjustments

Cost-of-living adjustments for fiscal years 1998 through 2002 will be made by a uniform percentage, that is no more than the percentage equal to the social security increase for that fiscal year. All increased monthly rates and limitations (other than increased rates and limitations equal to a whole dollar amount) will be rounded down to the next lower whole dollar amount.

How To Apply For Disability Compensation Benefits

In order to apply for disability compensation benefits from the VA, Form 21-526, Veteran's Application for Compensation or Pension, must be completed and returned to the VA Regional Office serving the veteran's area (refer to page 292 for a listing of regional offices). In addition to the application, the following documents must be submitted:

- Service Medical Records: In order to expedite processing of the claim, if an applicant has his or her service medical records, they should be submitted with the application. If not included with the application, VA will contact the veteran's service department to obtain them.

- Other Medical Records: Any medical records from private doctors or hospitals pertaining to the claim should be submitted along with the application.

- Dependency Documents: Copies of pertinent birth, marriage, death and divorce certificates should be submitted along with the application.

- Military Discharge / DD Form 214-Copy 4-Member Copy: In order to expedite processing of the claim, if an applicant has a copy of his or her DD-214, it should be submitted with the application. If not included with the application, VA will attempt to obtain verification from the veteran's service department.

- Copies of missing DD Forms 214 may be obtained form the National Personnel Records Center – 9700 Page Blvd. – St. Louis, MO – 63132-5100.

Special Note: If any of the pertinent supporting evidence is not immediately available, the applicant should send in the application anyway. The date VA receives the application is important! If VA approves the claim, benefit payments usually begin from the date the application is received, regardless of when the claim is approved.

Adjudication

Adjudication means a judicial decision made by the Veterans Administration in claims filed within their jurisdiction. There is an Adjudication Division in each regional office, under the direction of an adjudication officer, who is responsible for the preparation of claims.

Upon the receipt of an original application in the Adjudication Division, it will be referred to the Authorization Unit for review and development in accordance with established procedures. All reasonable assistance will be extended a claimant in the prosecution of his or her claim, and all sources from which

★★

information may be elicited will be thoroughly developed prior to the submission of the case to the rating board. Every legitimate assistance will be rendered a claimant in obtaining any benefit to which he or she is entitled, and the veteran will be given every opportunity to substantiate his or her claim. Information and advice to claimants will be complete, and will be given in words that the average person can understand.

VA personnel must at all times give to claimants and other properly interested and recognized individuals courteous and satisfactory service which is essential to good public relations. It is incumbent upon the claimant to establish his or her case in accordance with the law. This rule, however, should not be highly technical and rigid in its application. The general policy is to give the claimant every opportunity to substantiate the claim, to extend all reasonable assistance in its prosecution, and to develop all sources from which information may be obtained. Information and advice to claimants will be complete and expressed, so far as possible, in plain language, which can be easily read and understood by persons not familiar with the subject matter.

Benefits For Persons Disabled By Treatment Or Vocational Rehabilitation

Compensation shall be awarded for a qualifying additional disability or a qualifying death of a veteran in the same manner as if such additional disability or death were service-connected, provided:

- The disability or death was caused by hospital care, medical or surgical treatment, or examination was furnished under any law administered by the VA, either by a VA employee, or in a VA facility, and the proximate cause of the disability or death was:

    o Carelessness, negligence, lack of proper skill, error in judgment, or similar instance of fault on the part of the VA in furnishing the hospital care, medical treatment, surgical treatment, or examination; or

    o An event not reasonably foreseeable.

- The disability or death was proximately caused by the provision of training and rehabilitation services by the VA (including a service-provider used by the VA) as part of an approved rehabilitation program.

Effective December 1, 1962, if an individual is awarded a judgment against the United States in a civil action brought pursuant to Section 1346(b) of Title 28, or enters into a settlement or compromise under Section 2672 or 2677 of Title 28 by reason of a disability or death treated pursuant to this section as if it were service-connected, then no benefits shall be paid to such individual for any month beginning after the date such judgment, settlement, or compromise on account of such disability or death becomes final until the aggregate amount of benefits which would be paid out for this subsection equals the total amount included in such judgment, settlement, or compromise.

Person Heretofore Having A Compensable Status

The death and disability benefits outlined in this chapter, shall, notwithstanding the service requirements thereof, be granted to persons heretofore recognized by law as having a compensable status, including persons whose claims are based on war or peacetime service rendered before April 21, 1898.

★★

Aggravation

A preexisting injury or disease will be considered to have been aggravated by active military, naval, or air service, if there is an increase in disability during such service, unless there is a specific finding that the increase in disability is due to the natural progress of the disease.

Consideration To Be Accorded Time, Place And Circumstances Of Service

Consideration shall be given to the places, types, and circumstances of each veteran's service. The VA will consider the veteran's service record, the official history of each organization in which such veteran served, such veteran's medical records, and all pertinent medical and lay evidence. The provisions of Public Law 98-542 – *Section 5 of the Veterans' Dioxin and Radiation Exposure Compensation Standards Act* shall also be applied.

In the case of any veteran who engaged in combat with the enemy in active service with a military, naval, or air organization of the United States during a period of war, campaign, or expedition, the Secretary shall accept as sufficient proof of service-connection of any disease or injury alleged to have been incurred in or aggravated by such service, if consistent with the circumstances, conditions, or hardships of such service. This provision will apply even if there is no official record of such incurrence or aggravation in such service. Every reasonable doubt in such instance, will be resolved in favor of the veteran.

Service-connection of such injury or disease may be rebutted only by clear and convincing evidence to the contrary. The reasons for granting or denying service-connection in each case shall be recorded in full.

Disappearance

If a veteran who is receiving disability compensation disappears, the VA may pay the compensation otherwise payable to the veteran to such veteran's spouse, children, and parents. Payments made to such spouse, child, or parent shall not exceed the amounts payable to each if the veteran had died from a service-connected disability.

Combination Of Certain Ratings

The VA shall provide for the combination of ratings and pay compensation at the rates prescribed previously in this chapter to those veterans who served during a period of war and during any other time, who have suffered disability in the line of duty in each period of service.

Combined ratings can be figured out by the following formula:

1. Subtract the highest rating, for the major disability, from 100%

2. Multiply the rating for the next lower disability by the sum remaining after the first subtraction.

3. Add the product to the major rating to arrive at the combined rating for two disabilities.

★★★

If there are three rated service-connected disabilities, then, after the combined rating for the two larger ratings has been calculated, subtract such combined rating from 100% and multiply the rating for the third disability times the remainder, and add the resulting product to the combined rating of the first two disabilities to arrive at the combined rating for the three disabilities.

Thus, if a veteran has a 60% disability, a 40% disability, and a 20% disability, the following calculation would be done to arrive at the combined rating of 81%:

1. $100 - 60 = 40$
2. $40 \times .40 = 16$
3. $16 + 60 = 76$
4. $100 - 76 = 24$
5. $24 \times .20 = 4.8$ (round up to 5)
6. $76 + 5 = 81\%$

Tax Exemption

Compensation and pension may not be assigned to anyone, and are exempt from taxation (including income tax). No one can attach, levy, or seize a compensation or pension check either before or after receipt. Property purchased with money received from the government is not protected.

Protection Of Service Connection

Service connection for any disability or death granted under this title which has been in force for ten or more years shall not be severed on or after January 1, 1962, unless it is shown that the original grant of service connection was based on fraud, or it is clearly shown from military records that the person concerned did not have the requisite service or character of discharge. The mentioned period shall be computed from the date determined by the VA as the date on which the status commenced for rating purposes.

Special Consideration For Certain Cases Of Loss Of Paired Organs Or Extremities

If a veteran has suffered any of the following, the VA shall assign and pay to the veteran the applicable rate of compensation, as if the combination of disabilities were the result of a service-connected disability:

- Blindness in one eye as a result of a service-connected disability, and blindness in the other eye as a result of a non-service-connected disability not the result of the veteran's own willful misconduct; or

- The loss or loss of use of one kidney as a result of a service-connected disability, and involvement of the other kidney as a result of a non-service connected disability not the result of the veteran's own willful misconduct; or

- Total deafness in one ear as a result of a service-connected disability, and total deafness in the other ear as the result of non-service-connected disability not the result of the veteran's own willful misconduct; or

★★

- The loss or loss of use of one hand or one foot as a result of a service-connected disability and the loss or loss of use of the other hand or foot as a result of non-service-connected disability not the result of the veteran's own willful misconduct; or

- Permanent service-connected disability of one lung, rated 50% or more disabling, in combination with a non-service-connected disability of the other lung that is not the result of the veteran's own willful misconduct.

If a veteran described above receives any money or property of value pursuant to an award in a judicial proceeding based upon, or a settlement or compromise of, any cause of action for damages for the non-service-connected disability, the increase in the rate of compensation otherwise payable shall not be paid for any month following a month in which any such money or property is received until such time as the total of the amount of such increase that would otherwise have been payable equals the total of the amount of any such money received, and the fair market value of any such property received.

Payment Of Disability Compensation In Disability Severance Cases

The deduction of disability severance pay from disability compensation, as required by Section 1212(c) of Title 10, shall be made at a monthly rate not in excess of the rate of compensation to which the former member would be entitled based on the degree of such former member's disability, as determined on the initial Department rating.

Trial Work Periods And Vocational Rehabilitation For Certain Veterans With Total Disability Ratings

The disability rating of a qualified veteran who begins to engage in a substantially gainful occupation after January 31, 1985, may not be reduced on the basis of the veteran having secured and followed a substantially gainful occupation unless the veteran maintains such an occupation for a period of 12 consecutive months.

("Qualified Veteran" means a veteran who has a service-connected disability or disabilities, not rated as total, but who has been awarded a rating of total of disability by reason of inability to secure or follow a substantially gainful occupation as a result of such disability or disabilities.)

Counseling services, placement, and post placement services shall be available to each qualified veteran, whether or not the veteran is participating in a vocational rehabilitation program.

★★★

CHAPTER 3

AUTOMOBILES, ADAPTIVE EQUIPMENT AND CLOTHING ALLOWANCE FOR CERTAIN DISABLED VETERANS

AUTOMOBILE ASSISTANCE PROGRAM

The VA offers an automobile assistance program for eligible veterans. Following are highlights of the VA program:

Financial Assistance

Qualified veterans may receive a *one-time* payment from VA of up to $8,000 to be used toward the purchase of an automobile or other conveyance.

Eligibility Requirements For Receipt Of One-Time Payment:

Veterans or service members who are entitled to Disability Compensation under Chapter 11 of Title 38 due to one of the following service-connected losses:

- The loss or permanent loss of use of one or both feet; or
- The loss or permanent loss of use of one or both hands; or
- The permanent impairment of vision of both eyes of the following status:
  - Central visual acuity of 20/200 or less in the better eye, with corrective glasses, or central visual acuity of more than 20/200 if there is a field defect in which the peripheral field has contracted to such an extent that the widest diameter of visual field subtends an angular distance no greater than twenty degrees in the better eye.

ADAPTIVE EQUIPMENT

In addition to the one-time payment described above, VA will also pay for installation of adaptive equipment deemed necessary to insure that the eligible veteran will be able to safely operate the vehicle, and to satisfy the applicable State standards of licensure.

VA will also repair, replace, or reinstall adaptive equipment determined necessary for the operation of a vehicle acquired under this program, or for the operation of a vehicle an eligible veteran may previously or subsequently have acquired.

Eligibility Requirements For Receipt Of Adaptive Equipment:

- The loss or permanent loss of use of one or both feet; or
- The loss or permanent loss of use of one or both hands; or

★★

- The permanent impairment of vision of both eyes of the following status:
  - Central visual acuity of 20/200 or less in the better eye, with corrective glasses, or central visual acuity of more than 20/200 if there is a field defect in which the peripheral field has contracted to such an extent that the widest diameter of visual field subtends an angular distance no greater than twenty degrees in the better eye; or
- Ankylosis (immobility) of one or both knees; or
- Ankylosis (immobility) of one or both hips.

Adaptive Equipment Available for Installation

The term adaptive equipment, means generally, any equipment which must be part of or added to a vehicle manufactured for sale to the general public in order to make it safe for use by the claimant, and to assist him or her in meeting the applicable standards of licensure of the proper licensing authority.

Following is a partial list of adaptive equipment available under this program:

- Power steering
- Power brakes
- Power window lifts
- Power seats
- Special equipment necessary to assist the eligible person into and out of the automobile or other conveyance
- Air-conditioning equipment, if such equipment is necessary to the health and safety of the veteran and to the safety of others, regardless of whether the automobile or other conveyance is to be operated by the eligible person or is to operated for such person by another person
- Any modification of the size of the interior space of the automobile or other conveyance if necessary for the disabled person to enter or operate the vehicle
- Other equipment, not described above, if determined necessary by the Chief Medical Director or designee in an individual case

Eligible veterans are not entitled to adaptive equipment for more than 2 vehicles at any one time during any four-year period. (In the event an adapted vehicle is no longer available for use by the eligible veteran due to circumstances beyond his or her control, i.e. loss due to fire, theft, accident, etc., an exception to this four-year provision may be approved.)

SPECIALLY ADAPTED HOMES

Disabled veterans may be entitled to a ***one-time*** grant from VA for a home specially adapted to their needs, or for adaptations. There are two types of grants that may be payable:

★★★

$43,000 Grant

The VA may approve a grant of not more than 50% of the cost of building, buying, or remodeling adapted homes, or paying indebtedness on homes previously acquired, up to a maximum of $43,000.

To qualify for this grant, veterans must be entitled to compensation for permanent and total service-connected disability due to:

- Loss or loss of use of both lower extremities, which prevents movement without the aid of braces, crutches, canes, or a wheelchair; or
- Disability which includes:
  - o Blindness in both eyes, having only light perception; **with**
  - o Loss or loss of use of one lower extremity; or
- Loss or loss of use of one lower extremity together with:
  - o Residuals of organic disease or injury; **or**
  - o The loss or loss of use of one upper extremity, which so affects the functions of balance or propulsion as to preclude locomotion without using braces, canes, crutches, or a wheelchair.

$8,250 Grant

VA may approve a grant for the actual cost, up to a maximum of $8,250, for adaptations to a veteran's residence that are determined by VA to be reasonable necessary.

The grant may also be used to assist veterans in acquiring a residence that already has been adapted with special features for the veteran's disability.

To qualify for this grant, veterans must be entitled to compensation for permanent and total service-connected disability due to:

- Blindness in both eyes, with 5/200 visual acuity or less; or
- Anatomical loss or loss of use of both hands.

Supplemental Financing – Loan Guaranty

Veterans who have available loan guaranty entitlement may also obtain a guaranteed loan or possibly a direct loan from VA to supplement the grant to acquire a specially adapted home. Please refer to page 208 of this book for specific information on VA Loan Guaranties.

★★★

CLOTHING ALLOWANCE

The VA shall pay a clothing allowance of $565.00 per year (rate effective December 1, 2000) to each veteran who:

- Because of a service-connected disability, wears or uses a prosthetic or orthopedic appliance (including a wheelchair) which the VA determines tends to wear out or tear the clothing of the veteran; or

- Uses medication prescribed by a physician for a skin condition that is due to a service-connected disability, and which the VA determines causes irreparable damage to the veteran's outer garments.

★★

CHAPTER 4

NON-SERVICE CONNECTED DISABILITY PENSION

BENEFIT DESCRIPTION

Non-Service Connected Disability Pension is a Department of Veterans Affairs benefits program that provides financial support to wartime veterans having limited income. The amount payable under this program depends on the type and amount of income the veteran and family members receive from other sources. Monthly payments are made to bring a veteran's total annual income (including other retirement and Social Security income) to an established support level. (Unreimbursed medical expenses may reduce countable income.)

DEFINITIONS

The following definitions apply only to CHAPTER 4 – NON-SERVICE CONNECTED DISABILITY PENSION:

Indian Wars: means the campaigns, engagements, and expeditions of the United States military forces against Indian tribes or nations, service in which has been recognized heretofore as pensionable service.

World War I: means the period April 6, 1917, through November 11, 1918. In the case of a veteran who served with the United States military forces in Russia, the ending date is April 1, 1920.   Service after November 11, 1918 and before July 2, 1921 is considered World War I for compensation or pension purposes, if the veteran served in the active military, naval, or air service after April 5, 1917 and before November 12, 1918.

Civil War Veteran: includes a person who served in the military or naval forces of the Confederate States of America during the Civil War, and the term "active military or naval service" includes active service in those forces.

Period of War: means the Mexican border period, World War I, World War II, the Korean conflict, the Vietnam era, the Persian Gulf War, and the period beginning on the date of any future declaration of war by the Congress and ending on the date prescribed by Presidential proclamation or concurrent resolution of the Congress.

Permanently and Totally Disabled: for the purposes of this chapter, a person shall be considered to be permanently and totally disabled if such person is unemployable as a result of disability reasonably certain to continue throughout the life of the disabled person, or is suffering from:

• Any disability which is sufficient to render it impossible for the average person to follow a substantially gainful occupation, but only if it is reasonably certain that such disability will continue throughout the life of the disabled person; or

★★★

- Any disease or disorder determined by the VA Secretary to be of such a nature or extent as to justify a determination that persons suffering therefrom are permanently and totally disabled.

Regular Aid and Attendance: for the purposes of this chapter, a person shall be considered to be in need of regular aid and attendance if such person is:

- A patient in a nursing home; or
- Helpless or blind, or so nearly helpless or blind as to need or require the aid and attendance of another person.

Permanently Housebound: for the purposes of this chapter, the requirement of "permanently housebound" will be considered to have been met when the veteran is substantially confined to such veteran's house (ward or clinical areas, if institutionalized) or immediate premises due to a disability or disabilities, which it is reasonably certain will remain throughout such veteran's lifetime.

Annual Income: In determining annual income under this chapter, all payments of any kind or from any source (including salary, retirement or annuity payments, or similar income, which has been waived, irrespective of whether the waiver was made pursuant to statue, contract, or otherwise) shall be included except:

- Donations from public or private relief or welfare organizations;
- Payments under this chapter;
- Amounts equal to amounts paid by a spouse of a veteran for the expenses of such veteran's last illness, and by a surviving spouse or child of a deceased veteran for:
  - Such veteran's just debts;
  - The expenses of such veteran's last illness; and
  - The expenses of such veteran's burial to the extent such expenses are not reimbursed through Chapter 23 of Title 38, United States Code (Burial Benefits);
- Amounts equal to amounts paid:
  - By a veteran for the last illness and burial of such veteran's deceased spouse or child; or
  - By the spouse of a living veteran or the surviving spouse of a deceased veteran for the last illness and burial of a child of such veteran;
- Reimbursements of any kind for any casualty loss, but the amount excluded under this clause may not exceed the greater of the fair market value or reasonable replacement value of the property involved at the time immediately preceding the loss;
- Profit realized from the disposition of real or personal property other than in the course of a business;
- Amounts in joint accounts in banks and similar institutions acquired by reason of death of other joint owner;
- Amounts equal to amounts paid by a veteran, veteran's spouse, or surviving spouse, or by or on behalf of a veteran's child for unreimbursed

medical expenses, to the extent that such amounts exceed 5% of the maximum annual rate of pension (including any amount of increased pension payable on account of family members but not including any amount of pension payable because a person is in need of regular aid and attendance, or because a person is permanently housebound) payable to such veteran surviving spouse, or child.

- In the case of a veteran or surviving spouse pursuing a course of education or vocational rehabilitation or training, amounts equal to amounts paid by such veteran or surviving spouse for such course of education or vocational rehabilitation or training, including:

    o   Amounts paid for tuition, fees, books, and materials; and

    o   In the case of such a veteran or surviving spouse in need of regular aid and attendance, unreimbursed amounts paid for unusual transpiration expenses in connection with the pursuit of such course of education or vocational rehabilitation or training, to the extent that such amounts exceed the reasonable expenses which would have been incurred by a nondisabled person using an appropriate means of transportation (public transportation, if reasonably available); and

- In the case of a child, or any current-work income received during the year, to the extent that the total amount of such income does not exceed an amount equal to the sum of:

    o   The lowest amount of gross income for which an income tax return is required under section 6012(a) of the Internal Revenue Code of 1986, to be filed by an individual who is not married, is not a surviving spouse, and is not a head of household; and

    o   If the child is pursuing a course of postsecondary education or vocational rehabilitation or training, the amount paid by such child for such course of education or vocational rehabilitation or training, including the amount paid for tuition, fees, books, and materials.

Note: Where a fraction of a dollar is involved, annual income shall be fixed at the next lower dollar.

ELIGIBILITY

- Generally, a veteran must have 90 days or more of service, of which at least 1 day must have occurred during a period of war, and the veteran must have been discharged under conditions other than dishonorable.

- Additionally, the veteran must have a disability (ies) that VA evaluates as permanent and total (see definition of permanent and total disability in "Definitions" section of this chapter).

★★★

• In addition, the recipient's countable income must fall below an annual limit set by law.

AMOUNT OF VA PAYMENTS

If eligible, VA pays the difference between a recipient's countable family income and the annual income limit set by law (see following charts) for his or her status. This difference is generally paid in 12 equal monthly installments.

Family Income Limits

Improved Pension Annual Rates (PL-95-588) Effective December 1, 2000	
STATUS OF VETERAN:	**ANNUAL INCOME LIMITATION:**
Permanently and totally disabled veterans:	
Veteran alone	$ 9,304.00
Veteran with one dependent	12,186.00
Each additional dependent child	1,586.00
Veteran – Aid and Attendance:	
Veteran alone	15,524.00
Veteran with one dependent	18,405.00
Each additional dependent child	1,586.00
Veteran – Housebound:	
Veteran alone	11,372.00
Veteran with one dependent	14,253.00
Each additional dependent child	1,586.00
Two veterans married to one another:	12,186.00
One veteran entitled to A&A	18,405.00
Both veterans entitled to A&A	23,979.00
One veteran – housebound	14,253.00
Both veterans – housebound	16,322.00
One housebound and one A&A	20,470.00
Each additional dependent child	1,586.00
Add for Mexican Border Period or World War I Veterans:	2,109.00
Child Earned Income Exclusion effective 1-1-2000 - $7,200.00	

★★★

**Maximum Annual Income Limitations For Protected Pensions -
(Effective December 1, 2000)**

Pensioners entitled to benefits as of December 31, 1978, who do not elect to receive a pension under the Improved Pension Program, may continue to receive pension benefits at the rates they were entitled to receive on December 31, 1978 or June 30, 1960, as long as they remain permanently and totally disabled, do not lose a dependent, and their income does not exceed the income limitation, adjusted annually. Under the Old Law Disability Pensions, all veterans whose income was under the annual limitation received the same monthly amount. These monthly amounts are also listed below, following the annual income limitation charts.

Pension Law in Effect on December 31, 1978 (Section 306):	
(The rate entitled to on December 31, 1978 may be continued if the recipient's IVAP for 2000 is below the following limits:	
STATUS OF RECIPIENT:	**ANNUAL INCOME LIMITATION:**
Veteran / widow with no dependents	*$10,584.00*
Veteran / widow with one or more dependent	*14,228.00*
Child (no entitled veteran or surviving spouse)	*8,651.00*
Veteran with no dependents in receipt of A&A	*11,084.00*
Veteran with one dependent in receipt of A&A	*14,728.00*
Surviving spouse's income exclusion	*3,377.00*

Pension Law in Effect on June 30, 1960 (Old Law):	
(The rate entitled to on June 30, 1960 may be continued if the recipient's IVAP for 2000 is below the following limits:	
STATUS OF RECIPIENT:	**ANNUAL INCOME LIMITATION:**
Veteran / widow with no dependents	*$9,265.00*
Veteran / widow with one or more dependents	*13,357.00*
Child (no entitled veteran or surviving spouse)	*9,265.00*

Monthly Benefit Payable To Eligible Veterans Receiving Disability Pension Under Laws In Effect June 30, 1960 Or December 31, 1978	
VETERAN'S ENTITLEMENT:	**RATE PAYABLE:**
Basic Rates	*$ 66.15*
10 Years or Age 65	*78.75*
If Entitled To Aid & Attendance	*135.45*
If Entitled To Housebound	*100.00*

★★★

Indian And Spanish-American War Veterans

The VA shall pay to each veteran of the Indian Wars or Spanish-American War, who meets the service requirements established by the VA, a pension at the following monthly rates:

- $101.59; or
- $135.45 if the veteran is in need of regular aid and attendance.

Indian Wars Service Requirements:
Served in one of the Indian Wars for 30 days or more; or
For the duration of such Indian War

Spanish-American War Service Requirements:
Served in the active military or naval service for 90 days or more; or
Served in the active military or naval service and was discharged or released from such service for a service-connected disability

Veterans of the Spanish-American War who served between 70 and 90 days, may receive a pension at the following monthly rates:

- $67.73; or
- $88.04 if the veteran is in need of regular aid and attendance.

Any veteran eligible for pension under this section shall, if such veteran so elects, be paid pension at the rates payable to World War I veterans. If such an election is made, the election shall be irrevocable.

APPLYING FOR BENEFITS

Veterans can apply for a Disability Pension by completing VVA Form 21-526, Veteran's Application for Compensation or Pension. If available, the applicant should attach copies of dependency records (marriage and children's birth certificates) and current medical evidence (doctor and hospital reports). The completed form should be sent to the veteran's VA Regional Office (refer to Page 292 for a listing of all VA regional offices.)

Special Note: If any of the pertinent supporting evidence is not immediately available, the applicant should send in the application anyway. The date VA receives the application is important! If VA approves the claim, benefit payments usually begin from the date the application is received, regardless of when the claim is approved.

NET WORTH LIMITATION

The VA shall deny or discontinue the payment of pension to a veteran under this chapter when the corpus of the estate of the veteran, or, if the veteran has a spouse, the corpus of the estates of the veteran and of the veteran's spouse is such that under all the circumstances, including consideration of the annual income of the veteran, the veteran's spouse, and the veteran's children, it is reasonable that some part of the corpus of such estates be consumed for the veteran's maintenance.

★★

The VA shall deny or discontinue the payment of increased pension under this chapter on account of a child when the corpus of such child's estate is such that under all the circumstances, including consideration of the veteran's and spouse's income, and the income of the veteran's children, it is reasonable that some part of the corpus of such child's estate be consumed for the child's maintenance. During the period such denial or discontinuance remains in effect, such child shall not be considered as the veteran's child for purposes of this chapter.

PROOF OF INCOME AND OVERPAYMENT ADJUSTMENTS

As a condition of granting, or continuing payment of a Disability Pension for a Non-Service-Connected Disability, the VA:

- May require from any person who is an applicant or recipient, such information, proof, and evidence the VA determines to be necessary in order to determine the annual income and the value of the corpus of the estate of such person, and of any spouse or child for whom the person is receiving, or is to receive increased pension, and in the case of a child applying for or in receipt of benefits, of any person with whom such child is residing who is legally responsible for such child's support.

- May require that any such applicant or recipient file for a calendar year with the VA, a report showing:

  o The annual income which such applicant or recipient (and any spouse or dependent child) received during the preceding year, the corpus of the estate of such applicant or recipient (and of any such spouse or dependent child) at the end of such year, and in the case of a surviving child, the income and corpus of the estate of any person with whom such child is residing who is legally responsible for such child's support.

  o Such applicant's or recipient's estimate for the current year of the annual income such applicant or recipient (and any such spouse or dependent child) expects to receive, and of any expected increase in the value of the corpus of the estate of such applicant or recipient (and for any such spouse or dependent child); and

  o In the case of a surviving child, an estimate of the annual income of any person with whom such child is residing who is legally responsible for such child's support, and of any expected increase in the value of the corpus of the estate of such person;

- Shall require that any such applicant or recipient promptly notify the VA whenever there is a material change in the annual income of such applicant or recipient (or of any such spouse or dependent child) or a material change in the value of the corpus of the estate of such applicant or recipient (or of any such spouse or dependent child), and din the case of a surviving child, a material change in the annual income or value of the corpus of the estate of any person with whom such child is residing who is legally responsible for such child's support; and

- Shall require that any such applicant or recipient applying for or in receipt of increased pension on account of a person who is a spouse or child of such applicant or recipient promptly notify the VA if such person ceases to meet the applicable definition of spouse or child.

COMBINATION OF RATINGS

The VA shall provide that, for the purpose of determining whether or not a veteran is permanently and totally disabled, ratings for service-connected disabilities may be combined with ratings for non-service-connected disabilities.

Where a veteran is found to be entitled to a Non-Service-Connected Disability Pension, and is also entitled to Service-Connected Disability Compensation, the VA shall pay the veteran the greater benefit.

VOCATIONAL TRAINING FOR CERTAIN PENSION RECIPIENTS

In the case of a veteran who is awarded a Non-Service-Connected Disability Pension, the VA shall, based on information on file with the VA, make a preliminary finding whether such veteran, with the assistance of a vocational training program, has a good potential for achieving employment. If such potential is found to exist, the VA shall solicit from the veteran an application for vocational training. If the veteran thereafter applies for such training, the VA shall provide the veteran with an evaluation, which may include a personal interview, to determine whether the achievement of a vocational goal is reasonably feasible.

If the VA, based on the evaluation, determines that the achievement of a vocational goal by a veteran is reasonably feasible, the veteran shall be offered, and may elect to pursue a vocational training program.

If the veteran elects to pursue such a program, the program shall be designed in consultation with the veteran in order to meet the veteran's individual needs, and shall be set forth in an individualized written plan of vocational rehabilitation.

A vocational training program under this section:

- May not exceed 24 months unless, based on a determination by the VA that an extension is necessary in order for the veteran to achieve a vocational goal identified in the written plan formulated for the veteran, the VA grants an extension for a period not to exceed 24 months.

- May not include the provision of any loan or subsistence allowance, or any automobile adaptive equipment.

- May include a program of education at an institution of higher learning, only in a case in which the Secretary of the VA determines that the program involved is predominantly vocational in content.

When a veteran completes a vocational training program, the VA may provide the veteran with counseling, placement and post-placement services for a period not to exceed 18 months.

A veteran may not begin pursuit of a vocational training program under this chapter after the later of:

- December 31, 1995; or
- The end of a reasonable period of time, as determined by the VA, following either the evaluation of the veteran or the award of pension to the veteran.

In the case of a veteran who has been determined to have a permanent and total non-service-connected disability and who, not later than one year after the date the veteran's eligibility for counseling under this chapter expires, secures employment within the scope of a vocational goal identified in the veteran's individualized written plan of vocational rehabilitation (or in a related field which requires reasonably developed skills, and the use of some or all of the training or services furnished the veteran under such plan), the evaluation of the veteran as having a permanent and total disability may not be terminated be reason of the veteran's capacity to engage in such employment until the veteran first maintains such employment for a period of not less than 12 consecutive months.

PROTECTION OF HEALTH-CARE ELIGIBILITY

In the case of a veteran whose entitlement to pension is terminated after January 31, 1985, by reason of income from work or training, the veteran shall retain for a period of three years, beginning on the date of such termination, all eligibility for care and services that the veteran would have had if the veteran's entitlement to pension had not been terminated.

DISAPPEARANCE

When a veteran receiving a non-service-connected disability pension from the VA disappears, the VA may pay the pension otherwise payable to such veteran's spouse and children. Payments made to a spouse or child shall not exceed the amount to which each would be entitled if the veteran died of a non-service-connected disability.

★★

CHAPTER 5

DEPENDENCY AND INDEMNITY COMPENSATION FOR SERVICE-CONNECTED DEATHS

Dependency and Indemnity Compensation (DIC) payments may be available for:

- Surviving spouses who have not remarried;
- Unmarried Children under 18;
- Helpless children;
- Children between 18 and 23, if attending a VA-approved school; and
- Low-income parents of deceased servicemembers or veterans.

DEFINITIONS

The following definitions apply only to CHAPTER 5 – DEPENDENCY AND INDEMNITY COMPENSATION FOR SERVICE-CONNECTED DEATHS:

Veteran: in this chapter, the term includes a person who died in the active military, naval, or air service.

Social Security Increase: in this chapter, the term means the percentage by which benefit amounts payable under Title II of the Social Security Act (42 U.S.C. 401 et seq.) are increased for any fiscal year as a result of a determination under section 215(i) of such Act (42 U.S.C. 415(i)).

Permanently Housebound: for the purposes of this chapter, the requirement of "permanently housebound" will be considered to have been met when the individual is substantially confined to such individual's house (ward or clinical areas, if institutionalized) or immediate premises due to a disability or disabilities, which it is reasonably certain will remain throughout such individual's lifetime.

ELIGIBILITY

To receive Dependency and Indemnity Compensation (DIC), an individual must be an eligible survivor of a veteran who died from:

- A disease or injury incurred or aggravated while on active duty or active duty for training; or
- An injury incurred or aggravated in the line of duty while on inactive duty training.

If the veteran's death was not service-related, an individual may still be eligible if *EITHER* of the following conditions existed at the time of death:

- The veteran was receiving VA Disability Compensation for a total disability for the last 10 years. (Note: This also includes veterans who would have received VA compensation but did not, because they were receiving military retirement or disability pay.)

- The veteran was receiving VA Disability Compensation for a total disability continuously since released from active duty, *and* for at least 5 years.

(Special Note to Spouses of Former Prisoners of War: On November 30, 1999, the President signed into law the Veterans Millennium Healthcare and Benefits Act, Pub. L. 106-117. Section 501, a provision of the law, authorizes VA to pay DIC under 38 U.S.C. 1318 to the survivors of former Prisoners of War who died after September 30, 1999, and who were rated totally disabled continuously for a period of not less than one year immediately preceding death for a service-connected disability. This provision is effective November 30, 1999.)

To qualify as an eligible survivor, an individual must have proof of the following:

- Proof that he or she was married to the veteran for at least 1 year   (Note: If a child was born, there is no time requirement); AND

- Proof that the marriage was VALID; AND

- Proof that he or she lived with the veteran continuously until his/her death or, if separated, the surviving spouse wasn't at fault; AND

- Proof that he or she did not remarry. (Note: The remarriage of the surviving spouse of a veteran shall not bar the furnishing of DIC if the remarriage is terminated by death, divorce, or annulment, unless the VA determines that the divorce or annulment was secured through fraud or collusion.)

OR

- The individual is an unmarried child of a deceased veteran; AND

- The individual is under age 18, or between the ages of 18 and 23 and attending school.

Note: Certain helpless adult children and some parents of deceased veterans are entitled to DIC. Call VA toll free for the eligibility requirements for these survivors.

AMOUNT OF DIC PAYMENTS TO SURVIVING SPOUSES

- Surviving spouses of veterans who died after January 1, 1993, receive a basic monthly rate of **$911.00** (effective December 1, 2000).

- Surviving spouses entitled to DIC based on the veteran's death prior to January 1, 1993, receive the greater of:

  o   The basic monthly rate of $911, **or**

  o   An amount based on the veteran's pay grade. (See following sections for Pay Grade tables and Determination of Pay Grade.)

★★

There are additional DIC payments for dependent children. (Refer to the following charts.)

Additional Allowances For Surviving Spouses

- Add $197.00 to the basic monthly rate if, at the time of the veteran's death, the veteran was in receipt of, or entitled to receive compensation for a service-connected disability rated totally disabling (including a rating based on individual unemployability) for a continuous period of at least 8 years immediately preceding death **AND** the surviving spouse was married to the veteran for those same 8 years.

- Add $229.00 per child to the basic monthly rate for each dependent child under age 18.

- If the surviving spouse is entitled to Aid & Attendance, add $229.00 to the basic monthly rate.

- If the surviving spouse is Permanently Housebound, add $110.00 to the basic monthly rate.

SURVIVING SPOUSE DIC RATES IF VETERAN'S DEATH WAS PRIOR TO JANUARY 1, 1993–

PUBLIC LAW 106-118

Rates Effective December 1, 2000

Pay Grade	Monthly Rate	Pay Grade	Monthly Rate
E-1:	$911	W-4:	$1,090
E-2:	$911	O-1:	$962
E-3 (see footnote #1):	$911	O-2:	$995
E-4:	$911	O-3:	$1,063
E-5:	$911	O-4:	$1,125
E-6:	$911	O-5:	$1,239
E-7:	$942	O-6:	$1,396
E-8:	$995	O-7:	$1,509
E-9 (see footnote #2):	$1,038 or $1,119	O-8:	$1,653
W-1:	$962	O-9:	$1,771
W-2:	$1,001	O-10 (see footnote #3):	$1,943 or $2,083
W-3:	$1,031		

Footnotes to Table:
1. A surviving spouse of an Aviation Cadet or other service not covered by this table is paid the DIC rate for enlisted E-3 under 34.
2. $1,119 is for a veteran who served as Sergeant Major of the Army or Marine Corps, Senior Enlisted Advisor of the Navy, Chief Master Sergeant of the Air Force, or Master Chief Petty Officer of the Coast Guard.
3. $2,083 is for a veteran who served as Chairman of the Joint Chiefs of Staff, Chief of Staff of the Army or Air Force, Chief of Naval Operations, or Commandant of the Marine Corps.

★★

Determination Of Pay Grade

With respect to a veteran who died in the active military, naval, or air service, such veteran's pay grade shall be determined as of the date of such veteran's death, or as of the date of a promotion after death, while in a missing status.

With respect to a veteran who did not die in the active military, naval, or air service, such veteran's pay grade shall be determined as of:

- The time of such veteran's last discharge or release from active duty under conditions other than dishonorable; or

- The time of such veteran's discharge or release from any period of active duty for training or inactive duty training, if such veteran's death results from service-connected disability incurred during such period, and if such veteran was not thereafter discharged or released under conditions other than dishonorable from active duty.

If a veteran has satisfactorily served on active duty for a period of six months or more in a pay grade higher than that specified in the previous paragraphs of this section, and any subsequent discharge or release from active duty was under conditions other than dishonorable, the higher pay grade shall be used if it will result in greater monthly payments to such veteran's surviving spouse under this chapter. The determination as to whether an individual has served satisfactorily for the required period in a higher pay grade shall be made by the Secretary of the department in which such higher pay grade was held.

The pay grade of any person not otherwise described in this section, but who had a compensable status on the date of such person's death under laws administered by the Secretary, shall be determined by the head of the department under which such person performed the services by which such person obtained such status (taking into consideration such person's duties and responsibilities) and certified to the Secretary. For the purposes of this chapter, such person shall be deemed to have been on active duty while performing such services.

DIC PAYMENTS TO CHILDREN

Whenever there is no surviving spouse of a deceased veteran entitled to DIC, DIC shall be paid in equal shares to the children of the deceased veteran at the following monthly rates:

Number of Children	Total Payable (to be divided in equal shares):
1	$386
2	$556
3	$723
4	$863
5	$1,003
6	$1,143
7	$1,283

★★★

Additional Allowances For Children

- In the case of a child entitled to DIC who has attained the age of 18, and who, while under such age, became permanently incapable of self-support, the DIC paid monthly to such child shall be increased by $229.

- If DIC is payable monthly to a person as a surviving spouse, and there is a child (of such person's deceased spouse) who has attained the age of 18, and who, while under such age, became permanently incapable of self-support, DIC shall be paid monthly to each such child, concurrently with the payment of DIC to the surviving spouse, in the amount of $386.

- If DIC is payable monthly to a person as a surviving spouse, and there is a child (of such person's deceased spouse) who has attained the age of 18 and who, while under the age of 23, is pursuing a course of instruction at a VA-approved educational institution, DIC shall be paid monthly to each such child, concurrently with the payment of DIC to the surviving spouse, in the amount of $194.

DIC PAYMENTS FOR PARENTS

Parents whose child died in-service or from a service-connected disability may be entitled to DIC if they are in financial need. Parents may be biological, step, adopted, or *in loco parentis*.

The monthly payment for parents of deceased veterans depends upon their income. The following 3 charts outline the monthly rates payable, **effective December 1, 2000,** under various conditions.

Chart #1
Sole Surviving Parent Unremarried or
Remarried Living With Spouse

Income Not Over:	Monthly Rate:	Income Not Over:	Monthly Rate:
$ 800	$ 445	$ 3,700	$ 213
900	437	3,800	205
1,000	429	3,900	197
1,100	421	4,000	189
1,200	413	4,100	181
1,300	405	4,200	173
1,400	397	4,300	165
1,500	389	4,400	157
1,600	381	4,500	149
1,700	373	4,600	141
1,800	365	4,700	133
1,900	357	4,800	125
2,000	349	4,900	117
2,100	341	5,000	109
2,200	333	5,100	101
2,300	325	5,200	93
2,400	317	5,300	85
2,500	309	5,400	77
2,600	301	5,500	69

★★★

Chart #1 Continued –
Sole Surviving Parent Unremarried or Remarried Living With Spouse

Income Not Over:	Monthly Rate:	Income Not Over:	Monthly Rate:
$ 2,700	$293	$ 5,600	$ 61
2,800	285	5,700	53
2,900	277	5,800	45
3,000	269	5,900	37
3,100	261	6,000	29
3,200	253	6,100	21
3,300	245	6,200	13
3,400	237	6,300	5
3,500	229	6,301to **	5
3,600	221	If A&A add:	239
**If living w/spouse:	13,746	**If not living w/ spouse:	10,226

Chart #2
One of Two Parents Not Living With Spouse

Income Not Over:	Monthly Rate:	Income Not Over:	Monthly Rate:
$ 800	$ 320	$3,200	$ 132
900	314	3,300	124
1,000	307	3,400	116
1,100	300	3,500	108
1,200	292	3,600	100
1,300	284	3,700	92
1,400	276	3,800	84
1,500	268	3,900	76
1,600	260	4,000	68
1,700	252	4,100	60
1,800	244	4,200	52
1,900	236	4,300	44
2,000	228	4,400	36
2,100	220	4,500	28
2,200	212	4,600	20
2,300	204	4,700	12
2,400	196	4,787	5.04
2,500	188	4,788 to 10,584	5
2,600	180		
2,700	172	If A&A add:	239
2,800	164		
2,900	156		
3,000	148		
3,100	140		

★★

Chart #3

1 of 2 Parents Living with Spouse or Other Parent

Income Not Over:	Monthly Rate:	Income Not Over:	Monthly Rate:
1,000	$ 300	3,700	$ 153
1,100	297	3,800	145
1,200	294	3,900	137
1,300	291	4,000	129
1,400	288	4,100	121
1,500	285	4,200	113
1,600	281	4,300	105
1,700	277	4,400	97
1,800	273	4,500	89
1,900	269	4,600	81
2,000	264	4,700	73
2,100	259	4,800	65
2,200	254	4,900	57
2,300	249	5,000	49
2,400	244	5,100	41
2,500	238	5,200	33
2,600	232	5,300	25
2,700	226	5,400	17
2,800	220	5,500	9
2,900	214	5,549	5.08
3,000	207	5,550 to $14,228	5
3,100	200		
3,200	193		
3,300	185	If A&A add monthly:	239
3,400	177		
3,500	169		
3,600	161		

Miscellaneous Information Regarding Income Limitations For Parents

The VA may require, as a condition of granting or continuing DIC to a parent that such parent, other than one who has attained 72 years of age, and has been paid DIC during 2 consecutive calendar years, file for a calendar year with the VA, a report showing the total income which such parent expects to receive in that year, and the total income which such parent received in the preceding year. The parent or parents shall notify the VA whenever there is a material change in annual income.

In determining income under this section, all payments of any kind, or from any source shall be included except:

- Payments of a death gratuity
- Donations from public or private relief or welfare organizations;
- Payments under this chapter (DIC), Chapter 11 of Title 38, United States Code (Disability Compensation), and Chapter 15 of Title 38, United States Code (Non-Service Connected Disability/Death Pension);

★★★

- Payments under policies of servicemembers group life insurance, United States Government life insurance, or national service life insurance, and payments of servicemen's indemnity;

- 10% of the amount of payments to an individual under public or private retirement, annuity, endowment, or similar plans or programs;

- Amounts equal to amounts paid by a parent of a deceased veteran for:

  o A deceased spouse's just debts;

  o The expenses of the spouse's last illness, to the extent such expenses are not reimbursed under Chapter 51 of Title 38 of the United States Code;

  o The expenses of the spouse's burial to the extent that such expenses are not reimbursed under Chapter 23 or Chapter 51 of Title 38 of the United States Code;

- Reimbursements of any kind for any casualty loss (as defined in regulations which the VA shall prescribe), but the amount excluded under this clause may not exceed the greater of the fair market value or the reasonable replacement value of the property involved at the time immediately preceding the loss;

- Amounts equal to amounts paid by a parent of a deceased veteran for:

  o The expenses of the veteran's last illness, and

  o The expenses of such veteran's burial, to the extent that such expenses are not reimbursed under Chapter 23 of Title 38 of the United States Code;

- Profit realized from the disposition of real or personal property other than in the course of a business;

- Payments received for discharge of jury duty or obligatory civic duties;

- Payments of annuities elected under Subchapter I of Chapter 73 of Title 10.

Where a fraction of a dollar is involved, annual income shall be fixed at the next lower dollar.

The VA may provide by regulation for the exclusion from income under this section of amounts paid by a parent for unusual medical expenses.

Cost-Of-Living Adjustments

In the computation of cost-of-living adjustments for fiscal years 1998 through 2002 in the rates of Dependency and Indemnity Compensation payable under this chapter, such adjustments shall be made by a uniform percentage that is no more than the percentage equal to the social security increase for that fiscal year, with all increased monthly rates (other than increased rates equal to a whole dollar amount) rounded down to the next lower whole dollar amount.

★★

SPECIAL PROVISIONS RELATING TO SURVIVING SPOUSES

No Dependency and Indemnity Compensation shall be paid to the surviving spouse of a veteran dying after December 31, 1956, unless such surviving spouse was married to such veteran:

- Before the expiration of 15 years after the termination of the period of service in which the injury or disease causing the death of the veteran was incurred or aggravated; or

- For one year or more; or

- For any period of time if a child was born of the marriage, or was born to them before the marriage.

APPLYING FOR DEPENDENCY AND INDEMNITY COMPENSATION

Eligible surviving spouses and dependent children can apply for DIC by completing VA Form 21-534, *Application for Dependency and Indemnity Compensation or Death Pension by Surviving Spouse or Child.* If available, copies of dependency records (marriage records, divorce records, & children's birth certificates) should be attached to the application. A copy of the veteran's DD Form 214 and a copy of the veteran's death certificate should also be included with the completed application.

The completed form should be sent to the applicable VA Regional Office (refer to page 292 for a listing of all VA regional offices.)

Special Note: If any of the pertinent supporting evidence is not immediately available, the applicant should send in the application anyway. The date VA receives the application is important! If VA approves the claim, benefit payments usually begin from the date the application is received, regardless of when the claim is approved.

HELP FOR VETERAN'S WIDOWS

Tragedy Assistance Program for Survivors (TAPS)
2001 S Street, N.W., #300
Washington, D.C., 20009
1-800-959-TAPS

TAPS is a national non-profit organization made up of, and providing services to, all those who have lost a loved one on active duty with the Armed Forces. TAPS offers a national military survivor peer support network, grief counseling referral, caseworker assistance, and crisis information. Services are available 24-hours a day, free of charge.

★★

Gold Star Wives of America, Inc.
P.O. Box 361986
Birmingham, AL 35236
1-888-751-6350

Incorporated in 1945, the organization works for legislation, and exists to provide service widows with an organization dedicated to their needs, concerns, and welfare.

The Society of Military Widows
5535 Hempstead Way
Springfield, VA 22151
1-800-842-3451, extension 3009

The Society of Military Widows is a nationwide organization whose purpose is to:

- Benefit widows of members of all branches of the uniformed services of the United States;

- Give moral support, advice, referral service, and general help to the widows of career military members to return to the main stream of normal living;

- Educate the American public concerning the problems and needs of military widows in today's society; and

- Preserve the basic truths and enduring principles on which the government of the United States is founded.

★★

CHAPTER 6

DEATH PENSIONS TO SURVIVING SPOUSES AND CHILDREN

A Death Pension is a benefit paid to eligible dependents of deceased wartime veterans.

DEFINITIONS

The following definitions apply only to CHAPTER 6 – DEATH PENSIONS TO SURVIVING SPOUSES AND CHILDREN:

Veteran: as used in this chapter, includes a person who has completed at least 2 years of honorable active military, naval, or air service, as certified by the appropriate authority, but whose death in such service was not in line of duty.

Indian Wars: means the campaigns, engagements, and expeditions of the United States military forces against Indian tribes or nations, service in which has been recognized heretofore as pensionable service.

World War I: means the period April 6, 1917, through November 11, 1918. In the case of a veteran who served with the United States military forces in Russia, the ending date is April 1, 1920. Service after November 11, 1918 and before July 2, 1921 is considered World War I for compensation or pension purposes, if the veteran served in the active military, naval, or air service after April 5, 1917 and before November 12, 1918.

Civil War Veteran: includes a person who served in the military or naval forces of the Confederate States of America during the Civil War, and the term "active military or naval service" includes active service in those forces.

Period of War: means the Mexican border period, World War I, World War II, the Korean conflict, the Vietnam era, the Persian Gulf War, and the period beginning on the date of any future declaration of war by the Congress and ending on the date prescribed by Presidential proclamation or concurrent resolution of the Congress.

Regular Aid and Attendance: for the purposes of this chapter, a person shall be considered to be in need of regular aid and attendance if such person is:

- A patient in a nursing home; or
- Helpless or blind, or so nearly helpless or blind as to need or require the aid and attendance of another person.

Permanently Housebound: for the purposes of this chapter, the requirement of "permanently housebound" will be considered to have been met when the surviving spouse is substantially confined to such surviving spouse's house (ward or clinical areas, if institutionalized) or immediate premises due to a disability or disabilities, which it is reasonably certain will remain throughout such surviving spouse's lifetime.

★★

ELIGIBILITY REQUIREMENTS

Eligible dependents may qualify for a Death Pension if:

- The deceased veteran was discharged from service under other than dishonorable conditions; **AND**

- He or she served 90 days or more of active duty with at least 1 day during a war; **AND**

- The dependent is the surviving spouse or unmarried child of the deceased veteran; **AND**

- The dependent's countable income is below an annual limit set by law (See below for 2000 annual income limitations.)

NOTE: Separate provisions and monetary amounts are provided for eligible dependents of Civil War, Indian War, and Spanish-American War veterans. These benefits are described at the end of this chapter.

ANNUAL INCOME LIMITATIONS

DEATH PENSION RATE TABLE FOR SURIVING SPOUSES & CHILDREN – Rates Effective December 1, 2000

Maximum Annual Pension Rate (MAPR) Category	Annual Income Must Be Less Than:
Surviving Spouse Alone (No Dependent Child):	$6,237
Surviving Spouse With One Dependent Child:	$8,168
Child Alone:	$1,586
Housebound Spouse Without Dependents:	$7,625
Housebound Spouse With One Dependent:	$9,551
Surviving Spouse In Need Of Aid And Attendance (No Dependent Child):	$9,973
Surviving Spouse In Need Of Aid And Attendance With One Dependent Child:	$11,900
For Each Additional Child:	$1,586
Child Earned Income Exclusion Effective 1/1/2000:	$7,200

★★

Maximum Annual Income Limitations For Protected Pensions - (Effective December 1, 2000)

(Pensioners entitled to benefits as of December 31, 1978, who do not elect to receive a pension under the Improved Pension Program, may continue to receive pension benefits at the rates they were entitled to receive on December 31, 1978 or June 30, 1960, as long as they remain permanently and totally disabled, do not lose a dependent, and their income does not exceed the income limitation, adjusted annually.)

Pension Law in Effect on December 31, 1978 (Section 306):

(The rate entitled to on December 31, 1978 may be continued if the recipient's IVAP for 2000 is below the following limits:

STATUS OF RECIPIENT:	ANNUAL INCOME LIMITATION:
Surviving spouse with no dependents	$ 10,584.00
Surviving spouse with one or more dependents	14,228.00
Child (no entitled veteran or surviving spouse)	8,651.00

Pension Law in Effect on June 30, 1960 (Old Law):

(The rate entitled to on June 30, 1960 may be continued if the recipient's IVAP for 2000 is below the following limits:

STATUS OF RECIPIENT:	ANNUAL INCOME LIMITATION:
Surviving spouse with no dependents	9,265.00
Surviving spouse with one or more dependents	13,357.00
Child only (no entitled veteran or surviving spouse)	9,265.00

Note: Some income is not counted toward the yearly limit (for example, welfare benefits, some wages earned by dependent children, and Supplemental Security Income).

AMOUNT PAID BY VA

VA pays eligible spouses and dependents the difference between his or her countable income and the annual income limit outlined in the above table. The difference is generally paid in 12 equal monthly payments rounded down to the nearest dollar.

ADDITIONAL REQUIREMENTS

No Death Pension shall be paid under this chapter to a surviving spouse of a veteran unless the spouse was married to the veteran:

- Before:

    o   December 14, 1944, in the case of a surviving spouse of a Mexican Border period or World War I veteran; or

    o   January 1, 1957 in the case of a surviving spouse of a World War II veteran; or

    o   February 1, 1965, in the case of a surviving spouse of a Korean conflict veteran; or

    o   May 8, 1985, in the case of a surviving spouse of a Vietnam era veteran, or

    o   January 1, 2001, in the case of a surviving spouse of a veteran of the Persian Gulf War;

- For one year or more; or

- For any period of time if a child was born of the marriage, or was born to them before the marriage.

In determining the annual income of a surviving spouse, if there is a child of the veteran in the custody of the surviving spouse, that portion of the annual income of the child that is reasonably available to or for the surviving spouse shall be considered to be income of the surviving spouse, unless in the judgment of the VA, to do so would work a hardship on the surviving spouse.

NET WORTH LIMITATION

The VA shall deny or discontinue payment of pension to a surviving spouse when the corpus of the estate of the surviving spouse is such that under all the circumstances, including consideration of the income of the surviving spouse and the income of any child from whom the surviving spouse is receiving increased pension, it is reasonable that some part of the corpus of such estate be consumed for the surviving spouse's maintenance.

The VA shall deny or discontinue the payment of increased pension on account of a child when the corpus of such child's estate is such that under all the circumstances, including consideration of the income of the surviving spouse and such child and the income of any other child for whom the surviving spouse is receiving increased pension, it is reasonable that some part of the corpus of the child's estate be consumed for the child's maintenance. During the period such denial or discontinuance remains in effect, such child shall not be considered as the surviving spouse's child for purposes of this chapter.

The VA shall deny or discontinue payment of pension to a child when the corpus of the state of the child is such that under all the circumstances, including consideration of the income of the child, the income of any person with whom such child is residing who is legally responsible for such child's support, and the corpus of the estate of such person, it is reasonable that some part of the corpus of such estate be consumed for the child's maintenance.

★★

CIVIL WAR

Surviving Spouses Of Civil War Veterans

The VA shall pay to the surviving spouse of each Civil War veteran who met the service requirements, a pension at the following monthly rate:

- $40.64 if such surviving spouse is below 70 years of age; or
- $70.00 if such surviving spouse is 70 years of age or older.

If there is a child of the veteran, the rate of pension paid to the surviving spouse shall be increased by $8.13 per month for each such child.

A veteran met the service requirements of this section is such veteran served for 90 days or more in the active military or naval service during the Civil War, or if such veteran was discharged or released from such service upon a surgeon's certificate of disability.

No pension shall be paid to a surviving spouse of a Civil War veteran unless such surviving spouse was married to such veteran:

- Before June 27, 1905; or
- For one year or more; or
- For any period of time if a child was born of the marriage, or was born to them before the marriage.

Children of Civil War Veterans

Whenever there is no surviving spouse of a Civil War veteran entitled to a pension as described above, the VA shall pay to the children of each Civil War veteran who met the service requirements outlined above, a pension at the monthly rate of $73.13 for one child, plus $8.13 for each additional child, with the total amount equally divided.

INDIAN WAR

Surviving Spouses of Indian War Veterans

The VA shall pay to the surviving spouse of each Indian War veteran who met the service requirements (outlined below), a pension at the following monthly rate:

- $40.64 if such surviving spouse is below 70 years of age; or
- $70.00 if such surviving spouse s 70 years of age or older.

If there is a child of the veteran, the rate of pension paid to the surviving spouse shall be increased by $8.13 per month for each such child.

★★★

No pension shall be paid to a surviving spouse of an Indian War veteran unless such surviving spouse was married to such veteran:

- Before March 4, 1917; or
- For one year or more; or
- For any period of time if a child was born of the marriage, or was born to them before the marriage.

Indian Wars Service Requirements:
- Served in one of the Indian Wars for 30 days or more; or
- For the duration of such Indian War

Children of Indian War Veterans

Whenever there is no surviving spouse of an Indian War veteran entitled to a pension as described above, the VA shall pay to the children of each Indian War veteran who met the service requirements outlined above, a pension at the monthly rate of $73.13 for one child, plus $8.13 for each additional child, with the total amount equally divided.

SPANISH-AMERICAN WAR

Surviving Spouses of Spanish-American War Veterans

The VA shall pay to the surviving spouse of each Spanish-American War veteran who met the service requirements (outlined below), a pension at the monthly rate of $70.00, unless such surviving spouse was the spouse of the veteran during such veteran's service in the Spanish-American War, in which case the monthly rate shall be $75.00.

If there is a child of the veteran, the rate of pension paid to the surviving spouse shall be increased by $8.13 per month for each such child.

No pension shall be paid to a surviving spouse of a Spanish-American War veteran unless such surviving spouse was married to such veteran:

- Before January 1, 1938; or
- For one year or more; or
- For any period of time if a child was born of the marriage, or was born to them before the marriage.

Any surviving spouse eligible for pension under this section shall, if such surviving spouse so elects, be paid pension at the rates prescribed by Section 1541 of Title 38 of the United States Code – Surviving Spouses of A Period of War – and under the conditions (other than the service requirements) applicable to pension paid under that section to surviving spouses of veterans of a period of war. If pension is paid pursuant to such an election, the election shall be irrevocable.

Spanish-American War Service Requirements:
Served in the active military or naval service for 90 days or more; or
Served in the active military or naval service and was discharged or released from such service for a service-connected disability

Children of Spanish-American War Veterans

Whenever there is no surviving spouse of Spanish-American War veteran entitled to a pension as described above, the VA shall pay to the children of each Spanish-American War veteran who met the service requirements outlined above, a pension at the monthly rate of $73.13 for one child, plus $8.13 for each additional child, with the total amount equally divided.

APPLYING FOR DEATH PENSION BENEFITS

Eligible surviving spouses and dependent children can apply for Death Pension benefits by completing VA Form 21-534, *Application for Dependency and Indemnity Compensation or Death Pension by Surviving Spouse or Child.* If available, copies of dependency records (marriage & children's birth certificates) should be attached to the application. A copy of the veteran's DD Form 214 and a copy of the veteran's death certificate should also be included with the completed application.

The completed forms should be sent to the applicable VA Regional Office (refer to page 292 for a listing of all VA regional offices.)

Special Note: If any of the pertinent supporting evidence is not immediately available, the applicant should send in the application anyway. The date VA receives the application is important! If VA approves the claim, benefit payments usually begin from the date the application is received, regardless of when the claim is approved.

★★

CHAPTER 7

MISCELLANEOUS BENEFITS FOR SURVIVING SPOUSES AND CHILDREN

DEATH COMPENSATION FOR SURVIVING SPOUSES AND CHILDREN OF VETERANS WHO PASSED AWAY PRIOR TO JANUARY 1, 1957

The surviving spouse, child or children, and dependent parent or parents of any veteran who died before January 1, 1957 as the result of injury or disease incurred in or aggravated by active military, naval, or air service, in the line of duty during a period of war or peacetime, shall be entitled to receive the following monthly compensation rates:

Status:	Monthly Rate:
Surviving spouse, but no child:	$87
Surviving spouse with one child:	$121
Each additional child:	$29
No surviving spouse, but one child:	$67
No surviving spouse, but two children:	$94 (equally divided)
No surviving spouse, but three children:	$122 (equally divided)
Each additional child:	$23 (total amount to be equally divided)
Dependent parent:	$75
Both dependent parents:	$40 each
Additional amount payable if surviving spouse or dependent parent is a patient in a nursing home, or requires aid and attendance:	$79

Applying For Death Compensation

Eligible surviving spouses and dependent children can apply for Death Compensation by completing VA Form 21-534, *Application for Dependency and Indemnity Compensation or Death Pension by Surviving Spouse or Child.* If available, copies of dependency records (marriage records, divorce records, & children's birth certificates) should be attached to the application. A copy of the veteran's DD Form 214 and a copy of the veteran's death certificate should also be included with the completed application.

The completed form should be sent to the applicable VA Regional Office (refer to page 292 for a listing of all VA regional offices.)

★★

Special Note: If any of the pertinent supporting evidence is not immediately available, the applicant should send in the application anyway. The date VA receives the application is important! If VA approves the claim, benefit payments usually begin from the date the application is received, regardless of when the claim is approved.

SURVIVOR BENEFIT PLAN (SBP)

Since September 21, 1972, the Survivor Benefit Plan has been available for retired service personnel and commissioned officers of the Public Health Service. Eligible persons designate all or a part of retired pay as a basis for survivor's annuity.

Eligible surviving spouses of military retirees who did not participate in the plan, and who died prior to September 21, 1973 are eligible for SBP-MIW (Survivor Benefit Plan - Minimum Income Annuity). To be eligible the surviving spouse must not be remarried, must be eligible for VA death pension, and must have income for VA purposes, excluding any SBP annuity, of less than the MIW-SBP annuity limitation.

Effective December 1, 2000, the MIW-SBP annuity limitation is $6,237.

SBP survivor's annuity to a surviving spouse is subject to reduction or discontinuance if the spouse becomes eligible for Dependency and Indemnity Compensation (DIC).

However, concurrent payment of SBP and DIC to children or parents is not prohibited. For further information, interested parties should contact their respective military payment center.

Special Note: Any payments under MIW-SBP are considered income for VA purposes.

CHAPTER 8

BURIAL BENEFITS

REIMBURSEMENT OF BURIAL EXPENSES

The Veterans Benefits Administration administers a burial benefits program designed to assist claimants in meeting the funeral and burial costs of a deceased veteran. The type and amount of benefits payable depends on the veteran's individual service record and cause of death.

Service-Connected Death

If a veteran's death is service-connected, the VA will pay a burial allowance of up to $1,500. If the veteran is buried in a VA national cemetery, some or all of the cost of moving the deceased to the national cemetery nearest the veteran's home may also be reimbursed. There is no time limit for applying for a service-connected burial allowance. The person who bore the veteran's burial expense may claim reimbursement from any VA regional office.

Non-Service Connected Death

If a veteran's death is not service-connected, there are two types of payments the VA may make:

Burial and Funeral Expense Allowance

The VA will pay a burial and funeral allowance of $300, provided the veteran was discharged under conditions other than dishonorable; and:

- The veteran was receiving VA pension or compensation at the time of death, or would have been entitled to receive VA pension or compensation, but for receipt of military retirement or disability pay; or

- The veteran, at the time of death, had an original or reopened claim pending, and had been found entitled to compensation or pension from a date prior to the date of death; or

- The veteran's death occurred in a VA facility; or

- The veteran died while traveling, under proper authorization and at VA expense, to or from a specified place for the purpose of examination, treatment, or care; or

- The veteran died on or after October 9, 1996, while a patient at an approved State nursing home. (Contact a VA regional office for a complete listing of approved State nursing homes.)

A claim for reimbursement of the burial and funeral allowance for a non-service connected death must be filed within two years of the date of burial or cremation.

★★

Plot Allowance

In addition to the burial and funeral expense allowance, if a veteran is not buried in a cemetery that is under U.S. government jurisdiction, the VA will also pay a plot allowance of $150, provided that the veteran was discharged under conditions other than dishonorable; and:

- The veteran was discharged from active duty because of a disability incurred or aggravated in the line of duty; or

- The veteran was receiving VA pension or compensation at the time of death, or would have been entitled to receive VA pension or compensation, but for receipt of military retirement or disability pay; or

- The veteran died in a VA facility

The plot allowance may be paid to the state if a veteran is buried without charge for the cost of a plot or interment in a state-owned cemetery reserved solely for veteran burials. Burial expenses paid by the deceased veteran's employer or a state agency will not be reimbursed.

A claim for reimbursement of the plot allowance must be filed within two years of the date of burial or cremation.

Reimbursement Of Transportation Costs

The costs of transporting a veteran's body to the place of burial may be authorized if a veteran's death occurs while:

- Enroute for a VA authorized examination, treatment or care; or

- The veteran is properly hospitalized at an approved medical center domiciliary; or

- The veteran is in a nursing home under the direct jurisdiction of the VA; or if the veteran's death occurred on or after October 9, 1996, while a patient at an approved State nursing home.

- The costs of transporting the veteran's body to the place of burial may also be authorized if the veteran is buried in a national cemetery, and died of a service-connected condition. If burial is not in the national cemetery nearest the veteran's last place of residence, the total reimbursement will not be more than the amount which would have been payable for burial in the nearest national cemetery.

Filing Claim for Reimbursement of Expenses

Reimbursement of burial expenses may be applied for by submitting VA Form 21-530, Application for Burial Allowance. A certified copy of the death certificate, proof of the veteran's military service (Form DD-214), and itemized bills of the funeral and burial expenses must be submitted by the person(s) filing the claim(s). The itemized bills must clearly show the name of the veteran for whom services were performed, the nature and cost of the service rendered, all credits, and the name(s) of the person or persons by whom payment in whole or in part was made. If the undertaker's bill is not paid, he is entitled to file claim for reimbursement.

★★★

If more than one person is entitled to reimbursement, each claimant must submit a separate VA Form 21-530 containing the signature of the person who authorized services or the responsible official. Any burial allowance awarded will be apportioned according to the proportionate share paid by each, unless a waiver is executed in favor of one of such person by the other person or persons. However, in no case will there be allowed the person in whose favor payment is waived a sum greater than that which was paid by him/her toward the burial, funeral, and transportation expenses. If two or more persons have paid such expenses from their personal funds, and one or more of such persons dies before filing claim, no consideration will be given to the amount paid by the deceased person(s).

If applying for reimbursement of transportation expenses, a statement of account identifying the charges for transporting the body is required.

Unpaid Balance Due Persons who Performed Services

If there is an unpaid balance due the person who performed burial, funeral, and transportation services, such claim as a creditor for the statutory burial allowance will be given priority over any claim for reimbursement based on use of personal funds, unless there is executed by such creditor a waiver in favor of the person or persons whose personal funds were used in making the partial payment of the account.

No reimbursement may be made to a State, County, or other governmental subdivision.

Veteran's Estate

The representative of a deceased person's estate may file a claim for reimbursement, if estate funds were used to pay the expenses of the veteran's burial, funeral, and transportation. Accordingly, if otherwise in order, reimbursement may be made to the estate, regardless of whether such person pre-deceased the veteran or was deceased at the time the expenses were incurred or paid, or burial of the veteran actually occurred.

Death of Active Duty Personnel

The VA does not pay a burial or plot interment allowance if a veteran dies while on active military duty. However, such veteran is entitled to certain benefits from the military. Information should be obtained from the branch of the armed forces in which the person served at time of death.

Burial of Unclaimed Bodies

If the body of an eligible deceased veteran is unclaimed by relatives or friends, the Director of any regional VA office or any VA medical center is authorized to arrange for burial in either a national cemetery or in a cemetery or section of a cemetery, owned by a state, a state agency, or political subdivision of a state, and used solely for the interment of persons eligible for burial in a national cemetery.

If an organization provides a burial or furnishes a burial plot as a humanitarian measure, and not pursuant to a legal obligation, it may be reimbursed for its actual cost. Reimbursement to such organization cannot exceed the maximum benefits payable based on the veteran's eligibility.

★★★

Correction of Discharge to Honorable Conditions

Public Law 88-3 (H.R. 212) provides that where burial allowance was not payable at the time of a veteran's death because of the nature of his discharge from service, but after death his discharge is corrected by competent authority so as to reflect a discharge under conditions other than dishonorable, claim may be filed within two years from the date of correction of the discharge.

Legal Execution

The execution of a veteran as a lawful punishment for a crime does not of itself preclude a payment of the statutory burial allowances.

State Burial Allowance

There are some burial allowances allowed by states or counties for the burial of needy veterans, and in some instances, of their dependents. Check with the veteran's state or county of residence for specific information.

Assistance to Claimants

It is incumbent upon the claimant to establish his case in accordance with the law. This rule, however, will not be highly technical or rigid in its application. The general policy of the VA is to give the claimant every opportunity to substantiate his claim, to extend all reasonable assistance in its prosecution, and develop all sources from which information may be obtained. Assistance may also be secured from post, state, and national service officers or veterans' organizations.

Miscellaneous

If the deceased veteran is entitled to payment in full of burial expenses by the Employees' Compensation Commission, Workman's Compensation, or employer, the Veterans Administration will make no payment.

Appeal

An appeal may be made within one year from the date of denial of a claim. The appeal must be sent to the regional VA office that denied the claim. (For specific information regarding Appeals Procedures, refer to page 282 of this book.

BURIAL FLAGS

The VA shall furnish a United States flag, at no cost, for burial or memorial purposes in connection with the death of an eligible veteran who served honorably in the U.S. Armed Forces, or a reservist (if the reservist is entitled to military pay).

After the burial of the veteran, the flag shall be given to his next of kin. If no claim is made for the flag by the next of kin, it may be given, upon request, to a close friend or associate of the deceased veteran. If a flag is given to a close friend or associate of the deceased veteran, no flag shall be given to any other person on account of the death of such veteran.

When burial is in a national, state or post cemetery, a burial flag will automatically be provided. When burial is in a private cemetery, an American flag may be obtained by a service officer, an undertaker or other interested person from the nearest Veterans Administration office or most U.S. Post Offices. VA Form 2008, Application for United States Flag for Burial Purposes, must be completed and submitted along with a copy of the veteran's discharge papers. Generally, the funeral director will help the next of kin with this process.

The proper way to display the flag depends upon whether the casket is open or closed. VA Form 2008 provides the proper method for displaying and folding the flag. The burial flag is not suitable for outside display, because of its size and fabric.

After burial of a veteran, the flag should be folded in military style and presented to the next of kin at the cemetery. Local veteran organizations, when presenting the flag, usually say something like this:

> "In the name of the United States government and *name of veterans organization* (such as A.L., D.A.V., V.F.W., and American Veterans of World War II, etc.) we present you this flag, in loving memory of our departed comrade."

Presenting of the flag is sometimes a difficult task when there is a disagreement in the family. However, the Veterans Administration gives the following order of preference to be followed:

1. Widow or widower (even if separated but not divorced)
2. Children according to age (minor child may be issued flag on application signed by guardian)
3. Father, including adopted, step and foster father
4. Mother, including adopted, step and foster mother
5. Brothers or sisters, including brothers and sisters of half blood.
6. Uncles or aunts
7. Nephews or nieces
8. Cousins, grandparents, etc. (but not in-laws)

(If two relatives have equal rights, the flag will be presented to the elder one.)

Following a veteran's burial, the United States flag received by the next of kin may be donated to the VA, for use on national holidays at VA national cemeteries. If the next of kin chooses to make such a donation, it should be given or mailed to the Director of any national cemetery selected by the donor with a written request that the flag be flown at that location. If the flag is brought into a Veterans Service Division, it will be accepted and forwarded to the cemetery chosen by the donor. A Certificate of Appreciation is presented to the donor for providing their loved ones' burial flag to a national cemetery.

Please note that VA cannot provide flag holders for placement on private headstones or markers. These flag holders may be purchased from private manufacturing companies.

★★

The law allows the VA to issue one flag for a veteran's funeral. The VA cannot replace it if it is lost, destroyed, or stolen. However, if this occurs, a local veteran's organization or other community group may be able to assist you in obtaining another flag.

BURIAL IN NATIONAL CEMETERIES

The National Cemetery Administration honors Veterans with a final resting place and lasting memorials that commemorate their service to our nation.

Veterans and service members who meet the eligibility requirements, and their eligible dependents may be buried in one of the VA's national cemeteries. The National Cemetery Administration currently includes 119 national cemeteries. The Department of the Army administers 2 national cemeteries, and the Department of the Interior administers 14 national cemeteries, for a total of 135 national cemeteries. There are also numerous state cemeteries for veterans throughout the U.S. For a listing of all national cemeteries as well as state veterans cemeteries refer to the listing at the end of this chapter.

Eligibility

The VA national cemetery directors have the primary responsibility for verifying eligibility for burial in VA national cemeteries. A dependent's eligibility for burial is based upon the eligibility of the veteran. To establish a veteran's eligibility, a copy of the official military discharge document bearing an official seal or a DD 214 is usually sufficient. The document must show that release from service was under conditions other than dishonorable. A determination of eligibility is usually made in response to a request for burial in a VA national cemetery.

The cemeteries administered by the National Cemetery Administration and the Department of the Interior use the eligibility requirements that follow. The Department of the Interior can be contacted at:

U.S. Department of the Interior
National Park Service
1849 C Street, N.W.
Washington, D.C. 20240
(202) 208-4621

The Department of the Army should be contacted directly for inquiries concerning eligibility for interment in either of the two cemeteries under its jurisdiction (call 703-695-3250).

Eligibility requirements for burial in state veterans cemeteries are the same, or similar, to the eligibility requirements that follow. However, some states also have residency and other more restrictive requirements. Please contact the specific state cemetery for its eligibility requirements.

★★★

The following veterans and members of the Armed Forces (Army, Navy, Air Force, Marine Corps, Coast Guard) are eligible for burial in a VA national cemetery:

1. Any member of the Armed Forces of the U.S. who dies on active duty.

2. Any citizen of the U.S. who, during any war in which the U.S. has been engaged, served in the Armed Forces of any U.S. ally during that war, whose last active service terminated honorably by death or otherwise, and who was a citizen of the U.S. at the time of entry into such service and at the time of death.

3. Any veteran discharged under conditions other than dishonorable, and who has completed the required period of service. With certain exceptions, service beginning after September 7, 1980, as an enlisted person, and service after October 16, 1981, as an officer, must be for a minimum of 24 months or the full period for which the person was called to active duty.

4. Reservists and National Guard members with 20 years of qualifying service, who are entitled to retired pay, or would be entitled, if at least 60 years of age.

5. Members of reserve components who die under honorable conditions while hospitalized or undergoing treatment at the expense of the U.S. for injury or disease contracted or incurred under honorable conditions, while performing active duty for training, or inactive duty training, or undergoing such hospitalization or treatment.

6. Members of the Reserve Officers' Training Corps of the Army, Navy, or Air Force who die under honorable conditions while attending an authorized training camp or cruise, or while traveling to or from that camp or cruise, or while hospitalized or undergoing treatment at the expense of the U.S. for injury or disease contracted or incurred under honorable conditions while engaged in one of those activities.

7. Members of reserve components who, during a period of active duty for training, were disabled or died from a disease or injury incurred or aggravated in the line of duty, or, during a period of inactive duty training, were disabled or died from an injury incurred or aggravated in the line of duty.

8. A Commissioned Officer of the National Oceanic and Atmospheric Administration with full-time duty on or after July 29, 1945.

9. A Commissioned Officer of the National Oceanic and Atmospheric Administration who served before July 29, 1945, and:

    a. Was assigned to an area of immediate hazard described in the Act of December 3, 1942 (56 Stat. 1038; 33 U.S.C. 855a), as amended;

    b. Served in the Philippine Islands on December 7, 1941; or

    c. Transferred to the Department of the Army or the Department of the Navy under the provisions of the Act of May 22, 1917 (40 Stat. 87; 33 U.S.C. 855).

10. A Commissioned Officer of the Regular or Reserve Corps of the Public Health Service who served on full-time duty on or after July 29, 1945. If the service of such Officer falls within the meaning of active duty for training, he must have been disabled or died from a disease or injury incurred or aggravated in the line of duty.

★★

11. A Commissioned Officer of the Regular or Reserve Corps of the Public Health Service who performed full-time duty prior to July 29, 1945:

    a.   In time of war; or

    b.   On detail for duty with the Army, Navy, Air Force, Marine Corps, or Coast Guard; or

    c.   While the service was part of the military forces of the U.S. pursuant to Executive Order of the President.

12. A Commissioned Officer of the Regular or Reserve Corps of the Public Health Service serving on inactive duty training as defined in Section 101 (23), title 39, U.S. Code, whose death resulted from an injury incurred or aggravated in the line of duty.

13. U.S. Merchant Mariners with oceangoing service during the period of armed conflict, December 7, 1941 to December 31, 1946.

14. U.S. Merchant Mariners who served on blockships in support of Operation Mulberry during WWII.

15. The spouse or unremarried surviving spouse of an eligible person.

16. The spouse of a member of the U.S. Armed Forces lost or buried at sea, or officially determined to be missing or missing in action, or whose remains have been donated to science or cremated and the ashes scattered.

17. The surviving spouse of an eligible decedent, who remarries an ineligible individual, but whose remarriage is void, terminated by the ineligible individual's death, or dissolved by annulment or divorce.

18. The surviving spouse of an eligible decedent who remarries an eligible person.

19. The minor children of an eligible person. The child must be:

    a.   Under 21 years of age; or

    b.   Under 23 years of age and pursuing a course of instruction at an approved educational institution.

20. An unmarried adult child of an eligible person if the child is permanently incapable of self-support due to a physical or mental disability.

21. Any other persons or classes of persons as designated by the Secretary of Veterans Affairs or the Secretary of the Air Force.

The following are not eligible for burial in a VA national cemetery:

1.   A surviving spouse of an eligible decedent who later marries an ineligible individual and predeceases that individual.

2.   A former spouse of an eligible individual whose marriage to that individual has been terminated by annulment or divorce, if not otherwise eligible.

3.   Family members other than those specifically described in items #15 through #20, above.

4.   A person whose only separation from the Armed Forces was under dishonorable conditions, or whose character of service results in a bar to veterans benefits.

5.   A person ordered to report to an induction station, but not actually inducted into military service.

6. Any person convicted of subversive activities after September 1, 1959, even if the subversive activity occurred *prior* to the period of active military service. Eligibility will be reinstated if the President of the U.S grants a pardon.

7. A person whose only service is active duty for training or inactive duty training in the National Guard or Reserve Component, unless the individual meets any of the eligibility requirements outlined in items 1 through 21, above.

8. Members of groups whose service has been determined by the Secretary of the Air Force as not warranting entitlement to benefits administered by the Secretary of Veterans Affairs.

9. A person convicted of any Federal Capital crime, or any State capital crime involving the death of one or more persons.

If a veteran is discharged for undesirable, bad conduct, or any other type of discharge other than honorable, a VA Regional Office must determine his eligibility for burial in a VA National Cemetery.

Since 1997, persons convicted of federal or state capital crimes are not eligible for burial in National Cemeteries.

Requests for Gravesites in National Cemeteries

An eligible veteran or family member may be buried in the VA national cemetery of his choice, provided space is available. A veteran may not reserve a gravesite in his name prior to his death. However, any reservations made under previous programs will be honored. The funeral director or loved one making the burial arrangements must apply for a gravesite at the time of death. No special forms are required when requesting burial in a VA national cemetery. The person making burial arrangement should contact the national cemetery in which burial is desired at the time of need.

If possible, the following information concerning the deceased should be provided when the cemetery is first contacted:

- Full name and military rank;
- Branch of service;
- Social security number;
- VA claim number, if applicable;
- Date and place of birth;
- Date and place of death;
- Date of retirement or last separation from active duty; and
- Copy of any military separation documents (such as DD-214)

When a death occurs and eligibility for interment in a national cemetery is determined, grave space is assigned by the cemetery director in the name of the veteran or family member. One gravesite is permitted for the interment of all eligible family members, unless soil conditions or the number of family decedents necessitate more than one grave. There is no charge for burial in a national cemetery.

★★★

The availability of grave space varies among each National Cemetery. In many cases, if a national cemetery does not have space for a full-casket burial, it may still inter cremated remains. Full-casket gravesites occasionally become available in such cemeteries due to disinterment or cancellation of prior reservations. The cemetery director can answer such questions at the time of need.

Most national cemeteries do not typically conduct burials on weekends. However, weekend callers trying to make burial arrangements for the following week will be provided with the phone number of one of three strategically located VA cemetery offices that remains open during weekends.

Burial at Sea

The National Cemetery Administration cannot provide burial at sea. For information, contact:

U.S. Department of the Navy
Bureau of Medicine and Surgery
Naval Office of Medical / Dental Affairs
(MEDDEN AFFAIRS)
Mortuary Affairs, Building 38H
Great Lakes, IL 60085-5200
1-800-876-1131, ext. 629

Furnishing and Placement of Headstones and Markers

In addition to the gravesite, burial in a VA national cemetery also includes furnishing and placement of the headstone or marker, opening and closing of the grave, and perpetual care. Many national cemeteries also have columbaria or gravesites for cremated remains. (Some State Veterans' cemeteries may charge a nominal fee for placing a Government-provided headstone or marker.)

SPECIAL NOTES:

- *For person's with 20-years service in the National Guard or Reserves, entitlement to retired pay must be subsequent to October 27, 1992 in order to qualify for a Government-provided headstone or marker. A copy of the Reserve Retirement Eligibility Benefits Letter must accompany the application. Active duty service while in the National Guard or Reserves also establishes eligibility.*

- *Service prior to World War I requires detailed documentation to prove eligibility such as muster rolls, extracts from State files, military or State organizations where served, pension or land warrants, etc.*

By law, Government markers cannot be provided to be used as footstones, and should not be used to double-mark a veteran's grave. A government-provided headstone or marker should only be requested if the grave will not be marked with a private headstone or marker.

Flat bronze, granite, or marble grave markers and upright marble or granite headstones are available to mark graves in the style consistent with existing monuments in the national cemetery. Niche markers are also available for identifying cremated remains in columbaria. The following is a brief description of each type:

- *Upright Marble and Upright Granite:* 42 inches long, 13 inches wide, 4 inches thick, approximately 230 pounds.

- *Flat Bronze:* 24 inches long, 12 inches wide, ¾ inch rise, approximately 18 pounds. Anchor bolts, nuts and washers for fastening to base are supplied with marker. The government does not provide the base.

- *Flat Granite and Flat Marble*: 24 inches long, 12 inches wide, 4 inches thick, approximately 130 pounds.

- *Bronze Niche:* 8 ½ inches long, 5 ½ inches wide, 7/16 inch rise, approximately 3 pounds. Mounting bolts and washers are supplied with marker.

- There are also two special styles of upright marble headstones and flat markers available - one for those who served with the Union Forces during the Civil War or the Spanish-American War; and one for those who served with the Confederate Forces during the Civil War.

Inscriptions

Headstones and markers are inscribed with the name of the deceased, branch of service, year of birth, and year of death.

The word "Korea" may be included on Government headstones and markers for the graves of those members and former members of the United States Armed Forces who served within the areas of military operations in the Korean Theater between June 27, 1950 and July 27, 1954; and for headstones and markers for active duty decedents who lost their lives in Korea or adjacent waters as a result of hostile action subsequent to the 1953 Armistice.

The word "Vietnam" may be included on Government headstones and markers for the graves of those members and former members of the United States Armed Forces who died in Vietnam or whose death was attributable to service in Vietnam, and on the headstones and markers of all decedents who were on active duty on or after August 5, 1964.

The words "Lebanon" or "Grenada" may be included on Government headstones and markers for those killed as a result of those military actions.

The words "Panama" and "Persian Gulf" may be included on Government headstones and markers for those killed as a result of those military actions.

If desired, the following inscriptions can also be made (space permitting):

- Military grade

- Military rank

- Military rate

- Identification of war service

- Months and days of birth and death

- An authorized emblem of religious belief (see following list of available emblems)

- Military awards (documentation of award must be provided)
- Military organizations
- Civilian or veteran affiliations

With the VA's approval, terms of endearment that meet acceptable standards of good taste may also be added. Most optional inscriptions are placed as the last lines of the inscription. No other graphics are permitted on Government-provided headstones and markers, and inscriptions will be in English text only. Civilian titles such as "Doctor or Reverend" are not permitted on the name line of government-provided headstones and markers.

Available Emblems of Belief for Placement on Government Headstones and Markers:

- Christian Cross
- Buddhist (Wheel of Righteousness)
- Hebrew (Star of David)
- Presbyterian Cross
- Russian Orthodox Cross
- Lutheran Cross
- Episcopal Cross
- Unitarian Church (Flaming Chalice)
- United Methodist Church
- Aaronic Order Church
- Mormon (Angel Moroni)
- Native American Church of North America
- Serbian Orthodox
- Greek Cross
- Bahai (9 Pointed Star)
- Atheist
- Muslim (Crescent and Star)
- Hindu
- Konko-Kyo Faith
- Reorganized Church of Latter Day Saints
- Sufism Reoriented
- Tenrikyo Church
- Seicho-No-Ie
- Church of World Messianity (Izunome)
- United Church of Religious Science
- Christian Reformed Church
- United Moravian Church

★★★

- Eckankar
- Christian Church
- United Church of Christ
- Christian Scientist (Cross and Crown)
- Muslim (Islamic 5 Pointed Star)

Ordering a Headstone or Marker

For burial of a veteran in a national, state veteran, or military post cemetery, the cemetery will order the headstone or marker, and can give loved ones information on style, inscription, and shipment. Shipment and placement of the headstone or marker is provided at no cost.

For burial of a veteran outside of a national, state veteran, or military post cemetery, the headstone or marker must be applied for from the VA. The headstone or marker will be shipped at government expense, however the VA does not pay for placement of the headstone or marker. To apply for a headstone or marker, complete VA Form 40-1330, Application for Standard Government Headstone or Marker for Installation in a Private or State Veterans' Cemetery, and forward it along with a copy of the veteran's military discharge documents to:

Director
Memorial Programs Service (403A)
Department of Veterans Affairs
810 Vermont Avenue, NW
Washington, DC 20420

Headstones and Markers for Spouses and Children

The VA will issue a headstone or marker for an eligible spouse or child buried in a national, state veteran or military post cemetery (see pages 67-68 for eligibility requirements). However, the VA cannot issue a headstone or marker for a spouse or child buried in a private cemetery. The applicant can, however, request to reserve inscription space below the veteran's inscription, so that the non-veteran's commemorative information can be inscribed locally, at private expense, when the non-veteran is buried. The applicant may also choose to have his/her name and date of birth added at Government expense, when the headstone or marker is ordered. The date of death may then be added, at private expense, at the time of his/her death.

Commemoration of Unidentified Remains

Many national cemeteries have areas suitable to commemorate veterans whose remains were not recovered or identified, were buried at sea, or are otherwise unavailable for interment. In such instances, the VA will provide a memorial headstone or marker to be placed in that section of the cemetery. The words *"In Memory of"* must precede the authorized inscription.

Checking Order Status

To check the status of a previously ordered headstone or marker for placement in a private cemetery, applicants may call the VA's Applicant Assistance Line at

★★

1-800-697-6947. The line is open weekdays, from 8:00 A.M. to 5:00 P.M., Eastern Standard Time.

Replacement of Headstones and Markers

The Government will replace a previously furnished headstone or marker if it: becomes badly damaged, is vandalized, is stolen, becomes badly deteriorated, the inscription becomes illegible, is different from that ordered by the applicant, becomes damaged in transit, or the inscription is incorrect.

Government headstones or markers in private cemeteries damaged by cemetery personnel will not be replaced at Government expense.

If a marble or granite headstone or marker is permanently removed from a grave, it must be destroyed. Bronze markers must be returned to the contractor.

For guidance on obtaining a replacement headstone or marker, call 1-800-697-6947.

MILITARY HONORS

The rendering of Military Funeral Honors is a way to show the Nation's deep gratitude to those who have faithfully defended our country in times of war and peace. It is the final demonstration a grateful Nation can provide to the veterans' families.

The following service members are eligible for Military Funeral Honors:

- Military members on active duty or in the Selected Reserve at time of death
- Former military members who served on active duty and departed under conditions other than dishonorable
- Former military members who completed at least one term of enlistment or period of initial obligated service in the Selected Reserve, and departed under conditions other than dishonorable
- Former military members discharged from the Selected Reserve due to a disability incurred or aggravated in the line of duty

Military Funeral Honors have always been provided whenever possible. However, effective October 5, 1999, the law, under P.L. 105-261, Section 578, mandates that all eligible veterans receive basic Military Funeral Honors, if requested by the deceased veteran's family. As provided by law, an honor guard detail for the burial of an eligible veteran shall consist of not less than two members of the Armed Forces. One member of the detail shall be a representative of the parent Service of the deceased veteran. The honor detail will, at a minimum, perform a ceremony that includes the folding and presenting of the American flag to the next of kin, and the playing of Taps. Taps will be played by a bugler, if available, or by electronic recording.

Funeral Directors have the responsibility of assisting loved ones in requesting military honors. A toll-free telephone number has been established for funeral directors requesting military honors.

★★

The Department of Defense (DOD) has provided registered funeral home directors with a military funeral honors kit and information on how to contact the appropriate military organization to perform the honors ceremony. DOD recorded and distributed a "Military Honors" video to highlight an appropriate honors ceremony, and will soon record a video on how veterans' service organizations and military representatives can provide joint honors ceremonies. DOD will soon publish regulations concerning reimbursement to veterans' service organizations for participation in joint honors ceremonies.

Questions about the Military Funeral Honors program should be sent to:

Military Funeral Honors
9504 IH-35 North, Suite 320
San Antonio, TX 78233-6635

PREPARATIONS WHICH CAN BE MADE PRIOR TO DEATH

It is suggested that veterans and their families prepare in advance by discussing cemetery options, collecting the veteran's military information (including discharge papers), and by contacting the cemetery where the veteran wishes to be buried. If burial will be in a private cemetery and a Government headstone or marker will be requested, VA Form 40-1330 can be completed in advance and placed with the veteran's military discharge papers for use at the time of need.

BURIAL LOCATION ASSISTANCE

The VA National Cemetery Administration can provide limited burial location assistance to family members and close friends of decedents thought to be buried in a VA national cemetery.

The National Cemetery Administration will research its records to determine if the decedent is buried in one of VA's national cemeteries. A request can include a maximum of ten specific names to locate.

The National Cemetery Administration does not have information on persons buried in cemeteries other than its national cemeteries. Its records do not contain any personal, military or family information – only information regarding whether or not an individual is buried in a VA national cemetery, and if so, where, can be provided.

No form is required to request this information, and no fee is charged. The following information should be provided:

- Full name, including any alternate spellings, of decedent;
- Date and place of birth;
- Date and place of death;
- State from which the individual entered active duty;
- Military service branch;
- Mailing address and phone number of individual requesting the information.

Allow approximately 3 weeks for a reply.

Requests should be sent to:

> U.S. Department of Veterans Affairs
> National Cemetery Administration (402B)
> Burial Location Request
> 810 Vermont Avenue, N.W.
> Washington, D.C. 20420

U.S. MILITARY CEMETERIES AND MONUMENTS OVERSEAS

The *American Battle Monuments Commission (ABMC)* a small, independent agency of the U.S. government's executive branch, maintains 24 American military cemeteries, and 27 memorials, monuments, or markers. (The VA is not responsible for maintaining cemeteries and monuments honoring deceased veterans buried on foreign soil.)

ABMC Cemeteries

- Aisne Marne - South of Belleau, France
- Ardennes – Neupre (Neuville-enCondroz), Belgium
- Brittany – Southeast of St. James (Marche), France
- Brookwood – Brookwood, Surrey, England
- Cambridge – Cambridge, England
- Corozal – North of Panama City, Republic of Panama
- Epinal – Southeast of Epinal (Vosges), France
- Flanders Field – Waregem, Belgium
- Florence – South of Florence, Italy
- Henri-Chapelle – Northeast of Henri-Chapelle, Belgium
- Lorraine – North of St. Avold (Moselle), France
- Luxembourg – Luxembourg City, Luxembourg
- Manila – Southeast of Manila, Republic of Philippines
- Meuse Argonne – East of Romagne –sous-Montfaucon (Meuse), France
- Mexico City – Mexico City, Mexico
- Netherlands – Margraten, Netherlands
- Normandy – Colleville-sur Mer, France
- North Africa – near Carthage
- Oise-Aisne – East of Fere-en-Tardenois (Aisne), France
- Rhone – Draguignan (Var), France
- Sicily-Rome – Nettuno, Italy
- Somme – Southwest of Bony (Aisne), France
- St. Mihil – Thiaacourt, France
- Surresnes – West of Paris, France

ABMC Monuments

- AEF Memorial – Washington, D.C.
- Audenaude Monument – Oudenaarde (Audenarde), Belgium
- Bellicourt Monument – North of St. Quentin (Aisne), France
- Cabanatuan Memorial - Philippines
- Cantigny Monument – Cantigny (Somme), France
- Chateay-Thierry Monument – West of Chateay-Thierry, France

- Chaumont Marker – Chaumont, France
- East Coast Memorial – Battery Park, New York City
- Guadalcanal Memorial – Honiara, Guadalcanal, Solomon Islands
- Honolulu Memorial – Honolulu, Hawaii
- Kemmel Monument – South of Ieper (Ypres), Belgium
- Korean Memorial – Washington, D.C.
- Belleau Wood Monument – South of Belleau (Aisne), France
- Montfaucan Monument – Northwest of Verdun, France
- Montsec Monument – Montsec (Thiaucourt), France
- Naval Brest Monument – Brest, France
- Naval Gibraltar Monument – Straights of Gibraltar
- Pointe-du-Hoc Monument – Overlooks Omaha Beach, France
- Papua Marker – Papua, New Guinea
- Saipan Memorial – Saipan, Commonwealth of the Mariana Islands
- Sommepy Monument – Northwest of Sommepy – Tahure (Marne), France
- Souilly Marker – Souilly, France
- Tours Monument – Tours, France
- Utah Beach Monument – Sainte-Marie-du-Mont (Manche), France
- West Coast Memorial – San Francisco, California
- Western Task Force Marker – Casablanca, Morocco
- World War II Memorial – Washington, D.C.

ABMC Services

The ABMC can provide interested parties with:

- The name, location, plot, row and grave number of Honored War Dead;
- The best routes and modes of travel to foreign cemeteries or memorials;
- Letters authorizing no-fee passports for members of the immediate family traveling overseas to visit a grave or memorial site;
- Black and white photos of headstones and tablets of the Missing, on which the names of the dead or missing are engraved;
- Assistance making arrangements for floral decorations to be placed at grave and memorial sites; and
- Polaroid color photographs of donated floral decorations in place.

The ABMC maintains a listing of veterans interred at American military cemeteries overseas, and those Missing-in-Action from World War I, World War II, Korea and Vietnam. It also has a listing of war veterans buried at the Corozal American Cemetery, and those who lost their lives during the Korean War.

For further information, contact the ABMC at:

American Battle Monuments Commission
Arlington Court House Plaza II
2300 Clarendon Blvd., Suite 500
Arlington, VA 22201
(703) 696-6897

Passports to Visit Overseas Cemeteries

Family members who wish to visit overseas graves and memorial sites of World War I and World War II veterans are eligible for "no-fee" passports. Family

★★★

members eligible for the "no-fee" passports include surviving spouses, parents, children, sisters, brothers and guardians of the deceased veteran buried or commemorated in American military cemeteries on foreign soil. For further information contact the American Battle Monuments Commission at the address and phone number indicated in the previous section.

PRESIDENTIAL MEMORIAL CERTIFICATES

A Presidential Memorial Certificate is an engraved paper certificate that has been signed by the current president, honoring the memory of any honorably discharged deceased veteran. Presidential Memorial Certificates may be distributed to a deceased veteran's next of kin and loved ones. More than one certificate can be provided per family, and there is no time limit for applying for the certificate. Requests for a Presidential Memorial Certificate can be made in person at any VA regional office, or by U.S. Mail. There is no form to use when requesting a certificate. A copy of the veteran's discharge documents and a return mailing address should be included with any request. Written requests should be sent to:

U.S. Department of Veterans Affairs
National Cemetery Administration (403A)
810 Vermont Avenue, NW
Washington, DC 20420

LISTS OF NATIONAL CEMETERIES

Some national cemeteries can bury only cremated remains or casketed remains of eligible family members of those already buried. Contact the cemetery director for information on the availability of space

Department Of Veterans Affairs National Cemeteries

Alabama

Fort Mitchell National Cemetery
553 Highway 165
Seale, AL 36875
(334) 855-4731

Mobile National Cemetery
1202 Virginia Street
Mobile, AL 36604
For information please contact:
Barrancas National Cemetery (850) 452-3357

Alaska

Fort Richardson National Cemetery
Building #997, Davis Highway
P. O. Box 5-498
Fort Richardson, AK 99505
(907) 384-7075

Sitka National Cemetery
Box 1065
Sitka, AK 99835
For information please contact:
Fort Richardson National Cemetery
(907) 384-7075

Arizona

National Memorial Cemetery of Arizona
23029 North Cave Creek Road
Phoenix, AZ 85024
(602) 379-4615

★★

Prescott National Cemetery
500 Highway 89 North
Prescott, AZ 86301
For information please contact
National Memorial Cemetery of
Arizona (602) 379-4615

Arkansas

Fayetteville National Cemetery
700 Government Avenue
Fayetteville, AR 72701
(501) 444-5051

Fort Smith National Cemetery
522 Garland Avenue
Fort Smith, AR 72901
(501) 783-5345

Little Rock National Cemetery
2523 Confederate Boulevard
Little Rock, AR 72206
(501) 324-6401

California

Fort Rosecrans National Cemetery
P. O. Box 6237 Point Loma
San Diego, CA 92106
(619) 553-2084

Golden Gate National Cemetery
1300 Sneath Lane
San Bruno, CA 94066
(415) 761-1646 (San Francisco Co.)
(415) 589-7737 (San Mateo Co.)

Los Angeles National Cemetery
950 South Sepulveda Boulevard
Los Angeles, CA 90049
(310) 268-4494

Riverside National Cemetery
22495 Van Buren Boulevard
Riverside, CA 92518
(909) 653-8417

San Francisco National Cemetery
P. O. Box 29012
Presidio of San Francisco
San Francisco, CA 94129
For information please contact
Golden Gate National Cemetery
(415) 761-1646

San Joaquin Valley National
Cemetery
32053 West McCabe Road
Gustine, CA 95322
(209) 854-1040

Colorado

Fort Logan National Cemetery
3698 South Sheridan Boulevard
Denver, CO 80235
(303) 761-0117

Fort Lyon National Cemetery
VA Medical Center
Fort Lyon, CO 81038
For information please contact Fort
Logan National Cemetery
(303) 761-0117

Florida

Barrancas National Cemetery
Naval Air Station
Pensacola, FL 32508-1099
(850) 452-3357 or 4196

Bay Pines National Cemetery
P. O. Box 477
Bay Pines, FL 33504-0477
For information please contact
Florida National Cemetery
(352) 793-7740

Florida National Cemetery
6502 SW 102nd Avenue
Bushnell, FL 33513
(352) 793-7740 or 1074

St. Augustine National Cemetery
104 Marine Street
St. Augustine, FL 32084
For information please contact
Florida National Cemetery
(352) 793-7740

Georgia

Marietta National Cemetery
500 Washington Avenue
Marietta, GA 30060
For information please contact
Fort Mitchell National Cemetery
(334) 855-4731

Hawaii

National Memorial Cemetery of the Pacific
2177 Puowaina Drive
Honolulu, HI 96813-1729
(808) 566-1430

Illinois

Abraham Lincoln National
Cemetery
27034 South Diagonal Road
Elwood, IL 60421
(815) 423-9958
(815) 423-5824 (fax)

Alton National Cemetery
600 Pearl Street
Alton, IL 62003
For information please contact
Jefferson Barracks National
Cemetery (314) 260-8720

Camp Butler National Cemetery
5063 Camp Butler Road; RR #1
Springfield, IL 62707
(217) 492-4070

Danville National Cemetery
1900 East Main Street
Danville, IL 61832
(217) 431-6550

Mound City National Cemetery
P. O. Box 128
Mound City, IL 62963
For information please contact
Jefferson Barracks National
Cemetery
(314) 260-8720

Quincy National Cemetery
36th and Maine Street
Quincy, IL 62301
For information please contact
Rock Island National Cemetery
(309) 782-2094

Rock Island National Cemetery
Rock Island Arsenal
P. O. Box 737
Moline, IL 61265
Rock Island, IL 61299-7090
(309) 782-2094

Indiana

Crown Hill National Cemetery
700 West 38th Street
Indianapolis, IN 46208
For information please contact
Marion National Cemetery
(765) 674-0284

Marion National Cemetery
VA Medical Center
1700 East 38th Street
Marion, IN 46952
(765) 674-0284

New Albany National Cemetery
1943 Ekin Avenue
New Albany, IN 47150
For information please contact
Zachary Taylor National Cemetery
(502) 893-3852

Iowa

Keokuk National Cemetery
1701 J Street
Keokuk, IA 52632
For information please contact
Rock Island National Cemetery
(309) 782-2094

Kansas

Fort Leavenworth Natl Cemetery
Fort Leavenworth, KS 66027
For information please contact
Leavenworth National Cemetery
(913) 758-4105

Fort Scott National Cemetery
P. O. Box 917
Fort Scott, KS 66701
(316) 223-2840

Leavenworth National Cemetery
P. O. Box 1694
Leavenworth, KS 66048
(913) 758-4105

Kentucky

Camp Nelson National Cemetery
6980 Danville Road
Nicholasville, KY 40356
(606) 885-5727

Cave Hill National Cemetery
701 Baxter Avenue
Louisville, KY 40204
For information please contact
Zachary Taylor National Cemetery
(502) 893-3852

Danville National Cemetery
277 North First Street
Danville, KY 40442
For information please contact
Camp Nelson National Cemetery
(606) 885-5727

Lebanon National Cemetery
20 Highway 208
Lebanon, KY 40033
(502) 692-3390

Lexington National Cemetery
833 West Main Street
Lexington, KY 40508
For information please contact
Camp Nelson National Cemetery
(606) 885-5727

Mill Springs National Cemetery
Nancy, KY 42544
For information please contact
Camp Nelson National Cemetery
(606) 885-5727

Zachary Taylor National Cemetery
4701 Brownsboro Road
Louisville, KY 40207
(502) 893-3852

Louisiana

Alexandria National Cemetery
209 East Shamrock Street
Pineville, LA 71360
For information please contact
Natchez National Cemetery (601)
445-4981

Baton Rouge National Cemetery
220 North 19th Street
Baton Rouge, LA 70806
For information please contact
Port Hudson National Cemetery
(504) 389-0788

Port Hudson National Cemetery
20978 Port Hickey Road
Zachary, LA 70791
(504) 389-0788

Maine

Togus National Cemetery
VA Medical and Regional Office
Center
Togus, ME 04330
For information please contact
Massachusetts National Cemetery
(508) 563-7113

Maryland

Annapolis National Cemetery
800 West Street
Annapolis, MD 21401
For information please contact
Baltimore National Cemetery
(410) 644-9696

Baltimore National Cemetery
5501 Frederick Avenue
Baltimore, MD 21228
(410) 644-9696

Loudon Park National Cemetery
3445 Frederick Avenue
Baltimore, MD 21228
For information please contact
Baltimore National Cemetery
(410) 644-9696

Massachusetts

Massachusetts National Cemetery
Bourne, MA 02532
(508) 563-7113

Michigan

Fort Custer National Cemetery
15501 Dickman Road
Augusta, MI 49012
(616) 731-4164

Minnesota

Fort Snelling National Cemetery
7601 34th Avenue, South
Minneapolis, MN 55450-1199
(612) 726-1127

★★★

Mississippi

Biloxi National Cemetery
P. O. Box 4968
Biloxi, MS 39535-4968
(601) 388-6668

Corinth National Cemetery
1551 Horton Street
Corinth, MS 38834
For information please contact
Memphis National Cemetery (901)
386-8311

Natchez National Cemetery
41 Cemetery Road
Natchez, MS 39120
(601) 445-4981

Missouri

Jefferson Barracks National
Cemetery
2900 Sheridan Road
St. Louis, MO 63125
(314) 260-8720

Jefferson City National Cemetery
1024 East McCarty Street
Jefferson City, MO 65101
For information please contact
Jefferson Barracks National
Cemetery
(314) 260-8720

Springfield National Cemetery
1702 East Seminole Street
Springfield, MO 65804
(417) 881-9499

Nebraska

Fort McPherson National Cemetery
HCO1, Box 67
Maxwell, NE 69151
(308) 582-4433

New Jersey

Beverly National Cemetery
R.D. #1, Bridgeboro Road
Beverly, NJ 08010
(609) 877-5460

Finn's Point National Cemetery
RFD # 3, Fort Mott Road, Box 542
Salem, NJ 08079
For information please contact
Beverly National Cemetery
(609) 877-5460

New Mexico

Fort Bayard National Cemetery
P. O. Box 189
Fort Bayard, NM 88036
For information please contact
Fort Bliss National Cemetery
(915) 564-0201

Santa Fe National Cemetery
501 North Guadalupe Street
Santa Fe, NM 87501
(505) 988-6400

New York

Bath National Cemetery
VA Medical Center
Bath, NY 14810
(607) 776-5480, Ext. 1293

Calverton National Cemetery
210 Princeton Boulevard
Calverton, NY 11933-1031
(516) 727-5410 or 5770

Cypress Hills National Cemetery
625 Jamaica Avenue
Brooklyn, NY 11208
For information please contact
Long Island National Cemetery
(516) 454-4949

Long Island National Cemetery
2040 Wellwood Avenue
Farmingdale, NY 11735-1211
(516) 454-4949

Saratoga National Cemetery
200 Duell Road
Schuylerville, NY 12871-1721
(518) 581-9128
(518) 583-6975 (fax)

★★

Woodlawn National Cemetery
1825 Davis Street
Elmira, NY 14901
For information please contact
Bath National Cemetery
(607) 776-5480, Ext. 1293

North Carolina

New Bern National Cemetery
1711 National Avenue
New Bern, NC 28560
(252) 637-2912

Raleigh National Cemetery
501 Rock Quarry Road
Raleigh, NC 27610
For information please contact
Salisbury National Cemetery
(704) 636-2661

Salisbury National Cemetery
202 Government Road
Salisbury, NC 28144
(704) 636-2661

Wilmington National Cemetery
2011 Market Street
Wilmington, NC 28403
For information please contact New
Bern National Cemetery
(252) 637-2912

Ohio

Dayton National Cemetery
VA Medical Center
4100 West Third Street
Dayton, OH 45428-1008
(937) 262-2115

Ohio Western Reserve National
Cemetery
P.O. Box 8
10175 Rawiga Road
Rittman, OH 44270
(330) 335-3069
(330) 335-5087 (fax)

Oklahoma

Fort Gibson National Cemetery
1423 Cemetery Road
Fort Gibson, OK 74434
(918) 478-2334

Oregon

Eagle Point National Cemetery
2763 Riley Road
Eagle Point, OR 97524
(541) 826-2511

Roseburg National Cemetery
VA Medical Center
Roseburg, OR 97470
For information please contact
Willamette National Cemetery
(503) 273-5250

Willamette National Cemetery
11800 S.E. Mt. Scott Boulevard
Portland, OR 97266-6937
(503) 273-5250

Pennsylvania

Indiantown Gap National Cemetery
R. R. #2, P. O. Box 484
Annville, PA 17003-9618
(717) 865-5254

Philadelphia National Cemetery
Haines Street and Limekiln Pike
Philadelphia, PA 19138
For information please contact
Beverly National Cemetery
(609) 877-5460

Puerto Rico

Puerto Rico National Cemetery
P. O. Box 1298
Bayamon, PR 00960
(787) 798-6720

South Carolina

Beaufort National Cemetery
601 Boundary Street
Beaufort, SC 29902
(803) 524-3925

Florence National Cemetery
803 East National Cemetery Road
Florence, SC 29501
(803) 669-8783

★★

South Dakota

Black Hills National Cemetery
P. O. Box 640
Sturgis, SD 57785
(605) 347-3830 or 7299

Fort Meade National Cemetery
Old Stone Road
Sturgis, SD 57785
For information please contact
Black Hills National Cemetery
(605) 347-3830 or 7299

Hot Springs National Cemetery
VA Medical Center
Hot Springs, SD 57747
For information please contact
Black Hills National Cemetery
(605) 347-3830 or 7299

Tennessee

Chattanooga National Cemetery
1200 Bailey Avenue
Chattanooga, TN 37404
(423) 855-6590

Knoxville National Cemetery
939 Tyson Street, N.W.
Knoxville, TN 37917
For information please contact
Mountain Home National Cemetery
(423) 461-7935

Memphis National Cemetery
3568 Townes Avenue
Memphis, TN 38122
(901) 386-8311

Mountain Home National Cemetery
P. O. Box 8
Mountain Home, TN 37684
(423) 461-7935

Nashville National Cemetery
1420 Gallatin Road, South
Madison, TN 37115-4619
(615) 736-2839

Texas

Dallas-Fort Worth
National Cemetery
2191 Mountain Creek Parkway
Dallas, TX 75211
(214) 467-3333
(214) 467-3316 (fax)

Fort Bliss National Cemetery
5200 Fred Wilson Road
P. O. Box 6342
Fort Bliss, TX 79906
(915) 564-0201

Fort Sam Houston National
Cemetery
1520 Harry Wurzbach Road
San Antonio, TX 78209
(210) 820-3891

Houston National Cemetery
10410 Veterans Memorial Drive
Houston, TX 77038
(281) 447-8686

Kerrville National Cemetery
VA Medical Center
3600 Memorial Boulevard
Kerrville, TX 78028
For information please contact
Fort Sam Houston National
Cemetery
(210) 820-3891

San Antonio National Cemetery
517 Paso Hondo Street
San Antonio, TX 78202
For information please contact
Fort Sam Houston National
Cemetery
(210) 820-3891

Virginia

Alexandria National Cemetery
1450 Wilkes Street
Alexandria, VA 22314
For information please contact
Culpeper National Cemetery
(540) 825-0027

★★

Balls Bluff National Cemetery
Route 7
Leesburg, VA 22075
For information please contact
Culpeper National Cemetery
(540) 825-0027

City Point National Cemetery
10th Avenue and Davis Street
Hopewell, VA 23860
For information please contact
Fort Harrison National Cemetery
(804) 795-2031

Cold Harbor National Cemetery
Route 156 North
Mechanicsville, VA 23111
For information please contact
Fort Harrison National Cemetery
(804) 795-2031

Culpeper National Cemetery
305 U.S. Avenue
Culpeper, VA 22701
(540) 825-0027

Danville National Cemetery
721 Lee Street
Danville, VA 24541
For information please contact
Salisbury National Cemetery
(704) 636-2661

Fort Harrison National Cemetery
8620 Varina Road
Richmond, VA 23231
(804) 795-2031

Glendale National Cemetery
8301 Willis Church Road
Richmond, VA 23231
For information please contact
Fort Harrison National Cemetery
(804) 795-2031

Hampton National Cemetery
Cemetery Road at Marshall Avenue
Hampton, VA 23667
(757) 723-7104

Hampton National Cemetery
VA Medical Center
Emancipation Drive
Hampton, VA 23667
(757) 723-7104

Quantico National Cemetery
P. O. Box 10
18424 Joplin Road (Route 619)
Triangle, VA 22172
(703) 221-2183 (local)
(703) 690-2217 (metro)

Richmond National Cemetery
1701 Williamsburg Road
Richmond, VA 23231
For information please contact
Fort Harrison National Cemetery
(804) 795-2031

Seven Pines National Cemetery
400 East Williamsburg Road
Sandston, VA 23150
For information please contact
Fort Harrison National Cemetery
(804) 795-2031

Staunton National Cemetery
901 Richmond Avenue
Staunton, VA 24401
For information please contact
Culpeper National Cemetery
(540) 825-0027

Winchester National Cemetery
401 National Avenue
Winchester, VA 22601
For information please contact
Culpeper National Cemetery
(540) 825-0027

Washington

Tahoma National Cemetery
18600 Southeast 240th Street
Kent, WA 98042-4868
(425) 413-9614

West Virginia

Grafton National Cemetery
431 Walnut Street
Grafton, WV 26354
For information please contact
West Virginia National Cemetery
(304) 265-2044

West Virginia National Cemetery
Route 2, Box 127
Grafton, WV 26354
(304) 265-2044

★★

Wisconsin

Wood National Cemetery
5000 W National Ave, Bldg 1301
Milwaukee, WI 53295-4000
(414) 382-5300

DEPARTMENT OF THE INTERIOR NATIONAL CEMETERIES

District Of Columbia

Battleground National Cemetery
C/O Superintendent, Rock Creek
Park
3545 Williamsburg Lane, NW
Washington, DC 20008
(202) 282-1063

Georgia

Andersonville National Historic Site
Route 1, Box 800
Andersonville, GA 31711
(912) 924-0343

Louisiana

Chalmette National Cemetery
C/O Jean Lafitte National
Historical Park and Preserve
365 Canal Street, Suite 2400
New Orleans, LA 70130
(504) 589-3882
(504) 589-4430

Maryland

Antietam National Battlefield
Box 158
301) 432-5124
Sharpsburg, MD 21782-0158
(301) 432-5124

Mississippi

Vicksburg National Military Park
3201 Clay Street
Vicksburg, MS 39180
(601) 636-0583

Montana

Little Bighorn Battle
National Monument
Custer National Cemetery
P. O. Box 39
Crow Agency, MT 59022
(406) 638-2621

Pennsylvania

Gettysburg National Military Park
97 Taneytown Road
Gettysburg, PA 17325-2804
(717) 334-1124

Tennessee

Andrew Johnson National
Historic Site
P. O. Box 1088
Greeneville, TN 37744
(423) 638-3551

Fort Donelson National Battlefield
P. O. Box 434
Dover, TN 37058
(615) 232-5348

Shiloh National Military Park
Route 1, Box 9
Shiloh, TN 38376-9704
(901) 689-5275

Stones River National Battlefield
3501 Old Nashville Highway
Murfreesboro, TN 37129
(615) 893-9501

★★

Virginia

Fredericksburg and Spotsylvania
County Battlefields Memorial
National Military Park
120 Chatham Lane
Fredericksburg, VA 22405
(540) 371-0802

Poplar Grove National Cemetery
Petersburg National Battlefield
1539 Hickory Hill Road
Petersburg, VA 23803
(804) 732-3531

Yorktown Battlefield Cemetery
Colonial National Historical Park
P. O. Box 210
Yorktown, VA 23690
(757)898-3400

DEPARTMENT OF THE ARMY NATIONAL CEMETERIES

United States Soldiers' & Airmen's
Home National Cemetery
21 Harewood Road, NW
Washington, DC 20011
(202) 829-1829

Arlington National Cemetery
Interment Services Branch
Arlington, VA 22211
(703) 695-3250 or 3255

STATE VETERANS CEMETERIES

California

Veterans Memorial Grove Cemetery
Veterans Home of California
Yountville, CA 94599
(707) 944-4600

Colorado

Colorado State Veterans Cemetery
Colorado State Veterans Center
Box 97
Homelake, CO 81135
(719) 852-5118

Connecticut

Colonel Raymond F. Gates
Memorial Cemetery
Veterans Home and Hospital
287 West Street
Rocky Hill, CT 06067
(860) 721-5824

Spring Grove Veterans Cemetery
Darien, CT
C/O Veterans Home and Hospital
Rocky Hill, CT 06067
(860) 721-5824

Middletown Veterans Cemetery
C/O Veterans Home and Hospital
Rocky Hill, CT 06067
(860) 344-1961

Delaware

Delaware Veterans Memorial
Cemetery
2465 Chesapeake City Road
Bear, DE 19701
(302) 834-8046

Delaware Veterans Memorial
Cemetery-Sussex County
RD 5 Box 100
Bear, DE 19701(302) 934-5647

Hawaii

Director, Office of Veterans
Services
VAMROC E-Wing, Room 1A103
Tripler Army Medical Center
Honolulu, HI 96858
(808) 433-0420

Hawaii State Veterans Cemetery
45-349 Kamehameha Highway
Kaneohe, HI 96744
(808) 235-1596

East Hawaii Veterans
Cemetery - No. I
County of Hawaii
25 Aupuni Street
Hilo, HI 96720
(Island of Hawaii)
(808) 961-8311

East Hawaii Veterans
Cemetery - No. II
County of Hawaii
25 Aupuni Street
Hilo, HI 96720
(Island of Hawaii)
(808) 961-8311

Kauai Veterans Cemetery
County of Kauai Public Works
3021 Umi Street
Lihue, HI 96766
(Island of Kauai)
(808) 241-6649

Maui Veterans Cemetery
1295 Makawao Avenue, Box 117
Makawao, HI 96768
(Island of Maui)
(202) 243-7845

Hoolehua Veterans Cemetery
(Molokai)
P. O. Box 526
Kauna Kakai, HI 96748
(Island of Molokai)
(808) 553-3221

West Hawaii State
Veterans Cemetery
(Currently under construction –
located on the Island of Hawaii
near town of Kona)
(808) 961-8311

Lanai Veterans Cemetery
(Currently under construction –
located on the Island of Lanai)
(808) 565-7086

Illinois

Sunset Cemetery
Illinois Veterans Home
1707 North 12th Street
Quincy, IL 62301
(217) 782-7937

Indiana

Indiana State Soldiers Home
Cemetery
3851 North River Road
West Lafayette, IN 47906-3765
(317) 497-8501

Indiana Veterans Memorial
Cemetery
1415 North Gate Road
Madison, IN 47250
(812) 273-9220

Iowa

Iowa Veterans Home and Cemetery
13th & Summit Streets
Marshalltown, IA 50158
(515) 753-4309

Kansas

KSH Cemetery
Kansas Soldiers Home
Fort Dodge, KS 67843
(316) 227-2121

Maine

Maine Veterans Memorial Cemetery
Bureau of Maine Veterans Services
State House, Station #117
Augusta, ME 04333
(207) 626-4464

Maryland

Maryland State
Veterans Cemeteries
Federal Building-31 Hopkins Plaza
Baltimore, MD 21201
(410) 962-4700

Cheltenham Veterans Cemetery
11301 Crain Highway
P. O. Box 10
Cheltenham, MD 20623
(301) 372-6398

Crownsville Veterans Cemetery
1080 Sunrise Beach Road
Crownsville, MD 21032
(410) 987-6320 or
(301) 962-4700

★★

Eastern Shore Veterans Cemetery
6827 East New Market
Ellwood Road
Hurlock, MD 21643
(410) 943-3420

Garrison Forest Veterans Cemetery
P. O. Box 409
Owings Mills, MD 21117
(410) 363-6090

Rocky Gap Veterans Cemetery
Route #1, Box 82
Flintstone, MD 21530
(301) 777-2185

Massachusetts

Massachusetts State Veterans
Cemetery (Agawam & Winchendon)
239 Causeway Street, Suite 100
Boston, MA 02114
(617) 727-3578, Ext. 108

Michigan

Grand Rapids Home for Veterans
Cemetery
3000 Monroe, NW
Grand Rapids, MI 49505
(616) 364-5400

Minnesota

MN State Veterans Cemetery
1 Veterans Memorial Drive
Little Falls, MN 56345
(320) 632-3272

Missouri

St. James Missouri Veterans Home
Cemetery
620 North Jefferson
St. James, MO 65559
(573) 265-3271

Missouri Veterans Cemetery -
Higgensville, MO
20109 Bus. Hwy. 13
Higgensville, MO 64037
(660) 584-5252

Missouri Veterans Cemetery –
Springfield. MO
5201 South Southwood Road
Springfield, MO 65804
(417) 895-5893

Montana

State Veterans Cemetery
Fort William H. Harrison
Box 5715
Helena, MT 59604
(406) 444-6926

Montana Veterans Home Cemetery
P. O. Box 250
Columbia Falls, MT 59912
(406) 892-3256

Nebraska

Nebraska Veterans
Homes Cemetery
Burkett Station
Grand Island, NE 68803
(308) 385-6252, Ext. 230

Nevada

Commissioner of Veterans Affairs
1201 Terminal Way, Room 108
Reno, NV 89520
(775) 688-1155

Northern Nevada Veterans
Memorial Cemetery
14 Veterans Way
Fernley, NV 89408
(702) 575-4441

Southern Nevada Veterans
Memorial Cemetery
1900 Buchanan Boulevard
Boulder City, NV 89005
(702) 486-5920

New Hampshire

NH State Veterans Cemetery
4 Pembroke Road
Concord, NH 03301-5652
(603) 227-1594

★★

New Jersey

Brigadier General William C. Doyle
Veterans Memorial Cemetery
350 Provenceline Road, Route #2
Wrightstown, NJ 08562
(609) 758-7250

New Jersey Memorial Home
Cemetery (Closed)
524 N.W. Boulevard
Vineland, NJ 08360
(609) 696-6350

North Carolina

Western Carolina State Veterans
Cemetery
Old Highway 70
Black Mountain, NC 28711
(704) 669-0684

Coastal Carolina State Veterans
Cemetery
P. O. Box 1486
Jacksonville, NC 28541
(910) 347-4550 or 3570

Sandhills State Veterans Cemetery
P. O. Box 39
400 Murchison Road
Spring Lake, NC 28390
(910) 436-5630 or 5635

North Dakota

North Dakota Veterans Cemetery
Box 5511
Bismarck, ND 58502-5511
(701) 663-9893

Ohio

Ohio Veterans Home Cemetery
3416 Columbus Avenue
Sandusky, OH 44870
(419) 625-2454, Ext. 200

Oklahoma

Oklahoma Veterans Cemetery
Military Department (OKFAC)
3501 Military Circle N.E.
Oklahoma City, OK 73111-4398
(405) 425-8529

Pennsylvania

Pennsylvania Soldiers and
Sailors Home Cemetery
P. O. Box 6239
560 East Third Street
Erie, PA 16512-6239
(814) 871-4531

Rhode Island

Rhode Island Veterans Cemetery
301 South County Trail
Exeter, RI 02822-9712
(401) 884-7482

South Dakota

SD Veterans Home Cemetery
2500 Minnekahta Avenue
Hot Springs, SD 57747
(605) 745-5127

Tennessee

Director, State Veterans
Cemeteries and Administrative
Services
Tennessee Department of Veterans
Affairs
215 Eighth Avenue, North
Nashville, TN 37203
(615) 741-2930 or
(615) 532-9318

East Tennessee State
Veterans Cemetery
5901 Lyons View Pike
Knoxville, TN 37919
(423) 594-6776

Middle Tennessee
Veterans Cemetery
7931 McCrory Lane
Nashville, TN 37221
(615) 532-2238

West Tennessee
Veterans Cemetery
4000 Forest Hill/Irene Road
Memphis, TN 38125
(901) 543-7005

Utah

Utah State Veterans Cemetery
Utah Parks and Recreation
17111 South Camp Williams Road
Bluffdale, UT 84065
(801) 254-9036

Vermont

Vermont Veterans Home War
Memorial Cemetery
325 North Street
Bennington, VT 05201
(802) 442-6353, Ext. 347

Vermont Veterans Memorial
Cemetery
120 State Street
Montpelier, VT 05602-4401
(802) 654-0121

Virginia

Virginia Veterans Cemetery
10300 Pridesville Road
Amelia, VA 23002
(804) 561-1475

Washington

Washington Soldiers Home
Colony and Cemetery
1301 Orting-Kapowsin Highway
P. O. Box 500
Orting, WA 98360
(206) 840-6560

Washington Veterans Home
Cemetery
P. O. Box 698
Retsil, WA 98378
(360) 895-4700

Wisconsin

Wisconsin Veterans Memorial
Cemetery
Wisconsin Veterans Home
Highway QQ
King, WI 54946
(715) 258-4251

Southern Wisconsin
Veterans Memorial Cemetery
21731 Spring Street
Union Grove, WI 53182
(414) 878-5660

Wyoming

Oregon Trail Veterans Cemetery
89 Cemetery Road, Box 669
Evansville, WY 82636
(307) 235-6673

Territories

Guam Veterans Cemetery
Department of Parks
and Recreation
Agana, Guam 96919
(671) 477-9620 or 9621

Commonwealth of the
Northern Mariana Islands
CNMI is constructing a veterans
cemetery on Saipan
For information please contact
Department of Community and
Cultural Affairs
Saipan, Mariana Islands 96950
(670) 233-9556

NOTE:

All State cemeteries (except
Nevada, Pennsylvania, Wyoming
and Utah) restrict burials to State
residents.

California (cremations only),
Colorado, Indiana, Iowa, Kansas,
Missouri, Nebraska, Vermont
(Burlington), Washington, Montana
(Columbia Falls) and South Dakota
restrict burials to members of State
Veterans Homes.

CHAPTER 9

HEALTHCARE BENEFITS

In October 1996, Congress passed Public Law 104-262, the Veterans' Healthcare Eligibility Reform Act of 1996. This legislation paved the way for the creation of a Uniform Benefits Package - a standard enhanced health benefits plan available to all enrolled veterans. The Law also simplified the process by which veterans can receive services.

Public Law 104-262 was enacted to simplify the rules for providing healthcare to veterans and to introduce improvements in the quality and timeliness of the care veterans receive.

Note: Individuals are encouraged to contact the nearest VA benefits or healthcare facility to obtain the latest information regarding healthcare benefits. Legislation often changes the specific regulations regarding healthcare and nursing home care.

ELIGIBILITY

In order to qualify for enrollment in VA healthcare, the veteran must have:

Been discharged from active military service under honorable conditions.
Served a minimum of 2 years, if discharged after September 7, 1980 (prior to this date, there is no time limit).
If a National Guardsman or Reservist, served the entire period for which called to active duty other than for training purposes only.

Priority Groups

Once a veteran applies for enrollment, his or her application eligibility will be verified. Based on the individual's specific eligibility status, he or she is assigned a *priority group*.

The priority groups are as follows, ranging from 1-7 with 1 being the highest priority for enrollment. Under the Uniform Benefits Package, the same services are generally available to all enrolled veterans.

Priority Group 1
- Veterans with service-connected disabilities rated 50% or more disabling

Priority Group 2
- Veterans with service-connected disabilities rated 30% or 40% disabling

★★

Priority Group 3
Veterans who are former POWs

- Veterans whose discharge was for a disability that was incurred or aggravated in the line of duty
- Veterans with service-connected disabilities rated 10% or 20% disabling
- Veterans who are Purple Heart recipients (unless eligible for a higher Priority Group)
- Veterans awarded special eligibility classification under Title 38, U.S.C., Section 1151, "benefits for individuals disabled by treatment or vocational rehabilitation"

Priority Group 4

- Veterans who are receiving aid and attendance or housebound benefits
- Veterans who have been determined by VA to be catastrophically disabled

Priority Group 5

- Nonservice-connected veterans and service-connected veterans rated 0% disabled whose annual income and net worth are below the established dollar threshold. (Veterans in this priority group must provide VA with information on their annual income and net worth in order to determine whether they are below the "means test" threshold; or agree to co-payment requirements. The threshold is adjusted annually, and announced in January. In making the assessment, the veteran's household income is considered.

Priority Group 6
All other eligible veterans who are not required to make co-payments for their care, including:

- World War I and Mexican Border War veterans
- Veterans receiving care solely for disabilities resulting from exposure to toxic substances, radiation or for disorders associated with service in the Gulf War; or for any illness associated with service in combat in a war after the Gulf War or during a period of hostility after November 11, 1998
- *Compensable* 0% service-connected veterans

Priority Group 7

- Nonservice-connected veterans and noncompensable 0% service-connected veterans whose needed care cannot be provided by enrolling in any of the groups above and, who agree to pay specified co-payment.

UNIFORM BENEFITS PACKAGE

The Uniform Benefits Package will generally be provided to all enrolled veterans regardless of their priority group.

Public Law 104-262 called for VA to provide hospital care and outpatient care services that are defined as "needed". VA defines "needed" as care or service that will promote, preserve and restore health. This includes treatment, procedures, supplies or services. This decision of need will be based on the judgment of the healthcare provider, and in accordance with generally accepted standards of clinical practice.

The following three categories contain a list of healthcare services that are provided under the Uniform Benefits Package, a list of some that are not covered by VA and a list of other services that are provided under special authority.

Services Covered Under the Uniform Benefits Package

- Drugs, Biologicals, and Medical Devices approved by the Food and Drug Administration (FDA)
- Elective Sterilization (Tubal Ligation or Vasectomy)
- Emergency Care in VA Facilities
- Home Healthcare
- Hospice Care
- Hospital and Outpatient Care
- Maternity Benefits
- Medical and Surgical Care
- Mental Healthcare
- Palliative Care
- Preventive Care and Services
- Prosthetics and Orthotics
- Rehabilitation Care and Services
- Respite Care
- Substance Abuse Services

Services Not Covered Under the Uniform Benefits Package

- Abortions and Abortion Counseling
- Drugs, Biologicals, and Medical Devices not approved by the Food and Drug Administration (FDA)
- Gender Alterations
- Membership in Health Clubs and Spas
- Private Duty Nursing

Services Covered Under Special Authorities
- Adult Day Healthcare
- Dental Care
- Domiciliary Care
- Emergency Care in Non-VA Facilities
- Homeless Programs
- Non-VA Care
- Nursing Home Care
- Readjustment Counseling Service (Vet Centers)
- Sensori-Neural Aids(i.e., eyeglasses, contact lenses, hearing aids)
- Sexual Trauma Counseling

ENROLLMENT

VA healthcare enrollment is a new system providing veterans access to a comprehensive package of VA healthcare services. Veterans must answer a few questions, and are then are then assigned by VA to one of the priority groups

All veterans seeking VA healthcare are required to be enrolled unless they are in one of the following categories:

- VA rated the individual as having a service-connected disability of 50% or more
- It has been less than one year since the veteran was discharged from military service for a disability that the military determined was incurred or aggravated in the line of duty, and has not yet been rated by VA
- Veteran is seeking care from VA for a service-connected disability only

Veterans may apply for enrollment anytime during the year by completing an *Application for Benefits, VA Form 10-10 EZ*. This form may be obtained by contacting the local VA healthcare facility, County Veteran Service Office (VSO), or Veteran Service Organization.

The completed and signed form should be forwarded to the nearest VA healthcare facility. The application will be processed and forwarded to the VA Health Eligibility Center in Atlanta, GA. The Health Eligibility Center will notify the veteran of his or her status.

Veterans normally remain enrolled for one year. Enrollment is reviewed and renewed each year depending upon the veteran's priority group and available resources. If VA cannot renew enrollment for another year, the veteran will be notified in writing before their enrollment period expires.

★★★

Preferred Facility

An important aspect of enrollment is for the veteran to identify which VA location of care he or she chooses as the preferred facility. This can be a community-based outpatient clinic or a VA medical center.

A veteran's preferred facility designates where he or she prefers to receive primary care. The preferred facility is normally the facility closest to the veteran's home. However, acceptance in the VA healthcare system means that the veteran may receive the comprehensive benefits package through the VA's national healthcare system at any VA healthcare facility he or she chooses or are nearest to when requiring care.

If for any reason a selected facility is unable to provide the healthcare needed by an enrolled veteran, then that facility will make arrangements for referral to another VA healthcare facility or to one of VA's private sector affiliates to provide the required care.

Veterans can change their preferred facility at any time by simply notifying the VA location that has provided the care, the nearest VA healthcare facility or calling the toll-free number 1-877-222-VETS (1-877-222-8387).

Co-payments

After a veteran completes a financial assessment, if it is determined that the veteran's income is above the "means test" threshold, the veteran must agree to pay co-payments to be eligible for VA care. If a veteran does not agree to make the co-payments, the veteran will be ineligible for VA care.

VA holds these patients whose income is determined to be above the "means test" threshold responsible for the Medicare deductible for the first 90 days of care during any 365-day period. For each additional 90 days of hospital care, the patient is charged ½ the Medicare deductible. For each additional 90 days of nursing-home care, the patient is again charged the full Medicare deductible. In addition to these charges, the patient is charged $10 a day for hospital care, and $5 a day for VA nursing-home care. For outpatient care, the co-payment is 20% of the cost of an average outpatient visit.

Existing Healthcare Coverage

Veterans are allowed to keep their current healthcare coverage and are encouraged to do so. Veterans with private insurance or other coverage such as DoD, Medicare, or Medicaid may find these coverages to be a supplement to their VA enrollment. The use of other available healthcare coverage does not affect a veteran's enrollment status. VA does not charge the veteran for insurance company co-payments and deductibles.

When applying for medical care, all veterans will be asked to provide information pertaining to health insurance coverage, including policies held by spouses. VA is authorized to submit claims to insurance carriers for the recovery of costs for medical care provided to nonservice-connected veterans and service-connected veterans for nonservice-connected conditions. Veterans will not be responsible for portions of an insurance claim not covered by the policy. Veterans above certain income levels, however, are responsible for the co-payments required by federal law.

★★

Fee Basis Care

All veterans are potentially eligible for fee basis care; however, the decision to utilize such care is left to the facility providing the care. By law, fee basis care can only be provided when the treating facility cannot provide the veteran with the required care.

TRAVEL BENEFITS

Travel benefits vary from veteran to veteran, depending on specific situations. Please contact the VA directly at 1-877-222-VETS (1-877-222-8387) to determine eligibility.

HEARING AIDS AND EYEGLASSES

Generally, hearing aids and eyeglasses are not provided when the hearing and vision loss is the result of aging. However, if a veteran has a service-connected disability rating of 10% or greater, they will be provided.

Hearing aids and eyeglasses may also be provided in special circumstances.

NURSING HOMES

On November 30th, 1999 President Clinton signed into law the "Veterans Millennium Healthcare and Benefits Act", **Public Law 106-117.** **The Act amended the VA's statutory authority for providing nursing home care to eligible veterans.** Some of the key provisions of the Act Geriatrics and Extended Care are:

1. The VA is now required to operate and maintain extended care programs that include geriatric evaluations, VA and community-based nursing home care, domiciliary care, adult day healthcare, and respite care. In the past these Extended Care services were discretionary and based on the availability of resources. This Act now requires that they be provided.

2. The Act also requires the VA to provide, through the year 2003, needed nursing home care to veterans who are 70 percent service-connected or in need of nursing home care for a service-connected condition.

3. The VA must also provide alternatives to institutionalized care for veterans who are enrolled for VA care.

4. Under this Act, veterans who have no compensable service-connected disability, and whose income is above the pension level will be required to make a co-payment for VA nursing home care services of more than 21 days in a year. There are provisions in the act to insure that a spouse residing in the community would not be impoverished by this co-payment and that the veteran will retain a monthly personal allowance. This provision of the Act will not take effect immediately, as the procedures for implementing it still need to be developed.

5. The Act requires the establishment of a revolving fund in the Treasury in which to deposit co-payments. These funds will only be used to expand VA extended care services.

VA may also provide VA nursing-home care to other veterans. Veterans who have a service-connected disability are given first priority for nursing home care. Applicants who may be provided nursing home care without an income eligibility assessment include:

- Veterans with a compensable, service-connected disability;
- Veterans who were exposed to herbicides while serving in Vietnam;
- Veterans exposed to ionizing radiation during atmospheric testing or in the occupation of Hiroshima and Nagasaki;
- Veterans with a condition related to an environmental exposure in the Gulf War;
- Veterans who are former prisoners of war;
- Veterans on VA pension;
- Veterans of the Mexican Border period or World War I;
- Veterans who are eligible for Medicaid.

Nonservice-connected veterans and 0% noncompensable service-connected veterans requiring nursing home care for any nonservice-connected disability must complete the financial section on VA Form 10-10EZ, to determine whether they will be billed for nursing home care. Income assessment procedures are the same as for hospital care.

PRESCRIPTIONS

Veterans who are being provided VA treatment will also be provided with necessary prescriptions. A $2.00 co-payment is charged for each prescription provided for the treatment of a *nonservice-connected* disability. Exemptions from this co-payment requirement are provided for veterans with service-connected disability ratings of 50% or more, and for veterans whose income is less than the established dollar threshold.

Prescriptions By Non-VA Physicians

Only veterans with special eligibility, such as veterans in receipt of VA pension with aid and attendance benefits, are eligible to receive prescriptions at expense written by non-VA physicians.

★★★

MISCELLANEOUS HEALTHCARE BENEFITS INFORMATION

Treatment For Nonservice-Connected Conditions

Once enrolled, veterans may receive care that includes treatment for service-connected and nonservice-connected disabilities. The veteran's physician will determine what is medically indicated, and provide that care.

Veterans may have to agree to pay co-payments, including nonservice-connected veterans with incomes and net worth above the "means test" threshold, and 0% service-connected, noncompensable veterans needing care for any nonservice-connected disability.

Emergency Services

Urgent and limited emergency care services are available to enrolled veterans at VA healthcare facilities or non-VA healthcare facilities at which VA has a sharing agreement or contract. Only veterans with special eligibility may obtain emergency care, at VA expense, in a non-VA facility where VA does not have a sharing agreement or contract.

Limits On Days Of Care Or Outpatient Visits VA Will Provide

There are no limits on days of care or outpatient visits VA will provide. The veteran's primary care provider will determine what is appropriate and necessary hospital care or outpatient services and will provide such care consistent with current medical care practices.

SERVICES AND AIDS FOR BLIND VETERANS

On January 8, 1944, President Franklin D. Roosevelt made an extraordinary commitment to our nation's war-blinded servicemen, when he signed an executive order declaring:

"No blinded servicemen from World War II would be returned to their homes without adequate training to meet the problems of necessity imposed upon them by their blindness."

Meeting the demands of this obligation has resulted in various programs that have evolved throughout the years.

Blind veterans may be eligible for many of the benefits detailed throughout this book, including, but not limited to: Disability Compensation, Health Insurance, Adaptive Equipment, and Training & Rehabilitation. In addition to these benefits, there are a number of miscellaneous benefits due veterans of all wars who were blinded as the result of their war service. Many individual states offer special programs and benefits for the blind.

Veterans with corrected central vision of 20/200 or less in both eyes, or field loss to 20 degrees or less in both eyes are considered to be blind. Services are available at all VA medical facilities through Visual Impairment Services Team (VIST) coordinators.

★★★

The VIST Coordinator is a case manager who has major responsibility for the coordination of all services for legally blind veterans and their families. Duties include providing and/or arranging for appropriate treatment, identifying new cases of blindness, providing professional counseling, resolving problems, arranging annual healthcare reviews, and conducting education programs relating to blindness.

Blind veterans may be eligible for services at a VA medical center, or for admission to a VA blind rehabilitation center or clinic. In addition, blind veterans entitled to receive disability compensation may receive VA aids for the blind, which may include:

- A total health and benefits review by a VA Visual Impairment Services team;
- Adjustment to blindness training;
- Home Improvements and Structural Alterations to homes (HISA Program);
- Specially adapted housing and adaptations;
- Low-vision aids and training in their use;
- Electronic and mechanical aids for the blind, including adaptive computers and computer-assisted devices;
- Guide dogs, including the expense of training the veteran to use the dog, and the cost of the dog's medical care;
- Talking books, tapes, and Braille literature, provided from the Library of Congress.

The VA operates 9 blind rehabilitation centers in the United States and Puerto Rico. Rehabilitation centers offer comprehensive programs to guide individuals through a process that eventually leads to maximum adjustment to the disability, reorganization of the person's life, and return to a contributing place in the family and community. To achieve these goals, the rehabilitation centers offer a variety of skill courses to veterans, which are designed to help achieve a realistic level of independence. Services offered at rehabilitation centers include:

- Orientation and mobility;
- Living skills;
- Communication skills;
- Activities of daily living;
- Independent daily living program;
- Manual skills;
- Visual skills;
- Computer Access Training Section;
- Physical conditioning;
- Recreation;
- Adjustment to blindness;
- Group meetings.

★★

The VA also employs Blind Rehabilitation Outpatient Specialists (BROS) in several areas, including:

- Albuquerque, NM
- Ann Arbor, MI
- Bay Pines / St. Petersburg, FL
- Baltimore, MD
- Boston, MA
- Cleveland, OH
- Dallas, TX
- Gainesville, FL
- Los Angeles, CA
- Phoenix, AZ
- Portland, OR
- San Antonio, TX
- San Juan, PR
- Seattle, WA
- West Haven, CT

Blind Rehabilitation Outpatient Specialists are multi-skilled, experienced, blind instructors who teach skills in the veteran's home environment, and/or local VA facility.

SPECIAL CATEGORIES FOR MEDICAL CARE

Individual chapters of this book discuss the following special categories of veterans who may qualify for medical care, as well as other benefits:

- Gulf War Veterans (See Page 263)
- Veterans exposed to Agent Orange during the Vietnam War (See Page 226)
- Veterans exposed to atomic radiation, (See Page 230)
- Merchant Marine Seamen (See Page 252)
- Allied Veterans (See Page 250)

★★

HOME IMPROVEMENTS AND STRUCTURAL ALTERATIONS (HISA)

The Home Improvements and Structural Alterations (HISA) program provides funding for eligible veterans to make home improvements necessary for the continuation of treatment for disability access to the home and essential lavatory and sanitary facilities.

HISA grants provide for medically necessary improvements and/or structural changes to the veteran's residence for the following purposes:

- Allowing entrance to or exit from the veteran's residence;
- Use of essential lavatory and sanitary facilities;
- Allowing accessibility to kitchen or bathroom sinks or counters;
- Improving entrance paths or driveways in immediate area of the home to facilitate access to the home by the veteran;
- Improving plumbing or electrical systems made necessary due to installation of dialysis equipment in the home.

HISA benefits up to $4,100 (one-time payment) may be available for service-connected veterans and up to $1,200 (one-time payment) for nonservice-connected veterans may be provided. For application information, contact the prosthetic representative at the nearest VA medical center or outpatient clinic.

LISTING OF VA HEALTHCARE FACILITIES

Alabama
Medical Centers
Montgomery
Birmingham
Tuscaloosa

Clinics
Anniston
Decatur
Dothan
Gadsden
Huntsville
Jasper
Mobile
Shoals Area

Alaska
Clinic
Anchorage

Arizona
Medical Centers
Phoenix
Prescott

Tucson

Clinics
Bellemont
Casa Grande
Kingman
Mesa
Safford
Show Low
Sierra Vista
Sun City
Yuma

Arkansas
Medical Centers
Fayetteville
Little Rock

Clinics
Paragould

California
Medical Centers
Bakersfield
Loma Linda

★★

Long Beach
Los Angeles
Martinez
Palo Alto
San Diego
San Francisco Santa Barbara
Sepulveda
West Los Angeles

Clinics
Atwater
Auburn
Bakersfield
Capitola
Chico
Commerce
Eureka
Fairfield
Martinez
Modesto
Monterey
Oakland
Palm Desert
Redding
Sacramento
San Diego
San Francisco
San Jose
Santa Barbara
Santa Rosa
Seaside
Stockton
Sun City
Tulare
Vallejo
Victorville

Colorado
Medical Centers
Denver
Fort Lyon
Grand Junction

Clinics
Aurora
Colorado Springs
Greeley
Montrose
Sidney

Connecticut
Medical Centers
West Haven
Newington

Clinics
New London
Stamford
Waterbury
Windham
Winsted

Delaware
Medical Center
Wilmington

Clinic
Millsboro

District of Columbia
Medical Center
Washington D.C.

Florida
Medical Centers
Bay Pines
Gainesville
Lake City
Miami
Tampa
West Palm Beach

Clinics
Bartow
Brevard
Brooksville
Daytona Beach
Fort Myers
Fort Pierce
Homestead
Jacksonville
Key Largo
Key West
Manatee
N. Pinellas County
Oakland Park
Ocala
Orlando
Panama City
Pembroke Pines
Pensacola
Port Richey
Sarasota
S. St. Petersburg
Tallahassee

Georgia
Medical Centers
Augusta
Decatur

★★★

Dublin

Clinics
Albany
Columbus
Macon
Midtown Atlanta
Northeast Georgia
Savannah
Valdosta

Guam
Agana Heights

Hawaii
Medical Office
Honolulu

Idaho
Medical Center
Boise

Clinic
Pocatello

Illinois
Medical Centers
Chicago
Danville
Hines
Marion
North Chicago

Clinics
Aurora
Belleville
Decatur
Effingham
Elgin
Evanston
Evansville
Galesburg
Gurnee
Joliet
LaSalle
Manteno
McHenry
Mt. Vernon
Oak Park
Paducah
Peoria
Quincy
Rockford

Indiana
Medical Centers
Indianapolis
Fort Wayne
Marion

Clinics
Crown Point
Evansville
Lafayette
Munci/Anderson
South Bend

Iowa
Medical Centers
Des Moines
Knoxville
Iowa City

Clinics
Bettendorf
Dubuque
Marshalltown
Mason City
Waterloo

Kansas
Medical Centers
Leavenworth
Topeka
Wichita

Clinics
Abilene
Chanute
Dodge City
Emporia
Fort Riley
Garnett
Hays
Holton
Junction City
Kansas City
Lawrence
Liberal
Paola
Russell
St. Joseph, MO
Seneca

Kentucky
Medical Centers
Lexington
Louisville

★★

Clinic
Bellevue

Louisiana
Medical Centers
Alexandria
New Orleans
Shreveport

Clinics
Baton Rouge
Jennings
Monroe

Maine
Medical Center
Togus

Clinics
Bangor
Calais
Caribou
Machias
Rumford

Maryland
Medical Centers
Baltimore
Fort Howard
Perry Point

Clinics
Cumberland
Hagerstown

Massachusetts
Medical Centers
Bedford
Boston
Brockton
Northampton
West Roxbury

Clinics
Boston
Framingham
Haverhill
Hyannis
Lowell
Lynn
New Bedford
Pittsfield
Springfield

Winchendon
Worcester

Michigan
Medical Centers
Ann Arbor
Battle Creek
Detroit
Iron Mountain
Saginaw

Clinics
Gaylord
Grand Rapids
Hancock
Ironwood
Jackson
Lansing
Marquette
Menominee
Muskegon
Sault Ste. Marie
Traverse City
Yale

Minnesota
Medical Centers
Minneapolis
St. Cloud

Clinics
Brainerd
Fergus Falls
Hibbing Area
Mankato Area
Maplewood

Mississippi
Medical Centers
Biloxi
Jackson

Missouri
Medical Centers
Columbia
Kansas City
Poplar Bluff
St. Louis

Clinics
Belton
Cape Giradeau
Mt. Vernon
Nevada
St. Charles

99

West Plains
Whiteman

Montana
Medical Centers
Fort Harrison

Clinic
Billings

Nebraska
Medical Centers
Grand Island
Lincoln
Omaha

Clinics
Norfolk
North Platte

Nevada
Medical Center
Las Vegas
Reno

Clinics
Henderson
Pahrump

New Hampshire
Medical Center
Manchester

Clinics
Portsmouth
Tilton

New Jersey
Medical Centers
East Orange
Lyons

Clinics
Brick
Cape Mary
Elizabeth
Fort Dix
Hackensack
Jersey City
New Brunswick
Trenton
Ventnor
Vineland

New Mexico
Medical Center
Albuquerque

Clinics
Artesia
Clovis
Clayton
Farmington
Gallup
Hobbs
Las Cruces
Raton
Silver City

New York
Medical Centers
Albany
Batavia
Bath
Bronx
Brooklyn
Buffalo
Canandaigua
Castle Point
Montrose
New York City
Northport
St. Albans
Syracuse

Clinics
Alexandria Bay
Bennington
Binghamton
Brooklyn
Buffalo
Clifton Park
Dunkirk
Elizabethtown
Glens Falls
Islip
Jamestown
Kingston
Lindenhurst
Lockport
Lynbrook
Malone
Massena
Mt. Sinai
New York City
Niagara Falls
Oswego
Patchogue
Plainview
Plattsburgh

★★★

Riverhead
Rochester
Rome
Sayville
Schenectady
Sidney
Staten Island
Troy
Warsaw
White Plains
Yonkers

North Carolina
Medical Centers
Asheville
Durham
Fayetteville
Salisbury

Clinics
Charlotte
Greenville
Jacksonville
Winton-Salem

North Dakota
Medical Center
Fargo

Clinics
Bismarck
Grafton
Minot

Ohio
Medical Centers
Brecksville
Chillicothe
Cincinnati
Cleveland
Dayton

Clinics
Akron
Ashtabula
Athens
Canton
Cleveland/McCafferty
Cleveland/Otis Moss
Columbus
Lorain
Mansfiled
Middletown
Painesville
Portsmouth
St. Clairsville

Sandusky
Springfield
Toledo
Youngstown
Zanesville

Oklahoma
Medical Centers
Muskogee
Oklahoma City

Clinics
Ardmore
Bonham Area
Clinton
Lawton/Ft. Sill
Tulsa

Oregon
Medical Centers
Portland
Roseburg

Clinics
Bend
Bandon
Eugene

Pennsylvania
Medical Centers
Altoona
Butler
Coatesville
Erie
Lebanon
Philadelphia
Pittsburgh
Wilkes-Barre

Clinics
Aliquippa
Allentown
Camp Hill
DuBois
Frackville
Greensburg
Johnstown
Lancaster
Levittown
Meadville
Reading
Sayre
Schuylkill County
Schuylkill Haven
Smethport
Spring City

★★

Springfield
State College
Tobyhanna
Williamsport

Philippines
Outpatient Clinic
Manila

Puerto Rico
Medical Center
San Juan

Clinics
Arecibo
Mayaguez
Ponce
St. Croix
St. Thomas

Rhode Island
Medical Center
Providence

South Carolina
Medical Centers
Charleston
Columbia

Clinics
Florence
Greenville
Myrtle Beach
Rock Hill

South Dakota
Medical Centers
Fort Meade
Hot Springs
Sioux Falls

Clinics
Pierre
Rapid City

Tennessee
Medical Centers
Memphis
Mountain Home
Murfreesboro
Nashville

Clinics
Arnold AFB
Chattanooga
Cookville
Jonesboro
Knoxville
Mountain City
Smithville

Texas
Medical Centers
Amarillo
Big Spring
Bonham
Dallas
Houston
Kerrville
Marlin
San Antonio
Temple
Waco

Clinics
Abilene
Austin
Beaumont
Beeville
Bishop
Bonham
Brownsville
Brownwood
Childress
Cleburne
College Station
Corpus Christi
Dallas County
Decatur
Del Rio
Denton
Eagle Pass
Eastland
El Paso
Fort Worth
Fort Stockton
Greenville
Hamilton
Laredo
Lubbock
Lufkin
McAllen
Odessa
Palestine
San Angelo
San Antonio
San Diego
Stamford

★★★

Stratford
Texarkana
Tyler
Uvalde
Victoria
Wichita Falls

Utah
Medical Center
Salt Lake City

Vermont
Medical Centers
White River Junction

Clinics
Burlington
Bennington
Newport
St. Johnsbury
Wilder

Virginia
Medical Centers
Hampton
Richmond
Salem

Clinics
Danville
Harrisonburg
Stephens City
Tazewell

Washington
Medical Centers
Seattle
Tacoma
Spokane
Walla Walla

Clinics
Tri-Cities (Richland)

Yakima
West Virginia
Medical Centers
Beckley
Clarksburg
Huntington
Martinsburg

Clinics
Franklin
Gassaway
Parkersburg
Parsons
Petersburg

Wisconsin
Medical Centers
Madison
Milwaukee
Tomah

Clinics
Appleton
Baraboo
Beaver Dam
Chippewa Falls
Cleveland
Edgerton
LaCrosse
Loyal
Rhinelander
Superior
Union Grove
Wausau

Wyoming
Medical Centers
Cheyenne
Sheridan

Clinics
Cheyenne

CHAPTER 10

DENTAL BENEFITS

VA OUTPATIENT DENTAL BENEFITS

Outpatient dental benefits are provided by the Department of Veterans Affairs according to law. In some instances, the dental care may be extensive, while in other cases treatment may be limited.

Eligibility

Veterans are eligible for outpatient dental treatment if they are determined by VA to meet one of the following criteria:

- Those having a service-connected compensable dental disability or condition are eligible for any needed dental care.

- Those who were prisoners of war for 90 days or more are eligible for any needed dental care .

- Those whose service-connected disabilities have been rated at 100 percent, or who are receiving the 100 percent rate by reason of individual unemployability are eligible for any needed dental care. (Includes veterans with temporary ratings of 100 percent for duration of that rating.)

- Those who are participating in a VA rehabilitation program are eligible for dental care necessary to complete their program.

- Those having a service-connected noncompensable dental condition or disability may receive one-time treatment if it can be shown to have existed at the time of discharge or release from active duty of at least 150 days, and application is made within 90 days of separation from active duty.

- Those having a service-connected noncompensable dental condition or disability resulting from combat wounds or service trauma and those having a service-connected noncompensable dental condition or disability and were prisoners of war for less than 90 days are eligible for repeat care for the service-connected condition(s).

- Those having a dental condition clinically determined by VA to be currently aggravating a service-connected medical condition are eligible for dental care to resolve the problem.

- Those with nonservice-connected dental conditions or disabilities for which treatment was begun while in a VA medical center, when it is clinically determined to be necessary to complete such dental treatment on an outpatient basis.

- Those receiving outpatient care or scheduled for inpatient care may receive dental care if the dental condition is clinically determined to be complicating a medical condition currently under treatment

NOTE: Veterans of the Gulf War may receive a one-time dental treatment if the dental condition can be shown to have existed at discharge or release from active duty of at least 90 days.

TRICARE RETIREE DENTAL PROGRAM

The TRICARE Retiree Dental Program (TRDP) was established February 1, 1998. It provides dental care for Uniformed Service retirees, unremarried surviving spouses, and certain other family members. Enrollment in TRDP is voluntary. The TRDP is funded solely by enrollees, and receives **no** government subsidy.

The TRICARE Retiree Dental Program is administered by the Federal Services division of Delta Dental Plan of California. The TRICARE Retiree Dental Program is designed to provide Uniformed Services retirees and their families with optimum dental coverage at an affordable cost.

Eligible beneficiaries include:

- Military retirees, including those over age 65;
- Reserve members entitled to retired pay, but under age 60;
- Spouses of retirees;
- Children under age 21, or full-time students under age 23;
- A nonremarried surviving spouse or eligible child of a deceased member or member who died while on active duty for more than 30 days and who aren't eligible for the TRICARE Dental Program.

The information provided in this section is intended only as a brief overview. For complete information regarding eligibility, enrollment, premiums, and covered benefits, contact:

Delta Dental Plan of California
Federal Services
PO Box 537008
Sacramento, CA 95853-7008

Customer Service: 1-888-336-3260
Enrollment: 1-888-838-8737

TRICARE SELECTED RESERVE DENTAL PROGRAM BENEFITS

Individuals with at least one year of service commitment remaining who are serving in the Army Reserve, Naval Reserve, Air Force Reserve, Marine Corps Reserve, Coast Guard Reserve, Army National Guard or Air National Guard, may be eligible to enroll in the Tricare Selected Reserve Dental Program (TSRDP).

The Department of Defense works in conjunction with Humana Military Healthcare Services to offer and administer the TRICARE Selected Reserve Dental Program.

Coverage remains available as long as an individual maintains his or her Reserve status, and is shown as eligible on the DEERS record. Coverage is not available for family members.

The information provided in this section is intended only as a brief overview. Humana Military Healthcare Services has a staff of trained Beneficiary Services Representatives who are available to answer your questions. They can be reached at **1-800-211-3614.**

★★★

CHAPTER 11

CHAMPVA AND TRICARE

Although similar, CHAMPVA and TRICARE are completely separated programs, with totally different beneficiary populations. While the benefits provided are similar, the programs are administered separately, with significant differences in claim filing procedures and preauthorization requirements.

CHAMPVA

CHAMPVA (Civilian Health and Medical Program for the Veterans Administration) is a healthcare benefits program for:

- Dependents of veterans who have been rated by VA as having a total and permanent disability;

- Survivors of veterans who died from VA-rated service-connected conditions, or who at the time of death, were rated permanently and totally disabled from a VA-rated service-connected condition; and

- Survivors of persons who died in the line of duty, and not due to misconduct.

Under CHAMPVA, VA shares the cost of covered healthcare services and supplies with eligible beneficiaries.

The administration of CHAMPVA is centralized to the Health Administration Center in Denver, Colorado.

In general, CHAMPVA covers most healthcare services and supplies that are medically and psychologically necessary. Upon confirmation of eligibility, applicants will receive program material that specifically addresses covered and noncovered services and supplies.

CHAMPVA General Exclusions

- Services determined by VA to be medically unnecessary;
- Care as part of a grant, study, or research program;
- Care considered experimental or investigational;
- Care for persons eligible for benefits under other government agency programs, except Medicaid and State Victims of Crime Compensation programs;
- Care for which the beneficiary is not obligated to pay, such as services obtained at a health fair;
- Care provided outside the scope of the provider's license or certification;
- Custodial, domiciliary, or rest cures;

- Dental care (except treatment related to certain covered medical conditions);
- Medications that do no require a prescription (except insulin);
- Personal comfort and convenience items;
- Services rendered by providers suspended or sanctioned by other Federal entities.

Eligibility For CHAMPVA

The following persons are eligible for CHAMPVA benefits, providing they are not eligible for TRICARE or Medicare Part A as a result of reach the age of 65:

The spouse or child of a veteran who has been rated by a VA regional office as having a permanent and total service-connected condition / disability;
The surviving spouse or child of a veteran who died as a result of a VA-rated service-connected condition; or who, at the time of death, was rated permanently and totally disabled from a service-connected condition; and
The surviving spouse or child of a person who died in the line of duty, and not due to misconduct.

Applying for CHAMPVA And Filing Claims

Prospective applicants should contact the Health Administration Center at 1-800-733-8387.

Applications may also be requested by FAX at 1-303-331-7804

For inquiries, applications, appeals, and healthcare claims older than one year, please use:

VA Health Administration Center
CHAMPVA
PO Box 65023
Denver, CO 80206-9023

For submitting new (less than one year old) healthcare claim, please use:

VA Health Administration Center
CHAMPVA
PO Box 65024
Denver, CO 80206-9023

Generally, applicants can expect to receive written notification from the Health Administration Center within 45 days from the mailing of the application. To streamline the process, applicants are encouraged to complete the *Application for CHAMPVA Benefits, (VA 10D)* in its entirety and to attach all required documents. As further explained on the application, required documents include a copy of each applicant's Medicare card (if Medicare eligible) and a school certification for all applicant children between the ages of 18 and 23.

CHAMPVA As Secondary Payer

CHAMPVA is intended to serve as a safety net in the event other coverage is not available—rather than being the primary carrier. While families with other health insurance are not disqualified from CHAMPVA benefits, CHAMPVA's safety net protection only kicks in after the application of all other policies—including benefits available from the enrollment in a health maintenance organization (HMO).

(Exceptions to CHAMPVA's secondary payer status are supplemental CHAMPVA policies, Medicaid, and State Victims Compensation Programs—CHAMPVA assumes primary payer in these cases.)

Beneficiaries enrolled in an HMO cannot elect to waive the HMO benefits without forfeiting their CHAMPVA benefits. CHAMPVA benefits, however, do apply to covered services that are not covered by the HMO.

Healthcare Services At VA Facilities

Under the CHAMPVA In-house Treatment Initiative (CITI for short), CHAMPVA beneficiaries may receive cost-free healthcare services at participating VA facilities.

Although some VA facilities are not CITI participants due to the volume of veterans they are responsible for serving, most are. To find out if your local facility is participating and what services are offered, give them a call.

Medicare Impact:

Individuals, 65 or older, who lose CHAMPVA eligibility by becoming potentially eligible for Medicare Part A or who qualify for Medicare Part A benefits on the basis of disability, may re-establish CHAMPVA eligibility by submitting documentation from the Social Security Administration (SSA) certifying their non-entitlement to or exhaustion of Medicare Part A benefits.

Otherwise eligible individuals under age 65 who are enrolled in both Medicare Parts A&B are potentially eligible for CHAMPVA as secondary payer to Medicare. To determine CHAMPVA eligibility, SSA documentation of enrollment in both Parts A&B is required.

TRICARE

TRICARE (formally known as CHAMPUS), is a program administered by the Department of Defense for military retirees as well as families of active duty, retired, and deceased service members.

TRICARE was designed to make quality healthcare more accessible and easier to use than its predecessor, CHAMPUS. TRICARE contractors have been competitively selected to service 12 regions within the United States and overseas. Each regional contractor has developed a network of hospitals, physicians, pharmacies, and other healthcare professionals to complement the existing Military Treatment Facilities (MTFs).

★★

Active duty personnel are automatically enrolled into a program called TRICARE Prime. Their families and retired military may select among three plans:

- Prime (similar to health maintenance organizations (HMOs);
- Extra (preferred provider organization (PPO);
- Standard (fee-for-service model)

All plans limit out-of-pocket expenses (i.e. deductibles, copays, fees).

If an insured is also covered by other health insurance, such as a spouse's policy at work, all claims must be filed with that company first.

LIFETIME HEALTHCARE FOR MILITARY RETIREES

President Clinton signed the FY2001 National Defense Authorization Act on October 30, 2000, which brings many new initiatives to the TRICARE program including two dramatic improvements for Medicare-eligible uniformed services retirees, their spouses and survivors who are age 65 and over.

Key Features

- Effective April 1, 2001, eligible beneficiaries will receive pharmacy benefits to include access to military treatment facility pharmacies, the National Mail Order Pharmacy program and retail pharmacies.
- Effective October 1, 2001, eligible beneficiaries who continue to receive care from their current Medicare providers, will have TRICARE become second payer to Medicare. This means that TRICARE will pay out-of-pocket costs for services covered under Medicare, plus these beneficiaries will be eligible for TRICARE benefits not covered by Medicare.

For the Pharmacy Benefit:

- If an individual is currently age 65 or older or will be 65 before April 1, 2001, he or she will be eligible to use the retail and mail order pharmacy benefit without being enrolled in Medicare Part B.
- If the individual turns 65 on or after April 1, 2001, he or she will need to be enrolled in Medicare Part B in order to use the retail and mail order pharmacy benefit.

For the Medical Care (TRICARE as Second Payer) Benefit:

- Individuals must be eligible for Medicare Part A and enrolled in Medicare Part B to participate in the health program.
- If an individual is eligible, he or she should enroll in Medicare Part B if they haven't already. To enroll:

★★

Important Note

Eligible seniors should not immediately cancel their current Medigap insurance coverage. The Department of Defense (DoD) is working with the Healthcare Financing Administration, the organization that administers the Medicare benefit, to provide the most accurate information on the appropriateness of continued enrollment in Medigap insurance policies.

Other New Initiatives Coming Soon

The following are a few of the initiatives that were also included in the new law, but at the time of publication, specific information is not available:

- TRICARE Prime Remote for Families
- Elimination of Co-pays for Active Duty Family Members
- Catastrophic Cap Reduction
- Chiropractic Healthcare for Active Duty
- Individual Case Management Program

DEERS

The Defense Enrollment Eligibility Reporting System (DEERS) is a computerized data bank that lists all active and retired military members, and should also include family members. All TRICARE contractors use DEERS data to determine healthcare eligibility. All information in the DEERS files, such as home addresses and information about spouses and children, is listed and updated *only if the military sponsor specifically gives the information to DEERS.* An individual may be denied health benefits if a record is not up-to-date. Active and retired service members are automatically listed with DEERS when they enter the military service, but family members are not.

Individuals should notify their TRICARE Service Center if:

- A dependent has been added to an insured's record through marriage, birth, or adoption,
- If an individual is divorced, or
- A dependent has died

It is the responsibility of the TRICARE Service Center to initially notify DEERS of any additions to an insured's record.

★★

To make sure DEERS has up-to-date information, and to report any changes, they can be contacted at:

1-800-538-9552 (Continental U.S.)
1-800-334-4162 (California)
1-800-527-5602 (Alaska & Hawaii)

DEERS Support Office
ATTN: COA
400 Gigling Road
Seaside, CA 93955-6771

TRICARE ELIGIBILITY

TRICARE eligibility is determined by the various branches of the uniformed services. The persons listed below are eligible for benefits under TRICARE:

- Active-duty service members;
- (These individuals have top priority for care at military medical facilities, and are enrolled in TRICARE Prime. They cannot receive care under TRICARE Standard or TRICARE Extra.)
- Spouses and unmarried children of active-duty service members;
- Uniformed-service retirees, their spouses, and unmarried children;
- Unremarried spouses and unmarried children of active-duty or retired service members who have died;
- (Note: Family members of active-duty service members who died while on active duty, and who were on active duty for at least 30 days before death, are classified as dependents of a deceased member, but their claims will be cost-shared at the active-duty rate for one year after their active-duty sponsor dies.)
- Spouses and unmarried children of reservists who are ordered to active duty for more than 30 consecutive days. (They are covered only during the reservist's active-duty tour), or of reservists who die on active duty);
- Spouses and unmarried children of reservists who are injured or aggravate an injury, illness or disease during, or on the way to, active-duty training for a period of 30 days or less, or a period of inactive-duty training, and who die as a result of the specific injuries, illnesses or diseases;
- Former spouses of active or retired military who were married to a service member of former member who had performed at least 20 years of creditable service for retirement purposes at the time the divorce or annulment occurred.

  The former spouse must also be the following requirements:
  o Must not have remarried;
  o Must not be covered by an employer-sponsored health plan;
  o Must not be eligible for Part A of Medicare due to age, except under certain conditions;
  o Must not be the former spouse of a NATO (or "Partners for Peace" nation) member;

★★★

 o Must meet certain specific requirements regarding the years of marriage during years creditable in determining the member's eligibility for retirement pay.

TRICARE REGIONS

Region 1 - Northeast
Sierra Military Health Services, Inc.
Phone: 1-888-999-5195

Connecticut	Delaware	District of Columbia
Maine	Maryland	Massachusetts
New Hampshire	New Jersey	New York
Pennsylvania	Rhode Island	Vermont
Northern Virginia		

Region 2 - Mid Atlantic
Anthem Alliance For Health, Inc.
Phone: 1-800-931-9501
Southern Virginia
North Carolina

Region 3 - Southeast
Humana Military Healthcare Services
Phone: 1-800-444-5445

Florida
Georgia
South Carolina

Region 4 - Gulf South
Human Military Healthcare Services
Phone: 1-800-444-5445

Alabama	Mississippi
Tennessee	Western Panhandle of Florida
Eastern Louisiana	

Region 5 - Heartland
Anthem Alliance For Health, Inc.
Phone: 1-800-941-4501

Indiana	Illinois
Kentucky	Michigan
Ohio	West Virginia
Wisconsin	

Region 6 - Southwest
Foundation Health Federal Service, Inc.
Phone: 1-800-406-2832
Arkansas
Oklahoma
Texas (except for the extreme Western area)
Louisiana (major part)

★★

Regions 7 & 8 - Central
TriWest Healthcare Alliance, Inc.
Phone: 1-888-874-9378

Colorado	Idaho	Iowa
Kansas	Minnesota	Missouri
Montana	Nebraska	North Dakota
South Dakota	Utah	Wyoming
Arizona New Mexico	Nevada	
Extreme Western Texas		

Region 9 - Southern California
Foundation Health Federal Services, Inc.
Phone: 1-800-242-6788
Southern California

Region 10 - Golden Gate
Foundation Health Federal Services, Inc.
Phone: 1-800-242-6788
Northern California

Region 11 - Northwest
Foundation Health Federal Services, Inc.
1-800-404-0110
Washington
Oregon
Northern Idaho

Region 12 - Pacific
Foundation Health Federal Services, Inc.
Phone (Hawaii): 1-800-242-6788
Phone (Alaska): 1-888-777-8343
Alaska
Hawaii

Europe
Phone: 1-888-777-8343

Belgium	Germany	Greece
Iceland	Italy	The Netherlands
Portugal	Spain	Turkey
United Kingdom		

Region 15 - Latin America & Canada
Phone: 608-259-4847

Canada	Mexico
Central America	Puerto Rico
Bermuda	West Indies

★★★

PHARMACY BENEFITS

TRICARE offers several ways to have prescriptions filled depending on a family's specific needs: (Copayments may apply, and will vary for individuals, depending on specific situations.)

- Prescriptions may be filled (up to a 90-day supply for most medications) at a military treatment facility (MTF) pharmacy free of charge. Please be aware that not all medications are available at MTF pharmacies. Each facility is required to make available the medications listed in the basic core formulary (BCF). The MTF, through their local Pharmacy & Therapeutics Committee, may add additional medications to their local formulary based on the scope of care at that MTF.

- The National Mail Order Pharmacy (NMOP) is available for prescriptions taken on a regular basis. Insureds can receive up to a 90-day supply (for most medications) of a prescription through the mail by using the NMOP. (See below for further information.)

- Prescription medications that a doctor requires an insured to start taking immediately can be obtained though a TRICARE retail network pharmacy for a small copay. (See below for further information.)

National Mail Order Pharmacy (NMOP)

For prescriptions taken regularly — such as medication to reduce blood pressure, or to treat asthma or diabetes — the most convenient TRICARE pharmacy option may be the National Mail Order Pharmacy.

The Department of Defense National Mail Order Pharmacy is administered by Merck-Medco Rx Services. (Call 1-800-903-4680 for detailed information.) Through this program, insureds mail their healthcare provider's written prescription along with the required copay to the National Mail Order Pharmacy, and the medications are sent to the insured. Refills are available via mail, phone or Internet.

Prescriptions and correct copayments can be sent to:

Merck-Medco Rx Services
PO Box 1014
Summit, NJ 07902-9895

A registered pharmacist is available for emergency consultations 24 hours a day, seven days a week at the toll-free Member Services number above.

★★

TRICARE Retail Network Pharmacies

If an insured needs a prescription filled right away and is unable to use an MTF pharmacy, he or she may use one of the civilian pharmacies that are approved by TRICARE — otherwise known as "retail network pharmacies."

Through the retail network pharmacies, TRICARE beneficiaries can obtain up to a 30-day supply of most prescription medications for a small copay. While the National Mail Order Pharmacy is more cost effective for long-term medications, it may be easier to use a retail network pharmacy for new prescriptions a healthcare provider has required an individual to start taking immediately.

To use a retail network pharmacy, an insured simply presents the pharmacist with the written prescription, along with the military identification card. Depending on the TRICARE region, he or she may need to present the TRICARE card.

Individuals should contact their regional TRICARE service Center for a listing of approved retail network pharmacies.

To be eligible for the TRICARE benefit at a retail network pharmacy, a family's information must be up to date in the Defense Enrollment Eligibility Reporting System (DEERS).

★★

CHAPTER 12

VOCATIONAL REHABILITATION AND EMPLOYMENT SERVICES FOR VETERANS WITH SERVICE-CONNECTED DISABILITIES

OVERVIEW

Vocational Rehabilitation is a program which helps eligible disabled veterans get and keep lasting, suitable jobs. It also helps seriously disabled veterans achieve independence in daily living.

The program offers a number of services to help each eligible disabled veteran reach his or her rehabilitation goal. These services include:

- Vocational and personal counseling;
- Evaluation of abilities, skill and interests;
- Assistance finding and keeping a suitable job, including special employer incentives;
- If needed, education and training such as certificate, two, or four year college programs;
- Financial aid;
- If needed, training such as on-the-job and non-paid work experiences;
- Supportive rehabilitation services and additional counseling;
- Medical and dental treatment, if needed;
- Education and training benefits for dependent children with the birth defect spina bifida, caused by a veteran-parent's service in the Vietnam theater.
- Vocational and educational guidance and counseling to certain veteran's dependents eligible for one of VA's educational benefit programs.

If entitled to Vocational Rehabilitation, the law provides for a maximum of 48 months of services. These limitations may be extended in certain circumstances.

ELIGIBILITY

Usually, a veteran must first be awarded a monthly VA Disability Compensation payment. In some cases, veterans may be eligible if they are not getting VA compensation (for example, if they are awaiting discharge from the service because of a disability, OR they are entitled to VA compensation but have decided not to reduce their military retirement or disability pay).

Eligibility is also based on meeting the following conditions:

- The veteran served on or after September 16, 1940; and
- The veteran's discharge or release from active duty was under was under other than dishonorable conditions; and
- The veteran's service-connected disabilities are rated at least 20% disabling by VA (**NOTE:** Effective October 1, 1993, a veteran may be eligible for Vocational Rehabilitation if he or she is rated 10% disabled, and has a serious employment handicap.); and
- The veteran needs Vocational Rehabilitation to overcome an employment handicap; and
- It has been less than 12 years since VA notified the veteran of his or her eligibility. (A veteran may have longer than 12 years to use this benefit if certain conditions prevented him or her from training.)

AMOUNT OF VA PAYMENTS

If a veteran needs training, VA will pay his or her training costs, such as:

- Tuition and fees;
- Books;
- Supplies;
- Equipment; and
- Special services (such as prosthetic devices, lip-reading training, or signing for the deaf), if needed

While a veteran is in training, VA will also pay him or her a monthly benefit to help with living expenses, called a subsistence allowance. Details are provided in the next section of this chapter.

SUBSISTENCE ALLOWANCE (CHAPTER 31)

In some cases, a veteran requires additional education or training in order to become employable. A Subsistence Allowance may then be paid each month, and is based on the rate of attendance (full0time or part-time) and the number of dependents. The charts on the following page reflect the rates as of October 1, 2000.

INSTITUTIONAL TRAINING

Rates Effective October 1, 2000

# Of Dependents	Full Time	¾ Time	½ Time
None	$433.06	$325.41	$217.73
One	$537.19	$403.49	$269.77
Two	$633.04	$473.29	$317.11
Each Add'l	$46.14	$35.48	$23.67

QUARTER TIME RATES –
Payable For Extended Evaluation Only

Rates Effective October 1, 2000

# of Dependents	¼ Time
None	$108.85
One	$134.89
Two	$158.55
Each Add'l	$11.82

FARM COOPERATIVE, APPRENTICE, OR
ON-THE-JOB TRAINING

Rates Effective October 1, 2000

# of Dependents	Full Time
None	$378.65
One	$457.91
Two	$527.72
Each Add'l	$34.32

★★

PROGRAM FOR UNEMPLOYABLE VETERANS

Veterans awarded 100% disability compensation based upon unemployability may still request an evaluation, and, if found eligible, may participate in a vocational rehabilitation program and receive help in getting a job. A veteran who secures employment under the special program will continue to receive 100% disability compensation until the veteran has worked continuously for at least 12 months.

VOCATIONAL TRAINING FOR CHILDREN WITH SPINA BIFIDA

To qualify for entitlement to a vocational training program an applicant must be a child:

- To whom VA has awarded a monthly allowance for spina bifida; and
- For whom VA has determined that achievement of a vocational goal is reasonably feasible.

A vocational training program may not begin before a child's 18th birthday, or the date of completion of secondary schooling, whichever comes first. Depending on the need, a child may be provided up to 24 months of full-time training.

INDEPENDENT LIVING SERVICES

These services can help an individual with disabilities so severe that he or she cannot work. These services can lessen the individual's need to rely on others by giving him or her the skills needed to live as independently as possible at home and in the community.

Independent living services include:

- Extended evaluation of the individual's independent living needs;
- Training in activities of daily living;
- Case management;
- Personal adjustment counseling;
- Assistive technology;
- Training to improve the individual's chances of reaching a vocational goal

APPLYING FOR BENEFITS

Interested veterans can apply by filling out VA Form 28-1900, Disabled Veterans Application for Vocational Rehabilitation, and mailing it to the VA regional office serving his or her area. (For a complete list of VA Regional Offices, refer to page 292 of this book.)

CHAPTER 13

VET CENTERS

Vet Centers serve veterans and their families by providing a continuum of quality care that adds value for veterans, families, and communities. Care includes:

- Professional readjustment counseling;
- Professional counseling for posttraumatic stress disorder;
- Marital and family counseling;
- Substance abuse information and referral;
- Community education;
- Outreach to special populations, including disenfranchised and unserved veterans;
- The brokering of services with community agencies;
- Provides a key access link between the veteran and other services in the U.S. Department of Veterans Affairs;
- Promotion of wellness activities with veterans to help them reach quality health and life goals, and diminish the need for more intensive healthcare.

ELIGIBILITY

Legislation passed by Congress and signed into law by the President changed eligibility for Vet Center services, and extended the definition of the Vietnam era for war zone veterans (P.L. 104-262 and P.L. 104-275.)

Vet Centers serve the following veterans:

War Zone Veterans- all eras, including:

- **Vietnam War** – February 28, 1961 to May 7, 1975
- **Vietnam Era Veterans Not In The War Zone** – August 5, 1964 to May 7, 1975 (Veterans must request services at a Vet Center prior to January 1, 2004, to guarantee eligibility.)
- **Korean War** – June 27, 1950 to July 27, 1954 (eligible for the Korean Service Medal)
- **World War II** – There are 3 eligible categories:
    - o European-African-Middle Eastern Campaign Medal –
      December 7, 1941 to November 8, 1945
    - o Asiatic-Pacific Campaign Medal –
        - December 7, 1941 to March 2, 1946
    - o American Campaign Medal –
        - December 7, 1941 to March 2, 1946

★★★

- **Lebanon** – August 25, 1982 to February 26, 1984
- **Grenada** – October 23, 1983 to November 21, 1983
- **Panama** – December 20, 1989 to January 31, 1990
- **Persian Gulf** – August 2, 1990 to a date to be set by law or Presidential Proclamation
- **Somalia** – September 17, 1992 to a date to be set by law or Presidential Proclamation

Sexual Trauma and Harassment – Veterans of both sexes, and all eras

VET CENTER LOCATIONS

Alabama
Birmingham Vet Center
1500 5th Avenue South
Birmingham, AL 35205
(205) 731-0550

Mobile Vet Center
2577 Government Boulevard
Mobile, AL 36606
(334) 478-5906

Alaska
Anchorage Vet Center
4201 Tudor Centre Dr, Suite 115
Anchorage, AK 99508
(907) 563-6966

Fairbanks Vet Center
542 4th Avenue
Suite 100
Fairbanks, AK 99701
(907) 456-4238

Kenai Vet Center
445 Coral Street
Kenai, AL 99611
(907) 283-5205

Wasilla Vet Center
851 East Westpoint Ave, Suite 109
Wasilla, AK 99654
(907) 376-4318

Arizona
Phoenix Vet Center
141 East Palm Lane
Suite 100
Phoenix, AZ 85004
(602) 379-4769

Prescott Vet Center
161 South Granite Street
Prescott, AZ 86303
(520) 778-3469

Tucson Vet Center
3055 North 1st Avenue
Tucson, AZ 85719
(520) 882-0333

Arkansas
North Little Rock Vet Center
201 West Broadway
Suite A
Little Rock, AR 72114
(501) 324-6395

California
Anaheim Vet Center
859 South Harbor Boulevard
Anaheim, CA 92805
(714) 776-0161

★★

Chico Vet Center
25 Main St, Suite 100
Chico, CA 95928
(530) 899-8549

Chula Vista Vet Center
835 3rd Avenue
Chula Vista, CA 91910
(619) 409-1600

Commerce Vet Center
5400 East Olympic Blvd., #140
Commerce, CA 90022
(323) 728-9966

Concord Vet Center
1899 Clayton Rd, Suite 140
Concord, CA 94520
(925) 680-4526

Eureka Vet Center
2830 G Street, Suite A
Eureka, CA 95501
(707) 444-8271

Fresno Vet Center
3636 North 1st St, Suite 112
Fresno, CA 93726
(559) 487-5660

Los Angeles Vet Center
1045 W. Redondo Beach Blvd.
Gardena, CA 90247
(310) 767-1221

Los Angeles Vet Center
5730 Uplander Way
Culver City, CA 90230
(310) 641-0326

Marina Vet Center
455 Reservation Rd, Suite E
Marina, CA 93933
(408) 384-1660

Oakland Vet Center
1504 Franklin St, Suite 200
Oakland, CA 94612
(510) 763-3904

Redwood City Vet Center
2946 Broadway Street
Redwood City, CA 94062
(415) 299-0672

Riverside Vet Center
4954 Arlington Avenue, Suite A
Riverside, CA 92504
(909) 359-8967

Rohnert Park Vet Center
6225 State Farm Drive
Suite 101
Rohnert Park, CA 94928
(707) 586-3295

Sacramento Vet Center
1111 Howe Avenue
Suite 390
Sacramento, CA 95825
(916) 566-7430

San Bernardino Vet Center
155 West Hospitality Lane
Suite #140
San Bernardino, CA 92408
(909) 890-0797

San Diego Vet Center
2900 6th Avenue
San Diego, CA 92103
(619) 294-2040

San Francisco Vet Center
205 13th Street
Suite 3190
San Francisco, CA 94103
(415) 431-6021

San Jose Vet Center
278 North 2nd Street
San Jose, CA 95112
(408) 993-0729

Santa Barbara Vet Center
1300 Santa Barbara Street
Santa Barbara, CA 93101
(805) 564-2345

Sepulveda Vet Center
9737 Hascle Street
Sepulveda, CA 91343
(818) 892-9227

Upland Vet Center
313 North Mountain Avenue
Upland, CA 91786
(909) 982-0416

Vista Vet Center
1830 West Drive, Suite 103
Vista, CA 92083
(858) 945-8941

Colorado
Boulder Vet Center
2128 Pearl Street
Boulder, CO 80302
(303) 440-7306

Colorado Springs Vet Center
416 East Colorado Avenue
Colorado Springs, CO 80903
(719) 471-9992

Denver Vet Center
7465 E Academy Boulevard
Denver, CO 80220
(303) 326-0645

Connecticut
Hartford Vet Center
380 Market Street
Hartford, CT 06103
(860) 240-3543

New Haven Vet Center
141 Captain Thomas Boulevard
New Haven, CT 06516
(203) 932-9899

Norwich Vet Center
60 Main Street
Norwich, CT 06360
(860) 887-1755

Delaware
Wilmington Vet Center
1601 Kirkwood Highway
Wilmington, DE 19805
(302) 994-1660

District of Columbia
Washington, D.C. Vet Center
911 2nd Street, N.E.
Washington, DC 20002
(202) 543-8821

Florida
Fort Lauderdale Vet Center
713 NE 3rd Avenue
Fort Lauderdale, FL 33304
(954) 356-7926

Jacksonville Vet Center
300 East State Street
Jacksonville, FL 32202
(904) 232-3621

Miami Vet Center
2700 SW 3rd Avenue
Suite 1A
Miami, FL 33129
(305) 859-8387

Orlando Vet Center
5001 Orange Ave, Suite A
Orlando, FL 32809
(407) 857-2800

Palm Beach Vet Center
2311 10th Avenue, North #13
Palm Beach, FL 33461
(561) 585-0441

Pensacola Vet Center
202 West Jackson Street
Pensacola, FL 32501
(850) 435-8761

Sarasota Vet Center
4801 Swift Road
Sarasota, FL 34231
(941) 927-8285

St. Petersburg Vet Center
2837 1st Avenue, N.
St. Petersburg, FL 33713
(727) 893-3791

Tallahassee Vet Center
249 East 6th Avenue
Tallahassee, FL 32303
(850) 942-8810

★★★

Tampa Vet Center
1507 West Sligh Avenue
Tampa, FL 33604
(727) 228-2621

Georgia
Atlanta Vet Center
730 Peachtree Pl., N.W.
Atlanta, GA 30309
(404) 347-7264

Savannah Vet Center
8110A White Bluff Road
Savannah, GA 31406
(912) 652-4097

Guam
Agana Vet Center
222 Chalan Santo Papa Street
Reflection Center, Suite 102
Agana, Guam 96910
(671) 472-7160

Hawaii
Hilo Vet Center
120 Keawe Street
Suite 201
Hilo, HI 96720

Honolulu Vet Center
1680 Kapiolani Boulevard
Suite F3
Honolulu, HI 96814
(808) 973-8387

Kailua-Kona Vet Center
Pottery Terrace, Fern Building
75-5995 Kuakini Highway, #415
Kailua-Kona, HI 96470
(808) 329-0574

Lihue Vet Center
3367 Kuhlo Highway
Suite 101
Lihue, HI 96766
(808) 246-1163

Wailuku Vet Center
35 Lunalilo
Suite 101
Wailuku, HI 96793
(808) 242-8557

Idaho
Boise Vet Center
5440 Franklin Road, Suite 100
Boise, ID 83705
(208) 342-3612

Pocatello Vet Center
1800 Garrett Way
Pocatello, ID 83201
(208) 232-0316

Illinois
Chicago Vet Center
1514 East 63rd Street
Chicago, IL 60637
(773) 684-5500

Chicago Heights Vet Center
1600 Halsted Street
Chicago Heights, IL 60411
(708) 754-0340

East St. Louis Vet Center
1269 North 89th Street, Suite 1
East St. Louis, IL 62203
(618) 397-6602)

Evanston Vet Center
565 Howard Street
Evanston, IL 60202
(847) 332-1019

Moline Vet Center
1529 46th Avenue, #6
Moline, IL 61265
(309) 762-6954

Peoria Vet Center
3310 North Prospect Street
Peoria, IL 61603
(309) 671-7300

Springfield Vet Center
624 South 4th Street
Springfield, IL 62701
(217) 492-4955

Indiana
Evansville Vet Center
311 North Weinbach Avenue
Evansville, IN 47711
(812) 473-5993

★★

Fort Wayne Vet Center
528 West Berry Street
Fort Wayne, IN 46802
(219) 460-1456

Highland Vet Center
9105A Indianapolis Boulevard
Suite 301
Highland, IN 46322
(219) 923-2871

Indianapolis Vet Center
3833 Meridian, Suite 120
Indianapolis, IN 46208
(317) 927-6440

Iowa
Cedar Rapids Vet Center
1642 42nd Street, N.E.
Cedar Rapids, IA 52402
(319) 378-0016

Des Moines Vet Center
2600 Martin Luther King Jr.
Parkway
Des Moines, IA 50310
(515) 284-4929

Sioux City Vet Center
706 Jackson Street
Sioux City, IA 51101
(712) 255-3808

Kansas
Wichita Vet Center
413 South Pattie
Wichita, KS 67211
(316) 265-3260

Kentucky
Lexington Vet Center
301 East Vine Street, Suite C
Lexington, KY 40507
(606) 253-0717

Louisville Vet Center
1347 South 3rd Street
Louisville, KY 40208
(502) 634-1916

Louisiana
New Orleans Vet Center
1533 North Claiborne Avenue
New Orleans, LA 70116
(504) 943-8386

Shreveport Vet Center
2800 Youree Drive
Building 1, Suite 105
Shreveport, LA 71104
(318) 861-1776

Maine
Caribou Vet Center
456 York Street
Irving Complex
Caribou, ME 04736
(207) 496-3900

Lewiston Vet Center
Parkway Complex
29 Westminster Street
Lewiston, ME 04240
(207) 783-0068

Portland Vet Center
475 Stevens Avenue
Portland, ME 04103
(207) 780-3584

Sanford Vet Center
352 Harlow Street
Sanford, ME 04073
(207) 490-1513

Springvale Vet Center
23 Main Street
Springvale, ME 04083
(207) 490-1513

Maryland
Baltimore Vet Center
6666 Security Boulevard, Suite 2
Baltimore, MD 21207
(410) 277-3600

Elkton Vet Center
7 Elkton Commercial Plaza
South Bridge Street
Elkton, MD 21921
(410) 398-0171

Silver Spring Vet Center
1015 Spring St, Suite 101
Silver Spring, MD 20910
(301) 589-1073

Massachusetts
Boston Vet Center
665 Beacon Street
Boston, MA 02215
(617) 424-0665

Brockton Vet Center
1041-L Pearl Street
Brockton, MA 02401
(508) 580-2730

Lowell Vet Center
73 East Merrimack Street
Lowell, MA 01852
(978) 453-1151

New Bedford Vet Center
468 North Street
New Bedford, MA 02740
(508) 999-6920

Springfield Vet Center
1985 Main Street
Northgate Plaza
Springfield, MA 01103
(413) 737-5167

Worcester Vet Center
597 Lincoln Street
Worcester, MA 01605
(508) 856-7428

Michigan
Grand Rapids Vet Center
165 E. Apple Ave., Suite 201
Grand Rapids, MI 49507
(616) 243-0385

Lincoln Park Vet Center
1766 Fort Street
Lincoln Park, MI 48146
(313) 381-1370

Detroit Vet Center
4161 Cass Avenue
Detroit, MI 48201
(313) 831-6509

Minnesota
Duluth Vet Center
405 East Superior Street
Duluth, MN 55802
(218) 722-8654

St. Paul Vet Center
2480 University Avenue
St. Paul, MN 55114
(651) 644-4022

Mississippi
Biloxi Vet Center
313 Abbey Court
Biloxi, MS 39531
(228) 388-9938

Jackson Vet Center
4436 North State Street
Suite A3
Jackson, MS 39206
(601) 965-5727

Missouri
Kansas City Vet Center
3931 Main Street
Kansas City, MO 64111
(816) 753-1866

St. Louis Vet Center
2345 Pine Street
St. Louis, MO 63103
(314) 231-1260

Montana
Billings Vet Center
2345 King Avenue, W.
Billings, MT 59102
(406) 657-6071

Missoula Vet Center
500 North Higgins Avenue
Missoula, MT 59801
(406) 721-4918

Nebraska
Lincoln Vet Center
920 L Street
Lincoln, NE 68508
(402) 476-9736

★★★

Omaha Vet Center
2428 Cuming Street
Omaha, NE 68131
(402) 346-6735

Nevada
Las Vegas Vet Center
1040 East Sahara Avenue
Suite 102
Las Vegas, NV 89104
(702) 388-6369

Reno Vet Center
1155 West 4th Street
Suite 101
Reno, NV 89503
(775) 323-1294

New Hampshire
Manchester Vet Center
103 Liberty Street
Manchester, NH 03104
(603) 668-7060

New Jersey
Jersey City Vet Center
115 Christopher Columbus Drive
Room 200
Jersey City, NJ 07302
(973) 645-2038

Newark Vet Center
157 Washington Street
Newark, NJ 07102
(973) 645-5954

Trenton Vet Center
171 Jersey St., Building 36
Trenton, NJ 08611
(609) 989-2260

Ventnor Vet Center
6601 Ventnor Avenue, Suite 401
Ventnor, NJ 08406
(609) 487-8387

New Mexico
Albuquerque Vet Center
1600 Mountain Road, M.W.
Albuquerque, NM 87104
(505) 346-6562

Farmington Vet Center
4251 East Main, Suite B
Farmington, NM 87402
(505) 327-9684

Santa Fe Vet Center
2209 Brothers Road, Suite 110
Santa Fe, NM 87505
(505) 988-6562

New York
Albany Vet Center
875 Central Avenue
Albany, NY 12206
(518) 438-2505

Babylon Vet Center
116 West Main Street
Babylon, NY 11702
(631) 661-3930

Brooklyn Vet Center
25 Chapel Street, Suite 604
Brooklyn, NY 11201
(718) 330-2825

Bronx Vet Center
226 East Fordham Road
Room 220
Bronx, NY 10458
(718) 367-3500

Buffalo Vet Center
560 Delaware Avenue, Suite 1
Buffalo, NY 14202
(716) 882-0505

Harlem Vet Center
120 West 44th Street
Harlem, NY 10036
(212) 426-2200

New York City Vet Center
55 West 125th Street
New York, NY 10027
(212) 828-5265
(212) 426-2200

Rochester Vet Center
205 St. Paul Street
Rochester, NY 14604
(716) 232-5040

★★★

Staten Island Vet Center
150 Richmond Terrace
Staten Island, NY 10301
(718) 816-4799

Syracuse Vet Center
716 East Washington Street
Syracuse, NY 13210
(315) 478-7127

White Plains Vet Center
300 Hamilton Avenue
White Plains, NY 10601
(914) 682-6251

Woodhaven Vet Center
75-10B 91st Avenue
Woodhaven, NY 11421
(718) 296-2871

North Carolina
Charlotte Vet Center
223 South Brevard Street
Suite 103
Charlotte, NC 28202
(704) 333-6107

Fayetteville Vet Center
4140 Ramsey St., Suite 110
Fayetteville, NC 28311
(910) 488-6252

Greensboro Vet Center
2009 South Elm-Eugene Street
Greensboro, NC 27406
(336) 333-5366

Greenville Vet Center
150 Arlington Blvd., Suite B
Greenville, NC 27858
(252) 355-7920

Raleigh Vet Center
1649 Old Louisburg Road
Raleigh, NC 27604
(919) 856-4616

North Dakota
Fargo Vet Center
3310 Fiechtner Drive, Suite 100
Fargo. MD 58103
(701) 237-0942

Minot Vet Center
2041 3rd Street, N.W.
Minot, ND 58701
(701) 852-0177

Bismarck Vet Center
1684 Capital Way
Bismarck, ND 58501
(701) 244-9751

Ohio
Cincinnati Vet Center
801-B West 8th Street
Cincinnati, OH 45203
(513) 763-3500

Cleveland Heights Center
2022 Lee Road
Cleveland Heights, OH 44118
(216) 932-8471

Columbus Vet Center
30 Spruce Street
Columbus, OH 43215
(614) 257-5550

Dayton Vet Center
111 West 3rd St., Suite 101
Dayton, OH 45402
(937) 461-9150

Pama Vet Center
5700 Pearl Rd., Suite 102
Pama, OH 44129
(440) 845-5023

Oklahoma
Oklahoma City Vet Center
3033 North Walnut, Suite 101W
Oklahoma City, OK 73105
(405) 270-5184

Tulsa Vet Center
1408 South Harvard
Tulsa, OK 74112
(918) 748-5105

Oregon
Eugene Vet Center
1255 Pearl Street
Eugene, OR 97403
(541) 465-6918

★★

Grants Pass Vet Center
211 S.E. 10th Street
Grants Pass, OR 97526
(541) 479-6912

Portland Vet Center
8383 N.E. Sandy Blvd, Suite 110
Portland, OR 97220
(503) 273-5370

Salem Vet Center
617 Chemeketa St., N.E.
Salem, OR 97301
(503) 362-9911

Pennsylvania
Erie Vet Center
1001 State Street
Suites 1 & 2
Erie, PA 16501
(814) 453-7955

Harrisburg Vet Center
1007 North Front Street
Harrisburg, PA 17102
(717) 782-3954

McKeesport Vet Center
2001 Lincoln Way
McKeesport, PA 15132
(412) 678-7704

Philadelphia Vet Center
801 Arch Street, Suite 102
Philadelphia, PA 19107
(215) 627-0238

Philadelphia Vet Center
101 East Olney Avenue
Box C-7
Philadelphia, PA 19152
(215) 924-4670

Pittsburgh Vet Center
954 Penn Avenue
Pittsburgh, PA 15222
(412) 765-1193

Scranton Vet Center
1002 Pittston Avenue
Scranton, PA 18505
(570) 344-2676

Williamsport Vet Center
805 Penn Street
Williamsport, PA 17701
(570) 327-5281

Puerto Rico
Arecibo Vet Center
52 Gonzalo Marin Street
Arecibo, Puerto Rico 00612-4702
(787) 879-4510
(787) 879-4581

Ponce Vet Center
35 Mayor Street
Ponce, Puerto Rico 00731
(787) 841-3260

San Juan Vet Center
Condominio Medical Center Plaza
Suite LC8A and LC9
La Riviera
San Juan, Puerto Rico 00921
(787) 749-4409

Rhode Island
Cranston Vet Center
789 Park Avenue
Cranston, RI 02910
(401) 467-2046

South Carolina
Columbia Vet Center
1513 Pickens Street
Columbia, SC 29201
(803) 765-9944

Greenville Vet Center
14 Lavinia Avenue
Greenville, SC 29601
(864) 271-2711

North Charleston Vet Center
5603A Rivers Avenue
North Charleston, SC 29406
(843) 747-8387

South Dakota
Rapid City Vet Center
610 Kansas City Street
Rapid City, SD 57701
(605) 348-0077

★★

Martin Vet Center
East Highway 18
Martin, SD 57551
(605) 685-1300

Sioux Falls Vet Center
601 S. Cliff Ave., Suite C
Sioux Falls, SD 57104
(605) 332-0856

Tennessee

Chattanooga Vet Center
951 Eastgate Loop Road
Building 5700, Suite 300
Chattanooga, TN 37411
(423) 855-6570

Johnson City Vet Center
1615A West Market Street
Johnson City, TN 37604
(423) 928-8387

Knoxville Vet Center
2817 East Magnolia Avenue
Knoxville, TN 37914
(423) 545-4680

Memphis Vet Center
1835 Union, Suite 100
Memphis, TN 38104
(901) 544-0173

Texas
Amarillo Vet Center
3414 Olsen Blvd., Suite E
Amarillo, TX 79109
(806) 354-9779

Austin Vet Center
1110 W William Cannon Dr
Suite 301
Austin, TX 78745
(512) 416-1314

Corpus Christi Vet Center
4646 Corona, Suite 110
Corpus Christi, TX 78411
(361) 854-9961

Dallas Vet Center
5232 Forest Lane, Suite 111
Dallas, TX 75244
(214) 361-5896

El Paso Vet Center
Sky Park II
6500 Boeing
Suite L-112
El Paso, TX 79925
(915) 772-5368

Fort Worth Vet Center
1305 West Magnolia, Suite B
Forth Worth, TX 76104
(817) 921-9095

Houston Vet Center
503 Westheimer
Houston, TX 77006
(713) 523-0884

Houston Vet Center
701 N. Post Oak Rd., Suite 102
Houston, TX 77024
(713) 682-2288)

Laredo Vet Center
6020 McPherson Road, #1A
Laredo, TX 78041
(956) 723-4680

Lubbock Vet Center
3208 34th Street
Lubbock, TX 29410
(806) 792-9782

McAllen Vet Center
801 Nolana Loop, Suite 115
McAllen, TX 78504
(956) 631-2147

Midland Vet Center
3404 W. Illinois, Suite 1
Midland, TX 79703
(915) 697-8222

San Antonio Vet Center
231 West Cypress Street
San Antonio, TX 78212
(210) 472-4025

★★

Utah
Provo Vet Center
750 North 200 West
Suite 105
Provo, UT 84601
(801) 377-1117

Salt Lake City Vet Center
1354 East 3300 South
Salt Lake City, UT 84106
(801) 584-1294

Vermont
South Burlington Vet Center
359 Dorset Street
South Burlington, VT 05403
(802) 862-1806

White River Junction Vet Center
Gilman Office Center
Building #2
Holiday Inn Drive
(802) 295-2908
1-800-649-6603

Virginia
Alexandria Vet Center
8796 Sacramento Drive
Suites D & E
Alexandria, VA 22309
(703) 360-8633

Norfolk Vet Center
2200 Colonial Avenue, Suite 3
Norfolk, VA 23517
(757) 623-7584

Richmond Vet Center
4202 Fitzhugh Avenue
Richmond, VA 23230
(804) 353-8958

Roanoke Vet Center
350 Albemarle Avenue, S.W.
Roanoke, VA 24016
(540) 342-9726

Virgin Islands
St. Croix Vet Center
Box 12
R.R. 02, Village Mall, #113
St. Croix, Virgin Islands 00850
(340) 778-5553

St. Thomas Vet Center
9800 Buccaneer Mall, Suite 8
St. Thomas, Virgin Islands 00802

Washington
Bellingham Vet Center
3800 Byron Avenue, Suite 124
Bellingham, WA 98226
(360) 733-9226

Seattle Vet Center
2309 9th Avenue, Suite 210
Seattle, WA 98121
(206) 553-2706

Spokane Vet Center
W. 1708 Mission Avenue
Spokane, WA 99201
(509) 327-0274

Tacoma Vet Center
4916 Center Street, Suite E
Tacoma, WA 98409
(253) 565-7038

Toppenish Vet Center
219 South Toppenish Avenue
Toppenish, WA 98498

Yakima Vet Center
310 North 5th Avenue
Yakima, WA 98901
(509) 457-2736

West Virginia
Beckley Vet Center
101 Ellison Avenue
Beckley, WV 25801
(304) 252-8220

★★

Charleston Vet Center
512 Washington Street, West
Charleston, WV 25302
(304) 343-3825

Huntington Vet Center
1005 6th Avenue
Huntington, WV 25701
(304) 523-8387

Martinsburg Vet Center
105 South Spring Street
Martinsburg, WV 25401
(304) 263-6776

Morgantown Vet Center
1191F Pineview Drive
Morgantown, WV 26505
(304) 285-4001

Princeton Vet Center
905 Mercer Street
Princeton, WV 24740
(304) 425-5653

Wheeling Vet Center
1206 Chapline Street
Wheeling, WV 26003
(304) 232-0587

Wisconsin
Madison Vet Center
147 South Butler Street
Madison, WI 53703
(608) 264-5342

Milwaukee Vet Center
5401 North 76th Street
Milwaukee, WI 53218
(414) 536-1301

Wyoming
Casper Vet Center
111 South Jefferson
Casper, WY 82601
(307) 261-5355

Cheyenne Vet Center
3130 Henderson Drive
Cheyenne, WY 82001
(307) 778-7370

CHAPTER 14

EDUCATION BENEFITS

The Veterans' Administration administers nine educational assistance programs, each with different eligibility criteria. Typically, a veteran's eligibility is based on his or her dates of active duty. Generally, only the VA can determine an applicant's eligibility. Specific information regarding educational benefits can be obtained from the Education Service of the VA (1-888-GI-BILL-1) or any VA regional office.

The basic categories of VA educational assistance programs are:

- Montgomery G.I. Bill - Active Duty (MGIB - Chapter 30)
- Montgomery G.I. Bill - Selected Reserve (Chapter 1606)
- Veterans' Educational Assistance Program (VEAP - Chapter 32)
- Educational Assistance Test Program (Section 901)
- Educational Assistance Pilot Program (Section 903)
- Survivors' and Dependents' Educational Assistance Program (Chapter 35)
- Restored Entitlement Program for Survivors (REPS)
- Vocational Rehabilitation (Chapter 31) *(This topic is discussed in detail beginning on page 363.)*
- Omnibus Diplomatic Security and Antiterrorism Act

An individual can be eligible for more than one of the above education benefits. If so, he or she must elect which benefit to receive. Payments for more than one benefit at a time may not be made. *The VA strongly encourages individuals who qualify for more than one type of education benefit to discuss their education plans with a Veterans Benefits Counselor so that all options can be explored, and maximum benefits can be paid.*

The Montgomery G.I. Bill-Active Duty and the Montgomery G.I. Bill-Selected Reserve are discussed in the following two chapters. This chapter discusses the remaining seven educational assistance programs.

VETERANS EDUCATIONAL ASSISTANCE PROGRAM (VEAP) – CHAPTER 32

The Post-Vietnam Veterans' Educational Assistance Program is also known as VEAP or chapter 32. VEAP provides education and training opportunities to eligible persons who contributed to the program while on active duty. If an individual did not contribute, or received a refund of contributions, he or she is not eligible for VEAP benefits. Veterans who first entered active duty between January 1, 1977 and June 30, 1985 were able to voluntarily contribute to an education account to establish eligibility for this program. The initial contribution must have been made by March 31, 1987. The maximum contribution by any individual participant is $2,700. A participating member's contributions are matched on a $2 for $1 basis by the Government.

VEAP Eligibility

To qualify for VEAP benefits, individuals must have:

- Entered active duty for the first time between January 1, 1977 and June 30, 1985; and

- Enrolled in and contributed to VEAP before April 1, 1987; and

- Served for a continuous period of 181 days or more (Individuals may be eligible if discharged from a shorter period of active duty for a service-connected disability.); and

- Been discharged or released from service under conditions other than dishonorable; and

- Completed 24 continuous months of active duty if enlisted for the first time after September 7, 1980, or entered active duty as an officer or enlistee after October 16, 1981. (Individuals meet this requirement if they completed a shorter period of active duty to which the service department called or ordered the individual.)

Individuals may be eligible for VEAP benefits if they did not complete 24 continuous months of active duty if they:

- Received VA disability compensation or military disability retirement; or

- Served a period of at least 24 continuous months of active duty before October 17, 1981; or

- Were discharged or released for early out, hardship, or service-connected disability.

Individuals may be eligible for VEAP benefits while still on active duty if they:

- Entered active duty for the first time after December 31, 1976, and before July 1, 1985; and

- Enrolled in and contributed to VEAP before April 1, 1987, and have at least three months of contributions available (For an elementary or high school program, at least one month of contributions must be available.); and

- Served for a continuous period of 181 days or more; and

- Completed their first active duty commitment.

The following types of active duty do not establish eligibility:

- Time assigned by the military to a civilian institution for the same course provided to civilians;

- Time served as a cadet or midshipman at a service academy;

- Time spent on active duty for training in the National Guard or Reserve.

NOTE: Individuals are not eligible for VEAP if they are eligible for the Montgomery GI Bill-Active Duty based on prior eligibility for Vietnam Ear Veterans' Educational Assistance.

Approved Courses

VEAP benefits may be received for a wide variety of training, including:
- Training for a high school diploma or the equivalent
- Undergraduate or graduate degrees from a college or university
- Cooperative training programs
- Accredited independent study programs leading to standard college degrees
- Courses leading to certificates or diplomas from business, technical or vocational schools
- Vocational flight training (Individuals must have a private pilot's license and meet the medical requirements for a desired license before beginning training, and throughout the flight training program)
- Apprenticeship or job training programs offered by a company or union
- Correspondence courses
- VA may approve programs offered by institutions outside of the United States, when they are pursued at educational institutions of higher learning, and lead to a college degree. Individuals must receive VA approval prior to attending or enrolling in any foreign programs.
- **Update: Effective March 1, 2001**, benefits will be payable for licensing or certification tests. The tests are those needed to enter, maintain, or advance into employment in a civilian vocation or profession. The eligible veteran or family member may receive payment of the fee charged for the test or $2,000, whichever is less. *The tests must be approved for VA benefits.*

If an individual is seeking a college degree, the school must admit him or her to a degree program by the start of the third term.

Restrictions on Training
- Bartending and personality development courses
- Non-accredited independent study courses
- Any course given by radio
- Self-improvement courses such as reading, speaking, woodworking, basic seamanship, and English as a second language
- Any course which is avocational or recreational in character
- Farm cooperative courses
- Audited courses
- Courses not leading to an educational, professional, or vocational objective
- Courses an individual has previously taken and successfully completed
- Courses taken by a Federal government employee under the Government Employees' Training Act
- Courses paid for in whole or in part by the Armed Forces while on active duty
- Courses taken while in receipt of benefits for the same program from the Office of Workers' Compensation Programs

★★★

The VA must reduce benefits for individuals in Federal, State or local prisons after being convicted of a felony.

An individual may not receive benefits for a program at a proprietary school if he or she is an owner or official of the school.

Benefits are generally payable for 10 years following a veteran's release from active duty.

Part-Time Training

Individuals unable to attend school full-time should consider going part-time. Benefit rates and entitlement charges are less than the full-time rates. For example, if a student receives full-time benefits for 12 months, the entitlement charge is 12 months. However, if the students receives ½ time benefits for 12 months, the charge is 6 months. VA will pay for less than ½ time training if the student is not receiving Tuition Assistance for those courses.

Remedial, Deficiency And Refresher Training

Remedial and deficiency courses are intended to assist a student in overcoming a deficiency in a particular area of study. In order for such courses to be approved, the courses must be deemed necessary for pursuit of a program of education.

Refresher training is for technological advances that occurred in a field of employment. The advance must have occurred while the student was on active duty, or after release.

There is an entitlement charge for these courses.

Tutorial Assistance

Students may receive a special allowance for individual tutoring if they entered school at one-half time or more. To qualify, the student must have a deficiency in a subject. The school must certify the tutor's qualifications, and the hours of tutoring. Eligible students may receive a maximum monthly payment of $100.00. The maximum total benefit payable is $1,200.00.

There is no entitlement charge for the first $600.00 of tutorial assistance.

To apply for tutorial assistance, students must submit VA Form 22-1990t, Application and Enrollment Certification for Individualized Tutorial Assistance. The form should be given to the certifying official in the office handling VA paperwork at the school for completion.

Months of Benefits / Entitlement Charged

Eligible members may be entitled to receive up to 36 months of VEAP benefits. Usually, the number of monthly payments for full-time training is the same as the number of months an individual contributed to VEAP.

★★★

Individuals qualifying for more than one VA education program may receive a maximum of 48 months of benefits. For example, if a student used 30 months of Dependents' Educational Assistance, and is eligible for chapter 1606 benefits, he or she could have a maximum of 18 months of entitlement remaining.

Individuals are charged one full day of entitlement for each day of full-time benefits paid. For correspondence and flight training, one month of entitlement is charged each time VA pays one month of benefits. For cooperative programs, one month of entitlement is used for each month of benefits paid.

For apprenticeship and job training programs, the entitlement charge changes every 6 months. During the first 6 months, the charge is 75% of full time. For the second 6 months, the charge is 55% of full time. For the remainder of the program, the charge is 35% of full time.

Rates of Educational Assistance Pay

The total dollar amount of VEAP benefits is:

- An individual's total contributions, plus
- Matching funds equal to 2 times the individual's contributions, plus
- Any additional contributions or kickers made by the Department of Defense

The amount of money an individual receives each month depends on the type of training and the training time.

Institutional Training:

The monthly benefit payment will vary depending on the amount and number of contributions. Divide the total contributions by the number of months contributed, and this equals the full-time institutional rate.

Example:

Step 1:

$1,800	individual contributions
+3,600	matching funds (2 times individual contribution)
+ -0-	kicker

$5,400   TOTAL ENTITLEMENT

Step 2:

$5,400 divided by 36 months of contributions = $150 monthly full-time institutional rate

(No amount in excess of an individual's total entitlement can be paid.)

★★

Correspondence Training

An individual can be reimbursed for the entire established charges paid for a correspondence course. However, no amount in excess of an individual's total entitlement can be paid.

Flight Training

Individuals taking flight training will receive 60% of the approved charges for the course, including solo hours. (VA does not pay for solo hours before October 1, 1992.) No amount in excess of an individual's total entitlement can be paid.

Apprenticeship or Job Training

The monthly benefit amount is:

- 75% of the full-time rate for the first 6 months of training;
- 55% of the full-time rate for the second 6 months of training;
- 35% of the full-time rate for the rest of the training.

Monthly payments are reduced if an individual works less than 120 hours a month.

Cooperative Training

Individuals may receive payment at 80% of the rate to which he or she is entitled for institutional training.

Eligibility Periods

Benefits end 10 years from the date of the individual's last discharge or release from active duty.

VA can extend the 10-year period by the amount of time a service member was prevented from training during the period due to a disability or being held by a foreign government or power.

VA may extend the 10-year period if the individual reenters active duty for 90 days or more after becoming eligible. The extension ends 10 years from the date of discharge or release from the later period. Periods of active duty of less than 90 days can qualify for extensions only if discharge or release was due to:

- A service-connected disability; or
- A medical condition existing before active duty; or
- Hardship; or
- A reduction in force.

If a discharge is upgraded by the military, the 10-year period begins on the date of the upgrade.

If an individual is in an apprenticeship or job-training program, he or she will receive a form to report the hours worked each month. The form must be signed and given to the certifying official for the company or union. The certifying official must complete the form and send it to the appropriate VA regional office. After processing, VA will release a check.

If an individual is taking a correspondence course, he or she will receive a form each quarter, on which the student must show the number of lessons completed that quarter. The completed form should be sent to the school for certification of the number of lessons serviced during the quarter. The school will send the form to the appropriate VA regional office. After processing, VA will release a check. Payments are based on the number of lessons serviced by the school.

VA will send flight schools a supply of blank monthly certification of flight training forms. The school must complete the form by entering the number of hours, the hourly rate, and the total charges for flight training received during the month. The student should review and sign the completed form, and send it to the appropriate VA regional office. After processing, VA will release a check.

NOTE: It is against the law for schools to cash VA checks under a Power of Attorney Agreement.

Timely Receipt of Verification Forms And Checks

Students taking courses leading to a degree at a college or university should receive their checks for each month by the fifth of the next month. If it is not received by then, the VA should be immediately contacted so that appropriate action can be taken.

Students taking courses leading to a certificate or diploma from a business, technical, or vocational school should receive their verification forms for each month by the fifth of the following month. If it is not received by then, the VA should be immediately contacted so that another form can be issued.

Once a completed verification form has been submitted, the student should receive a check within 2 weeks. If a check is not received by then, the VA should immediately be contacted so that appropriate action can be taken.

Advance Payments

An advance payment for the initial month, or partial month and the following month may be made, if:

- The school agrees to handle advance payments; and
- Training is one-half time or more; and
- A request is made by the individual in writing; and
- The VA receives the enrollment certification at least 30 days prior to the start of classes.

Advance payments are made out to the individual, and sent to the applicable school for delivery to the individual registration. VA cannot issue a check more than 30 days before classes start. Before requesting an advance payment, students should verify with the school certifying official that the school has agreed to process advance payments.

Requests for advance payments must be on VA Form 22-1999, Enrollment Certification, or a sheet of paper attached to the enrollment certification.

Once a student receives an advance payment at registration, the school must certify to VA that the student received the check. If a student reduces enrollment, or withdraws from all courses during the period covered by an advance payment, he or she must repay the overpayment to VA.

If an individual believes that the amount of a VA check is incorrect, the VA should be contacted before the check is cashed.

Direct Deposit

Payments can be sent directly to a student's savings or checking account through Direct Deposit (Electronic Funds Transfer). To sign up for direct deposit by phone, students must call 1-877-838-2778.

Student Responsibilities

To ensure timely receipt of correct payments, students should be sure to promptly notify the VA of:

- Any change in enrollment
- Any change in address

In addition, students should use reasonable judgment when accepting and cashing a check. All letters from VA about monthly rates and effective dates should be read carefully. If a student thinks the amount of a VA check is wrong, VA should be contacted *before* cashing the check. Any incorrect checks should be returned to VA.

If a student cashes a check for the wrong amount, he or she will be liable for repayment of any resulting overpayment.

Recovery of Overpayments

VA must take prompt and aggressive action to recover overpayments. Students have the right to request a waiver of the overpayment, or verification that the amount is correct. If an overpayment is not repaid or waived, VA may add interest and collection fees to the debt. VA may also take one or more of the following actions to collect the debt:

- Withhold future benefits to apply to the debt;
- Refer the debt to a private collection agency;
- Recover the debt from any Federal income tax refund;
- Recover the debt from the salary (if student is a Federal employee);

★★

- File a lawsuit in Federal court to collect the debt;
- Withhold approval of a VA home loan guarantee.

An individual's reserve component will act to collect penalties caused by unsatisfactory participation in the reserve.

Changes in Enrollment

If a student withdraws from one or more courses after the end of the school's drop period, VA will reduce or stop benefits on the date of reduction or withdrawal. Unless the student can show that the change was due to *mitigating circumstances*, the student may have to repay **all** benefits for the course.

VA defines *mitigating circumstances* as "unavoidable and unexpected events that directly interfere with the pursuit of a course, and which are beyond the student's control."

Examples of reasons VA may accept include:

- Extended illness;
- Severe illness or death in immediate family;
- Unscheduled changes in employment; and
- Lack of child care

Examples of reasons VA may not accept include:

- Withdrawal to avoid a failing grade;
- Dislike of the instructor; and
- Too many courses attempted

(VA may ask the student to furnish evidence to support the reason for change, such as physician or employer written statements.)

The first time a student withdraws from up to 6 credit hours, VA will "excuse" the withdrawal, and pay benefits for the period attended.

- If a student receives a grade that does not count toward graduation, all benefits for the course may have to be repaid.

If a student receives a non-punitive grade, the school will notify VA, and VA may reduce or stop benefits. The student may not have to repay the benefits if he or she can show that the grades were due to mitigating circumstances.

Work-Study Programs

Students may be eligible for an additional allowance under a work-study program that allows students to perform work for VA in return for an hourly wage. Students may perform outreach services under VA supervision, prepare and process VA paperwork, work at a VA medical facility or National Cemetery, or perform other approved activities.

Students must attend school at the three-quarter of full-time rate.

★★★

VA will select students for the work study program based on different factors. Such factors include:

- Disability of the student
- Ability of the student to complete the work-study contract before the end of his or her eligibility for education benefits
- Job availability within normal commuting distance to the student
- VA will give the highest priority to a veteran who has a service-connected disability or disabilities rated by VA at 30% or more

The number of applicants selected will depend on the availability of VA-related work at the school or at VA facilities in the area.

Students may work during or between periods of enrollment, and can arrange with VA to work any number of hours during his or her enrollment. However, the maximum number of hours a student may work is 25 times the number of weeks in the enrollment period.

Students will earn an hourly wage equal to the Federal or State minimum wage, whichever is greater. If a student works at a college or university, the school *may* pay the difference between the amount VA pays and the amount the school normally pays other work-study students doing the same job.

Students interested in taking part in a work-study program must complete VA Form 22,8691, Application for Work-Study Allowance. Completed forms should be sent to the nearest VA regional office.

Educational Counseling

VA can provide services to help eligible individuals understand their educational and vocational strengths and weaknesses and to plan:

- An educational or training goal, and the means by which the goal can be reached; or
- An employment goal for which an individual qualifies on the basis of present training or experience.

VA can also help plan an effective job search.

Counseling is available for:

- Service members eligible for VA educational assistance; or
- Service members on active duty and within 180 days of discharge; or
- Veterans with discharges that are not dishonorable, who are within one year from date of discharge.

Vocational Rehabilitation

Veterans may qualify for Training and Rehabilitation under Chapter 31 of Title 38, United States Code, if:

- The veteran has a service-connected disability or disabilities rated by VA at 20% or more; and

★★

- The veteran received a discharge from active duty that was not dishonorable; and
- The veteran has an employment handicap.

Veterans may also qualify with a service-connected disability or disabilities rated by VA at 10%, and:

- The veteran has a serious employment handicap; or
- The veteran first applied for vocational rehabilitation benefits before November 1, 1990, reapplied after that date, and has an employment handicap.

Vocational rehabilitation helps disabled veterans become independent in daily living. Veterans may also receive assistance in selecting, preparing for, and securing employment that is compatible with their interests, talents, skills, physical capabilities, and goals.

To apply for vocational rehabilitation, VA for 28-1900, Disabled Veterans Application for Vocational Rehabilitation, must be completed and sent to the nearest VA regional office.

For detailed information on vocational rehabilitation, refer to page 117 of this book.

Refund of VEAP Benefits

If a service member does not wish to use his or her VEAP benefits, he or she must apply to the nearest VA regional office for a refund of his or her contributions.

Appeal of VA Decision

VA decisions on education benefits may be appealed within one year of the date an individual receives notice of a VA decision.

For detailed information on filing an appeal, please refer to page 282 of this book.

EDUCATIONAL AND ASSISTANCE TEST PROGRAM (SECTION 901)

This program was included as part of the "Department of Defense Authorization Act of 1981". The test program is funded by the Department of Defense, and administered by the VA. "Section 901" has been used to identify the program since its inception. However, the title "chapter 107" may also be used.

Section 901 is a noncontributory program in which an eligible participant, or in some cases his or her dependent(s), may receive an educational assistance and subsistence allowance while training at an accredited institution.

Basic eligibility to section 901 benefits was limited to a small group of servicepersons who enlisted between September 30, 1980 and October 1, 1981, met strict guidelines and were selected by the Department of Defense. The Waco Regional Office processes all section 901 payments.

★★★

EDUCATIONAL ASSISTANCE PILOT PROGRAM (SECTION 903)

Section 903 is a modified Chapter 32 (VEAP) program, in which the Service Department makes the individual's monthly contributions. Eligibility was limited to a small group of participants, selected by the service department, who enlisted between November 30, 1980 and October 1, 1981. Individuals must have been selected for the pilot program

SURVIVORS' AND DEPENDENTS EDUCATIONAL ASSISTANCE PROGRAM (DEA) – CHAPTER 35

The Survivors' and Dependents Educational Assistance Program (DEA) was enacted by Congress to provide education and training opportunities to eligible dependents of certain veterans. The program offers up to 45 months of education benefits.

Eligibility Requirements

To qualify, one must be the son, daughter or spouse of:

- A veteran who died, or is permanently and totally disabled as the result of a service-connected disability, which arose out of active service in the Armed Forces.

- A veteran who died from any cause while such service-connected disability was in existence.

- A service member who is missing in action or captured in the line of duty by a hostile force.

- A service member who is being forcibly detained or interned in the line of duty by a foreign power.

Pension, Compensation, and DIC Programs

A son or daughter who is eligible for Chapter 35 benefits, as well as pension, compensation, or Dependency & Indemnity Compensation (DIC) based on school attendance, must elect which benefit to receive. An election of Chapter 35 benefits is a bar to further payment of pension, compensation, or DIC after the age of 18.

NOTE: If a program will last longer than 45 months, the son or daughter may find it to his or her advantage to defer Chapter 35 benefits. He or she could continue to receive pension, compensation, or DIC benefits which are payable as a result of school attendance. *The VA strongly encourages individuals who qualify for more than one type of education benefit to discuss their education plans with a Veterans Benefits Counselor so that all options can be explored, and maximum benefits can be paid.*

★★★

Approved Courses

Individuals may receive benefits for a wide variety of training, including:

- Undergraduate degrees from a college or university
- Graduate degrees from a college or university
- Cooperative training programs
- Accredited independent study programs leading to a college degree
- Courses leading to a certificate or diploma from business, technical, or vocational schools
- Apprenticeship or job training program offered by a company or union
- Correspondence courses (spouses only)
- Farm cooperative courses
- Secondary school programs for individuals who are not high school graduates
- Secondary school deficiency or remedial courses to qualify for admission to an educational institution

Update: Effective November 1, 2000, persons eligible for DEA can receive benefits for VA-approved preparation courses for college and graduate school entrance exams. (The law also allows children to pursue these courses before age 18.)

Update: Effective March 1, 2001, benefits will be payable for licensing or certification tests. The tests are those needed to enter, maintain, or advance into employment in a civilian vocation or profession. The eligible veteran or family member may receive payment of the fee charged for the test or $2,000, whichever is less. *The tests must be approved for VA benefits.*

VA may approve programs offered by institutions outside of the United States, when they are pursued at educational institutions of higher learning, and lead to a college degree. Individuals must receive VA approval prior to attending or enrolling in any foreign programs.

An eligible son or daughter who is handicapped by a physical or mental disability that prevents pursuit of an educational program may receive Special Restorative Training. This may involve speech and voice correction, language retraining, lip reading, auditory training, Braille reading and writing, etc.

An eligible spouse or son or daughter over age 14 who is handicapped by a physical or mental disability that prevents pursuit of an educational program may receive Specialized Vocational Training This includes specialized courses, alone or in combination with other courses, leading to a vocational objective that is suitable for the person and required by reason of physical or mental handicap.

A State agency or VA must approve each program offered by a school or company.

If an individual is seeking a college degree, the school must admit the individual to a degree program by the start of the individual's third term.

Restrictions on Training

Benefits are not payable for the following courses:

- Non-accredited independent study courses
- Bartending and personality development courses
- Correspondence courses (if you are a dependent or surviving child)
- Any course given by radio
- Vocational flight training
- Self-improvement courses such as reading, speaking, woodworking, basic seamanship, and English as a 2nd language
- Any course which is avocational or recreational in character
- Audited courses
- Courses not leading to an educational, professional, or vocational objective
- Courses previously taken and successfully completed
- Courses taken by a Federal government employee under the Government Employee's Training Act
- Courses taken while in receipt of benefits for the same program from the Office of Workers' Compensation Programs

VA must reduce benefits for individuals in Federal, State, or local prisons after being convicted of a felony.

An individual may not receive benefits for a program at a proprietary school if her or she is an owner or official of the school.

An individual may not receive benefits under this program while serving on active duty in the Armed Forces.

Part-Time Training

Individuals unable to attend school full-time should consider going part-time. Benefit rates and entitlement charges are less than the full-time rates. For example, if a student receives full-time benefits for 12 months, the entitlement charge is 12 months. However, if the students receives ½ time benefits for 12 months, the charge is 6 months. VA will pay for less than ½ time training if the student is not receiving Tuition Assistance for those courses.

Remedial, Deficiency and Refresher Training

Remedial and deficiency courses are intended to assist a student in overcoming a deficiency in a particular area of study.

Refresher training is available only at the elementary or secondary level. It is for reviewing or updating material previously covered in a course satisfactorily completed.

There is no entitlement charge for these courses for the first 5 months of training.

Tutorial Assistance

Students may receive a special allowance for individual tutoring performed after September 30, 1992, if they entered school at one-half time or more. To qualify, the student must have a deficiency in a subject. The school must certify the tutor's qualifications, and the hours of tutoring. Eligible students may receive a maximum monthly payment of $100.00. The maximum total benefit payable is $1,200.00.

There is no entitlement charge for the first $600.00 of tutorial assistance.

To apply for tutorial assistance, students must submit VA Form 22-1990t, Application and Enrollment Certification for Individualized Tutorial Assistance. The form should be given to the certifying official in the office handling VA paperwork at the school for completion.

Months of Benefits / Entitlement Charged

Eligible individuals may be entitled to receive up to 45 months of education benefits.

Individuals qualifying for more than one VA education program may receive a maximum of 48 months of benefits. For example, if a student used 30 months of his or her own benefits as a veteran under the Montgomery GI Bill – Active Duty Educational Assistance Program, and is eligible as a dependent, he or she could have a maximum of 18 months of entitlement remaining.

Individuals are charged one full day of entitlement for each day of full-time benefits paid. For spouses pursuing correspondence training, one month of entitlement is charged each time VA pays one month of benefits.

Period of Eligibility for Sons or Daughters

Sons or daughters who wish to receive benefits for attending school or job training must be between the ages of 18 and 26. (In certain circumstances, it is possible to begin or end before or after these dates.) Marriage does not disqualify a son or daughter from this benefit. However, an eligible child may not receive benefits while on active duty in the Armed Forces.

To pursue training after military service, the son or daughter's discharge must not be under dishonorable conditions.

VA can extend a son or daughter's period of eligibility by the number of months and days equal to the time spent on active duty. This extension cannot go beyond his or her 31st birthday.

Period of Eligibility for Spouses

For surviving spouses who are eligible because the veteran has a permanent and total service-connected disability, benefits end 10 years from one of the following dates:

- The effective date of the veteran's permanent and total disability evaluation; or

- The date VA notifies the spouse of the veteran's permanent and total disability evaluation; or

- The beginning date the spouse chooses, between the date he or she became eligible and the date VA notifies him or her of eligibility.

★★

For surviving spouses who are eligible because the veteran died from a service-connected disability, benefits end 10 years from one of the following dates:

- The date of death; or

- The date VA determines that death was due to a service-connected disability; or

- The beginning date the spouse chooses, between the date of death and the date VA determines that death was due to a service-connected disability.

If a surviving spouse is eligible because the veteran had a permanent and total service-connected disability at the time of death, the beginning date of the 10-year period is the date of death.

If a spouse is eligible because the veteran or serviceperson is being held as a prisoner of war, is missing in action, or is being forcibly held by a foreign government or power, the period of eligibility ends 10 years from the 90th day after the veteran or serviceperson is listed as a captive or missing. If the veteran or serviceperson is released from captivity, or is determined to be alive and no longer missing, the period of eligibility ends on that date.

Rates of Educational Assistance

The following basic monthly rates are effective November 1, 2000:

Basic Monthly Rates Survivors' And Dependents Educational Assistance Program (DEA)					
Type of Training	Full-Time	Three-Quarter Time	One-Half Time	Less than ½ Time, But More Than ¼ Time	One-Quarter Time
Institutional	$588.00	$441.00	$294.00	Tuition & Fees, not to exceed $294.00	Tuition & Fees, not to exceed $147.00
Farm Cooperative Training	$475.00	$356.00	$238.00		
Correspondence Training	Entitlement charged at the rate of one month for each $588.00 paid. *(Payment for correspondence courses is made at 55% of the approved charges for the course. Only spouses are eligible for correspondence courses.)*				
Apprenticeship On-The-Job Training	First six months: $428.00 Second six months: $320.00 Third six months: $212.00 Remainder of program: $107.00				

Note: If an eligible student is training at less than ½ time, he or she will receive the lesser of:

- The monthly rate based on the tuition and fees for the course(s); or
- $242 per month for less than ½ time or $121 per month for ¼ time.

★★

Change of Program

Any change in educational, professional or vocational objectives is considered a *"change of program."* VA will not charge a change of program when a student enrolls in a new program, provided he or she successfully completed the immediately preceding program.

Spouse, Widow or Widower of Veteran
A spouse, widow, or widower of a veteran may make one change of program without prior VA approval if attendance, conduct, and progress in the last program were satisfactory. VA may approve additional changes if the proposed programs are suitable to the student's abilities, aptitudes, and interests.

Child of Veteran
VA may approve a change of program for sons or daughters if it finds that the new program is suitable to the student's abilities, aptitudes, and interests.

Attendance, Conduct and Progress

Once an individual starts receiving benefits, he must maintain satisfactory attendance, conduct and progress. The VA may stop benefits if an individual does not meet the standards set by the school. VA may later resume benefits if the individual reenters the same program at the same school, and the school approves the reentry, and certifies it to VA.

If the individual does not reenter the same program at the same school, VA may resume benefits if the cause of unsatisfactory attendance, conduct or progress has been removed; and the program that the student intends to pursue is suitable to his or her abilities, aptitudes and interests.

Application For Benefits

When the individual finds a school, company or apprenticeship, there are two important steps that must be followed:

1. Make sure the program is approved for VA training. Contact the local VA regional office if there are any questions.
2. Compete VA Form 22-5490, Application for Survivors' and Dependents' Educational Assistance. The completed form should be sent to the VA regional office with jurisdiction over the State where training will occur. (See Page 139 for Areas of VA jurisdiction.) Sons or daughters under legal age must have the application signed by a parent or guardian. Sons or daughters of age can apply alone.

Following receipt of an application, VA will review it and advise if anything else is needed.

If an individual has started training, the application and Notice of Basic Eligibility should be taken to the school, employer or union. The certifying official should complete VA Form 22-1999, Enrollment Certification, and send all the forms to VA.

Procedures For Receipt of Monthly Payments

After selecting a school and submitting an application to VA, the school official must complete an enrollment certification, and submit it to the appropriate VA regional office. If a student meets the basic eligibility requirements for benefits, and the program or course is approved, VA will process the enrollment based on certified training time.

If a student is enrolled in a degree program at a college or university, he or she will receive payment after the first of each month for the training during the preceding month. If a student is enrolled in a certificate or diploma program at a business, technical, or vocational school, he or she will not receive payment until they have verified their attendance. Students will receive a *Student Verification of Enrollment Form 22-8979* each month, and must complete and return it to the appropriate VA regional office. After processing, VA will release a check.

If an individual is in an apprenticeship or job-training program, he or she will receive a form to report the hours worked each month. The form must be signed and given to the certifying official for the company or union. The certifying official must complete the form and send it to the appropriate VA regional office. After processing, VA will release a check.

If an individual is taking a correspondence course, he or she will receive a form each quarter, on which the student must show the number of lessons completed that quarter. The completed form should be sent to the school for certification of the number of lessons serviced during the quarter. The school will send the form to the appropriate VA regional office. After processing, VA will release a check. Payments are based on the number of lessons serviced by the school.

NOTE: It is against the law for schools to cash VA checks under a Power of Attorney Agreement.

Update: Effective November 1, 2000, VA education benefits can be paid (with some exceptions) for school breaks, if the breaks do not exceed 8 weeks; and the terms before and after the breaks are not shorter than the break. Prior to November 1 2000, VA education benefits could be paid only if the breaks did not exceed a calendar month.

Timely Receipt of Verification Forms And Checks

Students taking courses leading to a degree at a college or university should receive their checks for each month by the fifth of the next month. If it is not received by then, the VA should be immediately contacted so that appropriate action can be taken.

Students taking courses leading to a certificate or diploma from a business, technical, or vocational school should receive their verification forms for each month by the fifth of the following month. If it is not received by then, the VA should be immediately contacted so that another form can be issued.

One a completed verification form has been submitted, the student should receive a check within 2 weeks. If a check is not received by then, the VA should immediately be contacted so that appropriate action can be taken.

Advance Payments

An advance payment for the initial month, or partial month and the following month may be made, if:

- The school agrees to handle advance payments; and
- Training is one-half time or more; and
- A request is made by the individual in writing; and
- The VA receives the enrollment certification at least 30 days prior to the start of classes.

Advance payments are made out to the individual, and sent to the applicable school for delivery to the individual registration. VA cannot issue a check more than 30 days before classes start. Before requesting an advance payment, students should verify with the school certifying official that the school has agreed to process advance payments. .

Requests for advance payments must be on VA Form 22-1999, Enrollment Certification, or a sheet of paper attached to the enrollment certification.

Once a student receives an advance payment at registration, the school must certify to VA that the student received the check. If a student reduces enrollment, or withdraws from all courses during the period covered by an advance payment, he or she must repay the overpayment to VA.

If an individual believes that the amount of a VA check is incorrect, the VA should be contacted before the check is cashed.

Direct Deposit

Payments can be sent directly to a student's savings or checking account through Direct Deposit (Electronic Funds Transfer). To sign up for direct deposit by phone, students must call 1-877-838-2778. the request

Student Responsibilities

To ensure timely receipt of correct payments, students should be sure to promptly notify the VA of:

- Any change in enrollment

- Any change in address

- Any change in marital status (separation from the veteran, divorce from the veteran, or remarriage following the death of the veteran)

In addition, students should use reasonable judgment when accepting and cashing a check. All letters from VA about monthly rates and effective dates should be read carefully. If a student thinks the amount of a VA check is wrong, VA should be contacted **before** cashing the check. Any incorrect checks should be returned to VA.

If a student cashes a check for the wrong amount, he or she will be liable for repayment of any resulting overpayment.

★★

Recovery of Overpayments

VA must take prompt and aggressive action to recover overpayments. Students have the right to request a waiver of the overpayment, or verification that the amount is correct. If an overpayment is not repaid or waived, VA may add interest and collection fees to the debt. VA may also take one or more of the following actions to collect the debt:

- Withhold future benefits to apply to the debt;
- Refer the debt to a private collection agency;
- Recover the debt from any Federal income tax refund;
- Recover the debt from the salary (if student is a Federal employee);
- File a lawsuit in Federal court to collect the debt;
- Withhold approval of a VA home loan guarantee.

Changes in Enrollment

If a student withdraws from one or more courses after the end of the school's drop period, VA will reduce or stop benefits on the date of reduction or withdrawal. Unless the student can show that the change was due to *mitigating circumstances*, the student may have to repay **all** benefits for the course.

VA defines *mitigating circumstances* as "unavoidable and unexpected events that directly interfere with the pursuit of a course, and which are beyond the student's control.

Examples of reasons VA may accept include:

- Extended illness;
- Severe illness or death in immediate family;
- Unscheduled changes in employment; and
- Lack of child care

Examples of reasons VA may not accept include:

- Withdrawal to avoid a failing grade;
- Dislike of the instructor; and
- Too many courses attempted

(VA may ask the student to furnish evidence to support the reason for change, such as physician or employer written statements.)

The first time a student withdraws from up to 6 credit hours, VA will "excuse" the withdrawal, and pay benefits for the period attended.

If a student receives a grade that does not count toward graduation, all benefits for the course may have to be repaid.

If a student receives a non-punitive grade, the school will notify VA, and VA may reduce or stop benefits. The student may not have to repay the benefits if he or she can show that the grades were due to mitigating circumstances.

Work-Study Programs

Students may be eligible for an additional allowance under a work-study program that allows students to perform work for VA in return for an hourly wage. Students may perform outreach services under VA supervision, prepare and process VA paperwork, work at a VA medical facility or National Cemetery, or perform other approved activities.

Students must attend school at the three-quarter of full-time rate.

VA will select students for the work study program based on different factors. Such factors include:

- Disability of the student
- Ability of the student to complete the work-study contract before the end of his or her eligibility for education benefits
- Job availability within normal commuting distance to the student
- VA will give the highest priority to a veteran who has a service-connected disability or disabilities rated by VA at 30% or more

The number of applicants selected will depend on the availability of VA-related work at the school or at VA facilities in the area.

Students may work during or between periods of enrollment, and can arrange with VA to work any number of hours during his or her enrollment. However, the maximum number of hours a student may work is 25 times the number of weeks in the enrollment period.

Students will earn an hourly wage equal to the Federal or State minimum wage, whichever is greater. If a student works at a college or university, the school **may** pay the difference between the amount VA pays and the amount the school normally pays other work-study students doing the same job.

Students interested in taking part in a work-study program must complete VA Form 22,8691, Application for Work-Study Allowance. Completed forms should be sent to the nearest VA regional office.

Educational Counseling

Upon request, VA will provide counseling services, including testing, to help qualified individuals:

- Select an educational, vocational, or professional objective;
- Develop a plan to achieve the above objective;
- Overcome any personal or academic problems that may interfere with the successful achievement of the stated objective.

Qualified VA personnel are available to provide counseling services free of charge to qualified individuals. Individuals must pay the cost of any travel to and from the place at which VA provides counseling.

VA requires and provides counseling for each disabled child who needs special services to pursue a program of education and for certain other eligible children.

VA requires and provides counseling for disabled spouses and those who need specialized programs of vocational training as a result of the handicapping effects of their disabilities.

Individuals should contact the nearest VA regional office to make counseling appointments.

Appeal of VA Decision

VA decisions on education benefits may be appealed within one year of the date an individual receives notice of a VA decision.

For detailed information on filing an appeal, please refer to page 282 of this book.

RESTORED ENTITLEMENT PROGRAM FOR SURVIVORS (REPS)

The Restored Entitlement Program for Survivors (REPS) is authorized by Section 156 of Public Law 97-377. This program restores social security benefits that were reduced or terminated by Public Law 97-35, the Omnibus Budget Reconciliation Act of 1981. This act eliminated the "parent with child in care" benefit when a surviving spouse's last child in care attained age 16. REPS restores the benefit until the youngest child in care attains 18, unless entitled to another Social Security benefit of equal or greater value.

The REPS program is funded by the Department of Defense, based on Social Security rules, and administered by the VA.

REPS benefits are payable to certain spouses and children of veterans who died while on active duty before August 13, 1981, or died from disabilities incurred in active duty before August 13, 1981. If a surviving spouse remarries, his or her benefits are terminated. If the child in care leaves the parent's custody, marries or dies, REPS entitlement ends. REPS benefits are reduced by $1 for each $2 of earned income over the exempt amount for Social Security (announced by Social Security Administration at the beginning of each calendar year).

REPS benefits are payable to unmarried children between the ages of 18 and 22 who are full-time students at approved schools beyond the high school level. Benefits are awarded on a school year basis. Each year verification must be received before any additional benefits can be awarded. If the child marries or reduces to less than full-time attendance, benefits will be discontinued. If the child has earned income or wages, REPS benefits are reduced.
REPS benefits are not payable based on service in the commissioned corps of the National Oceanic and Atmospheric Administration, or the Public Health Service.

★★★

To apply for REPS benefits, VA Form 21-8924, Application of Surviving Spouse or Child for REPS Benefits must be completed and sent to the local VA regional VA office for basic eligibility determination.

Once completed, the application will be forwarded to the St. Louis office for processing. A *Student Beneficiary Report* is mailed to each student receiving REPS benefits each March. The report confirms enrollment, and allows students to report any earnings.

For specific information, contact the nearest regional VA office.

VOCATIONAL REHABILITATION (CHAPTER 31)

This topic is discussed in detail beginning on page 117 of this book.

OMNIBUS DIPLOMATIC SECURITY AND ANTITERRORISM ACT

Public Law 99-399, The Omnibus Diplomatic Security and Antiterrorism Act of 91986 (the Antiterrorism Act) became effective January 21, 1981. This program is designed to provide educational assistance for persons held as captives, and their dependents.

Under this Act, VA may provide education benefits to:

- Former captives who were employees of the United States Government. Individuals providing personal services to the United States similar to that provided by civil service employees may also be eligible. This includes foreign nationals and resident aliens of the United States.

- Former captives taken during hostile action resulting from their relationship with the United States.

- Family members of individuals in captivity or individuals who die while in captivity.

VA will provide educational benefits to persons eligible under the Antiterrorism Act that are identical to those provided to eligible persons under Chapter 35 of title 38, U.S. Code (Survivors' and Dependents' Educational Assistance Program).

All inquiries regarding this Act should be directed to the nearest VA regional office.

SCHOLARSHIPS

The American Legion publishes a college financial aid guide called Need A Lift? This 128-page guide lists scholarships, grants, and loans. It also contains a scholarship research service application called CASHE. Using the information provided on an individual's application form, a database of over 150,000 entries will be searched to match awards to the individual.

To order a copy of Need A Lift?, send a $3.00 check or money order to:

NEED A LIFT?
Emblem Sales
P.O. Box 1050
Indianapolis, IN 4620

★★★

CHAPTER 15

EDUCATION BENEFITS - MONTGOMERY G.I. BILL (MGIB), CHAPTER 1606

ELIGIBILITY REQUIREMENTS

The Montgomery G.I. Bill (MGIB) establishes education benefits for four categories of individuals, based on active duty service. The benefits available under each category may vary depending on individual situations and lengths of active duty service. The eligibility requirements for each category are as follows:

Category I

- The veteran must have entered active duty for the first time on or after July 1, 1985, and had his military pay reduced by $100 per month for 12 months. This amount is nonrefundable.

  Update: Effective May 1, 2001, service members will be able to increase their benefits substantially by making contributions above the $1,200 at any time while on active duty. As of May 1, 2001, they will be able to make additional payments to VA in $4 increments up to a maximum of $600. Their monthly full-time MGIB benefit will be increased by an additional $1 per month for each $4 contributed.

  Important Time Limit: Participants who are discharged between November 1, 2000 and April 30, 2001 must elect to make contributions for additional benefits **by July 31, 2001.**

- The veteran must have served continuously for three years.

- If the veteran is currently on active duty, only two years of active duty may be required, provided:

  o The veteran first enlisted for two years of active duty; or

  o The veteran enlisted for 2 years of active duty, with an obligation to serve 4 years in the Selected Reserve (this is referred to as the 2 by 4 program). The veteran must have entered the Selected Reserve within 1 year of release from active duty.

  Update: Effective November 1, 2000, the above "length of service" requirements will no longer be based on the *initial* period of active duty. Veterans still have to serve their obligated period of service, but that time does not have to be only from their first period of service. They can now serve the required number of years in a later period of service. Likewise, veterans who were discharged for convenience of the government still have to serve 20 months, if they had a 2-year obligation, or 30 months, if they had an obligation of 3 years or more. However, effective November 1, 2000, that time can no be from a later period of service.

★★★

- If the veteran is separated from active duty, the character of discharge must specifically be listed as "Honorable." "Under Honorable Conditions," or a "General" discharge do not establish eligibility. (See the section titled *Discharges and Separations* on page 222 for additional discharge information.)

Under Category I, if a veteran elects not to participate in the program, he may not change his decision at a later date, unless eligibility can be established under Category 3 below.

A veteran may also qualify under Category I if:

- The veteran was on active duty between December 1, 1988 and July 30, 1989; and
- The veteran withdrew the election not to participate; and
- The veteran had his military pay reduced by $100 a month for 12 months; and
- The veteran completed the period of active duty he was obligated to serve on December 1, 1988. If he did not complete the period, discharge must be for one of the reasons listed in the paragraph on page 222 regarding Discharges and Separations.
- Members of the National Guard who first entered active duty on or after November 28, 1989, under Title 32 U.S.C. (Active Guard Reserve or AGR), and who never served on active duty before entering AGR service, may use this active duty to establish eligibility. (Military pay must have been reduced by $1200, which is non-refundable.)
- A veteran must obtain a high school diploma or an equivalency certificate before his first period of active duty ends. Completion of 12 hours toward a college degree meets this requirement. (There is a *special extension* for veterans on active duty on August 2, 1990 who were discharged without obtaining a high school diploma or an equivalency certificate, if either document is received before October 28, 1994. Under this *special extension*, you may not use 12 hours toward a college degree to meet the requirement. **(Update: Effective November 1, 2000, veterans and reservists can become eligible by meeting this requirement *before* they apply for MGIB benefits.)**

Individuals who graduated from a service academy and received a commission after December 31, 1976 are not eligible under Category I.

Category II

- The veteran had remaining entitlement under the Vietnam Era Veterans' Educational Assistance Program (chapter 34 of Title 38, U.S. Code) on December 31, 1989; and

- The veteran served on active duty for any number of days during the period October 19, 1984 to June 30, 1985, and

★★★

- The veteran continued on active duty without a break from July 1, 1985 through:

    o June 30, 1988; or

    o June 30, 1987, and the veteran served four years in the Selected Reserve after release from active duty. The veteran must have entered the Selected Reserve within one year of release from active duty.

- The veteran must have obtained a high school diploma or an equivalency certificate before December 31, 1989. Completion of 12 hours toward a college degree meets this requirement.

- If the veteran is separated from active duty, the character of discharge must specifically be listed as "Honorable." "Under Honorable Conditions," or a "General" discharge do not establish eligibility. (See the section titled *Discharges and Separations* on page 222 for additional discharge information.)

Military pay is not reduced for veterans qualifying under Category II. Veterans who qualify under Category II will receive the basic MGIB rate plus ½ of the Vietnam Era GI Bill wage, including the allowance paid for veterans with dependents. Veterans will receive this rate only as long as they have Chapter 34 entitlement remaining. After that, they will receive the basic Chapter 30 rate.

Individuals who graduated from a service academy and received a commission after December 31, 1976 are not eligible under Category II.

Category III

Effective February 3, 1991, the law was amended to allow certain individuals who were involuntarily separated from service as a result of reduction in personnel, who would not otherwise be eligible, to have the opportunity to elect MGIB benefits before separation. A veteran may qualify if:

- The veteran was on active duty on September 30, 1990, and was involuntarily separated after February 2, 1991; or

- The veteran was involuntarily separated on or after November 30, 1993.

- Effective October 23, 1992, the law was expanded to allow the same opportunity to elect MGIB benefits before separation to members voluntarily separated under either the Voluntary Separation Incentive (VSI) or Special Separation Benefit (SSB) program.

- The veteran must obtain a high school diploma or an equivalency certificate before applying for benefits. Completing 12 credit hours toward a college degree meets this requirement.

- If the member was eligible for the Post Vietnam Era Veterans' Educational Assistance Program (VEAP), he must elect to receive MGIB benefits, and apply for a refund of contributions to Chapter 32.

- The member must have had his military pay reduced by $1,200 before discharge.

- If the veteran is separated from active duty, the character of discharge must specifically be listed as "Honorable." "Under Honorable Conditions," or a "General" discharge do not establish eligibility. (See the following section titled *Discharges and* for additional discharge information.)

Members qualifying under Category III based on a voluntary or involuntary separation are not eligible for MGIB benefits until the day following discharge.

(If a veteran eligible under Category 3 had a chapter 32 *kicker,* VA will pay the basic chapter 30 rate and an additional amount based upon the amount of the remaining kicker.)

Category IV

Individuals may qualify under Category IV if they were on active duty on October 9, 1996, and were VEAP participants with money in the VEAP fund. These individuals must have elected MGIB, and paid $1,200 by October 9, 1997.

Individuals may also be eligible if they served on full time active duty in the National Guard between June 10, 1985 and November 29, 1989, and elected to have their National Guard service count toward establishing eligibility for MGIB benefits by July 9, 1997.

If the veteran is separated from active duty, the character of discharge must specifically be listed as "Honorable." "Under Honorable Conditions," or a "General" discharge do not establish eligibility. (See the following section titled *Discharges and Separations* for additional discharge information.)

Update: Effective November 1, 2000, VEAP participants, whether they have contributions in their accounts or not, can become eligible for MGIB if they:

- Make an irrevocable election to receive MGIB; and

- Were VEAP participants on or before October 9, 1996; and

- Continuously served on active duty from October 9, 1996 through April 1, 2000; and

- Make a payment of $2,700. The payment will be made by reducing their basic pay before their discharge from service. If $2,700 is not collected before discharge from pay reductions, veterans must make payments to the military service in the amount needed to bring the total to $2,700. The additional amount can also be collected by DoD by reducing retired or retainer pay. **(NOTE: This payment, unlike earlier contributions to VEAP is *not refundable.* ** The payment does not go into the VEAP account, it is deposited into the Treasury of the United States as miscellaneous receipts; and

- Meet other VEAP eligibility requirements.

- **VEAP participants must make this election on or before October 31, 2001.**

★★

Important update, effective November 1, 2000

The Floyd D. Spence National Defense Authorization Act for Fiscal Year 2001 (Public Law 106-398), which was signed into law by the President on October 30, 2000, gives many members of the Armed Forces a chance to receive increased payment for off-duty training and education.

- **Before this law**—the military services in most cases could pay up to 75% of the tuition or expenses charged by the school. This program is known as Tuition Assistance. Eligible service members had to find additional financing, or pay the remaining expenses, from their own pockets. A service member eligible for the Montgomery GI Bill (MGIB), a VA education benefit, wasn't allowed to receive both Tuition Assistance and the MGIB for the same course.

- **Now, with this law**—the military services can pay up to 100% of the tuition and expenses charged by the school. If a service department pays less than 100%, a service member eligible for MGIB can elect to receive MGIB benefits for all or a part of the remaining expenses.

A service member who receives MGIB benefits as a result of the provision will receive a lower rate once he or she is discharged. The full-time monthly rate will be the rate that would have been payable to him or her had he or she not used the MGIB in service for tuition assistance, reduced by the amount of payments received in service, divided by 36.

DISCHARGES AND SEPARATIONS

As previously mentioned, if the veteran is separated from active duty, the character of discharge must specifically be listed as "Honorable." "Under Honorable Conditions," or a "General" discharge do not establish eligibility. A discharge for one of the following reasons may result in a reduction of the required length of active duty to qualify for benefits under the MGIB:

- Convenience of the Government; or
- Disability; or
- Hardship; or
- Medical conditions existing before entry into Service; or
- Force reductions; or
- Medical condition which is not a disability due to misconduct, but which prevents satisfactory performance of duty.

ROTC Programs

Individuals who received a commission after completing an ROTC scholarship program after December 31, 1976 are not eligible under Categories I or II. (This scholarship pays a stipend and all educational expenses.)

★★

However, graduates of an ROTC program may still be eligible for MGIB benefits under one of the following conditions:

- The graduate received a commission after becoming eligible for MGIB benefits; or
- The graduate completed ROTC without a full scholarship; or
- The graduate received a commission after September 30, 1996, provided he received less than $2,000 during each year of the ROTC program.

Certain Types of Active Duty Which Do Not Establish Eligibility

The following types of active duty do not establish eligibility for MGIB benefits:

- Time assigned by the military to a civilian institution to take the same course provided to civilians.
- Time served as a cadet or a midshipman at a service academy.
- Time spent on active duty for training in the National Guard or Reserve.

(Please note: Time assigned by the military to a civilian institution, and time served at a service academy does not break the continuity of active duty required to establish eligibility for MGIB benefits. Active duty for training does count toward the four years in the Selected Reserve under the 2 by 4 program.)

Approved Courses

This program provides veterans up to 36 months of education benefits. The benefits may be used for:

- Undergraduate or graduate degrees from a college or university
- Cooperative training programs
- Accredited independent study programs leading to standard college degrees
- Courses leading to certificates or diplomas from business, technical or vocational schools
- Vocational flight training (from September 30, 1990 only – Individuals must have a private pilot's license and meet the medical requirements for a desired license before beginning training, and throughout the flight training program)
- Apprenticeship or job training programs offered by a company or union
- Correspondence courses
- VA may approve programs offered by institutions outside of the United States, when they are pursued at educational institutions of higher learning, and lead to an associate or higher degree, or the equivalent. Individuals must receive VA approval prior to attending or enrolling in any foreign programs.

- **Update: Effective March 1, 2001**, benefits will be payable for licensing or certification tests. The tests are those needed to enter, maintain, or advance into employment in a civilian vocation or profession. The eligible veteran or family member may receive payment of the fee charged for the test or $2,000, whichever is less. *The tests must be approved for VA benefits.*

If an individual is seeking a college degree, the school must admit the individual to a degree program by the start of the individual's third term.

Under certain circumstances, remedial, deficiency and refresher courses may be approved. A special allowance for tutorial assistance, vocational counseling, and work-study programs may also be payable to individuals

Restrictions on Training

- Bartending and personality development courses
- Non-accredited independent study courses
- Any course given by radio
- Self-improvement courses such as reading, speaking, woodworking, basic seamanship, and English as a second language
- Any course which is avocational or recreational in character
- Farm cooperative courses
- Audited courses
- Courses not leading to an educational, professional, or vocational objective
- Courses an individual has previously taken and successfully completed
- Courses taken by a Federal government employee under the Government Employees' Training Act
- Courses paid for in whole or in part by the Armed Forces while on active duty
- Courses taken while in receipt of benefits for the same program from the Office of Workers' Compensation Programs

The VA must reduce benefits for individuals in Federal, State or local prisons after being convicted of a felony.

An individual may not receive benefits for a program at a proprietary school if he or she is an owner or official of the school.

Benefits are generally payable for 10 years following a veteran's release from active duty.

Part-Time Training

Individuals unable to attend school full-time should consider going part-time. Benefit rates and entitlement charges are pro-rated as follows:

Individuals who are on active duty or training at less than one-half time, will receive the lesser of:

- The monthly rate based on tuition and fees for the course(s); or
- The maximum monthly rate based on training time.

Individuals training at less than one-half time will receive payment in one sum for the whole enrollment period.

Remedial, Deficiency And Refresher Training

Remedial and deficiency courses are intended to assist a student in overcoming a deficiency in a particular area of study. In order for such courses to be approved, the courses must be deemed necessary for pursuit of a program of education.

Refresher training is for technological advances that occurred in a field of employment. The advance must have occurred while the student was on active duty, or after release.

There is an entitlement charge for these courses.

Tutorial Assistance

Students may receive a special allowance for individual tutoring, if attending school at one-half time or more. To qualify, the student must have a deficiency in a subject. The school must certify the tutor's qualifications, and the hours of tutoring. Eligible students may receive a maximum monthly payment of $100.00. The maximum total benefit payable is $1,200.00.

There is no entitlement charge for the first $600.00 of tutorial assistance.

To apply for tutorial assistance, students must submit VA Form 22-1990t, Application and Enrollment Certification for Individualized Tutorial Assistance. The form should be given to the certifying official in the office handling VA paperwork at the school for completion.

Months of Benefits / Entitlement Charged

Individuals who complete their full period of enlistment may receive up to 36 months of MGIB benefits. Individuals are considered to have completed their full enlistment period if they are discharged for the convenience of the government after completing 20 months of an enlistment of less than three years; or 30 months of an enlistment of three years or more.

Individuals will earn only one month of entitlement for each month of active duty after June 39, 1985, if they are discharged for other specific reasons (i.e. service-connected disability, reduction in force, hardship, etc.) before completing the enlistment period.

Individuals will earn one month of entitlement for each four months in the Selected Reserve after June 30, 1985.

Individuals qualifying for more than one VA education program may receive a maximum of 48 months of benefits. For example, if a student used 30 months of Dependents' Educational Assistance, and is eligible for chapter 1606 benefits, he or she could have a maximum of 18 months of entitlement remaining.

Individuals are charged one full day of entitlement for each day of full-time benefits paid. For correspondence and flight training, individuals use one month of entitlement each time the VA pays the equivalent of one month of full-time benefits. Individuals pursuing a cooperative program use one month for each month of benefits paid.

For apprenticeship and job-training programs, the entitlement charge during the first 6 months is 75% of full-time. For the second six months, the charge is 55% of full-time. For the rest of the program, the charge is 35% of full-time.

VA can extend entitlement to the end of a term, quarter, or semester if the ending date of an individual's entitlement falls within such period. If a school does not operate on a term basis, entitlement can be extended for 12 weeks.

Rates of Educational Assistance Pay

The following basic monthly rates are effective November 1, 2000:

BASIC MONTHLY RATES Montgomery G.I. Bill - Active Duty (MGIB), Chapter 30					
Type of Training	Full-Time	Three-Quarter Time	One-Half Time	Less than ½ Time, But More Than ¼ Time	One-Quarter Time
Institutional	$650.00	$487.50	$325.00	Tuition & Fees, not to exceed $325.00	$162.50
Cooperative Training	$650.00 (Full-Time Only)				
Correspondence Training	Entitlement charged at the rate of one month for each $650.00 paid				
Apprenticeship On-The-Job Training	First six months: $487.50 Second six months: $357.50 Remainder of program: $227.50				
Flight Training	Entitlement charged at the rate of one month for each $650.00 paid				

★★★

BASIC MONTHLY RATES FOR PERSONS WHOSE INITIAL ACTIVE DUTY OBLIGATION WAS LESS THAN THREE YEARS, AND WHO SERVED LESS THAN THREE YEARS (EXCLUDING 2 X 4 PARTICIPANTS)

Type of Training	Full-Time	Three-Quarter Time	One-Half Time	Less than ½ Time, But More Than ¼ Time	One-Quarter Time
Institutional	$528.00	$396.00	$264.00	Tuition & Fees, not to exceed $264.00	$132.00
Cooperative Training	$528.00 (Full-Time Only)				
Correspondence Training	Entitlement charged at the rate of one month for each $528.00 paid				
Apprenticeship On-The-Job Training	First six months: $396.00 Second six months: $290.40 Remainder of program: $184.80				
Flight Training	Entitlement charged at the rate of one month for each $528.00 paid				

BASIC INSTITUTIONAL RATES FOR PERSONS WITH REMAINING ENTITLEMENT UNDER CHAPTER 34 OF TITLE 38, U.S.C.

Time	No Dependents	One Dependent	Two Dependents	Each Add'l Dependent
Full	$838.00	$874.00	$905.00	$16.00
Three-Quarter	$629.00	$655.50	$679.00	$12.00
One-Half	$419.00	$437.00	$452.50	$8.50
Less Than 1/2, But More Than 1/4	Tuition and fees, not to exceed the rate of $419.00			
One-Quarter	Tuition and fees, not to exceed the rate of $209.50			
Cooperative	$838.00	$874.00	$905.00	$16.00

**BASIC JOB TRAINING RATES FOR PERSONS WITH REMAINING
ENTITLEMENT UNDER CHAPTER 34 OF TITLE 38, U.S.C.**

Time	No Dependents	One Dependent	Two Dependents	Each Add'l Dependent
First six months	$590.25	$602.63	$613.50	$5.25
Second six months	$413.88	$423.23	$430.93	$3.85
Third six months	$251.30	$257.43	$262.15	$2.45
Remainder	$239.40	$245.18	$250.43	$2.45

SPECIAL NOTES:

- Monthly checks may include *kickers*, which are amounts contributed by the Department of Defense to an education fund on behalf of individuals to encourage enlistment or retention in the Armed Forces, usually in specialized areas. VA only pays *kickers* to individuals authorized by DOD. If payment includes a *kicker,* the *kicker* is not increased, but the basic rate is increased.

- Cooperative Training is full time only.

- Individuals taking correspondence courses will receive 55% of the approved charges for the course.

- Individuals taking flight training will receive 60% of the approved charges for the course, including solo hours.

Eligibility Periods

Benefits generally end 10 years from the date of an individual's last discharge or release from active duty. The VA may extend the 10-year period by the amount of time an individual is prevented from training due to a disability, or the individual being held by a foreign government or power.

The VA may extend the 10-year period if an individual reenters active duty for 90 days or more after becoming eligible. The extension ends 10 years from the date of discharge or release from the later period. Periods of active duty of less than 90 days may qualify for extensions, only if the discharge or release was for:

- A service-connected disability; or
- A medical condition existing before active duty; or
- Hardship; or
- A reduction in force

If an individual's discharge is upgraded by the military, the 10-year period begins on the date of the upgrade.

Special Note For Individuals Eligible Under Category Ii:

If an individual is eligible under Category II, and discharge was before December 31, 1989,he had until January 1, 2000 to use his entitlement. In most cases, the VA will subtract periods an individual was not on active duty between January 1, 1977 and June 30, 1985, from the individual's 10-year period.

Special Note For Individuals Eligible Under The 2 By 4 Program

If an individual is eligible based upon two years of active duty followed by four years in the Selected Reserve, the individual may have 10 years from release from active duty, or 10 years from the completion of the four-year Selected Reserve obligation to use benefits, whichever is later.

Miscellaneous Information

- Any change in educational, professional or vocational objectives is considered a *"change of program."* The law permits one change of program without prior VA approval, provided an individual's attendance, conduct and progress in the last program were satisfactory. Additional *"changes of program"* require prior VA approval. VA will not charge a *change of program* if the individual enrolls in a new program after successful completion of the immediately preceding program.

- Once an individual starts receiving benefits, he must maintain satisfactory attendance, conduct and progress. The VA may stop benefits if an individual does not meet the standards set by the school. VA may later resume benefits if the individual reenters the same program at the same school, and the school approves the reentry, and certifies it to VA.

- If the individual does not reenter the same program at the same school, VA may resume benefits if the cause of unsatisfactory attendance, conduct or progress has been removed; and the program that the student intends to pursue is suitable to his or her abilities, aptitudes and interests.

- **Update: Effective November 1, 2000,** VA education benefits can be paid (with some exceptions) for school breaks, if the breaks do not exceed 8 weeks; and the terms before and after the breaks are not shorter than the break. Prior to November 1 2000, VA education benefits could be paid only if the breaks did not exceed a calendar month.

Application For Benefits

VA Form 22-1990, "Application for Education Benefits" must be completed. The form may be obtained from individual schools, from any VA regional office, or by calling 1-888-GI-BILL.

The completed form should be sent to the VA regional office with jurisdiction over the state in which the individual will train. (Refer to page 141 for a listing of Areas of VA Jurisdiction.)

★★

If an individual is not on active duty, copy 4 of DD Form 214 (Certificate of Release or Discharge from Active Duty), must also be sent to the VA. If an individual is on active duty, enrollment must be approved by the Base Education Services Officer, and service must be verified by the Commanding Officer.

If training has already started, the school, employer, or union should complete VA Form 22-1999 (Enrollment Certification) and submit it along with the application.

Procedures For Receipt of Monthly Payments

After selecting a school and submitting an application to VA, the school official must complete an enrollment certification, and submit it to the appropriate VA regional office. If a student meets the basic eligibility requirements for benefits, and the program or course is approved, VA will process the enrollment based on certified training time.

If a student is enrolled in a degree program at a college or university, or a certificate or diploma program at a business, technical, or vocational school, they will not receive payment until they have verified their attendance. Students will receive a *Student Verification of Enrollment Form 22-8979* each month, and must complete and return it to the appropriate VA regional office. After processing, VA will release a check.

Beginning in the Fall of 2000, VA announced a new way to verify enrollment. **All students who are receiving MGIB Active Duty (chapter 30) education benefits are now able to certify their monthly Verification of Enrollment (VAF 22-8979) over the by using a toll free phone system (Interactive Voice Response - IVR) or the internet (Web Automated Verification of Enrollment (WAVE).** Use of these systems eliminates the need for the student to sign and return the VA Form 22-8979 every month.

Once the IVR or WAVE system tells the student that he or she is certified, it is not necessary to return the Verification of Enrollment form.

If an individual is in an apprenticeship or job-training program, he or she will receive a form to report the hours worked each month. The form must be signed and given to the certifying official for the company or union. The certifying official must complete the form and send it to the appropriate VA regional office. After processing, VA will release a check.

If an individual is taking a correspondence course, he or she will receive a form each quarter, on which the student must show the number of lessons completed that quarter. The completed form should be sent to the school for certification of the number of lessons serviced during the quarter. The school will send the form to the appropriate VA regional office. After processing, VA will release a check. Payments are based on the number of lessons serviced by the school.

VA will send flight schools a supply of blank monthly certification of flight training forms. The school must complete the form by entering the number of hours, the hourly rate, and the total charges for flight training received during the month. The student should review and sign the completed form, and send it to the appropriate VA regional office. After processing, VA will release a check.

NOTE: It is against the law for schools to cash VA checks under a Power of Attorney Agreement.

★★

Timely Receipt of Verification Forms And Checks

Students should receive their verification forms for each month by the fifth of the following month. If it is not received by then, the VA should be immediately contacted so that another form can be issued.

One a completed verification form has been submitted, the student should receive a check within 2 weeks. If a check is not received by then, the VA should immediately be contacted so that appropriate action can be taken.

Advance Payments

An advance payment for the initial month, or partial month and the following month may be made, if:

1. The school agrees to handle advance payments; and
2. Training is one-half time or more; and
3. A request is made by the individual in writing; and
4. The VA receives the enrollment certification at least 30 days prior to the start of classes.

Advance payments are made out to the individual, and sent to the applicable school for delivery to the individual registration. VA cannot issue a check more than 30 days before classes start. Before requesting an advance payment, students should verify with the school certifying official that the school has agreed to process advance payments.

Requests for advance payments must be on VA Form 22-1999, Enrollment Certification, or a sheet of paper attached to the enrollment certification.

Once a student receives an advance payment at registration, the school must certify to VA that the student received the check. If a student reduces enrollment, or withdraws from all courses during the period covered by an advance payment, he or she must repay the overpayment to VA.

If an individual believes that the amount of a VA check is incorrect, the VA should be contacted before the check is cashed.

Direct Deposit

Chapter 30 payments can be sent directly to a student's savings or checking account through Direct Deposit (Electronic Funds Transfer). To sign up for direct deposit by phone, students must call 1-877-838-2778.

Student Responsibilities

To ensure timely receipt of correct payments, students should be sure to promptly notify the VA of:

- Any change in enrollment
- Any change in address
- Any change in selected reserve status
- Any changes affecting a student's dependents (if a student is receiving an allowance which includes an additional amount for dependents)

In addition, students should use reasonable judgment when accepting and cashing a check. All letters from VA about monthly rates and effective dates should be read carefully. If a student thinks the amount of a VA check is wrong, VA should be contacted **before** cashing the check. Any incorrect checks should be returned to VA.

If a student cashes a check for the wrong amount, he or she will be liable for repayment of any resulting overpayment.

Recovery of Overpayments

VA must take prompt and aggressive action to recover overpayments. Students have the right to request a waiver of the overpayment, or verification that the amount is correct. If an overpayment is not repaid or waived, VA may add interest and collection fees to the debt. VA may also take one or more of the following actions to collect the debt:

- Withhold future benefits to apply to the debt;
- Refer the debt to a private collection agency;
- Recover the debt from any Federal income tax refund;
- Recover the debt from the salary (if student is a Federal employee);
- File a lawsuit in Federal court to collect the debt;
- Withhold approval of a VA home loan guarantee.

Changes in Enrollment

If a student withdraws from one or more courses after the end of the school's drop period, VA will reduce or stop benefits on the date of reduction or withdrawal. Unless the student can show that the change was due to *mitigating circumstances*, the student may have to repay **all** benefits for the course.

VA defines *mitigating circumstances* as "unavoidable and unexpected events that directly interfere with the pursuit of a course, and which are beyond the student's control.

Examples of reasons VA may accept include:

- Extended illness;
- Severe illness or death in immediate family;
- Unscheduled changes in employment; and
- Lack of child care

★★

Examples of reasons VA may not accept include:

- Withdrawal to avoid a failing grade;
- Dislike of the instructor; and
- Too many courses attempted

(VA may ask the student to furnish evidence to support the reason for change, such as physician or employer written statements.)

The first time a student withdraws from up to 6 credit hours, VA will "excuse" the withdrawal, and pay benefits for the period attended.

If a student receives a grade that does not count toward graduation, all benefits for the course may have to be repaid. Affected students should check the school's grading policy with the office handling VA paperwork.

If a student receives a non-punitive grade, the school will notify VA, and VA may reduce or stop benefits. The student may not have to repay the benefits if he or she can show that the grades were due to mitigating circumstances.

Work-Study Programs

Students may be eligible for an additional allowance under a work-study program that allows students to perform work for VA in return for an hourly wage. Students may perform outreach services under VA supervision, prepare and process VA paperwork, work at a VA medical facility or National Cemetery, or perform other approved activities.

Students must attend school at the three-quarter of full-time rate.

VA will select students for the work study program based on different factors. Such factors include:

- Disability of the student
- Ability of the student to complete the work-study contract before the end of his or her eligibility for education benefits
- Job availability within normal commuting distance to the student
- VA will give the highest priority to a veteran who has a service-connected disability or disabilities rated by VA at 30% or more

The number of applicants selected will depend on the availability of VA-related work at the school or at VA facilities in the area.

Students may work during or between periods of enrollment, and can arrange with VA to work any number of hours during his or her enrollment. However, the maximum number of hours a student may work is 25 times the number of weeks in the enrollment period.

Students will earn an hourly wage equal to the Federal or State minimum wage, whichever is greater. If a student works at a college or university, the school **may** pay the difference between the amount VA pays and the amount the school normally pays other work-study students doing the same job.

Students may elect to be paid in advance for 40% of the number of hours in the work-study agreement, or for 50 hours, whichever is less. After completion of the hours covered by the first payment, VA will pay the student after completion of each 50 hours of service.

Students interested in taking part in a work-study program must complete VA Form 22,8691, Application for Work-Study Allowance. Completed forms should be sent to the nearest VA regional office.

Educational Counseling

VA can provide services to help eligible individuals understand their educational and vocational strengths and weaknesses and to plan:

- An educational or training goal, and the means by which the goal can be reached; or

- An employment goal for which an individual qualifies on the basis of present training or experience.

VA can also help plan an effective job search.

Counseling is available for:

- Service members who are on active duty, and are within 180 days of discharge, and are stationed in the United States; or

- Veterans with discharges that are not dishonorable, who are within one year from date of discharge.

Vocational Rehabilitation

Veterans may qualify for Training and Rehabilitation under Chapter 31 of Title 38, United States Code, if:

- The veteran has a service-connected disability or disabilities rated by VA at 20% or more; and

- The veteran received a discharge from active duty that was not dishonorable; and

- The veteran has an employment handicap.

Veterans may also qualify with a service-connected disability or disabilities rated by VA at 10%, and:

- The veteran has a serious employment handicap; or

- The veteran first applied for vocational rehabilitation benefits before November 1, 1990, reapplied after that date, and has an employment handicap.

★★

Vocational rehabilitation helps disabled veterans become independent in daily living.   Veterans may also receive assistance in selecting, preparing for, and securing employment that is compatible with their interests, talents, skills, physical capabilities, and goals.

To apply for vocational rehabilitation, VA for 28-1900, Disabled Veterans Application for Vocational Rehabilitation, must be completed and sent to the nearest VA regional office.

For detailed information on vocational rehabilitation refer to page 117 of this book.

Appeal of VA Decision

VA decisions on education benefits may be appealed within one year of the date an individual receives notice of a VA decision.

For detailed information on filing an appeal, please refer to page 282 of this book.

★★

CHAPTER 16

EDUCATION BENEFITS -
MONTGOMERY G.I. BILL – SELECTED RESERVE
(MGIB-SR), CHAPTER 1606

The Montgomery GI Bill-Selected Reserve Program is for members of the Selected Reserve, including the Army Reserve, Navy Reserve, Air Force Reserve, Marine Corps Reserve, Coast Guard Reserve, Army National Guard and Air National Guard. While the reserve components decide who is eligible for the program, VA makes the payments for the program. Chapter 1606 is the first educational program that does not require service in the *active* Armed Forces in order to qualify.

Eligibility Requirements:

- Member must have signed a 6-year obligation to serve in the Selected Reserve after June 30, 1985. (Officers must have agreed to serve 6 years in addition to his or her original obligation.) For some types of training, it is necessary to have a 6-year commitment that began after September 30, 1990. Call 1-888-GI-BILL for more information.
- Member must have completed his or her Initial Active Duty for Training (IADT)
- Member must meet the requirement to receive a high school diploma or equivalency certificate before completing IADT. **(Update: Effective November 1, 2000, veterans and reservists can become eligible by meeting this requirement *before they apply for MGIB benefits.***
- Member must remain in good standing while serving in an active Selected Reserve Unit.

Beginning on October 1, 1990, a member of the Selected Reserve with a bachelor's degree can become eligible by signing a new contract that will result in a 6 year reserve obligation. Beginning on November 30, 1993, a member of the Selected Reserve can become eligible for graduate degree training. A new 6 year contract is not required in order to pursue graduate training.

If an individual enters active duty in the Selected Reserve (AGR, TAR, FTS) after November 29, 1989, he or she must have been eligible *before* November 29, 1989 in order to remain eligible.

Approved Courses

Individuals may receive benefits for a wide variety of training, including:

- Undergraduate degrees from a college or university;
- Beginning November 30, 1993, graduate degrees from a college or university;
- Accredited independent study programs leading to standard college degrees;
- Technical courses for a certificate at a college or university.

Individuals with 6 year commitments beginning after September 30, 1990 may take the following types of training:

- Courses leading to a certificate or diploma from business, technical, or vocational schools
- Cooperative training
- Apprenticeship or job training programs offered by companies
- Correspondence training
- Independent study programs
- Flight training (Individuals must have a private pilot's license, and must meet the medical requirements for the desired license program before beginning training, and throughout the flight training program.)

VA may approve programs offered by institutions outside of the United States, when they are pursued at educational institutions of higher learning, and lead to a college degree. Individuals must receive VA approval prior to attending or enrolling in any foreign programs.

Eligibility for this program is determined by the Selected Reserve components. Payments for the program are made by the VA.

A State agency or VA must approve each program offered by a school or company.

If an individual is seeking a college degree, the school must admit the individual to a degree program by the start of the individual's third term.

Restrictions on Training

Benefits are not payable for the following courses:

- Courses paid by the military Tuition Assistance program , if student is enrolled at less than ½ time
- Courses taken while student is receiving a Reserve Officers' Training Corps scholarship
- Non-accredited independent study courses
- Bartending and personality development courses
- Any course given by radio
- Self-improvement courses such as reading, speaking, woodworking, basic seamanship, and English as a 2nd language
- Any course which is avocational or recreational in character
- Farm-cooperative courses
- Audited courses
- Courses not leading to an educational, professional, or vocational objective
- Courses previously taken and successfully completed
- Courses taken by a Federal government employee under the Government Employee's Training Act
- Courses taken while in receipt of benefits for the same program from the Office of Workers' Compensation Programs

VA must reduce benefits for individuals in Federal, State, or local prisons after being convicted of a felony.

★★★

An individual may not receive benefits for a program at a proprietary school if her or she is an owner or official of the school.

Part-Time Training

Individuals unable to attend school full-time should consider going part-time. Benefit rates and entitlement charges are less than the full-time rates. For example, if a student receives full-time benefits for 12 months, the entitlement charge is 12 months. However, if the students receives ½ time benefits for 12 months, the charge is 6 months. VA will pay for less than ½ time training if the student is not receiving Tuition Assistance for those courses.

Remedial, Deficiency and Refresher Training

Remedial and deficiency courses are intended to assist a student in overcoming a deficiency in a particular area of study. Individuals may qualify for benefits for remedial, deficiency, and refresher courses if they have a 6 year commitment that began after September 30, 1990. In order for such courses to be approved, the courses must be deemed necessary for pursuit of a program of education.

Refresher training is for technological advances that occurred in a field of employment. The advance must have occurred while the student was on active duty, or after release.

There is an entitlement charge for these courses.

Tutorial Assistance

Students may receive a special allowance for individual tutoring performed after September 30, 1992, if they entered school at one-half time or more. To qualify, the student must have a deficiency in a subject. The school must certify the tutor's qualifications, and the hours of tutoring. Eligible students may receive a maximum monthly payment of $100.00. The maximum total benefit payable is $1,200.00.

There is no entitlement charge for the first $600.00 of tutorial assistance.

To apply for tutorial assistance, students must submit VA Form 22-1990t, Application and Enrollment Certification for Individualized Tutorial Assistance. The form should be given to the certifying official in the office handling VA paperwork at the school for completion.

Months of Benefits / Entitlement Charged

Eligible members may be entitled to receive up to 36 months of education benefits. Benefit entitlement ends 10 years from the date the member becomes eligible for the program, or on the day the member leaves the Selected Reserve. (If a member's Reserve or National Guard unit was deactivated during the period October 1, 1991 through September 30, 1999, or if the member was involuntarily separated from service during this same period, eligibility for MGIB-SR benefits is retained for the full 10 year eligibility period. Eligibility for MGIB-SR benefits is also retained if a member is discharged due to a disability that was not caused by misconduct. Eligibility periods may be extended if a member is ordered to active duty.)

Individuals qualifying for more than one VA education program may receive a maximum of 48 months of benefits. For example, if a student used 30 months of Dependents' Educational Assistance, and is eligible for chapter 1606 benefits, he or she could have a maximum of 18 months of entitlement remaining.

Individuals are charged one full day of entitlement for each day of full-time benefits paid. For correspondence and flight training, one month of entitlement is charged each time VA pays one month of benefits. For cooperative programs, one month of entitlement is used for each month of benefits paid.

For apprenticeship and job training programs, the entitlement charge changes every 6 months. During the first 6 months, the charge is 75% of full time. For the second 6 months, the charge is 55% of full time. For the remainder of the program, the charge is 35% of full time.

Rates of Educational Assistance Pay

The following basic monthly rates are effective October 1, 2000:

BASIC MONTHLY RATES MONTGOMERY G.I. BILL – SELECTED RESERVE (MGIB-SR), CHAPTER 1606				
Type of Training	**Full-Time**	**Three-Quarter Time**	**One-Half Time**	**Less than ½ Time**
Institutional	$263.00	$197.00	$131.00	$65.75
Cooperative Training	$263.00 (Full-Time Only)			
Correspondence Training	Entitlement charged at the rate of one month for each $263.00 paid *(Payment for correspondence courses is made at 55% of the approved charges for the course.)*			
Apprenticeship On-The-Job Training	First six months: $197.25 Second six months: $144.65 Remainder of program: $92.05			
Flight Training	Entitlement charged at the rate of one month for each $263.00 paid *(Payment for flight training is made at 60% of the approved charges for the course, including solo hours.)*			

SPECIAL NOTES:

- Cooperative Training is full time only.
- Individuals taking correspondence courses will receive 55% of the approved charges for the course.
- Individuals taking flight training will receive 60% of the approved charges for the course, including solo hours.

Eligibility Periods

For individuals who remain in the Selected Reserve, benefits end 10 years from the date the individual became eligible for the program.

VA can extend the 10-year period if the student could not train due to a disability caused by Selected Reserve service.

Individuals may still use their full 10 years if they leave the Selected Reserve because:

- Of a disability that was not caused by misconduct; or

- The military unit was inactivated during the period from October 1, 1991 through September 30, 1999; or

- The individual was involuntarily separated under section 286 (b) of title 10, U.S. Code during the period from October 1, 1991 through September 30, 1999.

In all other cases, if an individual leaves the Selected Reserve before completion of his or her obligation, benefits will stop.

Miscellaneous Information

- Any change in educational, professional or vocational objectives is considered a *"change of program."* The law permits one change of program without prior VA approval, provided an individual's attendance, conduct and progress in the last program were satisfactory. Additional *"changes of program"* require prior VA approval. VA will not charge a *change of program* if the individual enrolls in a new program after successful completion of the immediately preceding program.

- Once an individual starts receiving benefits, he must maintain satisfactory attendance, conduct and progress. The VA may stop benefits if an individual does not meet the standards set by the school. VA may later resume benefits if the individual reenters the same program at the same school, and the school approves the reentry, and certifies it to VA.

- If the individual does not reenter the same program at the same school, VA may resume benefits if the cause of unsatisfactory attendance, conduct or progress has been removed; and the program that the student intends to pursue is suitable to his or her abilities, aptitudes and interests.

- **Update: Effective November 1, 2000,** VA education benefits can be paid (with some exceptions) for school breaks, if the breaks do not exceed 8 weeks; and the terms before and after the breaks are not shorter than the break. Prior to November 1 2000, VA education benefits could be paid only if the breaks did not exceed a calendar month.

Application For Benefits

When an individual becomes eligible for the program, his or her unit will provide the individual with a Notice of Basic Eligibility, DD Form 2384, or DD Form 2384-1 (for persons who establish eligibility on or after October 1, 1990). The unit will also code the eligibility into the Department of Defense personnel system.

★★

When the individual finds a school, program, company, apprenticeship or job-training program, there are two important steps that must be followed:

- Make sure the program is approved for VA training. Contact the local VA regional office if there are any questions.

- Compete VA Form 22-1990, Application for Education Benefits. The completed form should be sent to the VA regional office with jurisdiction over the State where training will occur. (See page 141 for Areas of VA jurisdiction.)

Following receipt of an application, VA will review it and advise if anything else is needed.

If an individual has started training, the application and Notice of Basic Eligibility should be taken to the school, employer or union. The certifying official should complete VA Form 22-1999, Enrollment Certification, and send all the forms to VA.

Procedures For Receipt of Monthly Payments

After selecting a school and submitting an application to VA, the school official must complete an enrollment certification, and submit it to the appropriate VA regional office. If a student meets the basic eligibility requirements for benefits, and the program or course is approved, VA will process the enrollment based on certified training time.

VA will accept the Notice of Basic Eligibility to pay benefits for 120 days after an individual's eligibility date. If the eligibility date is more than 120 days before the training program starts, VA will not approve the claim unless the Department of Defense personnel system shows that the individual is eligible. Only a student's reserve component can update the DoD personnel system. VA cannot change an individual's eligibility record.

When VA approves a claim, it will issue a letter with the details of the benefits payable. The first payment should be received within a few days of receipt of the letter.

If a student is enrolled in a degree program at a college or university, he or she will receive payment after the first of each month for the training during the preceding month. If a student is enrolled in a certificate or diploma program at a business, technical, or vocational school, he or she will not receive payment until they have verified their attendance. Students will receive a *Student Verification of Enrollment Form 22-8979* each month, and must complete and return it to the appropriate VA regional office. After processing, VA will release a check.

If an individual is in an apprenticeship or job-training program, he or she will receive a form to report the hours worked each month. The form must be signed and given to the certifying official for the company or union. The certifying official must complete the form and send it to the appropriate VA regional office. After processing, VA will release a check.

If an individual is taking a correspondence course, he or she will receive a form each quarter, on which the student must show the number of lessons completed that quarter. The completed form should be sent to the school for certification of the number of lessons serviced during the quarter. The school will send the form to the appropriate VA regional office. After processing, VA will release a check. Payments are based on the number of lessons serviced by the school.

VA will send flight schools a supply of blank monthly certification of flight training forms. The school must complete the form by entering the number of hours, the hourly rate, and the total charges for flight training received during the month. The student should review and sign the completed form, and send it to the appropriate VA regional office. After processing, VA will release a check.

NOTE: It is against the law for schools to cash VA checks under a Power of Attorney Agreement.

Timely Receipt of Verification Forms And Checks

Students taking courses leading to a degree at a college or university should receive their checks for each month by the fifth of the next month. If it is not received by then, the VA should be immediately contacted so that appropriate action can be taken.

Students taking courses leading to a certificate or diploma from a business, technical, or vocational school should receive their verification forms for each month by the fifth of the following month. If it is not received by then, the VA should be immediately contacted so that another form can be issued.

One a completed verification form has been submitted, the student should receive a check within 2 weeks. If a check is not received by then, the VA should immediately be contacted so that appropriate action can be taken.

Advance Payments

An advance payment for the initial month, or partial month and the following month may be made, if:

- The school agrees to handle advance payments; and
- Training is one-half time or more; and
- A request is made by the individual in writing; and
- The VA receives the enrollment certification at least 30 days prior to the start of classes.

Advance payments are made out to the individual, and sent to the applicable school for delivery to the individual registration. VA cannot issue a check more than 30 days before classes start. Before requesting an advance payment, students should verify with the school certifying official that the school has agreed to process advance payments.

Requests for advance payments must be on VA Form 22-1999, Enrollment Certification, or a sheet of paper attached to the enrollment certification.

Once a student receives an advance payment at registration, the school must certify to VA that the student received the check. If a student reduces enrollment, or withdraws from all courses during the period covered by an advance payment, he or she must repay the overpayment to VA.

★★

If an individual believes that the amount of a VA check is incorrect, the VA should be contacted before the check is cashed.

Direct Deposit

Payments can be sent directly to a student's savings or checking account through Direct Deposit (Electronic Funds Transfer). To sign up for direct deposit by phone, students must call 1-877-838-2778.

Student Responsibilities

To ensure timely receipt of correct payments, students should be sure to promptly notify the VA of:

- Any change in enrollment

- Any change in address

- Any change in selected reserve status (If an individual changes units or components, both the old and new units must report the change to VA through the components' eligibility data systems.)

In addition, students should use reasonable judgment when accepting and cashing a check. All letters from VA about monthly rates and effective dates should be read carefully. If a student thinks the amount of a VA check is wrong, VA should be contacted **before** cashing the check. Any incorrect checks should be returned to VA.

If a student cashes a check for the wrong amount, he or she will be liable for repayment of any resulting overpayment.

If an individual does not participate satisfactorily in the Selected Reserve, his or her eligibility ends. His or her component can require that a penalty be paid, based on a portion of payments received.

Recovery of Overpayments

VA must take prompt and aggressive action to recover overpayments. Students have the right to request a waiver of the overpayment, or verification that the amount is correct. If an overpayment is not repaid or waived, VA may add interest and collection fees to the debt. VA may also take one or more of the following actions to collect the debt:

- Withhold future benefits to apply to the debt;

- Refer the debt to a private collection agency;

- Recover the debt from any Federal income tax refund;

- Recover the debt from the salary (if student is a Federal employee);

- File a lawsuit in Federal court to collect the debt;

- Withhold approval of a VA home loan guarantee.

An individual's reserve component will act to collect penalties caused by unsatisfactory participation in the reserve.

Changes in Enrollment

If a student withdraws from one or more courses after the end of the school's drop period, VA will reduce or stop benefits on the date of reduction or withdrawal. Unless the student can show that the change was due to *mitigating circumstances*, the student may have to repay **all** benefits for the course.

VA defines *mitigating circumstances* as "unavoidable and unexpected events that directly interfere with the pursuit of a course, and which are beyond the student's control.

Examples of reasons VA may accept include:

- Extended illness;
- Severe illness or death in immediate family;
- Unscheduled changes in employment; and
- Lack of child care

Examples of reasons VA may not accept include:

- Withdrawal to avoid a failing grade;
- Dislike of the instructor; and
- Too many courses attempted

(VA may ask the student to furnish evidence to support the reason for change, such as physician or employer written statements.)

The first time a student withdraws from up to 6 credit hours, VA will "excuse" the withdrawal, and pay benefits for the period attended.

If a student receives a grade that does not count toward graduation, all benefits for the course may have to be repaid.

If a student receives a non-punitive grade, the school will notify VA, and VA may reduce or stop benefits. The student may not have to repay the benefits if he or she can show that the grades were due to mitigating circumstances.

Work-Study Programs

Students may be eligible for an additional allowance under a work-study program that allows students to perform work for VA in return for an hourly wage. Students may perform outreach services under VA supervision, prepare and process VA paperwork, work at a VA medical facility or National Cemetery, or perform other approved activities.

Students must attend school at the three-quarter of full-time rate.

VA will select students for the work study program based on different factors. Such factors include:

- Disability of the student
- Ability of the student to complete the work-study contract before the end of his or her eligibility for education benefits
- Job availability within normal commuting distance to the student
- VA will give the highest priority to a veteran who has a service-connected disability or disabilities rated by VA at 30% or more

The number of applicants selected will depend on the availability of VA-related work at the school or at VA facilities in the area.

Students may work during or between periods of enrollment, and can arrange with VA to work any number of hours during his or her enrollment. However, the maximum number of hours a student may work is 25 times the number of weeks in the enrollment period.

Students will earn an hourly wage equal to the Federal or State minimum wage, whichever is greater. If a student works at a college or university, the school **may** pay the difference between the amount VA pays and the amount the school normally pays other work-study students doing the same job.

Students interested in taking part in a work-study program must complete VA Form 22,8691, Application for Work-Study Allowance. Completed forms should be sent to the nearest VA regional office.

Educational Counseling

VA can provide services to help eligible individuals understand their educational and vocational strengths and weaknesses and to plan:

- An educational or training goal, and the means by which the goal can be reached; or
- An employment goal for which an individual qualifies on the basis of present training or experience.

VA can also help plan an effective job search.

Counseling is available for:

- Service members eligible for VA educational assistance; and
- Service members on active duty and within 180 days of discharge; or
- Veterans with discharges that are not dishonorable, who are within one year from date of discharge.

★★

Vocational Rehabilitation

Veterans may qualify for Training and Rehabilitation under Chapter 31 of Title 38, United States Code, if:

- The veteran has a service-connected disability or disabilities rated by VA at 20% or more; and
- The veteran received a discharge from active duty that was not dishonorable; and
- The veteran has an employment handicap.

Veterans may also qualify with a service-connected disability or disabilities rated by VA at 10%, and:

- The veteran has a serious employment handicap; or
- The veteran first applied for vocational rehabilitation benefits before November 1, 1990, reapplied after that date, and has an employment handicap.

Vocational rehabilitation helps disabled veterans become independent in daily living. Veterans may also receive assistance in selecting, preparing for, and securing employment that is compatible with their interests, talents, skills, physical capabilities, and goals.

To apply for vocational rehabilitation, VA for 28-1900, Disabled Veterans Application for Vocational Rehabilitation, must be completed and sent to the nearest VA regional office.

For detailed information on vocational rehabilitation, refer to page 117 of this book.

Appeal of VA Decision

VA decisions on education benefits may be appealed within one year of the date an individual receives notice of a VA decision. Examples of *VA decisions* include:

- Training time,
- Change of program,
- School or course approval

If a service member disagrees with a decision about his or her basic eligibility, he or she must contact the unit, National Guard Education Officer, or Army Reserve Education Services Officer. VA does not have authority under the law to reverse eligibility determinations. If the eligibility status is corrected, VA will pay benefits for periods during which the individual was eligible.

For detailed information on filing an appeal, please refer to page 282 of this book.

★★

CHAPTER 17

LIFE INSURANCE

VA insurance programs were developed to provide insurance benefits for veterans and servicemembers who may not be able to get insurance from private companies because of a service connected disability or because of the extra risks involved in military service.

VA has responsibility for veterans' and servicemembers' life insurance programs. Listed below are the eight life insurance programs managed by VA. The first four programs listed are closed to new issues. The last four are still issuing new policies.

WAR RISK INSURANCE ACT (1914)

The United States Government first became involved in the insurance business when war broke out in Europe in 1914. Although President Wilson declared America neutral, commercial merchant ships supplied war materials to the allies in the war against Germany. Owners of these merchant ships could not get marine insurance from commercial companies. Congress passed the War Risk Insurance Act on September 2, 1914, providing marine insurance protection for merchant ships supplying the allies.

America entered the war against Germany in April 1917. Life insurance issued by commercial life insurers either excluded protection against the extra hazards of war, or if such protection was included, the premium rates were much higher than the normal rate. The War Risk Insurance Act was amended on June 12, 1917, to cover merchant marine personnel. The act was again amended on October 6, 1917, authorizing, for the first time, issuance of government life insurance to members of the armed forces. Over 4 million policies were issued during World War I.

UNITED STATES GOVERNMENT LIFE INSURANCE – USGLI (1919-1940)
POLICY PREFIX – K

The United States Government Life Insurance program (USGLI) was established in 1919 and replaced War Risk policies. Individuals could keep this coverage after separation from service.

The program was established to meet the needs of World War I veterans, but remained open to servicemembers and veterans with service before October 8, 1940. The government became a self-insurer, since private insurance companies were unwilling to assume the unpredictable risks associated with a war.

★★

Premiums No Longer Paid

Because of the strong financial position of this program, all USGLI policies were declared paid-up as of January 1, 1983. *Premiums are no longer collected from policyholders in this program.*

Dividends Paid To USGLI Policyholders

Dividends are paid on all but a few USGLI policies.

* Reserves set aside in the trust funds continue to earn interest each year in excess of what is needed to pay future claims allowing VA to pay dividends.
* In 2000, VA paid approximately $3.5 million in dividends to USGLI policyholders. This is an average of $204.57 per policyholder.

Disability Provisions

USGLI policies (except Special Endowment at Age 96) contain a provision that matures the policy upon the insured's total permanent disability. Under this provision:

* Proceeds are payable in installments of $5.75 monthly per $1,000 of insurance, as long as the insured remains totally and permanently disabled, with 240 payments guaranteed.
* If the insured dies before all guaranteed installments have been paid, the balance is payable to his or her named beneficiary.
* No additional premium is charged.
* There is no limit as to the age at which a disability may occur.

Filing a Death Claim

To file a death claim, the beneficiary should complete *VA Form 29-4125, Claim for One Sum Payment.* The completed form should be mailed or faxed, along with a death certificate to:

Department of Veterans Affairs
Regional Office and Insurance Center
PO Box 7208
Philadelphia, PA 19101
Fax: (215) 381-3561

If the beneficiary desires monthly payments instead of one lump sum, additional information is needed. The beneficiary should call the Insurance Center at 1-800-669-8477 for instructions.

★★

Customer Service

Any questions regarding USGLI should be directed to the VA Life Insurance Program at 1-800-669-8477.

NATIONAL SERVICE LIFE INSURANCE (1940-1951)
POLICY PREFIX - V, H, N OR AN

The National Service Life Insurance program (NSLI) was established on October 8, 1940 to meet the insurance needs of World War II military personnel and veterans. Like USGLI coverage, insureds could keep their NSLI coverage after discharge from service.

Over 22 million policies were issued under the NSLI program. The majority of policies VA administers directly are NSLI policies. This program remained open until April 25, 1951, when two new programs were established for Korean War servicemembers and veterans.

The NSLI program provides for:

- A maximum amount of $10,000 insurance coverage. (However, this limit does not include *paid-up additional insurance* which can be purchased with the annual dividends.);
- Individual policies issued to each policyholder;
- Certain contractual rights whereby a policyholder can bring a suit against VA in a US District Court. Administrative decisions of the Board of Veterans Appeals can be appealed to the Court of Veterans Appeals.

Premium Rates "Capped" For Term Policies

NSLI "V" term policies can be renewed indefinitely. At the older ages, premium rates increase significantly to cover the higher death rates at those ages.

In 1984, the VA "capped" premium rates at the age 70 rate. This means that a term policyholder's premium will never increase over the age 70 -premium rate.

Dividends Paid To NSLI Policyholders

After the reserve level requirements are determined by the Insurance Actuarial Staff, any surplus funds are returned to policyholders as a dividend. In 2000, a total of $591.0 million in dividends was distributed to NSLI policyholders. This was an average dividend of $386.29 per policyholder.

Disability Provisions

All NSLI policies provide for

- A waiver of premiums at no extra cost if the insured becomes totally disabled for six months or longer prior to age 65.

- An optional "Total Disability Income Provision" covering disability before age 65, providing a monthly income of up to $100 per month, as long as total disability continues.

"H" Insurance

"H" policies were issued between August 1, 1946, and December 31, 1949, to veterans with service-incurred disabilities.

On November 11, 1998, the President signed into law the 'Veterans Programs Enhancement Act of 1998' (Public Law 105-368), which contained provisions affecting VA benefits. Included in the legislation was the merger of "H" policies into the regular NSLI "V" policies. Under the new law:

- All "H" policies were to be converted to "V" policies by January 1999.

- Converted policies now have the same premium rates and policy provisions as "V" policies.

- "H" policyholders now receive dividends.

Filing a Death Claim

To file a death claim, the beneficiary should complete *VA Form 29-4125, Claim for One Sum Payment.* The completed form should be mailed or faxed, along with a death certificate to:

Department of Veterans Affairs
Regional Office and Insurance Center
PO Box 7208
Philadelphia, PA 19101
Fax: (215) 381-3561

If the beneficiary desires monthly payments instead of one lump sum, additional information is needed. The beneficiary should call the Insurance Center at 1-800-669-8477 for instructions.

Customer Service

Any questions regarding NSLI should be directed to the VA Life Insurance Program at 1-800-669-8477.

SERVICEMEN'S INDEMNITY INSURANCE
(1951-1956)

In 1951, NSLI was replaced by Servicemen's Indemnity Insurance, which automatically covered active duty servicemembers for $10,000 at no cost to the individual. Servicemembers remained covered for 120 days after their discharge.

VETERANS' SPECIAL LIFE INSURANCE – VSLI
(1951-1956)
POLICY PREFIX – RS OR W

Discharged servicemembers who had Servicemen's Indemnity Insurance could replace their coverage with Veterans' Special Life Insurance (VSLI). VSLI was established in 1951 to meet the insurance needs of veterans who served during the Korean Conflict, and the post Korean period through January 1, 1957.

The VSLI program allowed these newly discharged servicemembers to apply for $10,000 of contract term insurance. Application had to be made during the 120-day period during which they remained covered by Servicemen's Indemnity Insurance. (The $10,000 policy limit does not include *paid-up additional insurance*, which can be purchased with the annual dividends.)

In the early 1950's, commercial life insurance companies began to view the government's life insurance programs for veterans as competition for their business and began lobbying Congress to remove the government from the life insurance business. As a result, the Veterans' Special Life Insurance program was closed to new issues at the end of 1956.

Features Of "RS" And "W" Policies:

There are two types of VSLI policies:

"RS" - five-year level premium term policies:
- These were the original policies available in this program.
- "RS" policies could remain in force as 5 Year Level Premium Term beyond the age of 50.
- To provide financial relief from the high premium rates at advanced ages, "RS" term premiums were capped at the age 70-renewal rate effective May 1, 1989. This meant that the annual premium for these policies would not exceed $69.73 per $1,000 of coverage.

"W" - five-year level premium term policies:
- A 1959 legislative change permitted "RS" policyholders to convert to permanent plans or to exchange their policies for a special lower premium term policy. These newer policies are identified by the prefix "W."

★★

- To avoid "W" term policyholders from keeping their policies into advanced ages (when premiums are very high), these policies had to be converted to permanent plans before age 50, or coverage ceased. There are no longer any "W" term policyholders eligible for this conversion.

Dividends Paid To VSLI Policyholders

In 2000, a total of $95.6 million in dividends was distributed to VSLI policyholders. This was an average dividend of $443.69 per policyholder.

Disability Provisions

All VSLI policies provide for:

- A waiver of premiums at no extra cost based on the insured's total disability lasting six months or longer and starting before age 65.

- An optional Total Disability Income Provision covering disability before age 65, providing a monthly income of $10 per $1,000 of insurance, is available at an extra cost.

Filing a Death Claim

To file a death claim, the beneficiary should complete *VA Form 29-4125, Claim for One Sum Payment.*

The completed form should be mailed or faxed, along with a death certificate to:

Department of Veterans Affairs
Regional Office and Insurance Center
PO Box 7208
Philadelphia, PA 19101
Fax: (215) 381-3561

If the beneficiary desires monthly payments instead of one lump sum, additional information is needed. The beneficiary should call the Insurance Center at 1-800-669-8477 for instructions.

Customer Service

Any questions regarding VSLI should be directed to the VA Life Insurance Program at 1-800-669-8477.

SERVICE-DISABLED VETERANS INSURANCE-S-DVI
(1951-PRESENT)
(POLICY PREFIX - RH OR ARH)

The only new insurance issued between 1957 and 1965 to either servicemembers or veterans was Service-Disabled Veterans Insurance. This insurance was (and still is) available to veterans with a service-connected disability.

S-DVI, also called "RH Insurance" is available in a variety of permanent plans, as well as term insurance. Policies are issued for a maximum face amount of $10,000.

S-DVI is open to veterans separated from the service on or after April 25, 1951, who receive a service-connected disability rating of 0% or greater. New policies are still being issued under this program.

Eligibility For S-DVI Insurance ("RH")

Veterans are eligible to apply for S-DVI if:

- They have received a rating for a service-connected disability.

- They apply for the insurance within two years from the date service-connection is established. (Public Law 102-86 extended the initial one-year limit for service-connection grants made on or after September 1, 1991.)

Eligibility For Supplemental S-DVI ("Supplemental RH")

The Veterans' Benefits Act of 1992, provided for $20,000 of supplemental coverage to S-DVI policyholders. ***Premiums may not be waived on this supplemental coverage.***

S-DVI policyholders are eligible for this supplemental coverage if:

- They are eligible for a waiver of premiums.

- They apply for the coverage within one year from notice of the grant of waiver.

Gratuitous S-DVI ("ARH")

Congress enacted legislation in 1959 to protect veterans who become incompetent from a service-connected disability while eligible to apply for S-DVI, but who die before an application is filed. "ARH" insurance is:

- Issued posthumously;

- Payable to a preferred class of the veteran's relatives;

- Payable in a lump sum only.

★★

Premiums For S-DVI Insurance

The premiums charged for this coverage are:

- Based on the rates a healthy individual would have been charged when the program began in 1951.

- Insufficient to pay all of the claims because the program insures many veterans with severe disabilities.

- Waived for totally disabled veterans (27% of S-DVI policyholders).

- Supplemented on an annual basis by Congressional appropriations.

Effective November 1, 2000, the VA "capped" premium rates at the age 70 rate. This means that a term policyholder's premium will never increase over the age 70 -premium rate.

There are no reserves or surplus funds in this program. Therefore, dividends are *not* paid.

Disability Provisions

S-DVI policies (except supplemental coverage) provide for the following disability benefits:

- A waiver of premiums at no extra premium based on the insured's total disability lasting six months or longer and starting before age 65;

- A total disability premium waiver in cases where the disability commenced prior to the effective date of the policy, providing the disability is service-connected.

The optional Total Disability Income Provision is not available under this program.

Filing a Death Claim

To file a death claim, the beneficiary should complete *VA Form 29-4125, Claim for One Sum Payment.* The completed form should be mailed or faxed, along with a death certificate to:

Department of Veterans Affairs
Regional Office and Insurance Center
PO Box 7208
Philadelphia, PA 19101
Fax: (215) 381-3561

If the beneficiary desires monthly payments instead of one lump sum, additional information is needed. The beneficiary should call the Insurance Center at 1-800-669-8477 for instructions.

Customer Service

Any questions regarding USGLI should be directed to the VA Life Insurance Program at 1-800-669-8477.

★★★

VETERANS' REOPENED INSURANCE - VRI
(1965-1966)
POLICY PREFIX - J, JR, OR JS

In 1964, Congress enacted legislation providing for a limited reopening of NSLI and VSLI. Beginning May 1, 1965, veterans who had been eligible to obtain insurance between October 8, 1940 and January l, 1957, could once again apply for government life insurance. They had one year to apply for this "reopened" insurance, which was available *only* to disabled veterans. Approximately 228,000 VRI policies were issued. No term insurance policies were issued in this program.

The maximum face amount of a policy is $10,000. However, this limit does not include *paid-up additional insurance*, which can be purchased with the dividends that are paid annually on these policies.

Premium Rates

Premium rates for this insurance depend on the nature and severity of the disability.

Disability Provisions

VRI policies provide for:

- A waiver of premium at no extra premium based on the insured's total disability lasting six months or longer, and starting prior to age 65.

- An optional total disability income benefit covering disability occurring before age 65 for "J" policyholders. (This is **not** available on policies prefixed by "JR" or "JS".) Payments are made at the rate of $10 monthly per $1,000 of coverage, as long as the insured remains totally disabled.

Dividends Paid To VRI Policyholders

The VRI program began paying dividends in 1980 in order to more equitably distribute the surplus earnings of the program. A total of $21.6 million in dividends was paid to VRI policyholders in 2000.

Filing a Death Claim

To file a death claim, the beneficiary should complete *VA Form 29-4125, Claim for One Sum Payment*. The completed form should be mailed or faxed, along with a death certificate to:

Department of Veterans Affairs
Regional Office and Insurance Center
PO Box 7208
Philadelphia, PA 19101
Fax: (215) 381-3561

★★

If the beneficiary desires monthly payments instead of one lump sum, additional information is needed. The beneficiary should call the Insurance Center at 1-800-669-8477 for instructions.

Customer Service

Any questions regarding VRI should be directed to the VA Life Insurance Program at 1-800-669-8477.

SERVICEMEMBERS' GROUP LIFE INSURANCE - SGLI (1965-PRESENT)

To meet the insurance needs of Vietnam Era servicemembers, the government entered into a cooperative effort with the private insurance industry. In 1965, the Servicemembers' Group Life Insurance (SGLI) program was established. This program provides low-cost term insurance protection to servicemembers through a group policy issued by a commercial life insurance company. Under this policy, the government agrees to pay the claim costs resulting from of the extra hazards of service. All other costs of the program are covered by the premiums deducted from the service member's pay.

SGLI is supervised by the Department of Veterans Affairs and is administered by the Office of Servicemembers' Group Life Insurance (OSGLI) under terms of a group insurance contract.

Eligibility For SGLI

Full-time coverage is available for:

• Commissioned, warrant and enlisted members of the Army, Navy, Air Force, Marine Corps and Coast Guard

• Commissioned members of the National Oceanic and Atmospheric Administration and the Public Health Service

• Cadets or midshipmen of the four United States Service Academies

• Ready Reservists scheduled to perform at least 12 periods of inactive training per year.

Part-time coverage is available for eligible members of the Reserves who do not qualify for full-time coverage.

Coverage Amounts

The SGLI program provides up to $200,000 **(effective April 1, 2001, the automatic maximum coverage will be increased to $250,000)** of life insurance coverage. This coverage is:

- Automatic at the time of entry into a period of active duty or reserve status.

- Available in $10,000 increments up to the maximum of $200,000 of insurance.

Members may decline coverage or may elect reduced coverage. If such a member later wishes to obtain or increase coverage, proof of good health will be required.

Coverage Periods

Full-time coverage is effective:

- Throughout a member's period of active duty or qualifying reserve status.

- For a 120-day free period following separation or release from active duty or reserve status.

- For up to one year for members who are totally disabled at the time of separation. This is free coverage and must be applied for to the OSGLI after separation.

Part-time coverage is effective:

- Only on the days of active duty or active duty for training and for periods of travel to and from such duty.

- For a free period of 120 days if a member under part-time coverage incurs a disability or aggravates a preexisting disability while performing a period of duty.

Premiums

Premium rates for SGLI coverage are as follows:

- Active duty members and Ready Reservists - 8 cents *per month* per $1,000:

- Part-time coverage - 10 cents *per year* per $1,000:

(Note: above premiums shown are accurate as of January 2000, but are subject to change.)

Beneficiary Selection

Any beneficiary can be named. If none is selected, the insurance is distributed, by law, in the following order:

- Spouse, or
- Children, or
- Parents, or
- Executor of estate, or
- Other next of kin.

★★★

An insured should designate a beneficiary by completing *Form SGVL 8286, Servicemembers' Group Life Insurance Election and Certificate.* The completed form should be submit to the individual's uniformed service.

Options For Payment Of Policy Proceeds

SGLI proceeds can be paid in a lump sum *or* over a 36-month period.

Alliance Account

If the proceeds are to be paid in a lump sum then beneficiaries of SGLI and VGLI will receive the payment of their insurance proceeds via an *"Alliance Account".* Rather than the traditional single check for the full amount of insurance proceeds, the beneficiary receives a checkbook for an interest bearing account from which the beneficiary can write a check for any amount from $250 up to the full amount of the proceeds. The Alliance Account

- Earns interest at a competitive rate
- Is guaranteed by Prudential
- Gives the beneficiary time to make important financial decisions while their funds are secure and earning interest
- Gives them instant access to their money at all times

Accelerated Benefits

On November 11, 1998, the President signed legislation authorizing the payment of "Accelerated Benefits" in the SGLI and VGLI programs subject to the following:

- Terminally ill insureds will have access of up to 50% of the face amount of their coverage during their lifetime.
- This money will be available in increments of $5,000.
- An insured must have a medical prognosis of life expectancy of 9 months or less.

Insurance Options After Separation From Service

When released from active duty or the Reserve, members with full-time SGLI coverage can convert their coverage to Veterans Group Life Insurance *or* to an individual commercial life insurance policy with any one of 99 participating commercial insurance companies.

Filing Death Claims

A beneficiary may file a claim for VGLI proceeds by submitting *Form SGLV 8283, Claim For Death Benefits*, to:

Office of Servicemembers' Group Life Insurance
213 Washington Avenue
Newark, NJ 07102-2999

★★

Taxation

SGLI proceeds that are payable at the death of the insured are excluded from gross income for tax purposes. (The value of the proceeds, however, may be included in determining the value of an estate, and that estate may ultimately be subject to tax.)

If SGLI proceeds are paid to a beneficiary in 36 equal installments, the interest portion included in these installments is also exempt from taxation. In addition, delayed settlement interest (interest accrued from the date of the insured's death to the date of settlement) is also exempt from taxation.

A beneficiary is not required to report to the Internal Revenue Service any installment interest or delayed settlement interest received in addition to the proceeds.

Customer Service

Any questions regarding SGLI should be directed to the office of Servicemembers' Group Life Insurance (OSGLI) at 1-800-419-1473.

VETERANS' GROUP LIFE INSURANCE – VGLI
(1974-PRESENT)

In 1974, the Veterans' Group Life Insurance (VGLI) program became available to veterans, providing term insurance protection after separation from service.

VGLI, like SGLI, is supervised by the Department of Veterans Affairs, but is administered by the Office of Servicemembers' Group Life Insurance (OSGLI). VGLI provides for the conversion of Servicemembers' Group Life Insurance to a five-year renewable term policy of insurance protection after a service member's separation from service.

Eligibility For VGLI

Full-time coverage is available for the following members:

- Full-time SGLI insureds that are released from active duty or the Reserves.

- Ready Reservists who have part-time SGLI coverage, and who, while performing active duty or inactive duty for training for a period of less than 31 days, incur a disability or aggravate a preexisting disability that makes them uninsurable at standard premium rates.

- Members of the Individual Ready Reserve (IRR) and Inactive National Guard (ING).

★★★

Coverage Amounts

VGLI is issued in multiples of $10,000 up to a maximum of $200,000, but not for more than the amount of SGLI coverage the member had in force at the time of separation from active duty or the reserves.

VGLI Renewal

Members may renew their VGLI coverage under the following conditions:

- Members who have separated from service may renew their VGLI coverage for life in 5-year term periods.

- Members of the IRR or ING may renew their VGLI for additional 5-year term periods, as long as they remain in the IRR or ING.

- Rather than renew, a member also has the right at any time to **convert** VGLI to an individual commercial life insurance policy with any one of 99 participating commercial insurance companies.

How To Apply For VGLI

VGLI applications are mailed to eligible members, generally within 60 days after separation, and again shortly before the end of the 16-month application period. Applications are mailed to the address shown on the member's DD-Form 214 or equivalent separation orders. *It is the member's responsibility, however, to apply within the time limits, even if they do not receive an application in the mail.*

Applications should be mailed to:

Office Of Servicemembers' Group Life Insurance
213 Washington Street
Newark, New Jersey 07102-2999.

Time Limits To Apply For VGLI

To be eligible, a member must apply for VGLI within the following time limits:

- Ordinarily, a member must submit an application to the OSGLI with the required premium within 120 days following separation from service.

- If a member is *totally disabled* at the time of separation from active duty *and* is granted extended free SGLI coverage, he or she may apply for VGLI anytime during the one-year period of extension.

- Individuals who are assigned to the IRR and ING have 120 days after assignment to apply, without evidence of good health, and one year after that with evidence of good health.

- If an application or the initial premium has not been submitted within the time limits above, VGLI may still be granted if an application, the initial premium and **evidence of insurability** (good health) are submitted to OSGLI within 1 year and 120 days following termination of SGLI. *Applications will not be accepted after one year and 120 days.*

- An application for an incompetent member may be made by a guardian, committee, conservator or curator. In the absence of a court appointed representative, the application may be submitted by a family member or anyone acting on the member's behalf.

VGLI Premiums Rates

VGLI premium rates are determined by age group and amount of insurance. To lessen the high cost of term insurance at the older ages, a Decreasing Term Option is available, starting at age group 60 to 64. Under this option an insured pays a level premium for life, while the insurance amount declines by 25% for three subsequent five-year renewals. At that point, coverage remains level at 25% of the original insurance amount.

Payment Of Premiums

Once the VGLI application is approved, the OSGLI will send the insured a certificate and a supply of monthly premium payment coupons.

Premiums may be paid:

- Monthly
- Quarterly
- Semiannually
- Annually
- By monthly allotment from military retirement pay
- By monthly deduction from VA compensation payments

If the insured does not pay the premium when it is due, or within a grace period of 60 days, the VGLI coverage will lapse. If VGLI lapsed due to failure to pay the premiums on time, the insured will receive a notification of the lapse and a reinstatement form. The insured may apply to reinstate coverage at any time within 5 years of the date of the unpaid premium. If the insured applies for reinstatement within 6 months from the date of lapse, the individual only needs to provide evidence that he or she is in the same state of health on the date of reinstatement as on the date of lapse. Otherwise, the individual may need to provide proof of good health.

Beneficiary Selection

Any **beneficiary** can be named. If none is selected, the insurance is distributed, by law, in the following order:

- Spouse, or
- Children, or
- Parents, or
- Executor of estate, or
- Other next of kin.

To name a beneficiary, the insured must submit *Form SGLV 8712, Beneficiary Designation-Veterans' Group Life Insurance.* The completed form should be sent to:

Office of Servicemembers' Group Life Insurance
213 Washington Avenue
Newark, NJ 07102-2999

When an insured converts SGLI to VGLI following separation from service, a new beneficiary designation form must be completed. If a new form is not filed, the SGLI beneficiary designation will be considered the VGLI designation for up to 60 days after the effective date of the VGLI. If a new beneficiary is not designated after this 60-day period, the proceeds would be paid "By Law" under the order of precedence in the law.

Options For Payment Of Policy Proceeds

Alliance Account

VGLI proceeds can be paid in a lump sum or over a 36-month period.
If the proceeds are to be paid in a lump sum then beneficiaries of SGLI and VGLI will receive the payment of their insurance proceeds via an *"Alliance Account"*.

Rather than the traditional single check for the full amount of insurance proceeds, the beneficiary receives a checkbook for an interest bearing account from which the beneficiary can write a check for any amount from $250 up to the full amount of the proceeds. The Alliance Account:

- Earns interest at a competitive rate
- Is guaranteed by Prudential
- Gives the beneficiary time to make important financial decisions while their funds are secure and earning interest
- Gives them instant access to their money at all times

Accelerated Benefits

On November 11, 1998, the President signed legislation authorizing the payment of *"Accelerated Benefits"* in the SGLI and VGLI programs subject to the following:

- Terminally ill insureds will have access of up to 50 percent of the face amount of their coverage during their lifetime.
- This money will be available in increments of $5,000.
- An insured must have a medical prognosis of life expectancy of 9 months or less.

Filing Death Claims

A beneficiary may file a claim for VGLI proceeds by submitting *Form SGLV 8283, Claim For Death Benefits*, to:

> Office of Servicemembers' Group Life Insurance
> 213 Washington Avenue
> Newark, NJ 07102-2999

Taxation

VGLI proceeds are exempt from taxation. Any installment interest or delayed settlement interest that a beneficiary receives in addition to the proceed is also exempt from taxation, and does not need to be reported to the IRS.

Customer Service

Any questions regarding VGLI should be directed to the office of Servicemembers' Group Life Insurance (OSGLI) at 1-800-419-1473.

VETERANS' MORTGAGE LIFE INSURANCE – VMLI (1971-PRESENT)

The Veterans' Mortgage Life Insurance (VMLI) program began in 1971, and is designed to provide financial protection to cover eligible veterans' home mortgages in the event of death. VMLI is issued to those severely disabled veterans who have received grants for Specially Adapted Housing from VA. (Refer to page 24 of this book for information regarding Specially Adapted Housing.) VMLI coverage ceases at age 70.

The maximum amount of VMLI allowed an eligible veteran is $90,000. The insurance is payable if the veteran dies before the mortgage is paid off. VA will pay the amount of money still owed on the mortgage up to $90,000. *The insurance is payable only to the mortgage lender.* The day-to-day operations of the program are handled by the Philadelphia VAROIC.

Coverage Amounts

VMLI coverage decreases as the insured's mortgage falls below $90,000. This reduced coverage cannot be reinstated. However, if the home is sold and a new home is purchased the veteran becomes eligible once again for the maximum amount of coverage.

Payment Of VMLI Proceeds

Certain conditions apply to the payment of VMLI benefits:

- The insurance is payable at the death of the veteran only to the mortgage holder.

- If the title of the property is shared with anyone other than the veteran's spouse, the insurance coverage is only for the percentage of the title that is in the veteran's name.

★★

- No insurance is payable if the mortgage is paid off before the death of the insured or if it was paid off by other mortgage insurance before the VMLI payment is made.

The insurance will be canceled for any of the following conditions:

- 1) The veteran's 70th birthday.
- 2) The mortgage is paid in full.
- 3) Termination of the veteran's ownership of the property securing the loan.
- 4) The request of the veteran.
- 5) Failure of the veteran to submit timely statements or other required information.

Premiums

Premiums are determined by the insurance age of the veteran, the outstanding balance of the mortgage at the time of application, and the remaining length of time the mortgage has to run. Veterans who desire insurance will be advised of the correct premium when it is determined.

Premiums **must** be paid by deduction from the veteran's monthly compensation or pension payments, if the veteran is receiving such payments. If such payments are not being received the veteran may make direct payments, on a monthly, quarterly, semiannual, or annual basis, to the VA Insurance Center in Philadelphia, Pennsylvania.

DIVIDEND OPTIONS

If a policyholder is eligible for a dividend, he or she may choose from several dividend options that are available:

- *Cash*, paid to policyholder by US Treasury check.
- *Credit*, held in account for the insured with interest. Can be used to prevent policy lapse. Will be refunded upon the insured's request, or will be included in the award to the beneficiary(ies) at the time of the insured's death.
- *Paid-Up Additions (PUA'S)*, used as a net single premium to purchase additional paid-up insurance. Available only on "V," "RS," "W," "J," "JR," and "JS" policies. PUA's will be whole life insurance if the basic insurance is an endowment policy.
- *Deposit*, held in account for insured with interest. Available only on permanent plan policies. Considered part of the policy's cash value for the purpose of purchasing reduced paid-up insurance, or if the policy lapses, extended insurance (except for "K" or "JS" policies). Will be refunded upon the insured's request. Will be included in the award to the beneficiary(ies) at the time of the insured's death.
- *Premium*, applied to pay premiums in advance.
- *Indebtedness*, applied toward a loan or lien on a policy.

- **Net Cash**, used to pay an annual premium with any remainder paid to the policyholder under the cash option.

- **Net PUA**, used to pan an annual premium with any remainder used to purchase paid-up additional insurance.

- **Net Loan-Lien**, used to pay an annual premium with any remainder used to reduce an outstanding loan or lien.

To change the method in which dividends are paid, individuals should speak with an Insurance Specialist at 1-800-669-8477

MISCELLANEOUS INFORMATION ABOUT GOVERNMENT LIFE INSURANCE POLICIES

Power of Attorney is not acceptable for executing a change of beneficiary for government life insurance, even if certain state statutes allow it. Only a court appointed guardian that is recognized by state statutes can execute a beneficiary designation. If the state statute does not give the guardian broad powers to authorize a beneficiary change, a specific court order is needed to effectuate a change.

Assignment of government life insurance is not allowed, for any reason, nor can ownership of a policy be transferred. Only the insured can exercise the rights and privileges inherent in the ownership of the policy.

Policy Loans are available on permanent plans of insurance. The policyholder can take up to 94% of the reserve value of the policy, less any indebtedness. The policy cannot be lapsed, and premiums must be paid or waived at least one year before a policy has a loan value. Changes in interest rates are made on October 1 of each year, if warranted. Rate changes are tied to the "ten year constant maturities", U.S. Treasury securities index.

A policyholder can apply for a loan by filing *VA Form 29-1546, Application for Policy Loan.* The completed form can be faxed to (215) 381-3580, or mailed to:

Department of Veterans Affairs
Regional Office and Insurance Center
PO Box 7327
Philadelphia, PA 19101

An Annual Insurance Policy Statement is mailed to the insured on the policy anniversary date of each policy. The statement provides the insured with information about his or her VA insurance. The statement should be reviewed for accuracy each year, and the VA should be contacted immediately if there are any discrepancies.

Dividend Hoax - Rumors that Congress approved a "Special Dividend" for veterans who do or do not have Government life insurance have been spread for over 30 years. These rumors are false. The only dividends being paid by VA are on active Government life insurance policies. Dividends on active policies have been paid annually for many years and policyholders do not need to apply for them.

"Special Dividend" rumors are spread by well-meaning people who want to help veterans but fail to check out their sources before passing the information along to others.   Notices have appeared in veterans' magazines, union newspapers, fraternal publications, newspapers and every other publication imaginable. The hoax has appeared in many forms and seems to change to fit the times.   It started in the 1960's as a rumor about veterans with WW II insurance.   More recently, it has been adapted to state that a dividend is being paid on Servicemembers' Group Life Insurance (SGLI) or Veterans' Group Life Insurance (VGLI) coverage.

Unfortunately, this misinformation unnecessarily raises the expectations of veterans and service personnel.   There has been no recent legislation authorizing any "special" dividends.

If you have any questions regarding this issue, feel free to contact the VA Insurance Center at 1-800-669-8477.

CHAPTER 18

HOME LOAN GUARANTIES

GENERAL INFORMATION

The purpose of the VA loan guaranty program is to help veterans and active duty personnel finance the purchase of homes with competitive loan terms and interest rates. The VA does not actually lend the money to veterans. VA guaranteed loans are made by private lenders, such as banks, savings & loans, or mortgage companies. The VA guaranty means the lender is protected against loss if the veteran fails to repay the loan.

The VA Loan Guaranty Service is the organization within the VA that has the responsibility of administering the home loan program.

VA guaranteed loans offer the following important features:

- Equal opportunity for all qualified veterans to obtain a VA guaranteed loan.
- No downpayment (unless required by the lender or the purchase price is more than the reasonable value of the property).
- Buyer is informed of reasonable value.
- Buyer's interest rate is negotiable.
- Buyer has the ability to finance the VA funding fee (plus reduced funding fees with a downpayment of at least 5%, and exemption for veterans receiving VA compensation).
- Closing costs are comparable with other financing types (and may be lower).
- No mortgage insurance premiums are necessary.
- An assumable mortgage may be available.
- Buyer has the right to prepay without penalty.
- A warranty from the builder, and assistance from VA to obtain cooperation of builder is offered for homes inspected by VA during construction.
- VA may offer assistance to a veteran borrow who is in default due to temporary financial difficulty .

VA guaranteed loans do not do the following:

- Guarantee that a home is free of defects (VA only guarantees the loan. It is the veteran's responsibility to assure that he or she is satisfied with the property being purchased. Veterans should seek expert advice as necessary, *before* legally committing to a purchase agreement.)
- If a veteran has a home built, VA cannot compel the builder to correct construction defects, although VA does have the authority to suspend a builder from further participation in the VA home loan program.

- VA cannot guarantee the veteran is making a good investment.
- VA cannot provide a veteran with legal service.

Uses For VA Loan Guaranties

VA loan guaranties can be used for the following:

- To purchase, construct, or improve a home.
- To purchase and improve a home concurrently.
- To purchase a residential condominium or townhouse unit in a VA approved project. (If one veteran is purchasing the property, the total number of separate units cannot be more than 4.)
- To purchase a manufactured home or a manufactured home and manufactured home lot.
- To purchase and improve a manufactured home lot on which to place a manufactured home which the veteran already owns and occupies.
- To refinance an existing home loan.
- To refinance an existing VA loan to reduce the interest rate, and make energy-efficient improvements.
- To refinance an existing manufactured home loan in order to acquire a lot.
- To improve a home by installing a solar heating and/or cooling system, or other energy efficient improvements.

Veterans must certify that they plan to live in the home they are buying or building in order to qualify for a VA loan guaranty.

VA loan guaranties are available only for property located in the United States, its territories, or possessions (Puerto Rico, Guam, Virgin Islands, American Samoa, and Northern Mariana Islands).

VA loan guaranties are not available for farm loans, unless there is a home on the property, which will be personally occupied by the veteran. Non-realty loans for the purchase of equipment, livestock, machinery, etc. are not made. Other loan programs for farm financing may be available through the Farmers Home Administration, which gives preference to veteran applicants. (Interested veterans should refer to the local telephone directory for the phone number of a local office.)

Although business loans are not available through VA, the Small Business Administration (SBA) has a number of programs designed to help foster and encourage small business enterprises, including financial and management assistance. Each SBA office has a veteran's affairs officer available to speak with. (Interested veterans should refer to the local telephone directory for the phone number of a local SBA office, or call 1-800-827-5722.)

★★★

ELIGIBILITY REQUIREMENTS

Individuals may qualify for VA home loan guaranties if their service falls within any of the following categories:

World War II Eligibility Requirements:

- Active duty on or after September 16, 1940 and prior to July 26, 1947; and
- Discharge or separation under other than dishonorable conditions; and
- At least 90 days of total service, unless discharged earlier for a service-connected disability.
- Unremarried widows of above-described eligible individuals who died as a result of service.

Post World War II Eligibility Requirements:

- Active duty on or after July 26, 1947 and prior to June 27, 1950; and
- Discharge or separation under other than dishonorable conditions; and
- At least 181 days continuous service, unless discharged earlier for a service-connected disability.
- Unremarried widows of above-described eligible individuals who died as a result of service.

Korean Conflict Eligibility Requirements:

- Active duty on or after June 27, 1950 and prior to February 1, 1955; and
- Discharge or separation under other than dishonorable conditions; and
- At least 90 days of total service, unless discharged earlier for a service-connected disability.
- Unremarried widows of above-described eligible individuals who died as a result of service.

Post-Korean Conflict Eligibility Requirements:

- Active duty on or after February 1, 1955 and prior to August 5, 1964; and
- Discharge or separation under other than dishonorable conditions; and
- At least 181 days continuous service, unless discharged earlier for a service-connected disability.
- Unremarried widows of above-described eligible individuals who died as a result of service.

★★★

Vietnam Eligibility Requirements:

- Active duty on or after August 5, 1964, and prior to May 8, 1975. (For those serving in the Republic of Vietnam, the beginning date is February 28, 1961.); and
- Discharge or separation under other than dishonorable conditions; and
- At least 90 days of total service, unless discharged earlier for a service-connected disability.
- Unremarried widows of above-described eligible individuals who died as a result of service.

Post-Vietnam Eligibility Requirements for Veterans With Enlisted Service Between May 8, 1975 and September 7, 1980 (if enlisted) or October 16, 1981 (if officer):

- At least 181 days of continuous service, all of which occurred on or after May 8, 1975, unless discharged earlier for a service-connected disability; and
- Discharge or separation under other than dishonorable conditions.
- Unremarried widows of above-described eligible individuals who died as a result of service.

Post-Vietnam Eligibility Requirements for Veterans Separated from Enlisted Service Between September 7, 1980 (October 17, 1981 for Officers) and August 1, 1990:

- At least 24 months of continuous active duty, or the full period (at least 181 days) for which individual was called or ordered to active duty, and discharged or separated under other than dishonorable conditions; or
- At least 181 days of continuous active duty, and discharged due to:
    - a hardship; or
    - a service-connected, compensable disability; or
    - a medical condition which preexisted service, and has not been determined to be service-connected; or
    - the convenience of the government as a result of a reduction in force; or
    - a physical or mental condition not characterized as a disability, and not the result of misconduct, but which did interfere with the performance of duty.
- Early discharge for a service-connected disability.
- Unremarried widows of above-described eligible persons who died as the result of service.

★★

Persian Gulf War Eligibility Requirements:

- At least 24 months of continuous active duty on or after August 2, 1990, or the full period for which the individual was called or ordered to active duty, and discharged or separated under other than dishonorable conditions; or
- At least 90 days of continuous active duty, and discharged due to:
- a hardship; or
- a service-connected, compensable disability; or
- a medical condition which preexisted service, and has not been determined to be service-connected; or
- the convenience of the government as a result of a reduction in force; or
- a physical or mental condition not characterized as a disability, and not the result of misconduct, but which did interfere with the performance of duty.
- Early discharge for a service-connected disability.
- Unremarried widows of above-described eligible individuals who died as the result of service.

(When law or Presidential Proclamation ends the Persian Gulf War, a minimum of 181 days of continuous active duty will be required for those who did not serve during wartime.)

Members of the Reserve and National Guard are eligible if activated after August 1, 990, served at least 90 days, and discharged or separated under other than dishonorable conditions.)

Active Duty Personnel Eligibility Requirements

Individuals currently on active duty are eligible after serving on continuous active duty for at least 90 days.

(Individuals who are six-month enlistees, and serve six months active duty for training only are not eligible for VA guaranteed loans. However, these individuals may be eligible for FHA home mortgage insurance for veterans. See page 380 of this book for further information.

Eligibility Requirements for Members of the Selected Reserve:

- At least 6 years in the Reserves or National Guard, or discharged earlier due to a service-connected disability; and
- Discharged or separated under other than dishonorable conditions; or
- Placed on the retired list; or
- Transferred to an element of the Ready Reserve other than the Selected Reserve; or
- Continue to serve in the Selected Reserve.
- Unremarried widows of above-described eligible persons who died as the result of service.

★★

Please note that eligibility for members of the Selected Reserve Expires on September 30, 2007.

Eligibility Requirements for Other Types of Service:

- Certain U.S. citizens who served in the armed forces of a U.S. ally in World War II.

- Members of organizations with recognized contributions to the U.S. during World War II. (Questions about this type of service eligibility can be answered at any VA regional office.)

- Spouses of American servicemen who are listed as missing-in-action, or prisoners-of-war for a total of 90 days or more.

CERTIFICATE OF ELIGIBILITY

The Certificate of Eligibility is the medium by which VA certifies eligibility for A VA loan guaranty.

Individuals may request a Certificate of Eligibility by completing VA Form 16, 1880, Request for a Certificate of Eligibility for VA Home Loan Benefits. The completed form should be submitted to a VA Eligibility Center along with acceptable proof of service.

Veterans separated after January 1, 1950 should submit DD Form 214, Certificate of Release or Discharge from active Duty.

Veterans separated after October 1, 1979 should submit copy 4 of DD Form 214.

Since there is no uniform document similar to the DD Form 214 for proof of service in the Selected Reserve a number of different forms may be accepted as documentation of service in the Selected Reserve:

- For those who served in the Army or Air National Guard and were discharged after at least 6 years of such service, NGB Form 22 may be sufficient.

- Those who served in the Army, Navy, Air Force, Marine Corps or Coast Guard Reserves may need to rely on a variety of forms that document at least 6 years of participation in paid training periods, or have paid active duty for training.

- Often it will be necessary to submit a combination of documents, such as an Honorable Discharge certificate together with a Retirement Points Statement. It is the reservist's responsibility to obtain and submit documentation of 6 years of honorable service.

★★★

In addition, if an individual is now on active duty, and has not been previously discharged from active duty service, he or she must submit a statement of service that includes the name of the issuing authority (base or command), and is signed by or at the direction of an appropriate official. The statement must identify the individual, include the social security number, provide the date of entry on active duty and the duration of any lost time.

The Certificate of Eligibility should be presented to the lender when completing the loan application. (However, if an individual does not have a Certificate, the lender may have the forms necessary to apply for the Certificate of Eligibility.)

VA Eligibility Centers

Specific questions regarding VA home loan eligibility, and all requests for Certificates of Eligibility should be sent to the appropriate Eligibility Center:

Los Angeles Eligibility Center
P.O. Box 240097
Los Angeles, CA 90024
1-888-487-1970

Alaska
Arizona
Arkansas
California
Colorado
Hawaii
Idaho
Illinois
Iowa
Kansas
Louisiana
Minnesota
Missouri
Montana
Nebraska
Nevada
New Mexico
North Dakota
Oklahoma
Oregon
South Dakota
Texas
Utah
Washington
Wisconsin
Wyoming

Winston-Salem Eligibility Center
P.O. Box 20729
Winston-Salem, NC 27120
1-888-244-6711

Alabama
Connecticut
District of Columbia
Delaware
Florida
Georgia
Indiana
Kentucky
Maine
Maryland
Massachusetts
Michigan
Mississippi
New Hampshire
New Jersey
New York
North Carolina
Ohio
Pennsylvania
Puerto Rico
Rhode Island
South Carolina
Tennessee
Vermont
Virginia
West Virginia

PROCEDURES FOR OBTAINING LOANS

1. Apply for a Certificate of Eligibility
2. Decide on a home the buyer wants to purchase, and sign a purchase agreement
3. Order an appraisal from VA. (Usually this is done by the lender.) Most VA regional offices offer a "speed-up" telephone appraisal system. Call the local VA office for details.
4. Apply to a mortgage lender for the loan. While the appraisal is being done, the lender (mortgage company, savings and loan, bank, etc.) can be gathering credit and income information. If the lender is authorized by VA to do automatic processing, upon receipt of the VA or LAPP appraised value determination, the loan can be approved and closed without waiting for VA's review of the credit application. For loans that must first be approved by VA, the lender will send the application to the local VA office, which will notify the lender of its decision.
5. Close the loan and the buyer moves in.

If a lender cannot be located, the local VA regional office can provide a list of lenders active in the VA program.

A VA loan guaranty does not guarantee approval of a loan. The veteran must still meet the financial institution's income and credit requirements. If a loan is approved, the VA guarantees the loan when it's closed.

GUARNTY OR ENTITLEMENT AMOUNT

The amount of the VA guaranty available to a veteran is called the entitlement. The lender may use the entitlement amount in place of a down payment. The amount of entitlement varies with the loan amount, as detailed in the following table:

Loan Amount	VA Guaranty	Maximum Guaranty
Up to $45,000	50%	$22,500
$45,001 - $144,000	40% - 50%	$36,000
Greater than $144,000	25%	$50,750
Manufactured Home or Lot	40%	$20,000

The VA does not establish a maximum loan amount, although lenders generally limit the maximum VA loan to $203,000, because most VA loans are sold in the secondary market, which limits VA loans to that amount.

No loan, however, may exceed the reasonable value of the property. When refinancing certain loans, the maximum loan is 90% of the value of the property, plus the funding fee, if required. When purchasing a manufactured home or lot, the maximum loan is 95% of the amount that would be subject to finance charges.

Home loan entitlement is generally good until used. However, the eligibility of service personnel is only available as long as they remain on active duty. If an individual is discharged or released from active duty before using his or her entitlement, a new determination of eligibility must be made, based on the length of service and the type of discharge received.

DOWN PAYMENTS

The VA does not require a down payment be made, provided that:

- The loan is not for a manufactured home or lot (a 5% down payment is required for manufactured home or lot loans); and

- The purchase price or cost does not exceed the reasonable value of the property, as determined by VA; and

- The loan does not have graduated payment features. (Because with a graduated payment mortgage, the loan balance will be increasing during the first years of the loan, a down payment is required to keep the loan balance from going over the reasonable value or the purchase price.)

Even though the VA may not require a down payment, the lender may require one.

CLOSING COSTS AND FEES

The VA regulates the closing costs that a veteran may be charged in connection with closing a VA loan. The closing costs and origination fees must be paid in cash, and cannot be included in the loan itself, except in the case of refinancing loans.

Although some additional costs are unique to certain localities, the closing costs generally include:

- VA appraisal

- Credit report

- Survey

- Title evidence

- Recording fees

- A 1% loan origination fee

- Discount points

A veteran is charged the customary fees for title search, credit report, appraisal and transfer fees, etc., the same as any other borrower, but he is not required to pay commission or brokerage fees for obtaining the loan. In home loans, the lender may also charge a reasonable flat charge, called a funding fee, to cover the costs of originating the loan.

FUNDING FEES

A VA funding fee is payable at the time of loan closing. This fee may be included in the loan and paid from the loan proceeds. The funding fee does not have to be paid by veterans receiving VA compensation for service-connected disabilities, or who but for the receipt of retirement pay, would be entitled to receive compensation for service-connected disabilities, or surviving spouses of veterans who died in service or from a service-connected disability.

The funding fee rates are as follows:

Loan Purpose	Percent of Loan for Veterans	Percent of Loan for Reservists
Purchase or construction loan with down payment of less than 5%; or Refinancing loan; or Home improvement loan	2.0	2.75
Purchase or construction loan with down payment between 5% and 10%	1.5	2.25
Purchase or construction loan with down payment of 10% or more	1.25	2.25
Manufactured home loan	1.0	1.0
Interest rate reduction loan	0.5	0.5
Assumption of VA guaranteed loan	0.5	0.5
Second or subsequent use without a down payment	3.0	3.0

FLOOD INSURANCE

If the dwelling is in an area identified by the Department of Housing and Urban Development as having special flood hazards, and the sale of flood insurance under the national program is available, such insurance is required on loans made since March 1, 1974. The amount of insurance must be equal to the outstanding loan balance, or the maximum limit of coverage available, whichever is less.

INTEREST RATES

The interest rate on VA loans varies due to changes in the prevailing rates in the mortgage market. One a loan is made, the interest rate set in the note remains the same for the life of the loan. However, if interest rates decrease, a veteran may apply for a new VA loan to refinance the previous loan at a lower interest rate.

★★★

REPAYMENT PERIOD

The maximum repayment period for VA home loans is 30 years and 32 days. However, the exact amortization period depends upon the contract between the lender and the borrower.

The VA will guarantee loans with the following repayment terms:

- Traditional Fixed Payment Mortgage
- (equal monthly payments for the life of the loan)
- Graduated Payment Mortgage – GPM
- (Smaller than normal monthly payments for the first few years – usually 5 years, which gradually increase each year, and then level off after the end of the "graduation period" to larger than normal payments for the remaining term of the loan. The reduction in the monthly payment in the early years of the loan is accomplished by delaying a portion of the interest due on the loan each month, and by adding that interest to the principal balance.)
- Buydown
- (The builder of a new home or seller of an existing home may "buy down" the veteran's mortgage payments by making a large lump sum payment up front at closing that will be used to supplement the monthly payments for a certain period, usually 1 to 3 years.)
- Growing Equity Mortgage (GEM)
- (Provides for a gradual annual increase in monthly payments, with all of the increase applied to the principal balance, resulting in early payoff of the loan.)

Prepayment of Loan

A veteran or serviceman may pay off his entire loan at any time without penalty or fee, or make advance payments equal to one monthly installment or $100, whichever is the lesser amount. Individuals should check with the mortgage holder for the proper procedure.

Loan Defaults

If a veteran fails to make payments as agreed, the lender may foreclose on the property.. If the lender takes a loss, the VA must pay the guaranty to the lender, and the individual must repay this amount to the VA. If the loan closed on or after January 1, 1990, the veteran will owe the VA in the event of default, only if there was fraud, misrepresentation, or bad faith on the veteran's part.

★★

RELEASE OF LIABILITY

Any veteran who sells or has sold a home purchased with a VA loan guaranty may request release from liability to the VA. (If the VA loan closed prior to March 1, 1988, the application forms for a release of liability must be requested from the VA office that guaranteed the loan. If the VA loan closed on or after March 1, 1988, then the application forms must be requested from the lender to whom the payments are made.) The loan must be current, the purchaser must assume full liability for the loan, and the purchaser must sign an Assumption of Liability Agreement. The VA must approve the purchaser from a credit standpoint.

For loans closed on or after March 1, 1988, release of liability is not automatic. To approve the assumer and grant the veteran release from liability, the lender or VA must be notified, and release of liability must be requested.

If the loan was closed prior to March 1, 1988, the purchaser may assume the loan without approval from VA or the lender. However, the veteran is encouraged to request a release of liability from VA, regardless of the loan's closing date. If a veteran does not obtain a release of liability, and VA suffers a loss on account of a default by the assumer, or some future assumer, a debt may be established against the veteran. Also, strenuous collection efforts will be made against the veteran if a debt is established.

The release of a veteran from liability to the VA does not change the fact that the VA continues to be liable on the guaranty.

RESTORATION OF ENTITLEMENT

Veterans who have used all or part of their entitlement may restore their entitlement amount to purchase another home, provided:

- The property has been sold, and the loan has been paid in full; or

- A qualified veteran buyer has agreed to assume the outstanding balance on the loan, and agreed to substitute his entitlement for the same amount of entitlement the original veteran owner used to get the loan. (The veteran buyer must also meet the occupancy, income, and credit requirements of the VA and the lender.)

- If the veteran has repaid the VA loan in full, but has not disposed of the property securing that loan, the entitlement may be restored ONE TIME ONLY.

Restoration of entitlement does not occur automatically. The veteran must apply for restoration by completing Form 26, 1880. Completed forms may be returned to any VA regional office or center (A copy of the HUD-1, Closing Statement, or other appropriate evidence of payment in full should also be submitted with the completed Form 26, 1880.) Application forms for substitution of entitlement can be requested from the VA office that guaranteed the loan.

★★

If the requirements for restoration of entitlement cannot be met, veterans who had a VA loan before may still have remaining entitlement to use for another VA loan. The current amount of entitlement available to eligible veterans has been increased over time by changes in the law.

For example, in 1974 the maximum guaranty entitlement was $12,500. Today the maximum guaranty entitlement is $36,000 (for most loans under $144,000). So, if a veteran used the $12,500 guaranty in 1974, even if that loan is not paid off, the veteran could use the $23,500 difference between the $12,500 entitlement originally used and the current maximum of $36,000 to buy another home with a VA loan guaranty.

DIRECT HOME LOANS

VA direct home loans are only available to:

- Native American veterans who plan to buy, build, or improve a home on Native American trust land; or

- Certain eligible veterans who have a permanent and total service-connected disability, for specially adapted homes.

Native American Veterans Living on Trust Lands

A VA direct loan can be used to purchase, construct, or improve a home on Native American trust land. These loans may also be used to simultaneously purchase and improve a home, or to refinance another VA direct loan made under this program in order to lower the interest rate. VA direct loans are generally limited to the cost of the home or $80,000, whichever is less.

To qualify for a VA direct loan, the tribal organization or other appropriate Native American group must be participating in the VA direct loan program. The tribal organization must have signed a *Memorandum of Understanding* with the Secretary of Veterans Affairs that includes the conditions governing its participation in the program.

Veterans should contact their regional VA office for specific information regarding direct home loans.

RESALE OF REPOSSESSED VA HOMES

The VA sells homes that it acquires after foreclosure of a VA guaranteed loan. These home are available to veterans and non-veterans.

The properties are available for sale to the general public through the services of private sector real estate brokers. The VA cannot deal directly with purchasers. Real estate brokers receive the keys to the properties and assist prospective purchasers in finding, viewing, and offering to purchase them.

Participating brokers receive instructional material regarding the sales program, and are familiar with VA sales procedures. VA pays the sales commission.

★★

Offers to purchase VA acquired properties must be submitted on VA forms. Offers cannot be submitted on offer forms generally used in the real estate industry.

VA financing is available for most, but not all, property sales. The downpayment requirements are usually very reasonable, the interest rate is established by VA based on market conditions. Any prospective purchaser who requests VA financing to purchase a VA-owned property must have sufficient income to meet the loan payments, maintain the property, and pay all other obligation. The purchaser must have acceptable credit, and must also have enough funds remaining for family support.

Anyone interested should consult a local real estate agent to find out about VA-acquired properties listed for sale in the area.

HUD / FHA LOANS

Veterans are not eligible for VA financing based on service in World War I, Active Duty for Training in the Reserves, or Active Duty for Training in the National Guard (unless "activated" under the authority of Title 10, U.S. Code). However, these veterans may qualify for a HUD / FHA veteran's loan.

The VA's only role in the HUD / FHA program is to determine the eligibility of the veteran, and issue a *Certificate of Veteran Status*, if qualified. Under this program, financing is available for veterans at terms slightly more favorable than those available to non-veterans.

A veteran may request a *Certificate of Veteran Status* by completing VA form 26-8261a. The completed form and required attachments should be submitted to the veteran's regional VA office for a determination of eligibility.

★★

CHAPTER 19

OVERSEAS BENEFITS

MEDICAL BENEFITS

The Foreign Medical Program (FMP) is a healthcare benefits program for U.S. veterans with VA-rated service-connected conditions who are residing or traveling abroad (except Canada and the Philippines). Services provided in Canada and the Philippines are under separate jurisdictions, as indicated later in this chapter.

Under the FMP, VA assumes payment responsibility for *certain necessary medical services associated with the treatment of* **service-connected conditions.**

The Foreign Medical Program Office in Denver, Colorado has jurisdiction over all foreign provided services, with the exception of medical services received in Canada and the Philippines. It is responsible for all aspects of the program, including application processing, verification of eligibility, authorization of benefits, and payments of claims.

Generally, as long as the service is medically necessary for the treatment of a VA rated service-connected condition, it will be covered by the FMP. Additionally, the services must be accepted by VA and / or the U.S. Medical community (such as the American Medical Association and the U.S. Food and Drug Administration.)

Exclusions to Medical Benefits

The following services are not covered by the Foreign Medical Program:

- Procedures, treatments, drugs, or devices that are experimental or investigational;
- Family planning services and sterilization;
- Infertility services;
- Plastic surgery primarily for cosmetic purposes;
- Chiropractic services;
- Procedures, services, and supplies related to sex transformations;
- Non-acute institutional care such as long-term inpatient psychiatric care and nursing home care;
- Day care and day hospitalization;
- Non-medical home care (aid and attendance);

★★

- Abortions, except when the life of the mother would be endangered if the fetus were carried to term;
- Travel, meals, and lodging (including transportation costs to return to the United States)

Prosthesis

If an individual residing in a foreign country requires a prosthesis for a VA rated service-connected condition, and the cost of the prosthetic appliance is less than $300 (U.S. currency), the individual may purchase the prosthetic appliance from a local healthcare provider, and send the invoice to the FMP Office for reimbursement, or the healthcare provider may bill the VA.

If the cost of the prosthetic appliance exceeds $300 (U.S. currency), the individual must obtain preauthorization for the VA Foreign Medical Program Office (see address below).

Application Process – Registration

Although pre-registration for eligible veterans is not necessary, veterans who are permanently relocating to a country under the FMP's jurisdiction are encouraged to notify the FMP once a permanent foreign address is established. At that time, FMP will provide detailed program material, such as benefit coverage, benefit limitations, selecting healthcare providers, and claim filing instructions.

Veterans who are simply traveling, and are not planning a permanent relocation do not need to notify the FMP of their travel plans. Program materials are available, however, upon request.

The FMP can be contacted at:

VA Health Administration Center
Foreign Medical Program (FMP)
P.O. Box 65021
Denver, CO 80206-9021
Phone: (303) 331-7590
Fax: (303) 331-7803

Medical Services in Canada

The VA Medical and Regional Office Center in White River Junction, Vermont, is responsible for determining eligibility of U.S. veterans for reimbursement of medical treatment while traveling or residing in Canada. The local offices of Veterans' Affairs-Canada assists veterans in obtaining authorizations for treatment, arranging for treatment (if necessary), and providing information about the medical treatment program.

The same exclusions listed earlier in this chapter also apply to medical services in Canada, and VA assumes payment responsibility only for *certain necessary medical services associated with the treatment of service-connected conditions.*

To receive reimbursed medical treatment, an authorization must be obtained from the White River Junction office **prior to treatment** (unless an emergency situation exists).

When required by the VA to support a claim for disability benefits, Veterans' Affairs-Canada will make arrangement for disability examinations for veterans residing in Canada. In some instances, arrangements will be made locally in Canada. In other instances, arrangements will be made at bordering VA medical facilities.

Information on how to obtain medical services in Canada, including procedures for filing claims, can be obtained by contacting the following office:

VAM & RO Center (136FC)
North Hartland Road
White River Junction, VT 05009-0001
Fax: 802-296-5174

Or

Veterans Affairs-Canada
Foreign Countries Operations
Room 1055
264 Wellington Street
Ottawa, Ontario, Canada K1A 0P4
(613) 943-7461

Medical Services in the Philippines

The Republic of the Philippines is the only foreign country in which the VA operates a regional office and outpatient clinic.

The same exclusions listed earlier in this chapter also apply to medical services in the Philippines, and VA assumes payment responsibility only for *certain necessary medical services associated with the treatment of service-connected conditions.*

To receive reimbursed medical treatment, an authorization must be obtained **prior to treatment** (unless an emergency situation exists).

Information on how to obtain medical services in the Philippines, including procedures for filing claims, can be obtained by contacting the following office:

VA Outpatient Clinic (358/00)
2201 Roxas Boulevard
Pasay City 1300
Republic of the Philippines
011-632-838-4566 or (632) 833-4566

OTHER OVERSEAS BENEFITS

Virtually all VA monetary benefits, including compensation, pension, educational assistance, and burial allowances, are payable regardless of an individual's place of residence.

However, there are some program limitations in foreign jurisdictions, including:

- Home-loan guaranties are available only in the United States and selected territories and possessions.

- Educational benefits are limited to approved degree-granting programs in institutions of higher learning

Information and assistance are available to U.S. veterans worldwide at American embassies and consulates. In Canada, information and assistance are provided by the local offices of Veterans Affairs-Canada. Individuals may call toll-free within Canada, 1-888-996-2242.

In the Philippines, service is available at the VA Regional Office and Outpatient Clinic in Manila:

VA Regional Office
1131 Roxas Boulevard
Manila, Philippines
011-632-521-7521

Direct Deposit

The conventional method of direct deposit is not available outside of the U.S. However, there are foreign banks with branches in the United States, through which direct deposit can be established. Once the funds are received in the U.S. branch through electronic funds transfer, the U.S. branch transfers the money to the foreign branch.

While this process may take a few days longer than direct deposit within the United States, it is still quicker than having checks mailed overseas through the Department of State or International Priority Airmail.

★★★

CHAPTER 20

AGENT ORANGE, MUSTARD GAS AND RADIATION

AGENT ORANGE

Agent Orange was an herbicide used in Vietnam to defoliate trees and remove cover for the enemy. Agent Orange spraying missions were flown in Vietnam between January 1965 and April 1970.

VA has offered special access to health services and studies since 1978, when it initiated a medical surveillance program for Vietnam veterans with health concerns. By 1981, VA offered priority medical care to Vietnam veterans with any health problems, which may have resulted from Agent Orange exposure. That program continues today.

Determination of Service-Connected Diseases

A disease specified below, becoming manifest in a veteran, who, during active military, naval, or air service, served in the Republic of Vietnam during the period beginning on January 9, 1962, and ending on May 7, 1975 shall be considered to have been incurred in or aggravated by such service, notwithstanding that there is no record of evidence of such disease during the period of such service.

The diseases referred to above are:

- Non-Hodgkin's lymphoma becoming manifest to a degree of disability of 10% or more.

- Each soft-tissue sarcoma becoming manifest to a degree of disability of 10% ore more other than osteosarcoma, chondrosarcoma, Kaposi's sarcoma, or mesothelioma.

- Chloracne or another acne form disease consistent with chloracne becoming manifest to a degree of disability of 10% or more within one year after the last date on which the veteran performed active military, naval, or air service in the Republic of Vietnam during the period beginning on January 9, 1962, and ending on May 7, 1975.

- Hodgkin's disease becoming manifest to a degree of disability of 10% ore more.

- Porphyria cutanea tarda becoming manifest to a degree of disability of 10% ore more within a year after the last date on which the veteran performed active military, naval, or air service in the Republic of Vietnam during the period beginning on January 9, 1962, and ending on May 7, 1975.

★★★

- Respiratory cancers (cancer of the lung, bronchus, larynx, or trachea) becoming manifest to a degree of 10% or more within 30 years after the last date on which the veteran performed active military, naval, or air service in the Republic of Vietnam during the period beginning on January 9, 1962, and ending on May 7, 1975.

- Multiple myeloma becoming manifest to a degree of disability of 10% or more.

- Acute and subacute peripheral neuropathy.

- Prostate cancer.

- On November 9, 2000, VA issued a News Release stating that Diabetes Mellitus (Type-II, adult onset diabetes) is being added to the list of presumptive diseases associated with herbicide exposure. As of the writing of this book, the VA is still writing the final rules for implementing this change. Interested veterans should contact the VA for the latest information.

- Each additional disease (if any) that the Secretary of the VA determines warrants a presumption of service-connection by reason of having positive association with exposure to an herbicide agent, becomes manifest within the period (if any) prescribed in such regulations in a veteran who, during active military, naval, or air service, served in the Republic of Vietnam during the period beginning on January 9, 1962 and ending on May 7, 1975, and while so serving was exposed to that herbicide agent.

Veterans having a disease referred to above, shall be presumed to have been exposed during such service to an herbicide agent containing dioxin or 2,4-dichlorophenoxyacetic acid, and may be presumed to have been exposed during such service to any other chemical compound in an herbicide agent, unless there is affirmative evidence to establish that the veteran was not exposed to any such agent during that service.

If the Secretary of the VA later determines that a previously established presumption of service-connection for one of the above diseases is no longer warranted, all veterans currently awarded compensation on the basis of the presumption shall continue to be entitled to receive compensation. Additionally, all survivors of any such veterans who were awarded dependency and indemnity compensation shall continue to be entitled to receive dependency and indemnity compensation on that basis.

Rates of Disability Compensation

Rates of compensation depend upon the degree of disability, and follow a payment schedule that is adjusted annually and applies to all veterans. Please refer to the charts beginning on page 4 of this book.

Agent Orange Registry

VA developed the Agent Orange Registry Examination Program in 1978 to identify Vietnam veterans concerned about Agent Orange exposure. Nearly 300,000 Vietnam veterans have been provided examinations under the Registry program as of December 1999. VA maintains a computerized registry of data from these examinations. Registrants receive periodic updates on Agent Orange studies and VA policy.

VA's Advisory Committees on Health-Related Effects of Herbicides & Environmental Hazards

The VA's Advisory Committee on Health-Related Effects Of Herbicides was established in 1979 to examine issues surrounding the possible health effects of herbicides on Vietnam veterans.

VA also established the Veterans' Advisory Committee on Environmental Hazards, consisting of non-VA experts in dioxin and radiation exposure as well as several lay members, to advise the Secretary on the results of Agent Orange-related research, and regulatory, administrative and legislative initiatives.

Since passage of a 1991 law (PL 102-4), which directs VA to request that the National Academy of Sciences (NAS) review diseases associated with herbicide exposure, the committee's work has been superseded by the NAS review.

National Academy of Sciences (NAS)

The NAS reviews and evaluates scientific literature about Agent Orange. NAS reviewed more than 6,000 abstracts of scientific or medical articles and analyzed 230 epidemiological studies before its initial July 1993 report, which led to the inclusion of additional diseases on the list for presumptive service-connection. The NAS review has been continuing, with acute and subacute peripheral neuropathy and prostate cancer added to VA's presumptive list after the NAS issued an updated report in March 1996. Also based on that report's findings of new "limited or suggestive evidence" of an association between herbicides and Spina Bifida in the children of Vietnam veterans, VA proposed legislation to aid children of Vietnam veterans who suffer from that disorder, and established a reproductive outcomes research center to investigate potential environmental hazards of military service.

A separate VA study led Secretary of Veterans Affairs Togo D. West Jr. to call for legislation to benefit children who suffer from birth defects that may have been caused by their mothers' Vietnam service, not necessarily by herbicide exposure. Secretary West also asked NAS to review a study by the National Institute of Occupational Safety and Health of dioxin-exposed production workers at two U.S. plants that revealed elevated rates of diabetes among workers. A decision whether to establish a presumption of service-connection for diabetes will be made once the additional review is completed.

MUSTARD GAS EXPOSURE AND LONG-TERM HEALTH EFFECTS

In 1991, the Department of Veterans Affairs (VA) relaxed requirements for evaluating mustard gas-related compensation claims because of the confidentiality of some of the World War II testing and a lack of military medical records and follow-up. At that time, a review of studies of the effects of mustard gas exposure led VA to publish regulations authorizing service-connection and disability compensation payments to veterans who were exposed to significant levels of mustard gas and who suffer from chronic forms of certain diseases.

An estimated 4,000 servicemen participated in tests using significant concentrations of mustard gas either in chambers or field exercises in contaminated areas during World War II. This secret testing was conducted in order to develop better protective clothing, masks and skin ointments. There is no central roster of World War II participants in either the laboratory or field tests. The Army conducted tests on Army personnel in the laboratory and in the field. The test sites included:

- Edgewood Arsenal, Maryland;
- Camp Sibert, Alabama;
- Bushnell, Florida;
- Dugway Proving Ground, Utah; and
- San Jose Island, Panama Canal Zone

Military personnel from the U.S. Navy Training Center, Bainbridge, Maryland., also were sent to the Naval Research Lab in Washington, D.C., to participate in tests. Gas testing facilities also were located at Great Lakes Naval Training Center in Illinois and Camp Lejeune, North Carolina.

Institute of Medicine Study

Also in 1991, VA contracted with the Institute of Medicine to conduct a study of medical and scientific literature worldwide to determine the long-term health effects of mustard gas and Lewisite. The $600,000 VA-funded study, entitled "Veterans at Risk: The Health Effects of Mustard Gas and Lewisite," was released Jan. 6, 1993. The study found a relationship between exposure and the subsequent development of certain diseases.

Veterans Who May Be Eligible for Compensation

VA policies generally authorize service-connection and compensation payments to veterans who were exposed to mustard gas and/or Lewisite and who suffer from a number of diseases or conditions, including:

- Full-body exposure to nitrogen or sulfur mustard together with the subsequent development of chronic conjunctivitis, keratitis, corneal opacities, scar formation, or the following cancers: nasopharyngeal; laryngeal; lung (except mesothelioma); or squamous cell carcinoma of the skin;

- Full-body exposure to nitrogen or sulfur mustard -- or exposure to Lewisite -- and the subsequent development of a chronic form of laryngitis, bronchitis, emphysema, asthma or chronic obstructive pulmonary disease;

- Full-body exposure to nitrogen mustard with the subsequent development of acute nonlymphocytic leukemia.

Service-connection is not allowed if the claimed condition is due to the veteran's own willful misconduct or if there is affirmative evidence that establishes some other nonservice-related condition or event as the cause of the claimed disability.

Veterans who were exposed to significant amounts of mustard gas and have health problems that may be compensable (or their survivors) may contact the nearest VA regional office at 1-800-827-1000 for more information about benefits.

VA PROGRAMS FOR VETERANS EXPOSED TO RADIATION

VA provides special priority for enrollment for health-care services to any veteran exposed to ionizing radiation in connection with:

- Onsite participation in a test involving the atmospheric detonation of a nuclear device (without regard to whether the nation conducting the test was the United States or another nation).

- The American occupation of Hiroshima and Nagasaki, Japan, during the period beginning August 6, 1945, and ending July 1, 1946.

- Internment as a prisoner of war in Japan (or service on active duty in Japan immediately following such internment) during World War II which (as determined by the Secretary of the VA) resulted in an opportunity for exposure to ionizing radiation comparable to that of veterans described above.

In addition, these veterans are eligible to participate in the VA ionizing radiation registry examination program. VA also pays compensation to veterans and their survivors if the veteran is determined to have a disability due to radiation exposure while in service.

Radiation Statistics

Some 195,000 service members have been identified as participants in the post-World War II occupation of Hiroshima and Nagasaki, Japan. In addition, approximately 210,000 mostly military members are confirmed as participants in U.S. atmospheric nuclear tests between 1945 and 1962 in the United States and the Pacific and Atlantic oceans prior to the 1963 Limited Test Ban Treaty. The Defense Threat Reduction Agency's Nuclear Test Personnel Review program since 1978 has maintained a database of participants in atmospheric nuclear test activities. About one-fourth of the participants received no measurable dose of ionizing radiation, with fewer than one per cent of the nuclear test participants identified as having a dose of 5 rem or higher. (The current federal guideline for U.S. workplace exposure is 5 rem per year.)

★★

Determination of Service-Connected Diseases

VA may pay compensation for radiogenic diseases under two programs specific to radiation-exposed veterans and their survivors:

STATUTORY LIST

Veterans who participated in nuclear tests by the U.S. or its allies, who served with the U.S. occupation forces in Hiroshima or Nagasaki, Japan, between August 1945 and July 1946, or who were similarly exposed to ionizing radiation while a prisoner of war in Japan, are eligible for compensation for cancers specified in legislation.

The 15 types of cancer covered by these laws are:

- All forms of leukemia except chronic lymphocytic leukemia;
- Cancer of the thyroid,
- Cancer of the breast,
- Cancer of the pharynx,
- Cancer of the esophagus,
- Cancer of the stomach,
- Cancer of the small intestine,
- Cancer of the pancreas,
- Cancer of the bile ducts,
- Cancer of the gall bladder,
- Cancer of the salivary gland
- Cancer of the urinary tract;
- Lymphomas (except Hodgkin's disease);
- Multiple myeloma;
- Primary liver cancer.

REGULATORY LIST

Disability compensation claims of veterans who were exposed to radiation in service and who develop a disease within specified time periods not specified in the statutory list are governed by regulation. Under the regulations, various additional factors must be considered in determining service-connection, including amount of radiation exposure, duration of exposure, and elapsed time between exposure and onset of the disease. VA regulations identify all cancers as potentially radiogenic, as well as certain other non-malignant conditions: posterior subcapsular cataracts; non-malignant thyroid nodular disease; parathyroid adenoma; and tumors of the brain and central nervous system.

A final rule that expanded the regulatory list from more than a dozen specific cancers to add "any other cancer" (any malignancy) was published Sept. 24,

★★★

1998. The rulemaking began following a 1995 review of the radiogenicity of cancer generally by the Veterans Advisory Committee on Environmental Hazards. It concluded that, on the basis of current scientific knowledge, exposure to ionizing radiation can be a contributing factor in the development of any malignancy. VA also will consider evidence that diseases other those specified in regulation may be caused by radiation exposure.

Rates of Disability Compensation

Rates of compensation depend upon the degree of disability and follow a payment schedule that is adjusted annually and applies to all veterans. Please refer to the charts beginning on page 4 of this book.

Ionizing Radiation Registry Program

In addition to special eligibility to enroll for VA healthcare for radiation-related conditions, atomic veterans are eligible to participate in VA's Ionizing Radiation Registry examination. Under the Ionizing Radiation Registry program, VA will perform a complete physical examination, including all necessary tests, for each veteran who requests it if the veteran was exposed to ionizing radiation while participating in the nuclear weapons testing program, or if he or she served with the U.S. occupation forces in Hiroshima or Nagasaki. Veterans need not be enrolled for general VA care to be eligible for the Ionizing Radiation Registry.

★★

CHAPTER 21

SPINA BIFIDA PROGRAM

Spina bifida is the most frequently occurring permanently disabling birth defect. It affects approximately one of every 1,000 newborns in the United States. Neural tube defects (NTD) are birth defects that involve incomplete development of the brain, spinal cord, and/or protective coverings for these organs. Spina bifida, the most common NTD, results from the failure of the spine to close properly during the first month of pregnancy. (Anencephaly and encephalocele are less common types of NTDs). In severe cases, the spinal cord protrudes through the back of and may be covered by skin or a thin membrane.

Some Vietnam veterans have children with spina bifida. While Vietnam veterans and their mates are now moving out of the age category usually associated with childbirth, it is anticipated that some future births will occur and that some of these children may have birth defects, including spina bifida. Some research efforts have suggested that there may be a relationship between exposure by Vietnam veterans to Agent Orange and/or other herbicides used in Vietnam and the subsequent development of spina bifida in some of their children

Effective October 1, 1997, Public Law Number 104-204 authorized the VA to provide monetary benefits, vocational training, rehabilitation, and certain healthcare benefits to children of Vietnam veterans for disability resulting from spina bifida.

For the purpose of the Spina Bifida Program, the term **Vietnam Veteran** means an individual who performed active military, naval, or air service in the Republic of Vietnam during the period beginning on January 9, 1962, and ending May 7, 1975, without regard to the characterization of the individual's service. Service in the Republic of Vietnam includes service in the waters offshore and service in other locations if the conditions of service involved duty or visitation in the Republic of Vietnam.

MONETARY BENEFITS

VA shall pay a monthly allowance based upon the level of disability to or for a child who is suffering from spina bifida, and who is a child of a Vietnam veteran. Receipt of this allowance shall not affect the right of the child, or the right of any individual based on the child's relationship to that individual, to receive any other benefit to which the child, or that individual, may be entitled under any law administered by VA. If a child suffering from spina bifida is the natural child of two Vietnam veterans, he or she is entitled to only one monthly allowance.

The monthly allowance is set at three levels, depending upon the degree of disability suffered by the child. VA shall determine the level of disability suffered by the child in accordance with the following criteria:

Level I

- The child is able to walk without braces or other external support (although gait may be impaired); and
- Has no sensory or motor impairment of upper extremities; and
- Has an IQ of 90 or higher; and
- Is continent of urine and feces.

Level II

Provided that none of the child's disabilities are severe enough to be evaluated at Level III, and the child is:

- Ambulatory, but only with braces or other external support; or
- Has sensory or motor impairment of upper extremities, but is able to grasp pen, feed self, and perform self care; or
- Has an IQ of at least 70 but less than 90; or
- Requires drugs or intermittent catheterization or other mechanical means to maintain proper urinary bladder function, or mechanisms for proper bowel function.

Level III

- The child is unable to ambulate; or
- Has sensory or motor impairment of upper extremities severe enough to prevent grasping a pen, feeding self, and performing self care; or
- Has an IQ of 69 or less; or
- Has complete urinary or fecal incontinence

SPINA BIFIDA BENEFIT RATE TABLE (Effective 12-01-2000)	
Disability Level	*Monthly Allowance*
Level I	$221.00
Level II	$770.00
Level III	$1,317.00

★★

VOCATIONAL TRAINING FOR CHILDREN WITH SPINA BIFIDA

To qualify for entitlement to a vocational training program an applicant must be a child:

- To whom VA has awarded a monthly allowance for spina bifida; and
- For whom VA has determined that achievement of a vocational goal is reasonably feasible.

A vocational training program may not begin before a child's 18th birthday, or the date of completion of secondary schooling, whichever comes first. Depending on the need, a child may be provided up to 24 months of full-time training.

HEALTHCARE BENEFITS

In addition to monetary allowances, vocational training and rehabilitation, the Department of Veterans Affairs (VA) also provides VA-financed healthcare benefits to Vietnam veterans' birth children diagnosed with spina bifida. For the purpose of this program, spina bifida is defined as all forms or manifestations of spina bifida (except spina bifida occulta), including complications or associated medical conditions related to spina bifida according to the scientific literature.

Eligibility for VA spina bifida healthcare benefits is limited to birth children of Vietnam veterans who have been diagnosed with spina bifida. Since benefits are based upon eligibility determinations made by VA regional offices, prospective beneficiaries must first contact a regional office to initiate the application process. The local VA regional office can be contacted at 1-800-827-1000.

Healthcare benefits available under this program are limited to those necessary for the treatment of spina bifida and related medical conditions. Beneficiaries should be aware that this program is not a comprehensive healthcare plan and does not cover care that is unrelated to spina bifida.

Administration of the program is centralized to VA's Health Administration Center (HAC) in Denver, Colorado. HAC is responsible for all aspects of the spina bifida healthcare program, including the authorization of benefits and the subsequent processing and payment of claims. All inquiries regarding healthcare benefits should be made directly to HAC.

Healthcare benefits may be claimed for services and supplies starting on the effective date specified in the VA regional office award letter.

Beneficiaries in receipt of a VA regional office spina bifida award will receive an identification card from the Health Administration Center.

In general, the program covers most healthcare services and supplies that are medically or psychologically necessary for the treatment of conditions related to spina bifida. While some services require specific advance approval or preauthorization , the following services are specifically excluded from coverage.

★★

- Care unrelated to spina bifida
- Care as part of a grant study or research program
- Care considered experimental or investigational
- Drugs not approved by the u.s. food and drug administration for commercial marketing
- Services, procedures or supplies for which the beneficiary has no legal obligation to pay, such as services obtained at a health fair
- Services provided outside the scope of the provider's license or certification
- Services rendered by providers suspended or sanctioned by a federal agency

Covered Benefits

The following services are covered and paid by VA providing they are determined to be medically necessary for the treatment of spina bifida and related conditions, and accepted by the U.S./VA medical community. (See also preauthorization requirements above.)

- Inpatient services
- Outpatient services
- Pharmacy services to include supplies and over-the-counter items
- Mental health and substance abuse services
- Dental services
- Emergency services
- Durable medical equipment (furnished through VA sources unless specifically approved for private purchase)
- Preventative care
- Rehabilitative care
- Home care
- Nursing home care
- Respite care
- Training family members
- Travel expenses to include meals, lodging, commercial travel tickets, ambulance or special mode travel, and attendant * from the beneficiary's residence to the place of medical treatment (includes travel to and from Shriners hospitals for children)
- Travel benefits for an attendant may be covered when it has been determined that the beneficiary's physical or mental condition requires the presence of an attendant. All requests for attendant travel benefits require preauthorization.

★★

Selecting Healthcare Providers

Beneficiaries may select the provider of their choice as long as the provider is an approved healthcare provider. Regardless of the providers selected, please be sure that they are aware of the program's benefit limitations, preauthorization requirements, claim filing instructions, as well as how to reach us for assistance.

In addition to approved healthcare providers, some services may also be obtained from VA healthcare facilities. An alternative source to VA-financed healthcare is cost-free healthcare available through the Shriners Hospitals for Children-a nonprofit charitable corporation offering comprehensive services to children under the age of 18. (See directory of Shriners Hospitals for Children below.)

CLAIMS

Claims are to be mailed directly to VA's Health Administration Center at the following address.

VA Health Administration Center
PO Box 65025
Denver CO 80206-9025

As a safeguard against claims getting lost in the mail, beneficiaries should keep copies of all claim documents submitted.

Filing Deadlines

Claims must be filed with the Health Administration Center no later than:

- One year after the date of service; or
- In the case of inpatient care, one year after the date of discharge; or
- In the case of a VA regional office award for retroactive eligibility, 180 days following beneficiary notification of the award.

Payments

Approved healthcare providers will be paid 100% of the VA-determined allowable charge for covered services. VA payment for covered services constitutes payment in full. Federal regulations prohibit providers from seeking any additional monies from beneficiaries and third party payers such as private insurers, for services paid by VA.

★★

Note: If the beneficiary pays for care and subsequently files a claim for reimbursement, VA payment to the beneficiary will be limited to the VA-allowed amount. For this reason, beneficiaries are advised not to pay their providers-but instead, have the providers bill HAC directly.

Other Health Insurance

While VA assumes full responsibility for the cost of services related to the treatment of spina bifida and associated conditions, third-party insurers including Medicare and Medicaid, assume payment responsibility for services unrelated to the VA-covered conditions.

Explanation of Benefits

Upon completion of claim processing, an EOB will be mailed to the beneficiary. If a provider files the claim, an EOB will be mailed to them also. The EOB is a summarization of the action taken on the claim and contains, at a minimum, the following information.

- Beneficiary name
- Description of services and/or supplies provided
- Dates of service or supplies provided
- Amount billed
- VA-allowed amount
- To whom payment, if any, was made
- Reasons for denial (if applicable)

Reconsideration of Claims / Appeals

If a healthcare provider, beneficiary or beneficiary's representative disagrees with a claim determination, including the VA-allowed amount, a request for reconsideration of the disputed determination may be made. To do so, the request must:

- Be in writing;
- Be accompanied by a copy of the EOB in question; and
- State the specific issue that is being disputed, why the VA determination is considered to be in error, and include any new and relevant information not previously considered.

To meet the filing deadline, requests for reconsideration are to be mailed to the following address within one year of the date of the initial EOB:

Chief, Administrative Division
VA Health Administration Center
PO Box 65025
Denver CO 80206-9025

★★

Upon complete review of the request and all the relevant documentation and evidence, a written determination will be mailed to the claimant.

★★★

CHAPTER 22

BENEFITS FOR POST-TRAUMATIC STRESS DISORDER AND SEXUAL TRAUMA

POST-TRAUMATIC STRESS DISORDER (PTSD)

PTSD is an anxiety disorder resulting from a psychologically stressful event beyond the scope of "normal" human experience. The trauma may be experienced alone (rape or assault) or in the company of groups of people (military combat). Stressors producing PTSD include natural disasters (floods, earthquakes), accidental man-made disasters (car accidents, airplane crashes, large fires) or deliberate man-made disasters (bombing, torture, death camps). Symptoms include recurrent thoughts of a traumatic event, reduced involvement in work or outside interests, hyper alertness, anxiety and irritability. The disorder apparently is more severe and longer lasting when the stress is of human design. Studies show that PTSD affects 30 percent of war zone veterans, including those who saw combat in World War II, Korea, Vietnam, the Persian Gulf and Bosnia.

Vet Centers

A nationwide system of community-based counseling centers, known as Vet Centers, provides counseling for psychological war trauma. Readjustment counseling features a non-medical setting, a mix of social services, community outreach activities, psychological counseling for war-related experiences, and family counseling. These services are designed to assist combat-affected and other veterans attain a well-adjusted post-war work and family life. Implemented by VA in 1979, Vet Centers were initially designed for Vietnam veterans. Current law has extended eligibility for the program to any veteran who has served in the military in combat operations during any period of armed hostility. VA operates more than 200 Vet Centers in all 50 states, Puerto Rico, the Virgin Islands, the District of Columbia and Guam. The centers are staffed by interdisciplinary teams including psychologists, social workers, nurses and paraprofessionals.

For a complete listing of Vet Centers, please refer to page 122 of this book.

VA Medical Center Programs

While PTSD treatment is available through all of VA's 171 medical centers, a VA network of 124 facilities offers specialized inpatient and outpatient treatment. One notable program consists of PTSD clinical teams that provide outpatient treatment but also work closely with other VA treatment programs, including Vet Centers, to coordinate services and provide information on PTSD throughout the medical center and the community.

In addition to 83 PTSD clinical teams, VA operates 22 specialized inpatient units around the country, plus 13 brief-treatment units, 11 residential rehabilitation programs, and four PTSD day hospitals. There also are four outpatient Women's Stress Disorder and Treatment Teams and eight outpatient-based PTSD Teams Substance Use Disorder demonstration projects. A special focus in the program expansions has included underserved and minority populations, such as African Americans, Hispanics and Native Americans. A specialized PTSD inpatient treatment unit serves women veterans at the Palo Alto, Calif., VA Medical Center's Menlo Park Division.

National PTSD Center

In 1989, VA established the National Center for Post-Traumatic Stress Disorder -- a center for clinical research, training and information on PTSD. The center initially consisted of five divisions with distinct, but complementary responsibilities:

- Behavioral Science,

- Clinical Neurosciences,

- Education,

- Evaluation, and

- Executive and Resource Center Divisions.

Growing recognition of the dimensions of PTSD has brought new programs, such as the Women's Health Sciences Division, located at the Boston VA Medical Center, and the Pacific Islands Division in Honolulu.

Disability Compensation

PTSD can be a service-connected disability.

The process of applying for a VA disability for PTSD can take several months, and can be both complicated and quite stressful. The Veterans Service Organizations provide Service Officers at no cost to help veterans and family members pursue VA disability claims.

Service Officers are familiar with every step in the application and interview process, and can provide both technical guidance and moral support. In addition, some Service Officers particularly specialize in assisting veterans with PTSD disability claims. Even if a veteran has not been a member of a specific Veterans Service Organization, the veteran still can request the assistance of a Service Officer working for that organization. In order to get representation by a qualified and helpful Service Officer, you can directly contact the local office of any Veterans Service Organization -- or ask for recommendations from other veterans who have applied for VA disability, or from a PTSD specialist at a VA PTSD clinic or a Vet Center.

★★

SEXUAL TRAUMA

Some veterans (women and men) suffered personal assault and/or sexual trauma while serving on active military duty. They might still struggle with fear, anxiety, embarrassment, or profound anger as a result of these experiences.

VA defines sexual trauma as any lingering physical, emotional, or psychological symptoms resulting from a physical assault of a sexual nature, or battery of a sexual nature. Examples of this are:

- Rape,
- Physical assault,
- Domestic Battering, and
- Stalking

Compensation for Disabilities

Disability Compensation is a monthly payment to a veteran disabled by an injury or a disease incurred or aggravated on active service. The veteran must have been discharged under other than dishonorable conditions to be eligible. The individual must currently be suffering from disabling symptoms to receive compensation. Refer to page 2 of this book for information regarding Disability Compensation.

★★★

CHAPTER 23

BENEFITS FOR FORMER PRISONERS OF WAR (POWS)

Former American POWs are eligible for special veterans benefits from the VA, including medical care in VA hospitals and disability compensation for injuries and disease presumed to be caused by internment. Studies have shown that the physical deprivation and psychological stress endured as a captive have life-long effects on subsequent health, social adjustment, and vocational adjustment.

In 1981, Congress passed Public Law 97-37 entitled, "Former Prisoners of War Benefit Act." This law accomplished several things. It established an Advisory Committee on Former Prisoners of War and mandated medical and dental care. It also identified certain diagnoses as presumptive service-connected conditions for former POWs. Other public laws passed since then, and a policy decision by the Secretary of Veterans Affairs in 1993, have added additional diagnoses to the list of presumptive conditions.

On November 30, 1999, the President signed into law the Veterans Millennium Healthcare and Benefits Act, Pub. L. 106-117. Section 501, a provision of the law, authorizes VA to pay DIC under 38 U.S.C. 1318 to the survivors of former Prisoners of War who died after September 30, 1999, and who were rated totally disabled continuously for a period of not less than one year immediately preceding death for a service-connected disability. This provision is effective November 30, 1999.

A POW Coordinator has been designated at each VA regional office. The POW Coordinator can furnish former POWs with information about the benefits and services available to them.

HEALTHCARE

Former POWs are recognized as a special category of veterans, and will be placed on one of the top three (out of seven) Priority Groups established for VA healthcare by Congress.

Veterans who were POWs for 90 days or more may receive complete dental care. (Veterans held less than 90 days should check with the nearest VA facility to see if they may qualify for dental care under other provisions of the law.)

Former POWs are eligible for any prosthetic item, including eyeglasses and hearing aids. A VA physician must order the prosthetic items, when medically indicated, for eligible veterans.

Veterans may enroll in VA healthcare by completing VA Form 10-10, Application for Medical Benefits.

★★

DISABILITY COMPENSATION

Veterans are encouraged to apply for VA disability Compensation for any disabilities related to service, whether they were a POW or not. Some disabilities are *presumptive*, which means that if a veteran is diagnosed with certain conditions, and the veteran was a POW for at least 30 days, the VA presumes the captivity caused the disability.

Presumptions Of Service-Connection Relating To Certain Diseases And Disabilities For Former Prisoners Of War

In the case of any veteran who is a former prisoner of war, and who was detained or interned for not less than thirty days, any of the following which became manifest to a degree of 10% or more after active military, naval or air service, shall be considered to have been incurred in or aggravated by such service, notwithstanding that there is no record of such disease during the period of service:

- Avitaminosis
- Beriberi (including beriberi heart disease, which includes Ischemic Heart Disease-coronary artery disease-for former POWs who suffered during captivity from edema-swelling of the legs or feet- also known as "wet" beriberi)
- Chronic dysentery
- Helminthiasis
- Malnutrition (including optic atrophy associated with malnutrition)
- Pellagra
- Any other nutritional deficiency
- Psychosis
- Any of the anxiety states
- Dysthymic disorder (or depressive neurosis)
- Organic residuals of frostbite, if the VA determines the veteran was interned in climatic conditions consistent with the occurrence of frostbite
- Post-traumatic osteoarthritis
- Peripheral neuropathy, except where directly related to infectious causes
- Irritable bowel syndrome
- Peptic ulcer disease

Former POWs should file a claim by completing VA Form 21-526, Application for Compensation or Pension. The VA also offers a POW protocol exam. This is a one-time exam available to all former POWs, and is conducted at a VA medical facility to help determine if any presumptive disabilities exist.

★★

PRISONER OF WAR MEDAL

A Prisoner of War Medal is available to any member of the U.S. Armed Forces taken prisoner during any armed conflict dating from World War I. Please refer to page 315 of this book for detailed information on how to obtain medals.

★★★

CHAPTER 24

BENEFITS FOR FILIPINO VETERANS

FOUR CATEGORIES

For purposes of VA benefits and services, the service of members of the Philippine armed forces can be categorized as service in one of four groups:

Regular Philippine Scouts (also called Old Philippine Scouts)

These veterans enlisted in the Armed Forces of the United States before October 6, 1945. Regular Philippine Scouts, or "old scouts" were Filipino-manned special forces, units of the U.S. Army whose officers were Americans.

Special Philippine Scouts (also called New Philippine Scouts)

These individuals enlisted or reenlisted in Filipino-manned units of the U.S. Army on or after October 6, 1945.

Commonwealth Army of the Philippines (also called the Philippine Army)

These individuals served in the Philippine Army, and were ordered into the service of the U.S. Armed Forces by the President on July 26, 1941. Their service in the U.S. Armed Forces was terminated June 30, 1946.

Recognized Guerillas

These are individuals who provided acceptable service in resistance units recognized by, and cooperating with the United States, during the period April 20, 1942, through June 30, 1946

ELIGIBILITY FOR VA BENEFITS

Regular Philippine Scouts

These veterans are entitled to all VA benefits, under the same criteria as veterans of the U.S. Armed Forces.

Monetary benefits are payable in Dollars, at the full rate authorized.

Special Philippine Scouts

These veterans and eligible dependents are entitled to:

• Disability Compensation

★★

- Clothing Allowance
- Dependency & Indemnity Compensation (DIC)
- Hospital care and Outpatient Treatment for service-connected conditions, provided treatment is in the U.S., or at a facility over which the VA has jurisdiction, or has contracted.

Note: Monetary benefits are payable at a rate of $.50 of each Dollar authorized. (Commissioned officers are paid at the full rate authorized.)

Benefit Programs Not Available:

- Non-service connected pension benefits for veterans and dependents;
- Hospital care and outpatient treatment for service-connected or non-service-connected conditions, if the care is provided outside of the U.S., or at facilities outside of the U.S. over which the VA has no jurisdiction, or has not contracted;
- Dental care
- VA loans such as home loan guarantees;
- Specially adapted homes;
- Automobile or other conveyances;
- Service-disabled veterans insurance (RH);
- Burial and funeral expense allowance;
- Plot or interment allowance;
- Burial flag;
- Burial in national cemeteries;
- Headstones and markers

Commonwealth Army:

These veterans and eligible dependents are entitled to:

- Disability Compensation
- Clothing Allowance
- Dependency & Indemnity Compensation (DIC)
- Burial Allowance
- Burial Flag
- Hospital care and Outpatient Treatment for service-connected conditions, provided treatment is in the U.S., or at a facility over which the VA has jurisdiction, or has contracted.

Note: Monetary benefits are payable at a rate of $.50 of each Dollar authorized.

★★

Benefit Programs Not Available:

- Non-service connected pension benefits for veterans and dependents;
- Hospital care and outpatient treatment for service-connected or non-service-connected conditions, if the care is provided outside of the U.S., or at facilities outside of the U.S. over which the VA has no jurisdiction, or has not contracted;
- Dental care
- VA loans such as home loan guarantees;
- Specially adapted homes;
- Automobile or other conveyances;
- Service-disabled veterans insurance (RH);
- Plot or interment allowance;
- Burial in national cemeteries;
- Headstones and markers

Recognized Guerilla

These veterans and eligible dependents are entitled to:

- Disability Compensation
- Clothing Allowance
- Dependency & Indemnity Compensation (DIC)
- Burial Allowance
- Burial Flag
- Hospital care and Outpatient Treatment for service-connected conditions, provided treatment is in the U.S., or at a facility over which the VA has jurisdiction, or has contracted.

Note: Monetary benefits are payable at a rate of $.50 of each Dollar authorized.

Benefit Programs Not Available:
- Non-service connected pension benefits for veterans and dependents;
- Hospital care and outpatient treatment for service-connected or non-service-connected conditions, if the care is provided outside of the U.S., or at facilities outside of the U.S. over which the VA has no jurisdiction, or has not contracted;
- Dental care
- VA loans such as home loan guarantees;
- Specially adapted homes;
- Automobile or other conveyances;

★★

- Service-disabled veterans insurance (RH);
- Plot or interment allowance;
- Burial in national cemeteries;
- Headstones and markers

Note: veterans may be eligible for additional healthcare services at the Veteran's Memorial Medical Center, a facility in Manila operated by the Philippine government.

SPECIAL UPDATE –

New Law Signed By President Clinton October 27, 2000 Expands Benefits To Certain Filipino Veterans

Bills signed into law by President Clinton aid certain Filipino veterans residing in the United States who fought alongside American troops during World War II.

Two new laws will enable VA to improve benefits and services to certain World War II veterans of the Philippine Commonwealth Army and recognized guerilla groups with service-connected conditions who reside permanently in the United States today.

Although the laws make no additional Filipino veterans eligible for VA disability compensation, those Filipino veterans living in the United States who are U.S. citizens or permanent aliens and who have an existing service-connected disability will now be paid at a full, rather than half, rate.

Currently, these veterans may receive care at VA facilities in the United States only for their service-connected conditions. Under the change in law, these service-disabled Filipino veterans will be provided hospital and nursing home care and outpatient medical services regardless of cause, service-related or not, under the same rules as for U.S. veterans. The new law also allows VA to treat non-service-related conditions of U.S. veterans and Old Philippine Scouts at its Manila Outpatient Clinic.

The "Veterans Benefits and Healthcare Improvement Act of 2000" contains provisions extending eligibility for future burial in VA national cemeteries to certain World War II veterans of the Philippine Commonwealth Army and recognized guerilla groups living in the United States. Eligible will be those who, at the time of death, either were citizens of the United States or had permanent residence status.

Monetary burial benefits, funeral expenses and plot allowances will be payable at an increased rate for certain disabled World War II veterans of the Philippine Commonwealth Army and recognized guerilla groups residing in the United States. They must have been either U.S. citizens or admitted for permanent residence.

(At the time of publication, specific information on when these increased benefits will take effect was unavailable. Please contact the VA at 1-800-827-1000 for up-to-date information.)

CHAPTER 25

BENEFITS FOR ALLIED VETERANS

In consideration of reciprocal services extended to the United States, the VA, upon request of the proper officials of the government of any nation allied or associated with the U.S. in World War I (except any nation which was an enemy of the U.S. during World War II), or in World War II, may furnish to discharged members of the armed forces of such governments, under agreements requiring reimbursement in cash for incurred expenses, medical, surgical, and dental treatment, hospital care, transportation and traveling expenses, prosthetic appliances, education, training, or similar benefits authorized by the laws of such nation for its veterans.

Hospitalization in a VA facility shall not be offered, except in emergencies, unless there are available beds surplus to the needs of veterans of the U.S. The VA may also pay the court costs and other expenses incident to the proceedings taken for the commitment of such discharged members who are mentally incompetent to institutions for the care or treatment of the insane.

The VA may contract for necessary services in private, State, and other Government hospitals.

All amounts received by the VA as reimbursement for such services shall be credited to the current appropriation of the VA from which expenses were made.

Persons who served in the active service in the armed forces of any government allied with the U.S. in World War II, and who, at time of entrance into such active service, were citizens of the U.S. shall, by virtue of such service, and if otherwise qualified, be entitled to the VA's Training and Rehabilitation Benefits and Housing and Small Business Loans to the same extent as veterans of World War II are entitled. No such benefit shall be extended to any person who is not a resident of the United States at the time of filing claim, or to any person who has applied for and received the same or similar benefit from the government in whose armed forces such person served.

Any person who served during World War I or World War II as a member of any armed force of the Government of Czechoslovakia or Poland, and participated while so serving in armed conflict with an enemy of the U.S., and has been a citizen of the U.S. for at least ten years shall, by virtue of such service, and upon satisfactory evidence thereof, be entitled to hospital and domiciliary care and medical services within the United States to the same extent as if such service had been performed in the Armed Forces of the United States, unless such person is entitled to, or would, upon application, to payment for equivalent care and services under a program established by the foreign government concerned for persons who served in its armed forces in World War I or World War II.

In order to assist the VA in making a determination of proper service eligibility, each applicant for these benefits must furnish an authenticated certification from the French Ministry of Defense or the British War Office as to records in either such Office which clearly indicate military service of the applicant in the Czechoslovakian or Polish armed forces, and subsequent service in or with the armed forces of France or Great Britain during the period of World War I or World War II.

★★

CHAPTER 26

BENEFITS FOR CERTAIN NON-MILITARY GROUPS

MERCHANT MARINE SEAMEN

The Department of Defense announced January 19, 1988, that certain Merchant Marine seamen now qualify as veterans. (The original dates were December 7, 1941 to August 14, 1945. On November 11, 1998, the qualifying dates were extended from August 15, 1945 through December 31, 1946.)

Merchant seamen who engaged in active, ocean-going service from December 7, 1941 to December 31, 1946 are eligible to apply for a certificate of release or discharge from the DoD. This certificate will then entitle the holder to apply for VA benefits currently available to World War II veterans. (Civil Service crew members aboard U.S. Army Transport Service and Naval Transportation vessels in ocean-going service or foreign waters were included in the DoD action.)

Generally, the newly designated veterans and their survivors are eligible to apply for the same benefits that are available to other World War II veterans. These benefits include:

- Medical care;
- Service-connected disability compensation;
- Pension;
- VA-guaranteed home loans;
- Burial benefits;
- Certain survivors' benefits.

These veterans are not eligible for A-administered education programs, although in certain limited circumstances they may establish eligibility for vocational rehabilitation.

Applying for Certificate of Release (Obtaining Veteran Status or Extension of Veteran Status)

Interested mariners or survivors should complete the following steps and mail to the proper address:

1. Compete Form DD2168 (available from all VA regional offices). Supply as much information as possible.
2. Include photocopies of discharges, identification, and any other supporting documents.

★★

3. Survivors need to include a certified death certificate. (The Coast Guard will issue documents for a person listed as an official casualty list without a death certificate.)

4. No fee is required if service was between December 7, 1941 and August 14, 1945.

5. If service was between August 15, 1945 and December 31, 1946, include a check or money order for $30 payable to U.S. Treasury.

6. Send to:

   U.S. Merchant Marine:
   World War II Merchant Mariner Qualifications
   Highland Community Bank
   P.O. Box 804118
   Chicago, IL 60601-4118

   U.S. Army Transport Service:
   U. S. Army Reserve Personnel Command
   Attention: PSV-V
   One Reserve Way
   St. Louis, MO 63132-5200

   U.S. Navy Transport Service:
   Naval Military Personnel Command (NMPC-3)
   Navy Department
   Washington, DC 20370-5300

OTHER NON-MILITARY GROUPS

Through the years, a number of non-military groups have provided military-related service to the United States. Many of these groups have been formally recognized by the Department of Defense, and granted VA benefits.

Service in the following groups has been certified as active military service for benefits purposes:

- Women's Air Force Service Pilots (WASPs)
- Signal Corps Female Telephone Operators Unit of World I
- Engineer Field Clerks
- Women's Army Auxiliary Corps (WAAC)
- Quartermaster Corps female clerical employees serving with the American Expeditionary Forces in World War I
- Civilian employees of Pacific naval air bases who actively participated in defense of Wake Island during World War II
- Reconstruction aides and dietitians in World War I
- Male civilian ferry pilots
- Wake Island defenders from Guam

- Civilian personnel assigned to OSS secret intelligence
- Guam Combat Patrol
- Quartermaster Corps members of the Keswick crew on Corregidor during World War II
- U.S. civilians who participated in the defense of Bataan
- U.S. merchant seamen who served on blockships in support of Operation Mulberry in the World War II invasion of Normandy
- American merchant marines in oceangoing service during World War II
- Civilian Navy IFF radar technicians who served in combat areas of the Pacific during World War II
- U.S. civilians of the American Field Service who served overseas in World War I
- U.S. civilians of the American Field Service who served overseas under U.S. armies and U.S. army groups in World War II
- U.S. civilian employees of American Airlines who served overseas in a contract with the Air Transport Command between Dec. 14, 1941, and Aug. 14, 1945
- Civilian crewmen of U.S. Coast and Geodetic Survey vessels who served in areas of immediate military hazard while conducting cooperative operations with and for the U.S. Armed Forces between Dec. 7, 1941, and Aug. 15, 1945
- Members of the American Volunteer Group (Flying Tigers) serving between Dec. 7, 1941, and July 18, 1942
- U.S. civilian flight crew and aviation ground support employees of United Air Lines who served overseas in a contract with Air Transport Command between Dec. 14, 1941, and Aug. 14, 1945
- U.S. civilian flight crew and aviation ground support employees of Transcontinental and Western Air, Inc. (TWA), who served overseas in a contract with the Air Transport Command between Dec. 14, 1941, and Aug. 14, 1945
- U.S. civilian flight crew and aviation ground support employees of Consolidated Vultee Aircraft Corp. (Consairway Division) who served overseas in a contract with Air Transport Command between Dec. 14, 1941, and Aug. 14, 1945
- U.S. civilian flight crew and aviation ground support employees of Pan American World Airways and its subsidiaries and affiliates, who served overseas in a contract with the Air Transport Command and Naval Air Transport Service between Dec. 14, 1941, and Aug. 14, 1945
- Honorably discharged members of the American Volunteer Guard, Eritrea Service Command, between June 21, 1942, and March 31, 1943
- U.S. civilian flight crew and aviation ground support employees of Northwest Airlines who served overseas under the airline's contract with Air Transport Command from Dec. 14, 1941, through Aug. 14, 1945

★★★

- U.S. civilian female employees of the U.S. Army Nurse Corps who served in the defense of Bataan and Corregidor during the period January 2, 1942 to February 3, 1945

- U.S. Flight crew and aviation ground support employees of Northeast Airlines Atlantic Division, who served overseas as a result of Northeast Airlines' contract with the Air Transport Command during the period December 7, 1941 through August 14, 1945

- U.S. civilian flight crew and aviation ground support employees of Braniff Airways, who served overseas in the North Atlantic or under the jurisdiction of the North Atlantic Wing, Air Transport Command, as a result of a contract with the Air Transport Command during the period February 26, 1942 through August 14, 1945

For the service to qualify as military-related service, the Defense Secretary must certify that the group has provided active military service. Individual members must be issued a discharge by the Defense Secretary, which can then be used to qualify for VA benefits.

★★★

CHAPTER 27

NATURALIZATION PREFERENCE

Aliens with honorable service in the U.S. Armed Forces during hostilities (periods of hostilities must be declared by the President) may be naturalized without having to comply with the general requirements for naturalization. To qualify for naturalization preference, an alien must have:

- Been lawfully admitted to the United States for permanent residence; or
- Been inducted, enlisted, reenlisted or extended an enlistment in the Armed Forces while within:
  - United States, or
  - Puerto Rico, or
  - Guam, or
  - Virgin Islands of the United States, or
  - Canal Zone, or
  - American Samoa, or
  - Northern Marianas, or
  - Swain's Island

Aliens with honorable service in the U.S. Armed Forces for three years or more during periods not considered periods of conflict or hostility by Executive Order may be naturalized, provided they have been lawfully admitted to the United States for permanent residence. Applications must be made while on active duty, or within six months of discharge.

Aliens who have served honorably for at least 12 years after Oct. 15, 1978, may be granted special immigrant status. To be eligible for this benefit the person must have enlisted outside the United States pursuant to a treaty or agreement between the United States and the Philippines, the Federated States of Micronesia or the Republic of the Marshall Islands. In addition, Filipinos with active-duty service during World War II in the Philippine Scouts, Commonwealth Army of the Philippines or a recognized guerrilla unit may be naturalized without having been admitted for lawful permanent residence or having enlisted or reenlisted in the United States. Such persons must have submitted their applications to the Immigration and Naturalization Service by Feb. 2, 1995.

Aliens who died as a result of wounds incurred or disease contracted during periods of hostilities declared by the President may receive recognition as U.S. citizens. An application may be submitted by the person's next of kin or other authorized representative. (This posthumous citizenship is honorary only, and does not confer any other benefits to the person's surviving relatives.) For assistance, contact the nearest office of the Immigration and Naturalization Service, Justice Department.

★★

CHAPTER 28

HOMELESS VETERANS

Approximately one-third of the adult homeless population living on the streets or in shelters have served their country in the armed services. Many other veterans are considered at risk because of poverty, lack of support from family and friends and precarious living conditions in overcrowded or substandard housing.

VA has many benefits and services to assist homeless veterans, including:

HEALTHCARE FOR HOMELESS VETERANS PROGRAMS (HCHV)

VA's Healthcare for Homeless Veterans Program (HCHV) operates at 76 sites, where extensive outreach, physical and psychiatric health exams, treatment, referrals, and ongoing case management are provided to homeless veterans with mental health problems, including substance abuse. As appropriate, HCHV program places homeless veterans needing longer-term treatment into one of its 200 contract community-based facilities

DOMICILIARY CARE FOR HOMELESS VETERANS PROGRAM (DCHV)

VA's Domiciliary Care for Homeless Veterans (DCHV) Program provides medical care and rehabilitation in a residential setting on VA medical center grounds to eligible ambulatory veterans disabled by medical or psychiatric disorders, injury or age and who do not need hospitalization or nursing home care.

The domiciliaries conduct outreach and referral; admission screening and assessment; medical and psychiatric evaluation; treatment, vocational counseling and rehabilitation; and post-discharge community support.

INPATIENT AND OUTPATIENT HEALTHCARE

VA hospitals and outpatient clinics provide eligible veterans with comprehensive physical and mental healthcare, alcohol and substance abuse treatment, rehabilitation treatment, and other specialized services.

READJUSTMENT COUNSELING CENTERS (VET CENTERS)

Vet Centers help veterans through community outreach. They offer specialized services, such as group, individual and family counseling, to help eligible veterans overcome psychological difficulties or to resolve conflicts that may be contributing to their homelessness. They also provide referral services, connecting veterans to VA programs and community services.

★★

BENEFITS AND ENTITLEMENTS

VA annually awards more than $17 billion in disability benefits to millions of veterans. For many of these veterans, the VA payments are the major source of income, and serve to prevent homelessness. VA's fiduciary Program provides specialized case management to over 67,000 veterans.

ACQUIRED PROPERTY SALES FOR HOMELESS PROVIDERS PROGRAM

Acquired Property Sales for Homeless Providers Program makes available properties VA obtains through foreclosures on VA-insured mortgages for sale to homeless provider organizations at a discount of 20 to 50 percent.

HUD-VA SUPPORTED HOUSING (VASH) PROGRAM

HUD-VA Supported Housing (VASH) Program, a joint program with the Department of Housing and Urban Development (HUD), provides permanent housing and ongoing treatment services to the harder-to-serve homeless mentally ill veterans and those suffering from substance abuse disorders.

VA'S SUPPORTED HOUSING PROGRAM

VA's Supported Housing Program is like the HUD-VASH program in that VA staff help homeless veterans secure long-term transitional or permanent housing and offer ongoing case management services to help them remain in housing at a low cost the veteran can afford. It differs from HUD-VASH in that dedicated Section 8 housing vouchers are not available to homeless veterans in the program. VA staff work with private landlords, public housing authorities and nonprofit organizations to find creative housing arrangements.

VA EXCESS PROPERTY FOR HOMELESS VETERANS INITIATIVE

VA Excess Property for Homeless Veterans Initiative provides for the distribution of Federal Excess Personal Property, such as clothing, footwear, socks, sleeping bags, blankets and other items to homeless veterans through VA Medical Centers Domiciliaries and other outreach activities.

HOMELESS PROVIDERS GRANT AND PER DIEM PROGRAM

The Homeless Providers Grant and Per Diem Program provides grants and per diem payments to assist public and nonprofit organizations to establish and operate new supportive housing and supportive service centers for homeless veterans. Grant funds may also be used to assist organizations in purchasing vans to conduct outreach or provide transportation for homeless veterans.

★★

PROJECT CHALLENGE

Project CHALENG (Community Homelessness Assessment, Local Education and Networking Groups) for Veterans is a nationwide initiative in which VA medical center and regional office directors work with other federal, state and local agencies and nonprofit organizations to assess the needs of homeless veterans, develop action plans to meet identified needs and develop directories that contain local community resources to be used by homeless veterans.

OTHER ASSISTANCE

- Many VBA regional offices have designated staff who serve as coordinators and points of contact for homeless veterans.

- The Homeless Eligibility Clarification Act enables eligible veterans without a fixed address to receive VA benefits checks at VA regional offices. VBA also has instituted procedures to reduce the processing times for homeless veterans' benefits claims.

- Drop-In Centers provide homeless veterans who sleep in shelters or on the streets at night with safe, daytime environments. Some of these centers offer therapeutic activities and programs to improve daily living skills, meals, and a place to shower and wash clothes. At these centers, veterans also participate in other VA programs that provide more extensive assistance, including a variety of therapeutic and rehabilitative activities. Linkage with longer-term assistance also is available.

- Compensated Work-Therapy (CWT) and Compensated Work-Therapy/Transitional Residence Programs offer structured work opportunities and supervised therapeutic housing for at-risk and homeless veterans with physical, psychiatric and substance abuse disorders. VA contracts with private industry and the public sector for work to be done by these veterans, who learn new job skills, relearn successful work habits and regain a sense of self-esteem and self-worth. The veterans are paid for their work and, in turn, make a monthly payment toward maintenance and upkeep of the residence.

★★

CHAPTER 29

BENEFITS FOR FEMALE VETERANS

Female veterans are entitled to all of the benefits available to male veterans, including:

- Disability Compensation For Service-Related Disabilities
- Disability Pension For Non-Service Related Disabilities
- Education Assistance Programs
- Work-Study Allowance
- Vocational Rehabilitation And Counseling
- Insurance
- Home Loan Benefits
- Medical Inpatient And Outpatient Care
- Substance Abuse Treatment And Counseling
- Sexual Trauma And Assault Counseling
- Nursing Home Care
- Burial Benefits
- Burial In A VA National Cemetery
- Employment Assistance
- Survivors' Benefit Programs

VA has designed services and programs to be responsive to the gender-specific needs of female veterans.. VA offers comprehensive healthcare services for female veterans, including:

- Counseling for sexual trauma
- Pap smears
- Mammography
- General reproductive healthcare

In 1983, Public Law 98-160 called for the creation of the Advisory Committee on Women Veterans. The Committee continues to review VA programs, policy and the healthcare services for female veterans, and publishes their findings.

In November 1994, Public Law 103-446 established the Center for Women Veterans in the Department of Veterans Affairs under the Office of the Secretary. The main mission of the Center is to review VA programs and services for female veterans, and assure that female veterans receive benefits

★★

and services on a par with male veterans, encounter no discrimination in their attempt to access services, and are treated with respect, dignity, and understanding by VA service providers.

VA has also established a division within the National Center for Post-Traumatic Stress Disorder, the Women's Health Science Division. The center is based at the Boston VA Medical Center, and conducts clinical research addressing trauma-related problems of female veterans. Veterans may contact the Center at:

VA Medical Center
Women's Health Sciences Division
150 South Huntington Avenue
Boston, MA 02130

Most VA regional offices, medical centers and vet centers have a designated Women Veterans' coordinator to assist female veterans in accessing VA benefits and healthcare services. Many vet centers employ full and part-time counselors who have specialized skills in providing counseling to women for the after-effects of sexual trauma. Female veterans who have served during any wartime or peacetime era are eligible for counseling. Nearly all VA medical centers also provide counseling on-site, with a few providing counseling by contract.

WOMEN VETERANS COMPREHENSIVE HEATH CENTERS

Eight Women Veterans Comprehensive Heath Centers have been established to develop and enhance programs focusing on the gender-specific healthcare needs of female veterans. The locations are as follows:

Boston VA Medical Center
Boston, Massachusetts
(617) 232-9500, extension 4276

Chicago Area Network
(Hines, Lakeside, North Chicago, and West Side VA Medical Centers)
(312) 666-6500, extension 3382

Durham VA Medical Center
Durham, North Carolina
(919) 286-6936

Minneapolis VA Medical Center
Minneapolis, Minnesota
(612) 725-2030

Southeast Pennsylvania Network
(Coatesville, Lebanon, Philadelphia and Wilmington VA Medical Centers)
(215) 823-44496

San Francisco VA Medical Center
San Francisco, California
(415) 221-4810, extension 2174

Sepulveda / West Los Angeles VA Medical Centers
Sepulveda, California and Los Angeles, California
(818) 891-7711, extension 9555

Tampa VA Medical Center
Tampa, Florida
(813) 972-2000, extension 3678

WOMEN VETERANS HEALTH PROGRAMS

PROGRAM	FACILITY	LOCATION	PHONE NUMBER
Women Veterans Health Programs	Office of Environmental Medicine and Public Health VA Central Office	Washington, D.C.	(202) 535-7182
Women Veterans Health National Training Program	Birmingham Regional Medical Education Center	Birmingham, Alabama	(205) 731-1800
National Center for Post-traumatic Stress Disorder	Women's Health Science Division National Center for Post-traumatic Stress Disorder	Boston, Massachusetts	(617) 232-9500, extension 4145
Women Veterans Clinical Post-traumatic Stress Disorder Services	Women's Inpatient Post-traumatic Stress Disorder Unit VA Medical Center	Palo Alto, California	(415) 493-5000, extension 2274
Women's Stress Disorder Treatment Teams	Boston VA Medical Center	Boston, Massachusetts	(617) 232-9500, extension 4145
Women's Stress Disorder Treatment Teams	Cleveland / Brecksville VA Medical Center	Brecksville, Ohio	(216) 526-3030, extension 7584
Women's Stress Disorder Treatment Teams	New Orleans VA Medical Center	New Orleans, Louisiana	(504) 568-0811, extension 5835
Women's Stress Disorder Treatment Teams	Loma Linda VA Medical Center	Loma Linda, California	(909) 825-7084, extension 2595

★★

CHAPTER 30

BENEFITS FOR GULF WAR VETERANS

With variation in exposures and veterans' concerns ranging from oil well fire smoke to possible contamination from Iraqi chemical/biological agents, VA has initiated wide-ranging research projects evaluating illnesses as well as environmental risk factors.

The Department of Veterans Affairs (VA) offers Gulf War veterans physical examinations and special eligibility for follow-up care, and it operates a toll-free hotline at 800-749-8387 to inform these veterans of the program and their benefits. Operators are trained to help veterans with general questions about medical care and other benefits. It also provides recorded messages that enable callers to obtain information 24 hours a day

STATISTICS

More than one million service members served in the Gulf from August 1990 through the end of 1997, nearly 697,000 of them serving in the first year.

Twenty-six percent of the service members who served in Dessert Storm are now considered "Disabled," using VA categorization. This is the highest disability rate for any modern U.S. combat experience.

PERSIAN GULF REGISTRY PROGRAM

A free, complete physical examination with basic lab studies is offered to every Gulf War veteran, whether or not the veteran is ill. Veterans do not have to be enrolled in VA healthcare to participate in registry examinations. Results of the examinations, which include review of the veteran's military service and exposure history, are entered into special, computerized registries. The registries enable VA to update veterans on research findings or new compensation policies through periodic newsletters. The registries could also suggest areas to be explored in future scientific research. Registry participants are advised of the results of their examinations in personal consultations and by letters.

SPECIAL ACCESS TO FOLLOW-UP CARE

VA has designated a physician at every VA medical center to coordinate the special registry examination program and to receive updated educational materials and information as experience is gained nationally. Where an illness possibly related to military service in the Southwest Asia theater of operations during the Gulf War is detected during the examination, follow-up care is provided on a higher-eligibility basis than most non-service-connected care.

STANDARDIZED EXAM PROTOCOLS

VA has expanded its special registry examination protocol as more experience has been gained with the health of Gulf veterans. The protocol elicits information about symptoms and exposures, calls the clinician's attention to diseases common to the Gulf region, and directs baseline laboratory studies including chest X-ray (if one has not been done recently), blood count, urinalysis, and a set of blood chemistry and enzyme analyses that detect the "biochemical fingerprints" of certain diseases. In addition to this core laboratory work for every veteran undergoing the Gulf War program exam, physicians order additional tests and specialty consults as they would normally in following a diagnostic trail -- as symptoms dictate. If a diagnosis is not apparent, facilities follow the "comprehensive clinical evaluation protocol." The protocol suggests 22 additional baseline tests and additional specialty consultations, outlining dozens of further diagnostic procedures to be considered, depending on symptoms.

RISK FACTORS OF CONCERN TO VETERANS

Veterans have reported a wide range of factors observed in the Gulf environment or speculative risks about which they have voiced concerns. Some are the subject of research investigations and none have been ruled out. There appears to be no unifying exposure that would account for all unexplained illnesses. Individual veterans' exposures and experiences range from ships to desert encampments, and differences in military occupational specialty frequently dictate the kinds of elements to which service members are exposed.

Veteran concerns include exposure to the rubble and dust from exploded shells made from depleted uranium; the possibility of exposure to the nerve agent sarin or some yet-unconfirmed Iraqi chemical-biological agent; and use of a nerve agent pre-treatment drug, pyridostigmine bromide. Many other risk factors also have been raised. In 1991, VA initially began to develop tracking mechanisms that matured into the Gulf War Registry as a direct consequence of early concerns about the environmental influence of oil well fires and their smoke and particulate.

Anyone with first-hand information about "incidents" that occurred in the Southwest Asia theater of operations during the Persian Gulf War that may be related to health problems experienced by military personnel who served in the war should call the Department of Defense "Incidents" hotline at 1-800-472-6719.

VA DISABILITY COMPENSATION FOR DIAGNOSED AND UNDIAGNOSED ILLNESSES

If an illness or injury associated with service in the Persian Gulf results in a persistent disability, the veteran may be eligible for disability compensation from the VA. Recent legislation also authorized disability compensation for Persian Gulf veterans with chronic, undiagnosed illness resulting in a permanent disability that developed after they left the Persian Gulf. (A disability is considered "chronic" if it has existed for at least 6 months.)

Eligibility for disability compensation for Persian Gulf War veterans with undiagnosed illnesses will terminate on December 31, 2003.

The following symptoms may be manifestations of an undiagnosed illness:

- Fatigue
- Skin disorders
- Headaches
- Muscle pain
- Joint pain
- Neurological symptoms
- Neuropsychological symptoms
- Symptoms involving the respiratory system
- Sleep disturbances
- Gastrointestinal symptoms
- Cardiovascular symptoms
- Abnormal weight loss
- Menstrual disorders

Rates of compensation depend upon the degree of disability, and follow a payment schedule that is adjusted annually and applies to all veterans. Please refer to the charts beginning on page 4 for the current rates payable.

OBTAINING COPIES OF HOSPITAL RECORDS

A program is in place to help Gulf War veterans obtain copies of their in-patient hospital records from hospitals established during the Persian Gulf War.

Although these records were always located in the National Personnel Records Center in St. Louis, MO, they were stored only by the name of the hospital and the date of treatment.

An electronic database has been created to cross-reference patient names and social security numbers with their theater hospitals and admission dates.

Veterans may call 1-800-497-6261 to find out if their inpatient record ahs been added to the database, and to obtain the paperwork necessary to request a copy.

VA-FUNDED EXAMINATION PROGRAM FOR THE SPOUSES AND CHILDREN OF GULF WAR VETERANS

In 1996, VA initiated a special program to fund health examinations for some spouses and children of Gulf War Veterans Registry participants. The results of these examinations, which are conducted under contract by non-VA physicians in non-VA medical facilities, are included in the Gulf War Registry. Funding for the program has been approved through December 31, 2003.

VA can provide examinations to any individual who:

- Is the spouse or child of a veterans, is listed in the Persian Gulf War Veterans Registry; and

- Is suffering from, or may have suffered from, an illness or disorder (including birth defect, miscarriage, or stillbirth) which cannot be disassociated from the veteran's service in the Southwest Asia theater of operations; and

- Has granted VA permission to include in the Registry relevant medical data from the evaluation.

Interested individuals should call the VA Persian Gulf Information Help line at 1-800-749-8387.

Alternative Program

Eligible family members of Gulf War veterans may also have their medical information entered into the Persian Gulf War Registry by undergoing a physical examination from their private physician. The physician must complete a Registry code sheet, containing the protocol examination, and submit it to VA for entry into the database. The veteran or family member choosing this option must assume the cost of the examination and code sheet completion.

Interested individuals should contact the Persian Gulf Registry Coordinator at the nearest VA medical center for forms and information.

CONTINUING RESEARCH

A large number of studies are now in progress that will hopefully contribute to our understanding of Gulf War illnesses, including epidemiologic studies that will compare the types and frequency of illnesses in Gulf War veterans compared to veterans who did not serve in the Gulf War.

Additionally, more than 90 research studies are under way that will examine possible health consequences of exposure to a variety of factors present in the Persian Gulf, such as depleted uranium, pesticides, pyridostigmine bromide, and chemical warfare agents.

Any changes in benefits payable to Gulf War veterans as a result of this continuing research will be addressed in subsequent editions of this book, as well as in our monthly supplements.

★★

CHAPTER 31

ENTITLEMENT AND BENEFITS FOR THOSE SERVING IN OPERATION JOINT GUARD

The following entitlements and benefits are offered to U.S. military personnel serving in Operation Joint Guard.

Reserves called to active duty in support of a contingency operation have the same entitlement to pay and allowances as active duty personnel. In addition to normal pay and allowances, U.S. troops in Bosnia-Herzegovina may be authorized the following pays:

Imminent Danger Pay -- $150 a month.

> Bosnia-Herzegovina and certain surrounding countries were designated an area of imminent danger June 22, 1992. This includes the land area and airspace of most of the former Yugoslavia; including Croatia, Bosnia-Herzegovina, Serbia, Montenegro and Macedonia, but excluding Slovenia. While it applies to airspace above these countries, it does not apply to nearby coastal waters. Aircrews flying off carriers and entering airspace above the designated areas would receive the pay; ship crew members would not. However, if a naval vessel were fired upon, the crew would then receive hostile fire imminent danger pay.

Family Separation Allowance -- $100 a month.

> Paid anytime members are involuntarily separated from their dependents for more than 30 days.

Certain Places (foreign duty) Pay -- From $8 to $22.50 a month

> Payable to enlisted members serving in the land area of the former Yugoslavia (i.e. Croatia, Bosnia-Herzegovina, Serbia, Montenegro, Macedonia or Slovenia.)

Incidental portion of the Per Diem Rate -- $105 a month.

★★

CHAPTER 32

SOLDIERS' AND SAILORS' CIVIL RELIEF ACT

The Soldiers' and Sailors' Civil Relief Act (SSCRA) is one of the most powerful and protective tools service members have in asserting their rights under the law while on active duty. The Act provides a wide range of protections for individuals entering or called to federal active duty in the military. . Reservists and members of the National Guard are also protected by SSCRA *while on active duty.*

The SSCRA is intended to postpone or suspend certain civil obligations to enable service members to devote full attention to duty. The act does not apply to criminal matters.

The origins of the Soldiers' and Sailors' Relief Act of 1940 can be traced back all the way to the Civil War. Many of the present-day provisions of the Act were first enacted early during the Civil War when Congress passed a total moratorium on civil actions brought against Union soldiers and sailors. In basic terms, civil litigation involving soldiers or sailors was put on hold until they returned from the war. Examples of civil matters included breach of contract, bankruptcy, foreclosure or divorce proceedings.

Congress' intent was to protect the national interests and those of service members. First, it wanted service members to fight the war without worrying about problems that might arise at home. Second, most of the soldiers and sailors were not well paid, so it was difficult for them to honor pre-service debts such as mortgages or other credit.

Congress again protected the rights of service members during World War I with the Soldiers' and Sailors' Relief Act of 1918. Like the Civil War-era moratorium, the 1918 legislation protected service members until it expired shortly after the war. The 1918 version offered only a partial moratorium on civil actions, but did protect service members from such things as repossessions, bankruptcy and foreclosures.

The present-day statute, passed in 1940 to protect the millions of service members activated for World War II, essentially re-enacts the 1918 law -- except Congress gave it no provisions for expiration. Thus, since 1940, service members have received uninterrupted protection. Indeed, congressional commitment and support has remained so strong that the act has been amended more than 11 times since 1940 to keep pace with a changing military and changing world. The last amendments were added only eight years ago, during the 1991 Gulf War. Though titled Soldiers' and Sailors' Civil Relief Act, the Act does protect others, including members of the Air Force.

It is important to remember that the SSCRA affords no relief to persons in the Service against the collection of debts or other obligations contracted or assumed by them **after** entering such Service.

★★

IMPACT OF SERVICE ON DEBT

The courts are vested with a wide latitude of discretion under the Act. In determining whether or not persons in the Service are entitled to the relief sought, the courts will in each case inquire into and ascertain whether or not the ability of such persons to pay their debts or obligations has been materially impaired by reason of their service. The court will then determine the proper relief to be given.

RENT

The SSCRA prohibits eviction, without a court order, of a service member and their dependents from rented housing, when the rent does not exceed $1,200 per month. The court may delay eviction proceedings for up to 3 months.

TERMINATION OF LEASES

The SSCRA allows individuals called to federal active duty to terminate pre-service leases, if they give the required notice to their landlord. (It's very important before taking any action to terminate a pre-service lease that an individual contact a judge advocate or civilian attorney first.)

This protection does not apply to leases entered into after entry on active duty. Full-time National Guard personnel (title 32 AGR, Technicians, ADSW), however, are not protected. Such personnel should consider requesting insertion of a military clause in their lease, if they anticipate the possibility they may be transferred before expiration of the lease period.

INSTALLMENT CONTRACTS

A service member who enters into an installment contract prior to entering active duty is protected if the member's ability to make payments is materially affected by military service. In these situations, the courts will compare the service member's pre-service income and military income to determine if the member's financial condition has been materially affected by military service. The creditor is prevented from exercising his rights of recession, termination, or repossession without a court order.

MAXIMUM RATE OF INTEREST

If, prior to entering federal active duty, a military member incurs a loan or obligation with an interest rate in excess of 6%, the member will, upon application to the creditor, not be obligated to pay interest in excess of 6% per year.

In order to qualify for the reduction, however, service members must be able to demonstrate what is called "material effect." "Material effect" is a term that refers to how military service impacts people's lives and their ability to meet their obligations. Basically, this means that service members entering active duty must be able to show their military income is less than their pre-service income and that the loss affects their ability to meet financial obligations.

Obtaining an interest rate reduction requires service members to notify their creditors and mortgage lenders in writing of their intent to invoke the 6 percent rate cap. Notification must include proof of mobilization and placement on active duty status, as well as documentation of reduced income, such as a leave and earnings statement.

The interest rate reduction is only temporary, and individuals are required to notify their creditors once their active duty service ends. The interest rate prior to deployment then would be reinstated.

STAY OF PROCEEDINGS

Courts have the discretion to delay a civil court proceeding when the requirements of military service prevent a member from either asserting or protecting a legal rights. Usually, requests for a stay are granted if the time period requested is limited (TDY, exercise, deployment). Availability of leave (including excess leave) and duty requirements are key factors.

DEFAULT JUDGMENTS

Before a court can enter a default judgment (for failure to respond to a lawsuit or appear at trial) against a military member, the person suing the member must provide to the court an affidavit stating the defendant is not in the military.

If the defendant is in the military, the court will appoint an attorney to represent the defendant's interest (usually only to seek a stay of proceedings).

If a default judgment is entered against the active duty service member, the judgment may be reopened if the member applies within 90 days of separation from active duty and demonstrates both prejudice and a legal defense.

INSURANCE

A service member's private life insurance policy is protected against lapse, termination or forfeiture for nonpayment of premiums for a period of military service plus two years. The insured or beneficiary must apply to the VA for protection. Also, any health insurance in effect on the day before active duty commenced is reinstated without waiting periods or physical conditions restrictions.

TAXATION

A service member's state of legal residence may tax military pay and personal property. A member does not lose residence solely because of a transfer to another state pursuant to military orders.

For example, if an Illinois resident who is a member of Illinois Army National Guard is activated to federal military service and sent to California for duty, that person remains an Illinois resident while in California. The service member is not subject to California's authority to tax his/her military income. However, if the service member has a part-time civilian job in California, California will tax his/her non-military income earned in the state.

ADVERSE ACTIONS

Creditors and insurers are prohibited from pursuing adverse actions (i.e., notifying credit agencies, denying credit, changing terms) against service members who exercise their rights under SSCRA.

RIGHT TO VOTE

In addition to the protections involving debt payments and civil litigation, the act guarantees service members the right to vote in the state of their home of record and protects them from paying taxes in two different states.

CAUTION

The SSCRA does not wipe out any of an individual's obligations. Rather, it temporarily suspends the right of creditors to use a court to compel an individual to pay, only if the court finds that the inability to pay is due to military service. The obligation to honor existing debts remains, and some day the individual must "pay up."

The Relief Act is highly technical. The above summary is intended only to give a general overview of the protection available. The specific nature of all the relief provided under the law is a matter about which an individual may need to contact an attorney. The Act is designed to deal fairly with military personnel and their creditors. While relief is very often available, individuals are expected and required to show good faith in repayment of all debts.

★★

CHAPTER 33

FILING CLAIMS AND PAYMENT OF BENEFITS

FILING CLAIMS

In order for benefits of any type to be paid, the appropriate claim form(s) must be filed with the VA. Upon request made in person or in writing by any person claiming or applying for benefits, the VA shall furnish such person, free of all expense, all such printed instructions and forms as may be necessary in establishing such claim. The claim number assigned by VA to the initial claim should be referred to in all subsequent correspondence.

The veteran's DD 214 form should be kept in a safe location accessible to the veteran and next of kin or designated representative. The following documents will be needed for claims processing related to a veteran's death:

- Veteran's marriage certificate for claims of a surviving spouse or children

- Veteran's death certificate if the veteran did not die in a VA health-care facility

- Children's birth certificates to determine children's benefits

- Veteran's birth certificate to determine parents' benefits

If a claimant's application for benefits is incomplete, the VA shall notify the claimant of the evidence necessary to complete the application. If such evidence is not received within one year from the date of notification, no benefits may be paid or furnished by reason of such application. (This provision does not apply to any application or claim for Government life insurance benefits.)

- A claim filed by a surviving spouse or child for compensation or dependency and indemnity compensation shall also be considered to be a claim for death pension and accrued benefits, and a claim by a surviving spouse or child for death pension shall be considered to be a claim for death compensation (or dependency and indemnity compensation) and accrued benefits.

- A claim by a parent for compensation or dependency and indemnity compensation shall also be considered a claim for accrued benefits.

- Any person who applies for, or is in receipt of any compensation or pension benefit under laws administered by the VA shall, if requested by the VA, shall provide the social security number of such person, and the social security number of any dependent or beneficiary on whose behalf, or based upon whom, such person applies for, or is in receipt of such benefit. A person is not required to furnish the VA with a social security number for any person to whom a social security number has not been assigned.

The VA shall deny the application, or terminate the payment of compensation or pension to any person who fails to furnish the VA with a requested social security number.

Decisions And Notices Of Decisions

The VA shall, on a timely basis, provide the claimant (and to the claimant's representative) notice of a decision regarding the claim. The notice shall include an explanation of the procedure for obtaining review of the decision.

In the case of a denied benefit, the notice must also include a statement of the reasons for the decision, and a summary of the evidence considered by the VA.

Joint Applications For Social Security And Dependency And Indemnity Compensation

The VA and the Social Security Administration (SSA) shall jointly prescribe forms for use by survivors of members and former members of the uniformed services in filing application for benefits. Each such form shall request information sufficient to constitute an application for benefits from both agencies.

When an application on such a form is filed with either the VA or SSA, it shall be deemed to be an application for benefits from both agencies. A copy of each such application, filed with either agency, together with any additional information and supporting documents (or certifications thereof) that may have been received by the VA or SSA shall be transmitted by the receiving agency to the other agency. Please note that either agency may still request the applicant to furnish any additional information that may be necessary.

Burden Of Proof – Benefit Of The Doubt

A person who submits a claim for benefits from the VA shall have the burden of submitting evidence sufficient to justify a belief by a fair and impartial individual that the claim is well grounded. The VA shall assist a claimant in developing the facts pertinent to the claim.

When, after consideration of all evidence, there is an approximate balance of positive and negative evidence regarding the merits of an issue pertinent in the determination of such matter, the benefit of the doubt in resolving each such issue shall be given to the claimant. (The preceding sentence shall not be interpreted to shift from the claimant to the VA the burden outlined in the above paragraph.)

Reopening Disallowed Claims

If new and material evidence is presented or obtained with respect to a claim that has been disallowed, the VA shall reopen the claim and review the former disposition of the claim.

★★

Independent Medical Opinions

When the VA determines an expert medical opinion, in addition to that available within the VA, is warranted by the medical complexity or controversy involved in a case, the VA may secure an advisory medical opinion from one or more independent medical experts who are not employees of the VA.

The VA will make necessary rearrangements with recognized medical schools, universities, or clinics to furnish such advisory medical opinions.

The VA must furnish a claimant with notice that an advisory medical opinion has been requested, and when the VA has received the opinion, a copy of such opinion must be furnished to the claimant.

Revision Of Decisions Due To Clear And Unmistakable Error

A decision by the VA is subject to revision on the grounds of clear and unmistakable error. If evidence establishes the error, the prior decisions shall be reversed or revised.

Review to determine whether clear and unmistakable error exists in a case may be instituted by the VA on its own motion, or upon request by the claimant. A request for revision of a decision due to clear and unmistakable error may be made at any time after the original decision is made. Any such request must be submitted to the VA, and will be decided in the same manner as any other claim.

If a reversal or revision of a prior decision is made based on a clear and unmistakable error, the effective date of benefits will be the same as if the reversal or revision had been made on the date of the prior decision.

Effective Dates of Awards

Unless specifically outlined elsewhere in this section, the effective date of an award based on an original claim, a claim reopened after adjudication, or a claim for increase, of compensation, dependency and indemnity compensation, or pension, shall be fixed in accordance with the facts found, but shall not be earlier than the date of receipt of an application.

- The effective date of an award of **DISABILITY COMPENSATION** shall be the day following the date of discharge or release, provided the application is received within one year from the date of discharge or release.

- The effective date of an award of **INCREASED COMPENSATION** shall be the earliest date as of which it is ascertainable that an increase in disability has occurred, provided application is received within one year from such date.

- The effective date of an award of **DISABILITY PENSION** to a veteran who is totally and permanently disabled, and who is prevented by a disability from applying for disability pension for a period of at least 30 days, beginning on the date on which the veteran became permanently and totally disabled, shall be the date of application, or the date on which the

★★★

veteran became permanently and totally disabled, if the veteran applies for a retroactive award within one year from such date, whichever is to the advantage of the veteran.

- The effective date of an award of **DISABILITY COMPENSATION FOR PERSONS DISABLED BY TREATMENT OR VOCATIONAL REHABILITATION** shall be the date of such injury or aggravation which was suffered, provided an application is received within one year from such date.

- The effective date of an award of **DEATH COMPENSATION or DEPENDENCY AND INDEMNITY COMPENSATION** shall be the first day of the month in which the death occurred, provided an application is received within one year from the date of death.

- The effective date of an award of **DEPENDENCY AND INDEMNITY COMPENSATINO TO A CHILD** shall be the first day of the month in which the child's entitlement arose, provided an application is received within one year from such date.

- The effective date of an award of **DEATH PENSION** for which application is received within 45 days from the date of death shall be the first day of the month in which the death occurred.

- The effective date of **ADDITIONAL COMPENSATINO DUE TO DEPENDENTS,** based on the original establishment of a disability rating in the percentage evaluation specified by law for the purpose, shall be the effective date of such rating, provided proof of dependents is received within one year from the date of notification of such rating action.

- If a **CHILD WHO IS 18 YEARS OF AGE OR OVER, AND WHO IMMEDIATELY BEFORE BECOMING 18 YEARS OF AGE WAS COUNTED FOR THE AMOUNT OF DEPENDENCY AND INDEMNITY COMPENSATION PAID MONTHLY TO THE SURVIVING SPOUSE,** the effective date of an award of dependency and indemnity compensation to such child shall be the date the child attains the age of 18, provided the application is received within one year from such date.

- If **COMPENSATION, DEPENDENCY AND INDEMNITY COMPENSATION, OR PENSION** is awarded or increased pursuant to any Act or administrative issue, the **EFFECTIVE DATE** of such award or increase shall be fixed in accordance with the facts found. In no event, shall the effective date be earlier than the effective date of the Act or administrative issue. In no event shall such award or increase be retroactive for more than one year from the date of application therefore, or the date of administrative determination of entitlement, whichever is earlier.

- If an award of **PENSION HAS BEEN DEFERRED, OR PENSION HAS BEEN AWARDED AT A RATE BASED ON ANTICIPATED INCOME FOR A YEAR,** and the claimant later establishes that income for that year was at a rate warranting entitlement or increased entitlement, the effective date of such entitlement or increase shall be fixed in accordance with the facts found, provided satisfactory evidence is received before the expiration of the next calendar year.

- If any **DISALLOWED CLAIM** is reopened, and thereafter allowed on the basis of new and material evidence resulting from the correction of military records, or the change, correction, or modification of a discharge or dismissal, or from other corrective action by competent authority, the effective date of commencement of the benefits so awarded shall be the date on which an application was filed for correction of the military record or for the change, modification, or correction of a discharge or dismissal, or the date such disallowed claim was filed, whichever date is later. However, in no event shall such award of benefits be retroactive for more than one year from the date of reopening of such disallowed claim. (This paragraph shall not apply to any application or claim for Government life insurance benefits.)

- In the event of a **FINDING OF DEATH** of any person in the active military, naval, or air service has been made by the proper authorities, the effective date of an award of death compensation, dependency and indemnity compensation, or death pension, as applicable, shall be the first day of the month fixed by the proper authorities as the month of death in such report or finding, provided application is received within one year from the date of such report or finding. However, such benefits shall not be payable to any person for any period for which such person has received, or was entitled to receive, an allowance, allotment, or service pay of the deceased.

- The effective date of the award of benefits to a surviving spouse, or of an award or increase of benefits based on recognition of a child, **UPON ANNULMENT OF A MARRIAGE** shall be the date the judicial decree of annulment becomes final, provided a claim is fined within one year from the date the judicial decree of annulment becomes final. In all other cases, the effective date shall be the date the claim is filed.

- The effective date of an award of benefits to a surviving spouse based upon a **TERMINATION OF A REMARRIAGE BY DEATH OR DIVORCE**, or of an award or increase of benefits based on **RECOGNITION OF A CHILD UPON TERMINATIN OF THE CHILD'S MARRIAGE BY DEATH OR DIVORCE,** shall be the date of death, or the date the judicial decree or divorce becomes final, provided an application is received within one year from such termination.

- The effective date of the award of any benefit or any increase therein by reason of **MARRIAGE or the BIRTH OR ADOPTION OF A CHILD** shall be the date of such event, provided proof of such event is received within one year from the date of the marriage, birth, or adoption.

Commencement Of Period Of Payment

Payment of monetary benefits based on an award or an increased award of compensation, dependency and indemnity compensation, or pension may not be made to an individual for any period before the first day of the calendar month following the month in which the award or increased award became effective.

During the period between the effective date of an award or increased award and the commencement of the period of payment based on such award, an individual entitled to receive monetary benefits shall be deemed to be in receipt of such benefits for the purposes of all laws administered by the VA.

★★★

If any person who is in receipt of retired or retirement pay would also be eligible to receive compensation or pension upon the filing of a waiver of such pay, such waiver shall not become effective until the first day of the month following the month in which such waiver is filed, and nothing shall prohibit the receipt of retired or retirement pay for any period before such effective date.

In the case of a temporary increase in compensation for hospitalization or treatment where such hospitalization or treatment commences and terminates within the same calendar month, the period of payment shall commence on the first day of such month.

Effective Dates Of Reductions And Discontinuances

Unless otherwise specified in this section, the effective date of reduction or discontinuance of compensation, dependency and indemnity compensation, or pension shall be fixed in accordance with the facts found.

The effective date of a reduction or discontinuance of compensation, dependency and indemnity compensation, or pension due to:

- Marriage, remarriage, or death of a payee shall be the last day of the month before such marriage, remarriage, or death occurs.

- Marriage, annulment, divorce, or death of a dependent payee shall be the last day of the month in which such marriage, annulment, divorce, or death occurs.

- Receipt of active service pay or retirement pay shall be the day before the date such pay began.

- A change in income shall be the last day of the month in which the change occurred.

- A change in corpus of estate shall be the last day of the calendar year in which the change occurred.

- A change in disability or employability of a veteran in receipt of pension shall be the last day of the month in which discontinuance of the award is approved.

- A change in law or administrative issue, a change in interpretation of a law or administrative issue, or, for compensation purposes, a change in service-connected or employability status or change in physical condition shall be the last day of the month following sixty days from the date of notice to the payee (at the payee's last address of record) of the reduction nor discontinuance.

- The discontinuance of school attendance of a payee or a dependent of a payee shall be the last day of the month in which such discontinuance occurred.

- Termination of a temporary increase in compensation for hospitalization or treatment shall be the last day of the month in which the hospital discharge or termination of treatment occurred; whichever is earlier.

★★

- An erroneous award based on an act of commission or omission by the beneficiary, or with the beneficiary's knowledge, shall be the effective date of the award.

- An erroneous award based solely on administrative error or error in judgment shall be the date of last payment.

The effective date of a discontinuance of pension, compensation or emergency officers' retirement pay due to hospital treatment or institutional or domiciliary care shall be the last day of the first month of such treatment or care during which the value of the veteran's estate equals or exceeds $1,500.

Effective Dates Of Educational Benefits

Effective dates relating to awards under:

- All-volunteer force educational assistance program
- Training and rehabilitation for veterans with service-connected disabilities
- Post-Vietnam era Veterans' Educational Assistance
- Veterans' Educational Assistance
- Survivors' and Dependents' Educational Assistance

shall, to the extent feasible, correspond to effective dates relating to awards of disability compensation.

The effective date of an adjustment of benefits under any of the above items, if made on the basis of a certification made by the veteran or person, and accepted by the VA, shall be the date of the change.

PAYMENT OF BENEFITS

Delivery

Monetary benefits under laws administered by the VA shall be paid by checks transmitted by mail to the payee at the payee's last known address. If the payee has moved and filed a regular change of address notice with the United States Postal Service, the payee's check will be forwarded to the payee. The envelope or cover of each check shall bear on the face the following notice: "POSTMASTER: PLEASE FORWARD if addressee has moved and filed a regular change-of-address notice. If addressee is deceased, return the letter with date of death, if known."

Postmasters, delivery clerks, letter carriers, and all other postal employees are prohibited from delivering any mail addressed by the United States and containing any such check to any person whomsoever if such person has died, or, in the case of a surviving spouse, if the postal employee believes that the surviving spouse has remarried (unless the mail is addressed to the surviving spouse in the name the surviving spouse has acquired by the remarriage).

★★

Whenever mail is not delivered because of the prohibition outlined in the preceding paragraph, such mail shall be returned by the postmaster with a statement of the reason for so doing, and the date of death or remarriage, if known. Checks returned under this section shall be canceled.

Monetary benefits may be paid other than by check, upon written request of the person to whom such benefits are paid, provided such noncheck payment is determined by the Secretary to be in the best interest of such payees and the management of monetary benefits programs by the VA.

Direct Deposit

Payments can be sent directly to a student's savings or checking account through Direct Deposit (Electronic Funds Transfer). The following information must be provided to VA, so they will know where your payment should go:

- Bank or financial institution's nine digit routing number (For checking accounts, the routing number is the first 9 digits on the bottom of the check. For savings accounts, students may need to ask their financial institution for their routing number.)
- The account number
- The type of account (savings or checking)
- If mailing the information to VA, include a voided check with the request

Whenever the first day of any calendar month falls on a Saturday, Sunday, or legal public holiday, the VA shall, to the maximum extent practicable, certify benefit payments for such month in such a way that such payments will be delivered by mail, or transmitted for credit to the payee's account on the Friday immediately preceding such Saturday or Sunday, or weekday immediately preceding such legal public holiday.

In the case of a payee who does not have a mailing address, payments of monetary benefits shall be made by an appropriate method or methods. To the maximum extent practicable, such method or methods shall be designed to ensure the delivery of payments in such cases.

Payment of Certain Accrued Benefits Upon Death Of A Beneficiary

Periodic monetary benefits (other than insurance and servicemen's indemnity) under laws administered by the VA to which an individual was entitled at death under existing ratings or decisions, or those based on evidence in the file at date of death (hereafter referred to as "accrued benefits") and due and unpaid for a period not to exceed two years, shall, upon the death of such individual, be paid as follows:

- Upon the death of a person receiving an apportioned share of benefits payable to a veteran, all or any part of such benefits to the veteran or to any other dependent or dependents of the veteran, as may be determined by the VA.
- Upon the death of a veteran, to the living person first listed below:

279
★★★

  o The veteran's spouse

  o The veterans' children (in equal shares)

  o The veteran's dependent parents (in equal shares)

- Upon the death of a surviving spouse or remarried surviving spouse, to the children of the deceased veteran.

- Upon the death of a child, to the surviving children of the veteran who are entitled to death compensation, dependency and indemnity compensation, or death pension.

- In all other cases, only so much of the accrued benefits may be paid, as may be necessary to reimburse the person who bore the expense of last sickness and burial.

No part of any accrued benefits shall be used to reimburse any political subdivision of the United States for expenses incurred in the last sickness or burial of any beneficiary.

Applications for accrued benefits must be filed within one year after the date of death. If a claimant's application is incomplete at the time it is originally submitted, the VA shall notify the claimant of the evidence necessary to complete the application. If such evidence is not received within one year from the date of such notification, no accrued benefits may be paid.

Cancellation Of Checks Mailed To Deceased Payees

A check received by a payee in payment of accrued benefits shall, if the payee died on or after the last day of the period covered by the check, be returned to the issuing office and canceled, unless negotiated by the payee or the duly appointed representative of the payee's estate.

Rounding Down Of Pension Rates

The monthly or periodic rate of pension payable to an individual, if not a multiple of $1, shall be rounded down to the nearest dollar.

Acceptance Of Claimant's Statement As Proof of Relationship

The VA may accept the written statement of a claimant as proof of the existence of any relationship specified below, for the purpose of acting on such individual's claim for benefits:

- Marriage
- Dissolution of a marriage
- Birth of a child
- Death of any family member

The VA may require the submission of documentation in support of the claimant's statement if:

★★

- The claimant does not reside within a State.
- The statement on its face raises a question as to its validity.
- There is conflicting information of record.
- There is reasonable indication, in the statement or otherwise, of fraud or misrepresentation.

Acceptance Of Reports Of Private Physician Examinations

For purposes of establishing any claim for Disability Compensation or Non-Service-Connected Disability or Death Pension, a report of a medical examination administered by a private physician that is provided by a claimant in support of a claim for benefits may be accepted without a requirement for confirmation by an examination by a physician employed by the Veterans Health Administration, provided the report is sufficiently complete to be adequate for the purpose of adjudicating such claim.

CHAPTER 34

APPEALS

Veterans and other claimants for VA benefits have the right to appeal decisions made by a VA regional office or medical center.

If a claimant wishes to appeal a VA decision, the appeal is first reviewed by the BOARD OF VETERANS APPEALS. If, after review by the Board of Veterans' Appeals, the claimant is still dissatisfied, he or she may appeal to the UNITED STATES COURT OF VETERANS APPEALS. Both entities, along with specific guidelines for the filing of appeals, are discussed in the remainder of this chapter.

BOARD OF VETERANS APPEALS

The Board of Veterans Appeals was established by law to decide appeals for benefits under laws administered by the Veterans Administration. The Board of Veterans' Appeals (BVA) is a part of the Department of Veterans Affairs, located in Washington, D.C. Decisions are made by the members of a section of the Board, appointed with the approval of the president. The Board members are attorneys experienced in veterans' law and in reviewing benefit claims. It is the mission of the Board to decide appeals with sympathetic understanding and as promptly as possible, in order to grant all benefits to which veterans and their dependents and beneficiaries are entitled. Decisions are based on a veteran's entire record.

General Information

Anyone who has filed a claim for benefits with VA and has received a determination from a local VA office is eligible to appeal to the Board of Veterans' Appeals. Some decisions, such as eligibility for medical treatment, issued by VA medical centers can also be appealed to the BVA. An appeal can be made based on a complete denial of a claim, or based on the level of benefit granted. For example, if a veteran files a claim for disability, and the local VA office awards a 10% disability, but the veteran feels he or she is more than 10% disabled, the veteran can appeal that determination to the Board of Veterans' Appeals.

Decisions concerning the need for medical care or the type of medical treatment needed (such as a physician's decision to prescribe or not to prescribe a particular drug, or whether to order a specific type of treatment, are not within the BVA's jurisdiction.

An appeal must be filed within one year from the date the VA regional office or medical center mails its initial decision on a claim. If an appeal is not filed within the year, the original decision is considered final, and cannot be appealed unless the decision involves clear and unmistakable error by VA.

★★

How to File an Appeal and Important Time Limits

No special form is required to begin the appeal process. All that is initially needed is a written statement that the veteran disagrees with a claim decision. This initial statement is known as the "Notice of Disagreement" (NOD). The NOD must include why the veteran disagrees with a regional office decision. (For example, perhaps the veteran feels that the office making the decision overlooked or misunderstood some evidence, or misinterpreted the law.)

The Notice of Disagreement should be filed at the VA regional office where the veteran's claims file is kept. Normally, this is the same VA regional office or medical facility that issued the decision being appealed. However, if a veteran moves after a filing a claim, his or her claims file is transferred to the appropriate VA regional office, and that is where the NOD should be sent.

After the local VA office reviews a Notice of Disagreement, it is possible that the local office will agree with the NOD, and will change its original decision. However, if the local VA office does not change its decision, it will prepare and mail the veteran a *Statement of the Case*, which includes a VA Form 9 - Substantive Appeal, which the veteran must complete and return. The Statement of Case will summarize the evidence and applicable laws and regulations, and provide a discussion of the reasons for arriving at the decision.

Within 60 days of the date the local VA office issue the Statement of Case, the veteran must submit a completed VA Form 9-Substantive Appeal. (Please note that if the one year period from the date the VA regional office or medical center mailed its original decision is later than this 60-day period, the veteran has until that later one-year date to file the VA Form 9-Substantive Appeal.)

Completion of the VA Form 9-Substantive Appeal is very important. The form should include a clear statement of the benefit being sought, as well as any mistakes the veteran feels VA made when issuing its decision. VA Form 9-Substantive Appeal should also identify anything in the Statement of Case the veteran disagrees with. In addition to VA Form 9, any additional evidence, such as records from recent medical treatments or evaluations may be included as part of the appeal.

In most instances, a veteran can obtain civilian medical records and other non-government documents supporting his or her case by calling or writing directly to the office that keeps those records. VA regional office personnel and VSO representatives are experienced in locating many items that can support your case, such as service medical records, VA treatment records, and other government records. The VA does have a duty to assist veterans in the developing of their cases. However, individual veterans need to assist the VA in identifying the evidence that can prove the case.

If new information or evidence is included with VA Form 9, the regional office will prepare a Supplemental Statement of the Case (SSOC). The SSOC is similar to the Statement of the Case, but addresses the new information or evidence. If a veteran is not satisfied with the SSOC, a written statement must be mailed to the regional office within 60 days from the mailing date of the SSOC.

★★

It is important to realize the importance of submitting the VA Form 9-Substantive Appeal on a timely basis, otherwise, the right to appeal may be lost. Remember, the VA Form 9 is due the later of:

1 year from Regional Office determination mailing date

or

60 days from Statement of Case (SOC) mailing date

(An extension of the 60-day period for filing VA Form 9-Substantive Appeal or the 60-day period following a Supplemental Statement of the Case **may** be approved if a written request is filed with the local VA office handling the appeal. An extension will only be approved if the veteran can show "good cause" (can offer a valid reason why the extra time is needed).

Docket

A veteran's VA Form 9-Substantive Appeal becomes part of his or her claims folder, and is the basis for adding the appeal to the Board's *docket.*

The Board's docket is the record of all appeals awaiting review by the Board, listed in the order that appeals (VA Form 9) are received.

When an appeal is placed on the Board's docket, it is assigned the next higher number than the one received before it. The Board reviews appeals in the order in which they were placed on the docket. Thus, the lower the docket number, the sooner the appeal will be reviewed.

Lawyers and Other Representatives

A veteran may represent himself or herself. However, over 90% of all people who appeal to the Board of Veterans' Appeals obtain representation. The majority choose to be represented by Veterans' Service Organizations (VSOs) or their state's veterans department.

A lawyer may also be hired for representation. There are strict guidelines about what a lawyer may charge for services, as well as restrictions on fees that a lawyer may charge for work performed prior to issuance of the Board's final decision.

In addition to VSOs and attorneys, some other agents are recognized by VA to represent appellants.

To authorize a VSO for representation, VA Form 21-22 must be completed. To authorize an attorney or recognized agent for representation, VA Form 22a must be completed. Both forms are available at all VA offices.

LENGTH OF APPEAL PROCESS

No one can determine exactly how long it will take form the time an appeal is filed until receipt of the Board's decision. However, veterans can expect an average of two years from the time an appeal is placed on the Board's docket until issuance of a BVA decision.

If a veteran believes his or her case should be decided sooner than others filed earlier, a *motion to advance on the docket* can be submitted. The motion should explain why the appeal should be moved ahead. Because most appeals involve some type of hardship, before a case can be advanced, there needs to be convincing proof of exceptional circumstances (i.e. terminal illness, danger of bankruptcy or foreclosure, or an error by VA that caused a significant delay in the docketing of an appeal. Veterans should be aware that, on average, fewer than 3 out of every 20 requests for advancement on the docket are granted.

To file a motion to advance on the docket, a written request should be sent to:

Board of Veterans' Appeals (014)
Department of Veterans Affairs
810 Vermont Avenue, NW
Washington, DC 20420

Personal Hearings

A personal hearing is a meeting between the veteran (and his/her representative) and an official from VA who will decide the case. During the hearing, the veteran presents testimony and other evidence supporting the case. There are two types of personal hearings:

• Regional office hearings (also called RO hearing or local office hearings); and

• BVA hearings.

A regional office hearing is a meeting held at a local VA office with a "hearing officer" from the local office's staff. To arrange a regional office hearing, a veteran should contact the local VA office or appeal representative as early in the appeal process as possible.

In a BVA hearing, the veteran presents his or her case in person to a member of the Board. Appellants in most areas of the country can choose whether to hold the BVA hearing at the local VA regional office, called a "Travel Board Hearing," or at the BVA office in Washington, D.C. Some regional offices are also equipped to hold BVA hearings by videoconference. (Check with the regional office for availability.)

The VA cannot pay for any lodging or travel expenses incurred in connection with a hearing.

The VA Form 9-SubstantiveAppeal has a section for requesting a BVA hearing. VA Form 9 is not used, however, to request a local office hearing. Even if a BVA hearing is not requested on the VA Form 9, a request can still be requested by writing directly to the Board. If a BVA hearing is requested, the request must clearly state where the hearing is requested – at the VA regional office, or at the Board's office in Washington, D.C. A BVA hearing cannot be held in both places.

(Travel Board hearings may not be available at regional offices located near Washington, D.C.)

The requested type and location of the hearing determines when it will be held. Generally, regional office hearings are held as soon as they can be scheduled on the hearing officer's calendar.

The scheduling of BVA hearings held at regional offices (Travel Board hearings) is more complicated, since Board members must travel from Washington, D.C. to the regional office. BVA videoconferenced hearings are less complicated to arrange, and can be scheduled more frequently than Travel Board hearings.

Hearings held at the Board's offices in Washington, D.C. will be scheduled for a time close to when BVA will consider the case – approximately three months before the case is reviewed by the BVA.

Location of Claims Folder

If a BVA hearing is not requested, the claims folder remains at the local VA office until shortly before the BVA begins its review, at which time it is transferred to the BVA.

If a Travel Board hearing is requested, the claims folder remains at the local VA office until the hearing is completed, at which time it is transferred to the BVA.

If a videoconferenced BVA hearing or a hearing held at the Board's office in Washington, D.C. is requested, the claims folder remains at the local VA office until shortly before the BVA hearing is held. It is transferred to the BVA in time for the hearing and the Board's review.

When a claims folder is transferred from the local VA office to Washington, D.C., the local VA office will send the claimant a letter advising that he or she has 90 days remaining (from the date of that letter) during which more evidence can be added to a file, a hearing can be requested, or a representative can be selected (or changed).

The BVA cannot accept items submitted after the 90-day period has expired, unless a written explanation (called a "motion") is also submit, explaining why the item is late and showing why the BVA should accept it (called "showing good cause"). A motion to accept items after the 90-day period will be reviewed by a Board member who will issue a ruling either allowing or denying the motion.

Checking on the Status of an Appeal

To check on the status of an appeal, veterans or their representatives should contact the office where the claims folder is located (see previous section).

If a claims file is at the Board, veterans or their representatives may call (202) 565-5436 to check on its status (be sure to have the claim number available).

★★

The Board Review Process

When the VBA receives an appeal from a local VA office, the veteran and/or representative will be notified in writing. The Board will then examine the claims folder for completeness, and will provide an opportunity to submit additional written arguments . The case is then assigned to a Board member for review. If a BVA hearing was requested, the Board member assigned the case will conduct the hearing prior to reaching a decision.

When the docket number for an appeal is reached, the file will be reviewed by a Board member and a staff attorney, who will check for completeness, review all evidence and arguments, as well as the regional office's Statement of the Case (and Supplement Statement of the Case, if applicable), the transcript of the hearing (if applicable), the statement of any representative, and any other information included in the claims folder. The staff attorney, if directed to do so by the Board member, may also conduct additional research and prepare recommendations for the Board member's review.

When, in the judgment of the Board member, expert medical opinion, in addition to that available within the VA, is warranted by the medical complexity or controversy involved in an appeal, the Board may secure an advisory medical opinion from one or more independent medical experts who are not employees of the VA.

The VA shall make necessary arrangements with recognized medical schools, universities, or clinics to furnish such advisory medical opinions at the request of the Chairman of the Board. Any such arrangement shall provide that the actual selection of the expert or experts to give the advisory opinion in an individual case shall be made by an appropriate official of such institution.

The Board shall furnish a claimant with notice that an advisory medical opinion has been requested, and shall furnish the claimant with a copy of such opinion when it is received by the Board.

Prior to reaching a decision, the Board member must thoroughly review all materials and recommendations. The Board member will then issue a decision.

The Board member's decision will be mailed to the home address that the Board has on file, so it is extremely important that the VA be kept informed of any address changes.

The BVA must attempt to make its decisions as understandable as possible. However, due to the nature of legal documents, laws, court cases, and medical discussions, decisions can be confusing. If an appeal is denied , the Board will send a "Notice of Appellate Rights" that describes additional actions that can be taken.

The Board annually produces a CD-ROM with the text of its decisions. Most VA regional offices have these CD-ROMS available for review, or the CD-Rom may be purchased from the Government Printing Office. For further information, contact:

★★

Department of Veterans Affairs
Board of Veterans' Appeals (01B)
Washington, D.C. 20420

Remands

Sometimes when reviewing a claims folder, the Board member determines additional development of the case is necessary. The appeal is then returned to the local VA office. This is called a "remand." After performing the additional work, the regional office may issue a new decision. If the claim is still denied, the case is returned to the Board for a final decision. (The case keeps its original place on the Board's docket, so it is reviewed soon after it is returned to the Board.)

Depending on the reason for the remand, the regional office may provide the veteran with a Supplement Statement of the Case (SSOC). The claimant then has 60 days from the date the local VA office mails the SSOC to comment on it.

APPEALING THE BOARD OF VETERANS' AFFAIRS DECISION

If a veteran is not satisfied with the Board's decision, the decision can be appealed to the United States Court of Veterans Appeals (the Court). The Court is an independent court that is not part of the Department of Veterans Affairs.

If it can be demonstrated that the Board made an obvious error of fact or law in its decision, a written "motion to reconsider" can be filed. Any such motions should be sent directed to the Board, not to the local VA office. A motion to reconsider should not be submitted simply because of disagreement with the BVA's decision. The claimant must be able to show that the Board made a mistake, and that the Board's decision would have been different if the mistake had not been made.

If a claimant has "new and material evidence," he or she can request that the case be re-opened. To be considered "new and material," the evidence submitted must be information related to the case that was not included in the claims folder when the case was decided.

To re-open an appeal, the claimant must submit the new evidence directly to the local VA office that handled the claim.

DEATH OF APPELLANT

According to the law, the death of an appellant generally ends the appellant's appeal, and the Board normally dismisses the appeal without issuing a decision. The rights of a deceased appellant's survivors are not affected by this action. Survivors may still file a claim at the regional office for any benefits to which they may be entitled.

GENERAL GUIDELINES FOR EFFICIENT PROCESSING OF CLAIMS

The following guidelines may help ensure that an appeal is not unnecessarily delayed:

- Consider having an appeal representative assist with the filing of the appeal.

- File the Notice of Disagreement and VA Form 9-Substantive Appeal as soon as possible

- Be as specific as possible when identifying the issues the Board should consider.

- Be as specific as possible when identifying sources of evidence for the VA to obtain. (For example, provide the full names and addresses of physicians, along with dates of treatment, and reasons for treatment.)

- Keep VA informed of current address, phone number, and number of dependents.

- When possible, provide clinical treatment records, rather than simply a statement from a physician.

- Be clear on the VA Form 9 about whether or not a BVA hearing is requested, and where the hearing should take place, if applicable.

- Include the claim number on any correspondence with the VA.

- Do not submit material that is not pertinent to the claim. This will only delay the process.

- Do not use the VA Form 9 to raise new claims for the first time. (VA Form 9 is only to be used to appeal decisions on previously submitted claims.)

- Do not use the VA Form 9 to request a local office hearing.

- Do not raise additional issues for the Board's review late in the appeal process. This may cause the appeal to be sent back to the regional office for additional work, and may result in a longer delay.

- Do not submit evidence directly to the Board unless a written or typed statement is included, stating that consideration by the regional office is waived. The statement must clearly indicate that the Board is to review the evidence, even though the regional office has not seen it. If a waiver is not included with any additional evidence submitted directly to the Board, the case may be remanded to the regional office for review, and may result in further delays.

- Do not submit a last minute request for a hearing or a last minute change to the type or location of a hearing unless it is unavoidable. Such a request will likely result in a delay in reaching a final decision.

- Do not miss a scheduled VA examination or hearing.

★★

UNITED STATES COURT OF VETERANS' APPEALS

The United States Court of Veterans' Appeals was created under Public Law 100-687, on November 18, 1988. The Court has seven judges, appointed by the President and confirmed by the Senate. Judges are appointed for a 15-year term. The major

If a claimant is not satisfied with the Board of Veterans' Appeals decision, an appeal can be filed with the United States Court of Veterans Appeals (referred to as the "Court"). The Court is an independent court that is not part of the Department of Veterans Affairs. The Court does not hold trials, receive new evidence, or hear witnesses. It reviews the BVA decision, the written record, and the briefs of the parties. Claimants do not need to appear in Washington, D.C. for an appeal. (In approximately 1% of decided cases, the Court holds oral arguments in its Washington courtroom, or occasionally, by telephone conference call.)

A claimant may represent himself or herself, but may want to get advice from an attorney or from a service officer in a veterans organization or a state or county veterans' affairs office. The VA will be represented by its attorney, and a claimant's case may be better presented if he or she is represented.

The Court does not recommend or appoint attorneys to represent claimants. However, the Court does have a *Public List of Practitioners* which shows who is allowed to represent appellants in the Court, and have said that they are available. Most attorneys charge a fee.

To appeal a Board of Veterans' Appeals decision, a claimant must file a "Notice of Appeal" with the Court within 120 days from the date the Board's decision is mailed. (The first day of the 120 days a claimant has to file an appeal to the Court is the day the BVA's decision is postmarked, not the day the decision is signed.)

If a claimant filed a motion to reconsider with the Board of Veterans' Appeals within the 120 day time-frame, and that motion was denied, the claimant has an additional 120 days to file the "Notice of Appeal" with the Court. (This 120 day period begins on the date the Board mails a notification that it has denied the motion to reconsider.) If the Board denies the motion to reconsider, a "Notice of Appellate Rights" will be mailed to the claimant.

In addition to the above 120 day limit, in order for the Court to consider an appeal, a Notice of Disagreement must have been filed with the VA regional office handling the case on or after November 18, 1988.

An original "Notice of Appeal" must be filed directed with the Court at:

United States Court of Veterans Appeals
625 Indiana Avenue, NW, Suite 900
Washington, D.C. 20004
Fax: (202) 501-5848
(Appeals cannot be filed by e-mail)

The fee for an appeal is $50.00, and should be included with the "Notice of Appeal." If a claimant is unable to pay this fee, a "Motion to Waive Filing Fee" form must be completed and returned with the "Notice of Appeal."

If a claimant appeals to the Court, a copy of the "Notice of Appeal" must also be filed with the VA General Counsel at:

Office of the General Counsel (027)
Department of Veterans Affairs
810 Vermont Avenue, NW
Washington, D.C. 20420

Please note that the *original* "Notice of Appeal" that is filed with the Court is the only document that protects a claimants right to appeal a BVA decision. The copy sent to the VA General Counsel does not protect that right, or serve as an official filing.

If the Court accepts an appeal, it will send a printed copy of the rules of practice and procedure to the claimant and his/her representative, if applicable.

To obtain more specific information about the "Notice of Appeal," the methods for filing with the Court, Court filing fees, and other matters covered by the Court's rules, a claimant should contact the Court directly at:

United States Court of Veterans Appeals
625 Indiana Avenue, NW, Suite 900
Washington, D.C. 20004
1-800-869-8654

The Court's precedential opinions are published in West's *Veterans Appeals Reporter*. They are also sent to the Government Printing Office for microfilm distribution to its nationwide depository library system.

If either party disagrees with the Court's ruling, an appeal may be filed with the U.S. Court of Appeals for the Federal Circuit, and, thereafter, may seek review in the Supreme Court of the United States.

CHAPTER 35

VA REGIONAL OFFICES & BENEFITS OFFICES

Department of Veterans Affairs
Headquarters
810 Vermont Avenue NW
Washington, DC 20420
(202) 273-5400

Alabama (SDN 5)
Montgomery Regional Office
345 Perry Hill Road
Montgomery, AL 36109

Alaska (SDN 8)
Anchorage Regional Office
2925 DeBarr Road
Anchorage, AK 99508-2989

Juneau Benefits Office
709 West 9th Street, #263
Juneau, AK 99802

Arizona (SDN 9)
Phoenix Regional Office
3225 North Central Avenue
Phoenix, AZ 85012

Arkansas (SDN 7)
North Little Rock Regional Office
Building 65
Fort Roots
PO Box 1280
Little Rock, AR 72115

California (SDN 9)
Los Angeles Regional Office
Federal Building
11000 Wilshire Boulevard
Los Angeles, CA 90024

Oakland Regional Office
1301 Clay Street
Room 1300 North
Oakland, CA 94612

San Diego Regional Office
8810 Rio San Diego Drive
San Diego, CA 92108

Commerce Benefits Office
5400 E. Olympic Blvd.
Commerce, CA 90022

Colorado (SDN 8)
Denver Regional Office
155 Van Gordon Street
Denver, CO 80225

Connecticut (SDN 1)
Hartford Regional Office
450 Main Street
Hartford, CT 06103

Delaware (SDN 3)
Wilmington Regional Office
1601 Kirkwood Highway
Wilmington, DE 19805

Florida
St. Petersburg Regional Office
9500 Bay Pines Boulevard
Bay Pines, FL 33708

Fort Myers Benefits Office
2070 Carrell Road
Fort Myers, FL 33901

Jacksonville Benefits Office
1833 Boulevard, Room 3109
Jacksonville, FL 32206

Oakland Park Benefits Office
5599 North Dixie Highway
Oakland Park, FL 33334

Pensacola Benefits Office
312 Kenmore Road
Room 1G250
Pensacola, FL 32503-7492

Georgia (SDN 4)
Atlanta Regional Office
1700 Clairmont Road
Decatur, GA 30033

Hawaii (SDN 9)
Honolulu Regional Office
459 Patterson Road
E-Wing
Honolulu, HI 96819-1522

Idaho (SDN 8)
Boise Regional Office
805 West Franklin Street
Boise, ID 83702

Illinois (SDN 6)
Chicago Regional Office
536 South Clark Street
Chicago, IL 60605-1523

Indiana (SDN 2)
Indianapolis Regional Office
575 North Pennsylvania Street
Indianapolis, IN 46204

Iowa (SDN 6)
Des Moines Regional Office
210 Walnut Street
Des Moines, IA 50309

Kansas (SDN 6)
Wichita Regional Office
5500 East Kellogg
Wichita, KS 67211

Kentucky (SDN 3)
Louisville Regional Office
545 South 3rd Street
Louisville, KY 40202

Louisiana (SDN 7)
New Orleans Regional Office
701 Loyola Avenue
New Orleans, LA 70113

Maine (SDN 1)
Togus VA Med/Regional Office
1 VA Center
Togus, ME 04330

Maryland (SDN 3)
Baltimore Regional Office
31 Hopkins Plaza Federal Bldg
Baltimore, MD 21201

Massachusetts (SDN 1)
Boston VA Regional Office
JFK Federal Building
Government Center
Boston, MA 02114

Michigan (SDN 2)
Detroit Regional Office
Federal Building
477 Michigan Avenue
Detroit, MI 48226

Minnesota (SDN 6)
St. Paul Regional Office
1 Federal Drive
Fort Snelling
St. Paul, MN 55111-4050

Mississippi (SDN 5)
Jackson Regional Office
1600 East Woodrow Wilson Ave.
Jackson, MS 39216

Missouri (SDN 6)
St. Louis Regional Office
Federal Building
400 South, 18th Street
St. Louis, MO 63103

Kansas City Benefits Office
Federal Office Building
601 East 12th Street
Kansas City, MO 64106

Montana (SDN 8)
Fort Harrison Regional Office
William Street
off Highway 12 West
Fort Harrison, MT 59636

★★

Nebraska (SDN 6)
Lincoln Regional Office
5631 South 48th Street
Lincoln, NE 68516

New Hampshire (SDN 1)
Manchester Regional Office
Norris Cotton Federal Bldg
275 Chestnut Street
Manchester, NH 03101

New Jersey (SDN 2)
Newark Regional Office
20 Washington Place
Newark, NJ 07102

New Mexico (SDN 8)
Albuquerque Regional Office
Dennis Chavez Federal Building
500 Gold Avenue, S.W.
Albuquerque, NM 87102

Nevada (SDN 9)
Reno Regional Office
1201 Terminal Way
Reno, NV 89520

Las Vegas Benefits Office
4800 Alpine Pl., Suite 11
Las Vegas, NV 89107

New York (SDN1)
Buffalo Regional Office
Federal Building
111 West Huron Street
Buffalo, NY 14202

New York Regional Office
245 West Houston Street
New York, NY 10014

Rochester Benefits Office
465 Westfall Road
Rochester, NY 14620

Syracuse Benefits Office
344 W. Genesee Street
Syracuse, NY 13202

North Carolina (SDN 4)
Winston-Salem Regional Office
Federal Building
251 North Main Street
Winston-Salem, NC 27155

North Dakota (SDN 6)
Fargo Regional Office
2101 North Elm Street
Fargo, ND 58102

Ohio (SDN 2)
Cleveland Regional Office
A.J. Celebrezze Federal Building
1240 East 9th Street
Cleveland, OH 44199

Cincinnati Benefits Office
36 East 7th Street, Suite 210
Cincinnati, OH 45202

Columbus Benefits Office
Federal Building - Room 309
200 North High Street
Columbus, OH 43215

Oklahoma (SDN 7)
Muskogee Regional Office
125 South Main Street
Muskogee, OK 74401

Oklahoma City Benefits Office
215 Dean A. McGee Avenue
Room 276
Oklahoma City, OK 73102

Oregon (SDN 8)
Portland Regional Office
1220 SW 3rd Avenue
Portland, OR 97204

Pennsylvania (SDN 2)
Philadelphia Regional Office
5000 Wissahickon Avenue
Philadelphia, PA 19101

Pittsburgh Regional Office
1000 Liberty Avenue
Pittsburgh, PA 15222

★★

Wilkes-Barre Benefits Office
Jewelcor Building, 2nd Floor
100 N. Wilkes-Barre Blvd.
Wilkes-Barr, PA 18702

Rhode Island (SDN 1)
Providence Regional Office
380 Westminster Mall
Providence, RI 02903

South Carolina (SDN 4)
Columbia Regional Office
1801 Assembly Street
Columbia, SC 29201

South Dakota (SDN 6)
Sioux Falls Regional Office
PO Box 5046
2501 West 22nd Street
Sioux Falls, SD 57117

Tennessee (SDN 4)
Nashville Regional Office
110 9th Avenue South
Nashville, TN 37203

Texas (SDN 7)
Houston Regional Office
6900 Almeda Road
Houston, TX 77030

Waco Regional Office
1 Veterans Plaza
701 Clay Avenue
Waco, TX 76799

Corpus Christi Benefits Office
5283 Old Brownsville Road
Corpus Christi, TX 78405

Dallas Benefits Office
Santa Fe Building
1114 Commerce Street
Dallas, TX 75242

Lubbock Benefits Office
3208 34th Street, Suite 10
Lubbock, TX 79410

San Antonio Benefits Office
5788 Eckert Road
San Antonio, TX 78240

Tyler Benefits Office
1700 SSE Loop 323, Suite 310
Tyler, TX 75701

Utah (SDN 8)
Salt Lake City Regional Office
125 South State Street
Salt Lake City, UT 84147

Vermont (SDN 1)
White River Junction
Regional Office
North Hartland Road
White River Junction, VT 05009

Virginia (SDN 3)
Roanoke Regional Office
210 Franklin Road SW
Roanoke, VA 24011

Washington (SDN 8)
Seattle Regional Office
Federal Building
915 2nd Avenue
Seattle, WA 98174

Fort Lewis Benefits Office
Waller Hall, Room 700
PO Box 331153
Fort Lewis, WA 98433

West Virginia (SDN 3)
Huntington Regional Office
640 Fourth Avenue
Huntington, WV 25701

Wisconsin (SDN 6)
Milwaukee Regional Office
5000 West National Avenue
Milwaukee, WI 53295

Wyoming (SDN 8)
Cheyenne Regional Office
2360 East Pershing Blvd.
Cheyenne, WY 82001

District of Columbia (SDN 3)
Washington DC Regional Office
1120 Vermont Avenue N.W.
Washington, DC 20421

★★★

Puerto Rico (SDN 5)
San Juan Regional Office
150 Carlos Chardon Avenue
Hato Rey, Puerto Rico 00918

Ponce Benefits Office

Mayaguez Benefits Office

Philippines (SDN 9)
Manila Regional Office
1131 Roxas Boulevard
Pasay City, Philippines 96440
Note: SDN = Service Delivery
Network

CHAPTER 36

STATE BENEFITS

Many states offer services and benefits to veterans in addition to those offered by the Department of Veterans' Affairs. To find out more about a particular state's programs, individuals should contact the following:

Alabama Department of Veterans' Affairs
P.O. Box 1509
770 Washington Ave, Suite 530
Montgomery, AL 36102-1509
(334) 242-5077

Alaska Department of Veterans' Affairs
P.O. Box 5800
Fort Richardson, AK 99505-5800
(907) 428-6068

Arizona Department of Veterans' Services
3225 North Central Ave, Suite 910
Phoenix, AZ 85012
(602) 225-3373

Arkansas Department of Veterans' Affairs
P.O. Box 1280
Fort Roots – Room 119 – Bldg 65
North Little Rock, AR 72115
(501) 370-3820

California Department of Veterans' Affairs
1227 O Street, Suite 300
Sacramento, CA 95814
(916) 653-2158

Colorado Division of Veterans' Affairs
789 Sherman Street, Suite 260
Denver, CO 80203-1714
(303) 894-7474

Connecticut Department of Veterans' Affairs
287 West Street
Rocky Hill, CT 06067
(860) 721-5891

Delaware Commission of Veterans' Affairs
Robbins Building
802 Silverlake Blvd, Suite 100
Dover, DE 19904
(302) 739-2792
1-800-344-9900 (in state only)

Florida Department of Veterans' Affairs
Mailing Address:
P.O. Box 31003
St. Petersburg, FL 33731
Location:
2540 Executive Center Circle West
Douglas Building, Suite 100
Tallahassee, FL 32301
(727) 319-7400

Georgia Department of Veterans' Affairs
Floyd Veterans Memorial Building
Suite E-970
Atlanta, GA 30334
(404) 656-2300

★★

Hawaii Office of Veterans' Services
Mailing Address:
459 Patterson Road
E-Wing, Room 1-A103
Honolulu, HI 96819
Location:
Tripler Army Med Center (Ward Road)
VAMROC, E-Wing, Room 1-A103
Honolulu, HI 96819
(808) 433-0420

Idaho Division of Veterans' Affairs
320 Collins Road
Boise, ID 83702
(208) 334-3513

Illinois Department of Veterans' Affairs
P.O. Box 19434
833 South Spring Street
Springfield, IL 62794-9432

Indiana Department of Veterans' Affairs
302 West Washington, Room E120
Indianapolis, IN 46204-2738
(317) 232-3910

Iowa Commission of Veterans' Affairs
7700 N.W. Beaver Drive
Camp Dodge - Building A6A
Johnston, IA 50131-1902
(515) 242-5331

Kansas Commission on Veterans' Affairs
Jayhawk Towers
Suite 701
700 S.W. Jackson Street
Topeka, KS 66603-3714
(785) 296-3976

Kentucky Department of Veterans' Affairs
1111 Louisville Road
NGAKY Building
Frankfort, KY 40601
(502) 564-1864

Louisiana Department of Veterans' Affairs
P.O. Box 94095
Capitol Station
1885 Wooddale Blvd., 10th Floor
Baton Rouge, LA 70804-9095
(225) 922-0500

Maine Bureau of Veterans' Services
State House Station, #117
CP Keyes Building 7, Room 100
Augusta, ME 04333
(207) 626-4464

Maryland Department of Veterans' Affairs
Room 110, Federal Building
31 Hopkins Plaza
Baltimore, MD 21201
(410) 962-4700

Massachusetts Department of Veterans' Services
239 Causewway Street, Suite 100
Boston, MA 02114
(617) 727-3578

Michigan Department of Veterans' Affairs
611 West Ottawa Street, 3rd Floor
P.O. Box 30026
Lansing, MI 48913
(517) 335-6523

Minnesota Department of Veterans' Affairs
State Veterans Service Building
20 West 12th Street, 2nd Floor
St. Paul, MN 55155-2079
(651) 296-2562

Mississippi State Veterans' Affairs Board
3466 Highway 80 East
P.O. Box 5947
Pearl, MS 39208-5947
(601) 576-4850

Missouri Veterans' Commission
Mailing Address:
Post Drawer 147
Jefferson City, MO 65102-0147
Location:
1719 Southridge Drive
Jefferson City, MO 65109
(573) 751-3779

Montana Veterans' Affairs Division
P.O. Box 5715
Helena, MT 59604
(406) 841-3740

Nebraska Department of Veterans' Affairs
State Office Building
301 Centennial Mall South
P.O. Box 95083
Lincoln, NE 68509-5083
(402) 471-2458

Nevada Commission for Veterans' Affairs
1201 Terminal Way, Room 108
Reno, NV 89520
(702) 688-1653

New Hampshire State Veterans' Council
275 Chestnut Street
Room 321
Manchester, NH 03101-2411
(603) 624-9230
1-800-622-9230 (in state only)

New Jersey Department of Veterans' Affairs
CN 340, Egcert Crossing Road
Trenton, NJ 08625-0340
(609) 530-7045

New Mexico Veterans' Service Commission
P. O. Box 2324
Santa Fe, NM 87503
(505) 827-6300

New York Division of Veterans' Affairs
5 Empire State Plaza
Suite 2836
Albany, NY 12223-1551
(518) 474-6114

North Carolina Division of Veterans' Affairs
Albemarle Building, Suite 1065
1315 Mail Service Center
325 North Salisbury Street
Raleigh, NC 27699-1315
(919) 733-3851

North Dakota Department of Veterans' Affairs
P.O. Box 9003
1411 32nd Street, South
Fargo, ND 58106-9003
(701) 239-7165

Ohio Governor's Office of Veterans' Affairs
State Office Tower
65 South Front Street
Room 426
Columbus, OH 43215
(614) 644-0898

Oklahoma Department of Veterans' Affairs
P.O. Box 53067
Oklahoma City, OK 73152
(405) 521-3684

Oregon Department of Veterans' Affairs
700 Summer Street, NE
Salem, OR 97310-1201
(503) 373-2388

Pennsylvania Department of Veterans' Affairs
Fort Indiantown Gap
Building S-O-47
Annville, PA 17003-5002
(717) 861-8901

★★

Rhode Island Division of Veterans' Affairs
480 Metacom Avenue
Bristol, RI 02809
(401) 222-2488

South Carolina Office of Veterans' Affairs
1205 Pendleton Street, Suite 226
Columbia, SC 29201
(803) 734-0200

South Dakota Division of Veterans' Affairs
Soldiers & Sailors War Memorial Bldg
500 East Capitol Avenue
Pierre, SD 57501-5070
(605) 773-3269

Tennessee Department of Veterans' Affairs
215 Eighth Avenue North
Nashville, TN 37243-1010
(615) 741-2930

Texas Veterans' Commission
P.O. Box 12277
10th & Colorado
Austin, TX 78711
(512) 463-5538

Utah Division of Veterans' Affairs
125 South State St, Room 5223
Federal Building
Salt Lake City, UT 84138-1102
(801) 524-6048

Vermont State Veterans' Affairs
Mailing Address:
120 State Street
Montpelier, VT 05620-4401
Location:
118 State Street
Montpelier, VT 05620
(802) 828-3379

Virginia Department of Veterans' Affairs
Poff Federal Building, Room 1012
270 Franklin RD. S.W
Roanoke, VA 24011-2215
(540) 857-7104

Washington Department of Veterans' Affairs
P.O. Box 41150
1011 Plum Street
Olympia, WA 98504-1150
(360) 725-2151

West Virginia Division of Veterans' Affairs
1321 Plaza East, Suite 101
Charleston, WV 25301-1400
(304) 558-3661

Wisconsin Department of Veterans' Affairs
P.O. Box 7843
30 West Mifflin Street
Madison, WI 53707
(608) 266-1311

Wyoming Veterans' Affairs Commission
Wyoming ANG Armory
5905 CY Avenue - Room 101
Casper, WY 82604
(307) 265-7372

American Samoa Veterans' Affairs
P. O. Box 8586
Pago Pago
American Samoa 96799
(001) 684-633-4206

Guam Veterans' Affairs Office
P.O. Box 3279
Agana, Guam 96910

★★

**Puerto Rico Public Advocate for
Veterans' Affairs**
Mercantile Plaza Bldg, Suite 401
San Juan, PR 00918-1625
(787) 758-5760

**Government of the Virgin
Islands Division of Veterans'
Affairs**
1013 Estate Richmond
Christiansted, St. Croix VI
00820-4349
(340) 773-6663

★★

CHAPTER 37

WHERE TO OBTAIN MILITARY PERSONNEL RECORDS

The U.S. Department of Veterans Affairs does not maintain veterans' military service records.

The personnel records of individuals currently in the military service, in the reserve forces, and those completely separated from military service are located in different offices. A nominal fee is charged for certain types of service. In most instances service fees cannot be determined in advance. If your request involves a service fee you will be notified as soon as that determination is made.

A veteran and spouse should be aware of the location of the veteran's discharge and separation papers. If a veteran cannot locate discharge and separation papers, duplicate copies may be obtained (further information regarding who to contact is included later in this chapter).

Use Standard Form 180, *Request Pertaining To Military Records*, which is available from VA offices and veterans organizations. Specify that a duplicate separation document or discharge is needed. The veteran's full name should be printed or typed so that it can be read clearly, but the request must also contain the signature of the veteran or the signature of the next of kin, if the veteran is deceased. Include branch of service, service number or Social Security number and exact or approximate date and years of service.

It is not necessary to request a duplicate copy of a veteran's discharge or separation papers solely for the purpose of filing a claim for VA benefits. If complete information about the veteran's service is furnished on the application, VA will obtain verification of service from the National Personnel Records Center or the service department concerned. In a medical emergency, information from a veteran's records may be obtained by phoning the National Personnel Records Center:

- Army 314-538-4261;
- Air Force, 314-538-4243;
- Navy, Marine Corps or Coast Guard, 314-538-4141.

WHO TO CONTACT

The various categories of military personnel records are described in the tables below. Please read the following notes carefully, to make sure an inquiry is sent to the right address. Please note especially that the record is not sent to the National Personnel Records Center as long as the person retains any sort of reserve obligation, whether drilling or non-drilling.

★★★

Special Notes For Following Tables:

- **Health & Personnel records:** In most cases involving individuals no longer on active duty, the personnel record, the health record, or both can be obtained from the same location, as shown in the following tables. However, some health records are available from the VA Records Management Center. If the person was discharged, retired, or released from active duty (separated) on or after the following dates, a request for a copy of the health record should be sent to the Records Management Center of the VA (address follows):

Army:	*October 16, 1992*
Navy:	*January 31, 1994*
Air Force:	*May 1, 1994*
Marine Corps:	*May 1, 1994*
Coast Guard:	*April 1, 1998*

Department of Veterans Affairs
Records Management Center
P.O. Box 5020
St. Louis, MO 63115-5020

- **Records at the National Personnel Records Center:** Note that it takes at least 3 months, and often 6 or 7, for the file to reach the National Personnel Records Center after the military obligation has ended (such as by discharge). If only a short time has passed, please send the inquiry to the address shown for active or current reserve members. Also, if the person has only been released from active duty, but is still in a reserve status, the personnel record will stay at the location specified for reservists. A person can retain a reserve obligation for several years, even without attending meetings or receiving annual training.

- **Definitions & Abbreviations:**

  Discharged – the individual has no current military status

  Health – records of physical exams, dental treatment, & outpatient medical treatment received while in a duty status (does not include records of treatment while hospitalized)

  NPRC-National Personnel Records Center

  TDRL-Temporary Disability Retirement List

- **Service completed before WWI:** The oldest records pertaining to military service veterans are at the National Archives, for service that was completed before the following dates:

Army enlisted:	11/1/1912
Army officer:	07/01/1917
Navy enlisted:	01/01/1886

Navy officer: 01/01/1903
Marine Corps: 01/01/1905
Coast Guard: 01/01/1898

National Archives Trust Fund forms must be used to request these records. For information, contact:

National Archives & Records Administration
Old Military & Civil Records
NWCTB-Military), Textual Services Division
700 Pennsylvania Avenue, N.W.
Washington, D.C. 20408-0001

- If there were two or more periods of service within the same branch, send your request (only one is necessary) to the office having the records for the LAST PERIOD OF SERVICE.)

AIR FORCE (USAF)	
Active Members (includes National Guard on active duty in the Air Force, TDRL, and general officers retired with pay	Air Force Personnel Center HQ AFPC / DPSRP 550 C Street West, Suite 19 Randolph AFB, TX 78150-4721
Reserve, retired reservists in nonpay status, current National Guard officers not on active duty in Air Force, and National Guard released from duty in Air Force	Air Reserve Personnel Center / DSMR 6760 E Irvington Pl. #4600 Denver, CO 80280-4600
Current National Guard enlisted, not on active duty in Air Force	The Adjutant General of the appropriate state, DC, or Puerto Rico
Discharged, deceased, and retired with pay (see note #1, above, if requesting health record)	National Personnel Records Center Military Personnel Records 9700 Page Boulevard St. Louis, MO 63132

ARMY	
Discharged, deceased, or retired (see note #1, above, if requesting health record)	National Personnel Records Center Military Personnel Records 9700 Page Boulevard St. Louis, MO 63132
Reserve, or active duty records of current National Guard members who performed service in the U.S. Army before 7/1/72	Commander U.S. Army Reserve Personnel Command ATTN: ARPC-ALQ-B 1 Reserve Way St. Louis, MO 63132-5200
Active enlisted (including National Guard on active duty in the U.S. Army) or TDRL enlisted	Commander – USAEREC Attn: PCRE-F 8899 E 56th Street Indianapolis, IN 46249-5301
Active officers (including National Guard on active duty in U.S. Army) or TDRL officers	U.S. Total Army Personnel Command 200 Stoval Street Alexandria, VA 22332-0400
Current National Guard enlisted not on active duty in the U.S. Army (including records of Army active duty performed after 6/30/72)	The Adjutant General of the appropriate state, DC, or Puerto Rico
Current National Guard officers not on active duty in the U.S. Army (including records of Army active duty performed after 6/30/72)	Army National Guard Readiness Center NGB-ARP 111 South George Mason Drive Arlington, VA 22204-1382

★★

COAST GUARD (USCG)	
Active, reserve, and TDRL members	Commandant – CGPC – Adm - 3 U.S. Coast Guard 2100 2nd Street, SW Washington, DC 20593-0001
Discharged, deceased and retired members (see next item) (see note #1, above, if requesting health record)	National Personnel Records Center Military Personnel Records 9700 Page Boulevard St. Louis, MO 63132

MARINE CORPS (USMC)	
Active, TDRL, and Selected Marine Corps Reserve members	Headquarters U.S. Marine Corps Personnel Management Support Branch (MMSB-10) 2008 Elliot Road Quantico, VA 22134-5030
Individual Ready Reserve and Fleet Marine Corps Reserve members	Marine Corps Reserve Support Command (Code MMI) 15303 Andrews Road Kansas City, MO 64147-1207
Discharged, deceased, and retired members (see next item) (see note #1, above, if requesting health record)	National Personnel Records Center Military Personnel Records 9700 Page Boulevard St. Louis, MO 63132

★★

NAVY (USN)	
Active, reserve, or TDRL	Naval Personnel Command 5720 Integrity Drive Millington, TN 38055-3130
Discharged, deceased, or retired (see note #1, above, if requesting health record)	National Personnel Records Center Military Personnel Records 9700 Page Boulevard St. Louis, MO 63132

FACTS ABOUT THE 1973 ST. LOUIS FIRE AND LOST RECORDS

A fire at the NPRC in St. Louis on July 12, 1973, destroyed about 80 percent of the records for Army personnel discharged between November 1, 1912, and January 1, 1960. About 75 percent of the records for Air Force personnel with surnames from "Hubbard" through "Z" discharged between September 25, 1947, and January 1, 1964, were also destroyed.

What Was Lost

It is hard to determine exactly what was lost in the fire, because:

- There were no indices to the blocks of records involved. The records were merely filed in alphabetical order for the following groups:
    - World War I: Army November 1, 1912 - September 7, 1939
    - World War II: Army September 8, 1939 - December 31, 1946
    - Post World War II: Army January 1, 1947 - December 31, 1959
    - Air Force September 25, 1947 - December 31, 1963
- Millions of records, especially medical records, had been withdrawn from all three groups and loaned to the Department of Veterans Affairs (VA) before the fire. The fact that one's records are not in NPRC files at a particular time does not mean the records were destroyed in the fire.

Reconstruction of Lost Records

If veterans learn that their records may have been lost in the fire, they may send photocopies of any documents they possess -- especially separation documents -- to the NPRC at:

★★★

National Personnel Records Center
Military Personnel Records
9700 Page Blvd.
St. Louis, MO 63132-5100.

The NPRC will add those documents to the computerized index and file them permanently.

Alternate Sources of Military Service Data

When veterans don't have copies of their military records and their NPRC files may have been lost in the St. Louis fire, essential information about their military service may be available from a number of other sources, including:

- The Department of Veterans Affairs (VA) maintains records on veterans whose military records were affected by the fire if the veteran or a beneficiary filed a claim before July 1973.

- Service information may also be found in various kinds of "organizational" records such as unit morning reports, payrolls and military orders on file at the NPRC or other National Archives and Records Administration facilities.

- There also is a great deal of information available in records of the State Adjutants General, and other state "veterans services" offices.

By using alternate sources, NPRC often can reconstruct a veteran's beginning and ending dates of active service, the character of service, rank, time lost on active duty, and periods of hospitalization. NPRC can issue NA Form 13038, "Certification of Military Service," considered the equivalent of a Form DD-214, "Report of Separation From Active Duty," to use in establishing eligibility for veterans benefits.

Necessary Information for File Reconstruction

The key to reconstructing military data is to give the NPRC enough specific information so the staff can properly search the various sources. The following information is normally required:

- Full name used during military service;
- Place of entry into service;
- Branch of service;
- Last unit of assignment;
- Approximate dates of service;
- Place of discharge;
- Service number or Social Security number

CHAPTER 38

CORRECTION OF RECORDS BY CORRECTION BOARDS

Each service department has a permanent Board for Correction of Military (Naval) records, composed of civilians, to act on applications for correction of records.

JURISDICTION

Correction boards are empowered to deal with all matters relating to error or injustice in official records. The boards cannot act until all other administrative avenues of relief have been exhausted. Discharges by sentence of Special Court-Martial and administrative discharges cannot be considered by correction boards unless:

- Application to the appropriate Discharge Review Board has been denied and rehearing is barred, or
- Application cannot be made to the Discharge review Board because the time limit has expired.

APPLICATION

DD Form 149, Application for Correction of Military or Naval record, must be used to apply for correction of military records.

Time Limitations

Initial application to a Board For Correction of Military (Naval) Records must be made within 3 years of discovery of an alleged error or injustice. The boards may excuse failure to timely file if a reasonable explanation is given.

Procedures

Applications and supporting evidence should be submitted through the veteran's local service officer organization, i.e., VFW Department Service Officer to the Chief, Military Claims, National Veterans Service, etc. Cases are considered on the content of the record including evidence submitted and briefs by counsel. After review, the board may allow the request, deny the request, or grant a formal hearing at which the applicant and/or counsel may present arguments, testimony and witnesses.

DECISIONS

In the absence of new and material evidence the decision of a correction board, as approved or modified by the Secretary of the Service Department, is final. Adverse decisions are subject to judicial review in a U.S. District Court.

★★★

Decisions of the Boards for Correction of Military or Naval Records must be made available for public inspection. Copies of the decisional documents will be provided on request.

★★

CHAPTER 39

DISCHARGE REVIEW

DISCHARGE REVIEW BOARDS

Each branch of service has discharge review boards to review the discharge or dismissal of former service members. (The Navy Board considers Marine Corps cases.)

Authority

Discharge review boards can, based on the official records and such other evidence as may be presented, upgrade a discharge or change the reason and authority for discharge. Discharge review boards cannot grant disability retirement, revoke a discharge, reinstate any person in the service, recall any person to active duty, act on requests for re-enlistment code changes or review a discharge issued by sentence of a general court-martial. Discharge review boards have no authority to address medical discharges.

Application

DD Form 293, *Application for Review of Discharge or Dismissal from the Armed Forces of the United States*, is used to apply for review of discharge. (If more than 15 years have passed since discharge, DD Form 149 should be used.) The individual or, if legal proof of death is provided, the surviving spouse, next-of-kin, or legal representative can apply. If the individual is mentally incompetent, the spouse, next-of-kin, or legal representative can sign the application, but must provide legal proof of incompetence. The instruction for completing DD Form 293 must be read and complied with.

Time Limitation

Initial application to a discharge review board must be made within 15 years after the date of discharge.

Personal Appearance

A personal appearance before the Discharge Review Board is a legal right. A minimum 30-day notice of the schedule hearing date is given unless the applicant waives the advance notice in writing. Reasonable postponements can be arranged if circumstances preclude appearance on the scheduled date. All expenses of appearing before the board must be paid by the applicant. If no postponement of a scheduled hearing date is requested and the applicant does not appear on the date scheduled, the right to a personal hearing is forfeited and the case will be considered on the evidence of record.

Hearings

Discharge review boards conduct hearings at various locations in the U.S. Information concerning hearing locations and availability of counsel can be obtained by writing to the appropriate board at the address shown on DD Form 293. Those addresses are listed at the end of this chapter.

Published Uniform Standards For Discharge Review

A review of discharge is conducted to determine if an individual was properly and equitably discharged. Each case is considered on its own merits.

- A discharge is considered to have been proper unless the discharge review determines:

  o That there is an error of fact, law, procedures, or discretion which prejudiced the rights of the individual, or

  o That there has been a change of policy which requires a change of discharge.

- A discharge is considered to have been equitable unless the discharge review determines:

  o That the policies and procedures under which the individual was discharged are materially different from current policies and procedures and that the individual probably would have received a better discharge if the current policies and procedures had been in effect at the time of discharge; or

  o That the discharge was inconsistent with the standards of discipline; or

  o That the overall evidence before the review board warrants a change of discharge. In arriving at this determination, the discharge review board will consider the quality and the length of the service performed, the individual's physical and mental capability to serve satisfactorily, abuses of authority which may have contributed to the character of the discharge issued, and documented discriminatory acts against the individual.

Decisions

An authenticated decisional document is prepared and a copy provided to each applicant and council.

- A copy of each decisional document, with identifying details of the applicant and other persons deleted to protect personal privacy, must be made available for public inspection and copying. These are located in a reading room in the Pentagon, Washington, DC.

- To provide access to the documents by persons outside the Washington,. D.C. area, the documents have been indexed. The index includes case number of each case; the date, authority and reason for, and character if

★★★

the discharge, and the issues addressed in the statement of findings, conclusions and reasons.

- Interested parties may contact the DVARO or the State veterans Agency for the location of an index. A copy of the index will be made available at the sites of traveling board hearings during the period the board is present.

- An individual can go through the index and identify cases in which the circumstances leading to discharge are similar to those in the individual's case. A copy of these case decisional documents can be requested by writing to:

> DA Military Review Boards Agency
> ATTN: SFBA (Reading Room)
> Room 1E520
> The Pentagon
> Washington, D.C. 20310.

Examination of decisional documents may help to identify the kind of evidence which was used in the case, and may indicate why relief was granted or denied. Decisional documents do not set precedence - each case is considered on its own merits.

Reconsideration

An application which has been denied can be reopened if:

- The applicant submits newly discovered evidence which was not available at the time of the original consideration.

- The applicant did not request a personal hearing in the original application and now desires to appear before the board. If the applicant fails to appear at the hearings, the case will be closed with no further action.

- The applicant was not represented by counsel in the original consideration and now desires counsel and the application for reconsideration is submitted within 15 years following the date of discharge.

- Changes in policy, law or regulations have occurred or federal court orders have been issued which substantially enhance the rights of the applicant.

SERVICE DEPARTMENT DISCHARGE REVIEW BOARD ADDRESSES

Army

Army Discharge Review Board
Attention: SFMR-RBB
Room 200A
1941 Jefferson Davis Highway
Arlington, VA 22202-4504

★★

Navy & USMC

Navy Discharge Review Board
801 North Randolph Street
Suite 905
Arlington, VA 22203

Air Force

Air Force Military Personnel Center
Attention: DP-MDOA1
Randolph AFB, TX 78150-6001

Coast Guard

Coast Guard
Attention: GPE1
Washington, DC 20593

★★★

CHAPTER 40

DECORATIONS, RIBBONS AND MEDALS

PURPOSE

The military decorations system has an important purpose – to provide tangible evidence of public recognition and national appreciation of acts of heroism performed and valuable services rendered. Military decorations are awarded in recognition of , and as a reward for heroic, extraordinary, outstanding, and meritorious acts, achievements, and services. Such visible evidence of recognition is meant to be cherished by the recipients, their comrades, and their families.

Not more than one of each military decoration will be issued to any one individual. In its place, for each succeeding award of the same decoration, an Oak-Leaf Cluster or Service Star will be issued (except in the cases of succeeding awards of the Legion of Merit and Medal of Freedom to foreigners, and posthumous awards of the Purple Heart.)

No decoration shall be awarded or presented to any individual whose entire service, subsequent to the time of the distinguished act, achievement, or service, shall not have been awarded.

MILITARY DECORATIONS AND REASONS FOR AWARD
(Year indicated in parentheses indicates year decoration was instituted)

MEDAL OF HONOR
ARMY – NAVY – AIR FORCE – MARINE CORPS – COAST GUARD
(Instituted by Army in 1862, Navy in 1861, Air Force in 1960 - prior to 1960, Airmen received the Army Medal)
For conspicuous gallantry and intrepidity at the risk of life, above and beyond the call of duty, in action involving actual conflict with an opposing armed force

UNITED STATES PERSONAL DECORATIONS

AERIAL ACHIEVEMENT MEDAL (1988)
AIR FORCE
For sustained meritorious achievement while participating in aerial flight

AIR FORCE ACHIEVEMENT MEDAL (1980)
Air Force
For outstanding achievement or meritorious service not warranting award of the Air Force Commendation Medal

AIR FORCE COMMENDATION MEDAL (1958)
AIR FORCE
> For outstanding achievement or meritorious service rendered on behalf of the United States Air Force

AIR FORCE CROSS (1960)
AIR FORCE
> For extraordinary heroism in action against an enemy of the U.S. while engaged in military operations involving conflict with an opposing foreign force, or while serving with friendly foreign forces

AIRMAN'S MEDAL (1960)
AIR FORCE
> For heroism involving voluntary risk of life under conditions other than those of actual conflict with an armed enemy

AIR MEDAL (1942)
ARMY – NAVY – AIR FORCE – MARINE CORPS – COAST GUARD
> For heroic actions or meritorious service while participating in aerial flight

ARMY ACHIEVEMENT MEDAL (1981)
ARMY
> For meritorious service or achievement while serving in a non-combat area

ARMY COMMENDATION MEDAL (1945-retroactive to 1941)
ARMY
> For heroism, meritorious achievement, or meritorious service

BRONZE STAR MEDAL (1944)
ARMY – NAVY – AIR FORCE – MARINE CORPS – COAST GUARD
> For heroic or meritorious achievement or service not involving participation in aerial flight

COAST GUARD ACHIEVEMENT MEDAL (1968)
COAST GUARD
> For professional and/or leadership achievement in a combat or noncombat situation

COAST GUARD COMMENDATION MEDAL (1947)
COAST GUARD
> For heroic or meritorious achievement or service; and meritorious service resulting in unusual or outstanding achievement

COAST GUARD MEDAL (1958)
COAST GUARD
> For heroism not involving actual conflict with an armed enemy of the United States

COMBAT ACTION RIBBON (1969)
NAVY - MARINE CORPS
    For active participation in ground or air combat during specifically listed military operations

COMMANDANT'S LETTER OF COMMENDATION RIBBON (1979)
COAST GUARD
    For receipt of a letter of commendation for an act or service resulting in unusual and/or outstanding achievement

DEFENSE DISTINGUISHED SERVICE MEDAL (1970)
ARMY - NAVY - AIR FORCE - MARINE CORPS - COAST GUARD (ISSUED BY SECRETARY OF DEFENSE)
    For exceptionally meritorious service to the United States while assigned to a Joint Activity in a position of unique and great responsibility

DEFENSE MERITORIOUS SERVICE MEDAL (1977)
ARMY - NAVY - AIR FORCE - MARINE CORPS - COAST GUARD
    For noncombat meritorious achievement or service while assigned to Joint Activity

DEFENSE SUPERIOR SERVICE MEDAL (1976)
ARMY - NAVY - AIR FORCE - MARINE CORPS - COAST GUARD (ISSUED BY SECRETARY OF DEFENSE)
    For superior meritorious service to the United States while assigned to a Joint Activity in a position of significant responsibility

DISTINGUISHED FLYING CROSS (1926)
ARMY - NAVY - AIR FORCE - MARINE CORPS - COAST GUARD
    For heroism or extraordinary achievement while participating in aerial flight

DISTINGUISHED SERVICE CROSS (1918)
ARMY
    For extraordinary heroism in action against an enemy of the U.S. while engaged in military operations involving conflict with an opposing foreign force, or while serving with friendly foreign forces

DISTINGUISHED SERVICE MEDAL
(Instituted by Army in 1918, Navy and Marine Corps in 1919, Air Force in 1960, Coast Guard in 1961)
ARMY - NAVY - AIR FORCE - MARINE CORPS - COAST GUARD
    For exceptionally meritorious service to the United States Government in a duty of great responsibility

GOLD LIFESAVING MEDAL (1874)
ARMY - NAVY - AIR FORCE - MARINE CORPS - COAST GUARD - CIVILIANS
    For heroic conduct at the risk of life during the rescue or attempted rescue of a victim of drowning or shipwreck

★★

JOINT SERVICE ACHIEVEMENT MEDAL (1983)
ARMY – NAVY – AIR FORCE – MARINE CORPS – COAST GUARD
(Issued by Secretary of Defense)
For meritorious service or achievement while serving with a Joint Activity

JOINT SERVICE COMMENDATION MEDAL (1963)
ARMY – NAVY – AIR FORCE – MARINE CORPS – COAST GUARD (Issued by Secretary of Defense)
For meritorious service or achievement while assigned to a Joint Activity

LEGION OF MERIT (1942)
ARMY – NAVY – AIR FORCE – MARINE CORPS – COAST GUARD
For exceptionally meritorious conduct in the performance of outstanding services to the United States

MERITORIOUS SERVICE MEDAL (1969)
ARMY – NAVY – AIR FORCE – MARINE CORPS – COAST GUARD
For outstanding noncombat meritorious achievement or service to the United States

NAVY AND MARINE CORPS ACHIEVEMENT MEDAL (1961)
Navy – Marine Corps
For meritorious service or achievement in a combat or noncombat situation based on sustained performance of a superlative nature

NAVY AND MARINE CORPS COMMENDATION MEDAL (1945 retroactive to 1941)
NAVY – MARINE CORPS
For heroic or meritorious achievement or service

NAVY AND MARINE CORPS MEDAL (1942)
NAVY - MARINE CORPS
For heroism not involving actual conflict with an armed enemy of the United States

NAVY CROSS (1919)
NAVY – MARINE CORPS – COAST GUARD
For extraordinary heroism in action against an enemy of the U.S. while engaged in military operations involving conflict with an opposing foreign force, or while serving with friendly foreign forces

PURPLE HEART (1932)
ARMY – NAVY – AIR FORCE – MARINE CORPS – COAST GUARD
Awarded to any member of the U.S. Armed Forces killed or wounded in an armed conflict

SILVER LIFESAVING MEDAL (1874)
ARMY – NAVY – AIR FORCE – MARINE CORPS – COAST GUARD – CIVILIANS
For heroic conduct during rescue or attempted rescue of a victim of drowning or shipwreck

★★

SILVER STAR (1932)
ARMY – NAVY – AIR FORCE – MARINE CORPS – COAST GUARD
For gallantry in action against an armed enemy of the United States, or while serving with friendly foreign forces

SOLDIER'S MEDAL (1926)
ARMY
For heroism not involving actual conflict with an armed enemy of the United States

SPECIAL SERVICE, GOOD CONDUCT, & RESERVE MERITORIOUS AWARDS

AIR FORCE GOOD CONDUCT MEDAL (1963)
AIR FORCE (Air Force used Army Good Conduct Medal until 1963)
For exemplary conduct, efficiency, and fidelity during three years of active enlisted service with the U.S. Air Force

AIR FORCE RECOGNITION RIBBON (1980)
AIR FORCE
For individual recipients of Air Force-level special trophies and awards

AIR RESERVE FORCES MERITORIOUS SERVICE MEDAL (1964)
AIR FORCE
For exemplary behavior, efficiency, and fidelity during three years of active enlisted service with the Air Force Reserve

ARMY GOOD CONDUCT MEDAL (1941)
ARMY – AIR FORCE
For exemplary conduct, efficiency and fidelity during three years of active enlisted service with the U.S. Army (1 year during wartime)

ARMY RESERVE COMPONENTS ACHIEVEMENT MEDAL (1971)
ARMY
For exemplary conduct, efficiency, and fidelity during three years of service with the U.S. Army Reserve or National Guard

COAST GUARD GOOD CONDUCT MEDAL (1921)
COAST GUARD
For outstanding proficiency, leadership, and conduct during three continuous years of active enlisted Coast Guard service

COAST GUARD RESERVE GOOD CONDUCT MEDAL (1963)
COAST GUARD
For outstanding proficiency, leadership and conduct during three years of enlisted service in the Coast Guard Reserve

COMBAT READINESS MEDAL (1964)
AIR FORCE
For specific periods of qualifying service in a combat or mission-ready status

FLEET MARINE FORCE RIBBON (1984)
NAVY

> For active participation by professionally skilled Navy personnel with the Fleet Marine Force

MARINE CORPS GOOD CONDUCT MEDAL (1896)
MARINE CORPS

> For outstanding performance and conduct during three years of continuous active enlisted service in the U.S. Marine Corps

NAVAL RESERVE MERITORIOUS SERVICE MEDAL (1964)
NAVY

> For outstanding performance and conduct during four years of enlisted service in the Naval Reserve

NAVY GOOD CONDUCT MEDAL (1888)
NAVY

> For outstanding performance and conduct during four years of continuous active enlisted service in the U.S. Navy

NAVY RESERVE SPECIAL COMMENDATION RIBBON (1946) (obsolete)
NAVY – MARINE CORPS

> For Reserve Officers with four years of successful command, and a total Reserve service of ten years

OUTSTANDING AIRMAN OF THE YEAR RIBBON (1968)
AIR FORCE

> For airmen selected to the "12 outstanding Airmen of the Year" competition

PRISONER OF WAR MEDAL (1985)
ARMY – NAVY – AIR FORCE – MARINE CORPS – COAST GUARD

> For any member of the U.S. Armed Forces taken prisoner during any armed conflict dating from World War I

SELECTED MARINE CORPS RESERVE MEDAL (1939)
MARINE CORPS

> For outstanding performance and conduct during four years of enlisted service in the Marine Corps Selected Reserve

UNITED STATES SERVICE MEDALS

AMERICAN CAMPAIGN MEDAL (1942)
ARMY – NAVY – AIR FORCE – MARINE CORPS – COAST GUARD

> For service outside the U.S. in the American theater for 30 days, or within the continental U.S. for one year during 1941-1946

AMERICAN DEFENSE SERVICE MEDAL (1941)
ARMY – NAVY – AIR FORCE – MARINE CORPS – COAST GUARD

> For 12 months of active duty service in the Army during 1939-1941; or any active duty service in Naval Services during 1939-1941

ANTARCTICA SERVICE MEDAL (1960)

★★

ARMY – NAVY – AIR FORCE – MARINE CORPS – COAST GUARD
For 30 calendar days of service on the Antarctic Continent from 1946 to the present

ARCTIC SERVICE MEDAL (1976)
COAST GUARD
For 21 days of service on vessels operating in polar waters north of the Arctic Circle from 1946 to the present

ARMED FORCES EXPEDITIONARY MEDAL (1961)
ARMY – NAVY – AIR FORCE – MARINE CORPS – COAST GUARD
For participation in military operations from 1958 to the present not covered by a specific war medal

ARMED FORCES RESERVE MEDAL (1950)
ARMY – NAVY – AIR FORCE – MARINE CORPS – COAST GUARD
For 10 years of honorable service in any reserve component of the United States Armed Forces Reserve or award of "M" device from 1949 to the present

ARMED FORCES SERVICE MEDAL (1996)
ARMY – NAVY – AIR FORCE – MARINE CORPS – COAST GUARD
For participation in military operations not covered by a specific war medal or the Armed Forces Expeditionary Medal from 1995 to the present

ARMY OF OCCUPATION MEDAL (1946)
ARMY – AIR FORCE
For 30 consecutive days of service in occupied territories of former enemies during 1945-1955 (Berlin: 1945-1990)

ASIATIC-PACIFIC CAMPAIGN MEDAL (1942)
ARMY – NAVY – AIR FORCE – MARINE CORPS – COAST GUARD
For service in the Asiatic-Pacific theater for 30 days or receipt of any combat decoration during 1941-1946

CHINA SERVICE MEDAL (1940)
NAVY – MARINE CORPS – COAST GUARD
For service ashore in China or on-board naval vessels during 1937-1939 or 1945-1957

EUROPEAN-AFRICAN-MIDDLE EASTERN CAMPAIGN MEDAL (1942)
ARMY – NAVY – AIR FORCE – MARINE CORPS – COAST GUARD
For service in the European-African-Middle Eastern theater for 30 days or receipt of any combat decoration during 1941-1945

HUMANITARIAN SERVICE MEDAL (1977)
ARMY – NAVY – AIR FORCE – MARINE CORPS – COAST GUARD
For direct participation in specific operations of a humanitarian nature from 1975 to the present

★★★

KOREAN SERVICE MEDAL (1950)
ARMY – NAVY – AIR FORCE – MARINE CORPS – COAST GUARD
For participation in military operations within the Korean area during 1950-1954

KOSOVO CAMPAIGN MEDAL (2000)
ARMY – NAVY – AIR FORCE – MARINE CORPS – COAST GUARD
For 30 consecutive or 60 non-consecutive days of service in the Kosovo Air Campaign between March 24, 1999 and June 10, 1999; or the Kosovo Defense Campaign from June 11, 1999 to the present

MARINE CORPS EXPEDITIONARY MEDAL (1919)
MARINE CORPS
For landings on foreign territory and operations against armed opposition for which no specific campaign medal has been authorized

MEDAL FOR HUMANE ACTION (1949)
ARMY – NAVY – AIR FORCE – MARINE CORPS – COAST GUARD
For 120 consecutive days of service participating in the Berlin Airlift or in support thereof (Medal was also awarded posthumously)

NATIONAL DEFENSE SERVICE MEDAL (1953)
ARMY – NAVY – AIR FORCE – MARINE CORPS – COAST GUARD
For any honorable active duty service during 1950-1954, 1961-1974, or 1990-1995

NAVAL RESERVE MEDAL (1938) (obsolete)
NAVY
For ten years of honorable service in the U.S. Naval Reserve during 1938-1958

NAVY EXPEDITIONARY MEDAL (1936)
NAVY
For landings on foreign territory and operations against armed opposition for which no specific campaign medal has been authorized

NAVY OCCUPATION SERVICE MEDAL (1947)
NAVY – MARINE CORPS – COAST GUARD
For 30 consecutive days of service in occupied territories of former enemies during 1945-1955 (Berlin: 1945-1990)

OUTSTANDING VOLUNTEER SERVICE MEDAL (1993)
ARMY – NAVY – AIR FORCE – MARINE CORPS – COAST GUARD
For outstanding and sustained voluntary service to the civilian community

SOUTHWEST ASIA SERVICE MEDAL (1991)
ARMY – NAVY – AIR FORCE – MARINE CORPS – COAST GUARD
For active participation in, or support of Operation Desert Shield and/or Operation Desert Storm during 1991-1995

U.S. ANTARCTIC EXPEDITION MEDAL (1945)
NAVY – COAST GUARD
  For members of the U.S. Antarctic Expedition of 1939-1941 (awarded in gold, silver, and bronze)

VIETNAM SERVICE MEDAL (1965)
ARMY – NAVY – AIR FORCE – MARINE CORPS – COAST GUARD
  For service in Vietnam, Laos, Cambodia, or Thailand during 1965-1973

WOMEN'S ARMY CORPS SERVICE MEDAL (1943)
ARMY
  For service with both the Women's Army Auxiliary Corps and Women's Army Corps during 1941-1946

WORLD WAR II VICTORY MEDAL (1945)
ARMY – NAVY – AIR FORCE – MARINE CORPS – COAST GUARD
  For service in the U.S. Armed Forces during 1941-1946

UNITED STATES MILITARY MARKSMANSHIP AWARDS

Following is a list of medals and ribbons awarded for attainment of the minimum qualifying score during prescribed shooting exercises:

- Coast Guard Expert Pistol Shot Medal
- Coast Guard Expert Rifleman Medal
- Coast Guard Pistol Marksmanship Ribbon
- Coast Guard Rifle Marksmanship Ribbon
- Naval Expert Rifleman Medal
- Navy Distinguished Marksman And Pistol Shot Ribbon (Obsolete)
- Navy Distinguished Marksman Ribbon (Obsolete)
- Navy Distinguished Pistol Shot Ribbon (Obsolete)
- Navy Expert Pistol Shot Medal
- Navy Pistol Marksmanship Ribbon
- Navy Rifle Marksmanship Ribbon
- Small Arms Expert Marksmanship Ribbon

FOREIGN DECORATIONS AND NON U.S. SERVICE AWARDS

AMRED FORCES HONOR MEDAL (REPUBLIC OF VIETNAM, 1953)
  For outstanding contributions to the training and development of RVN Armed Forces

CIVIL ACTIONS MEDAL (REPUBLIC OF VIETNAM, 1964)
  For outstanding achievements in the field of civic actions

CROIX DE GUERRE (FRANCE, 1941)
  For individual feats of arms as recognized by mention in dispatches

★★★

GALLANTRY CROSS (REPUBLIC OF VIETNAM, 1950)
For deeds of valor and acts of courage/heroism while fighting the enemy

INTER-AMERICAN DFENSE BOARD MEDAL (1981)
ARMY – NAVY – AIR FORCE – MARINE CORPS – COAST GUARD
For service with the Inter-American Defense Board for at least one year

KUWAITI MEDAL FOR THE LIBERATION OF KUWAIT (1995)
ARMY – NAVY – AIR FORCE – MARINE CORPS – COAST GUARD
For participation in, or support of, Operations Desert Shield and/or Desert Storm (1990-1993)

MULTINATIONAL FORCE AND OBSERVERS MEDAL (1982)
ARMY – NAVY – AIR FORCE – MARINE CORPS – COAST GUARD
For six months of service with the Multinational Force & Observers peacekeeping force in the Sinai Desert

NATO MEDAL (1992)
ARMY – NAVY – AIR FORCE – MARINE CORPS – COAST GUARD
For 30 days of service in, or 90 days outside the former Republic of Yugoslavia and the Adriatic Sea under NATO command in direct support of NATO operations

NATO MEDAL (2001)
ARMY – NAVY – AIR FORCE – MARINE CORPS – COAST GUARD
For service members and civilians who participated in operations related to Kosovo

PHILIPPINE DEFENSE MEDAL (REPUBLIC OF THE PHILIPPINES, 1945, ARMY 1948)
For service in defense of the Philippines between December 8, 1941 and June 15, 1942

PHILIPPINE INDEPENDENCE MEDAL (REPUBLIC OF THE PHILIPPINES, 1946, ARMY 1948)
For receipt of both the Philippines Defense and Philippines Liberations medals

PHILIPPINE LIBERATION MEDAL (REPUBLIC OF THE PHILIPPINES, 1945, ARMY 1948)
For service in the liberation of the Philippines between October 17, 1944 and September 3, 1945

REPUBLIC OF KOREA WAR SERVICE MEDAL (1951)
ARMY – NAVY – AIR FORCE – MARINE CORPS – COAST GUARD
For service in Korea between June 25, 1950 and July 27, 1953
(This medal was retroactively approved for Korean War veterans in May 2000.)

★★

REPUBLIC OF VIETNAM CAMPAIGN MEDAL (1966)
ARMY – NAVY – AIR FORCE – MARINE CORPS – COAST GUARD
For six months of service in the Republic of Vietnam between 1965 and 1973; or if wounded, captured, or killed in action during the above period

SAUDI ARABIAN MEDAL FOR THE LIBERATION OF KUWAIT (1991)
ARMY – NAVY – AIR FORCE – MARINE CORPS – COAST GUARD
For participation in, or support of, Operation Desert Storm (January & February 1991)

UNITED NATIONS MEDAL (1964)
ARMY – NAVY – AIR FORCE – MARINE CORPS – COAST GUARD
For six months of service with any authorized UN Peacekeeping mission

UNITED NATIONS SERVICE MEDAL (1951)
ARMY – NAVY – AIR FORCE – MARINE CORPS – COAST GUARD
For service on behalf of the United Nations in Korea between June 27, 1950 and July 27, 1954

U.S. "RIBBONS-ONLY" - AWARDS HAVING NO MEDALS

AIR FORCE LONGEVITY SERVICE AWARD (1957)
AIR FORCE
For successful completion of an aggregate total of four years of honorable active service

AIR FORCE TRAINING RIBBON (1980)
AIR FORCE
For successful completion of an Air Force accession training program

ARMY OVERSEAS SERVICE RIBBON (1981)
ARMY
For successful completion of normal overseas tours not recognized by any other service award

ARMY RESERVE COMPONENTS OVERSEAS TRAINING RIBBON (1984)
ARMY
For successful completion of annual training or active duty training for 10 consecutive duty days on foreign soil

ARMY SERVICE RIBBON (1981)
ARMY
For successful completion of initial entry training

BASIC MILITARY TRAINING HONOR GRADUATE RIBBON (1976)
AIR FORCE
For demonstration of excellence in all academic and military training phases of basic Air Force entry training

★★★

COAST GUARD BASIC TRAINING HONOR GRADUATE RIBBON (1984)
COAST GUARD
For successful attainment of the top 3 percent of the class during Coast Guard recruit training

COAST GUARD RECRUITING SERVICE RIBBON (1995)
COAST GUARD
For successful completion of 3 consecutive years of recruiting duty

COAST GUARD SEA SERVICE RIBBON (1984)
COAST GUARD
For satisfactory completion of a minimum of 12 months of cumulative sea duty

MARINE CORPS DRILL INSTRUCTOR RIBBON (1997-retroactive to 1952)
MARINE CORPS
For successful completion of a tour of duty as a drill instructor (staff billets require completion of 18 months to be eligible)

MARINE CORPS RECRUITING RIBBON (1995-retroactive to 1973)
MARINE CORPS
For successful completion of 3 consecutive years of recruiting duty

MARINE CORPS RESERVE RIBBON (1945-obsolete)
MARINE CORPS
For successful completion of 10 years of honorable service in any class of the Marine Corps Reserve

MARINE SECURITY GUARD RIBBON (1997-retroactive to 1949)
MARINE CORPS
For successful completion of 24 months of cumulative security guard duty service at a foreign service establishment

NAVAL RESERVE SEA SERVICE RIBBON (1987)
NAVY
For 24 months of cumulative service embarked on Naval Reserve vessels or an embarked Reserve unit

NAVY AND MARINE CORPS OVERSEAS SERVICE RIBBON (1987)
NAVY – MARINE CORPS
For 12 months consecutive or accumulated duty at an overseas shore base duty station

NAVY ARCTIC SERVICE RIBBON (1987)
NAVY – MARINE CORPS
For 28 days of service on naval vessels operating above the Arctic Circle

NAVY RECRUITING SERVICE RIBBON (1989)
NAVY
For successful completion of 3 consecutive years of recruiting duty

★★

NAVY SEA SERVICE DEPLOYMENT RIBBON (1981)
NAVY – MARINE CORPS
For 12 months active duty on deployed vessels operating away from their home port for extended periods

N.C.O. PROFESSIONAL DEVELOPMENT RIBBON (1981)
ARMY
For successful completion of designated NCO professional development courses

N.C.O. PROFESSIONAL MILITARY EDUCATION GRADUATE RIBBON (1962)
AIR FORCE
For successful completion of a certified NCO professional military education school

OVERSEAS SERVICE RIBBON – SHORT TOUR (1980)
AIR FORCE
For successful completion of an overseas tour designated as "short term" by appropriate authority

OVERSEAS SERVICE RIBBON – LONG TOUR (1980)
AIR FORCE
For successful completion of an overseas tour designated as "long term" by appropriate authority

RESTRICTED DUTY RIBBON (1984)
COAST GUARD
For successful completion of a tour of duty at remote shore stations (LORAN stations, light ships, etc.) without family

SPECIAL OPERATIONS SERVICE RIBBON (1987)
COAST GUARD
For participation in a Coast Guard special noncombat operation not recognized by another service award

UNITED STATES AND FOREIGN UNIT AWARDS

AIR FORCE ORGANIZATIONAL EXCELLENCE AWARD (1969)
AIR FORCE
For exceptionally meritorious achievement or meritorious service by unique unnumbered organizations performing staff functions

AIR FORCE OUTSTANDING UNIT AWARD (1954)
AIR FORCE
For exceptionally meritorious achievement or meritorious service

AIR FORCE PRESIDENTIAL UNIT CITATION (1957)
AIR FORCE
For extraordinary heroism in action against an armed enemy

★★★

ARMY MERITORIOUS UNIT COMMENDATION (1944)
ARMY

For exceptionally meritorious conduct in the performance of outstanding service

ARMY PRESIDENTIAL UNIT CITATION (1942)
ARMY

For extraordinary heroism in action against an armed enemy

ARMY SUPERIOR UNIT AWARD (1985)
ARMY

For meritorious performance in difficult and challenging peacetime missions

ARMY VALOROUS UNIT AWARD (1963)
ARMY

For outstanding heroism in armed combat against an opposing armed force

COAST GUARD BICENTENNIAL UNIT COMMENDATION (1990)
COAST GUARD

For all Coast Guard personnel serving satisfactorily at any time between June 4, 1989 and June 4, 1990

COAST GUARD "E" RIBBON (1990)
COAST GUARD

For U.S. Coast Guard ships and cutters which earn the overall operational readiness efficiency award

COAST GUARD MERITORIOUS TEAM COMMENDATION (1993)
COAST GUARD

For valorous or meritorious achievement by smaller U.S. Coast Guard

COAST GUARD MERITORIOUS UNIT COMMENDATION (1973)
COAST GUARD

For valorous or meritorious achievement (combat or noncombat)

COAST GUARD UNIT COMMENDATION (1963)
COAST GUARD

For valorous or extremely meritorious service not involving combat

DEPARTMENT OF TRANSPORTATION OUTSTANDING UNIT AWARD (1995)
COAST GUARD

For valorous or extremely meritorious service on behalf of the Transportation Department

JOINT MERITORIOUS UNIT AWARD (1981)
ARMY – NAVY – AIR FORCE – MARINE CORPS – COAST GUARD

For meritorious achievement or service in combat or extreme circumstances

★★

KOREAN PRESIDENTIAL UNIT CITATION (1951)
ARMY – NAVY – AIR FORCE – MARINE CORPS – COAST GUARD
> Awarded to certain units of the U.S. Armed Forces for services rendered during the Korean War

NAVY "E" RIBBON (1976)
NAVY – MARINE CORPS
> For ships or squadrons which have won battle efficiency competitions

NAVY MERITORIOUS UNIT COMMENDATION (1967)
NAVY – MARINE CORPS
> For valorous actions or meritorious achievement (combat or noncombat)

NAVY PRESIDENTIAL UNIT CITATION (1942)
NAVY – MARINE CORPS
> For extraordinary heroism in action against an armed enemy

NAVY UNIT COMMENDATION (1944)
NAVY – MARINE CORPS
> For outstanding heroism in action or extremely meritorious service

PHILIPPINE PRESIDENTIAL UNIT CITATION (1948)
ARMY – NAVY – AIR FORCE – MARINE CORPS – COAST GUARD
> For service in the war against Japan and/or for 1970 and 1972 disaster relief

REPUBLIC OF VIETNAM CIVIL ACTIONS UNIT CITATION (1966)
ARMY – NAVY – AIR FORCE – MARINE CORPS – COAST GUARD
> Awarded to certain units of the U.S. Armed Forces for meritorious service during the Vietnam War, March 1, 1961 – March 28, 1974

REPUBLIC OF VIETNAM GALLANTRY CROSS UNIT CITATION (1966)
ARMY – NAVY – AIR FORCE – MARINE CORPS – COAST GUARD
> Awarded to certain units of the U.S. Armed Forces for valorous combat achievement during the Vietnam War, March 1, 1961 – March 28, 1974

VIETNAM PRESIDENTIAL UNIT CITATION (1954)
ARMY – NAVY – MARINE CORPS – COAST GUARD
> Awarded to certain units of the U.S. Armed Forces for humanitarian service in the evacuation of civilians from North and Central Vietnam

UNITED NATIONS MEDALS CURRENTLY AUTHORIZED FOR U.S. PERSONNEL

Korean War (1950 - 1953)
UN Advance Mission in Cambodia (1991 – 1992)
UN Iraq – Kuwait Observation Mission (1991 – Present)
UN Military Observer Group, in India and Pakistan (1949 – Present)
UN Mission for the Referendum in Western Sahara (1991 – Present)
UN Mission in Haiti (1993 – 1996)

★★

UN Operation in Somalia (1993 – 1995)
UN Protective Force in Former Yugoslavia (1992 – 1995)
UN Security Force on West New Guinea (1962 – 1963)
UN Transitional Authority in Cambodia (1992 – 1993)
UN Truce Supervision Organization (1948 - Present)

EARLIER SERVICE MEDALS

Earlier Service Medals \include the Civil War Campaign Medal, the Indian Campaign Medal, the Spanish Campaign Medal, the Spanish War Service Medal, the Army of Cuban Occupation Medal, the Army of Puerto Rican Occupations Medal, the Philippine Campaign Medal (1899-1913), Philippine Congressional Medal (1898-1902), China Campaign Medal (1900-1901), Army of Cuban Pacification Medal, Mexican Service Medal, Mexican Border Service Medal, Haitian Campaign Medal (April 1, 1919-June 15, 1920), Second Nicaraguan Campaign Medal (August 27, 1926-January 2, 1933), and the Yangtze Service Medal (September 3, 1926-October 21, 1927).

World War I Medals

Medals related to WWI include WWI Victory Medal and the Army of Occupation of Germany Medal. Specific WWI Campaigns are recognized not by separate medals, but by clasps to be attached to WWI Victory Medal's suspension ribbon. These clasps include battle clasps and service clasps.

World War I veterans who received an honorable discharge from Armed Forces for service between April 6, 1917 and November 11, 1918, or served with the American Expeditionary Forces in European Russia between November 12, 1918 and August 5, 1919, or in Siberia between November 12, 1918 and April 1, 1920, were entitled to receive the bronze wreathed star lapel button. Wounded veterans were entitled to receive a silver one.

WEAR OF DECORATIONS, RIBBONS AND MEDALS

Decorations, ribbons and medals which have been awarded may be worn on a uniform or civilian clothing of honorably discharged and retired Armed Force members. However, it is not considered appropriate to wear skill or qualification badges on civilian attire. It is customary to wear only the highest award in miniature form on the lapel of civilian clothing. These decorations have been awarded in recognition of honorable service, and should be worn on every occasion which will reflect credit on them. Retirees are also encouraged to wear their retired pin, and World War II veterans are encouraged to wear their Honorable Discharge Pin (sometimes referred to by veterans as the "ruptured duck".

★★★

GOLD STAR LAPEL BUTTON

A Gold Star lapel button is available to identify widows, parents, and next of kin of members of the armed forces who:

- Lost their lives during World War I, World War II, or during any subsequent period of armed hostilities in which the United States was engaged before July 1, 1958;
- Lost or lose their lives after June 30, 1958 while:
  - o Engaged in an action against an enemy of the U.S.
  - o Engaged in military operations involving conflict with an opposing foreign force; or
  - o Serving with friendly foreign forces engaged in an armed conflict in which the U.S. is not a belligerent party against an opposing armed force; or
- Lost or lose their lives after March 28, 1973, as a result of:
  - o An international terrorist attack against the U.S. or a foreign nation friendly to the U.S., recognized as such an attack by the Secretary of Defense; or
  - o Military operations whiles serving outside the U.S. (including the commonwealths, territories, and possessions of the U.S.) as part of a peacekeeping force.

Upon application, the Secretary of Defense shall furnish one gold star lapel button without cost to the widow and to each parent and next of kin of any member of the Armed Services who loses his or her life under any of the above-mentioned circumstances.

In this section, the following guidelines apply:

- The term "widow" includes widower;
- The term "parents" includes mother, father, stepmother, stepfather, mother through adoption, father through adoption, and foster parents who stood in loco parentis;
- The term "next of kin" includes only children, brothers, sister, half brothers, and half sisters;
- The term "children" includes stepchildren and children through adoption;
- The term "World War I" includes the period from April 6, 1917 to March 3, 1921;
- The term "World War II" includes the period from September 8, 1939, to July 25, 1947, at 12:00 P.M.;
- The term "military operations" includes those operations involving members of the armed forces assisting in U.S. Government sponsored training of military personnel of a foreign nation;

★★

- The term "peacekeeping force" includes those personnel assigned to a force engaged in a peacekeeping operation authorized by the United Nations Security Council

WHERE TO ORDER MEDALS / REPLACEMENT OF MEDALS

The Armed Forces typically issue decorations and service medals as they are awarded or earned.

Discharged veterans may request replacement of lost, stolen, or destroyed medals. Requests may also be made for awards that were earned, but never issued. The next-of-kin of deceased veterans may also make such requests. (Replacements will be issued for United States awards only, not foreign awards.)

All requests should include:

- The veteran's full name (printed or typed)
- The signature of the veteran or next-of-kin, if the veteran is deceased
- The veteran's branch of service
- The veteran's service number or social security number
- The exact or approximate dates of service
- If available, a copy of the discharge or separation document

Requests should be sent to the following locations:

Navy, Marine Corps And Coast Guard:

U.S. Navy Liaison Office (N314)
Room 3475
9700 Page Boulevard
St. Louis, MO 63132-5100

Army

U.S. Army Reserve Personnel Center
Attn: DARP-PAS-EAW
9700 Page Boulevard
St. Louis, MO 63132-5100

Air Force

Air Force Reference Branch NCPMF
National Personnel Records Center
(Military Personnel Records)
9700 Page Boulevard
St. Louis, MO 63132-5100

★★

PRESIDENTIAL MEMORIAL CERTIFICATES

A Presidential Memorial Certificate is an engraved paper certificate that has been signed by the current president, honoring the memory of any honorably discharged deceased veteran. Presidential Memorial Certificates may be distributed to a deceased veteran's next of kin and loved ones. More than one certificate can be provided per family, and there is no time limit for applying for the certificate. Requests for a Presidential Memorial Certificate can be made in person at any VA regional office, or by U.S. Mail. There is no form to use when requesting a certificate. A copy of the veteran's discharge documents and a return mailing address should be included with any request. Written requests should be sent to:

U.S. Department of Veterans Affairs
National Cemetery Administration (403A)
810 Vermont Avenue, NW
Washington, DC 20420

CHAPTER 41

SPECIAL PROVISIONS RELATING TO BENEFITS

VA ENCOURAGES VETERANS TO SETTLE DELINQUENT DEBTS

In July 2000, the VA sent letters to over 270,000 veterans to remind them that they owe the federal government and that money can now be taken from other federal checks to settle their debts.

For the first time, portions of a monthly Social Security check can be withheld by the Department of the Treasury to settle debts that veterans owe to VA. Veterans affected by the withholding will always receive the first $750 of each month's Social Security payment. Only 15 percent of the amount greater than $750 can be withheld.

Deductions will begin in the spring of 2001. Veterans can avoid any loss of Social Security or other federal payments by voluntarily settling their debts with VA.

Federal law says that when veterans owe more than $25 to VA and the debts are more than 90 days overdue, VA officials must report the debts to the U. S. Treasury Department.

The Treasury Department is responsible for collecting the debts from other income the veterans receive from the federal government, including income tax refunds, federal salary or federal retired pay, military pay or military retired pay, Social Security (but not Supplemental Security Income), Railroad Retirement Board benefits (but not "Tier 2" benefits), Black Lung Program payments (Part B) and other federal payments to individuals.

Many of the veterans affected have been treated in VA medical facilities for healthcare conditions not related to their military service. For that care, they are responsible for co-payments. Co-payments range from $2 for a 30-day supply of a drug to hundreds of dollars as the veteran's share of hospitalization costs.

Veterans being treated for service-connected disabilities are exempt from all co-payments, as are low-income veterans. Purple Heart recipients without service-connected disabilities are exempt from all co-payments except pharmacy costs.

Historically, VA has collected debts by withholding money from VA payments such as disability compensation and pension. In the spring of 2001, those offsets will also come from Social Security payments.

Veterans with questions about whether they have VA debts should contact the VA medical centers where they received care.

★★

NONASSIGNABILITY AND EXEMPT STATUS OF BENEFITS

Payments of benefits due or to become due under any law administered by the VA shall not be assignable to the extent specifically authorized by law, and such payments made to, or on account of, a beneficiary shall be:

- Exempt from taxation;
- Exempt from the claim of creditors; and
- Exempt from attachment, levy, or seizure by or under any legal or equitable process whatever, either before or after receipt by the beneficiary.

The preceding shall not apply to claims of the United States arising under such laws, nor shall the exemption from taxation extend to any property purchased in part or wholly out of such payments.

The provisions of the preceding paragraph shall not be construed to prohibit the assignment of insurance otherwise authorized, or of servicemen's indemnity. In any case where a payee of an educational assistance allowance has designated the address of an attorney-in-fact authority to negotiate such benefit check, such action shall be deemed to be an assignment, and is prohibited.

Also prohibited is the collection by setoff or otherwise out of any benefits payable pursuant to any law administered by the VA and relating to veterans, their estates, or their dependents, of any claim of the United States or any agency thereof against:

- Any person other than the indebted beneficiary or the beneficiary's estate; or
- Any beneficiary or the beneficiary's estate, except amounts due the United States by such beneficiary or the beneficiary's estate by reason of overpayments or illegal payments made under such laws to such beneficiary or the beneficiary's estate, or the beneficiary's dependents as such.

If the benefits referred to above are insurance payable by reason of yearly renewable term insurance, United States Government life insurance, or National Service Life Insurance issued by the United States, the exemption provided in this section shall not apply to indebtedness existing against the particular insurance contract upon the maturity of which the claim is based, whether such indebtedness is in the form of liens to secure unpaid premiums or loans, or interest on such premiums or loans, or indebtedness arising from overpayments of dividends, refunds, loans, or other insurance benefits.

The VA may, after receiving a request relating to a veteran, collect by offset of any compensation or pension payable to the veteran under laws administered by the VA the uncollected portion of the amount of any indebtedness associated with the veteran's participation in a plan prescribed in Chapter 73 of Title 10.

If the VA has been unsuccessful in the collection of an amount described in the above paragraph, and has determined that the uncollected portion of such amount is not collectible from amounts payable by that Secretary to the veteran or that the veteran is not receiving any payment from that Secretary, that Secretary may request the VA to make collection in the case of such veteran as authorized in the preceding paragraph.

Payments of benefits under laws administered by the VA shall not be exempt from levy under subchapter D of Chapter 64 of the Inter Revenue Code of 1986 (26 U.S.C. 6331 et seq.).

In the case of a person who:

- Has been determined to be eligible to receive pension or compensation under laws administered by the VA, but for the receipt by such person of pay pursuant to any provision of law providing retired or retirement pay to members or former members of the Armed Forces or commissioned officers of the National Oceanic and Atmospheric Administration or of the Public Health service; and

- Files a waiver of such pay in the amount of such pension or compensation before the end of the one-year period beginning on the date such person is notified by the VA of such person's eligibility for such pension or compensation; then

the retired or retirement pay of such person shall be exempt from taxation, in an amount equal to the amount of pension or compensation which would have been paid to such person but for the receipt by such person of such pay.

Waiver Of Recovery Of Claims By The United States

There shall be no recovery of payments or overpayments (or any interest thereon) of any benefits under any of the laws administered by the VA whenever the VA determines that recovery would be against equity and good conscience, if an application for relief is made within 180 days from the date of notification of the indebtedness by the VA to the payee, or within such longer period as the VA determines is reasonable in a case in which the payee demonstrates to the satisfaction of the VA that such notification was not actually received by such payee within a reasonable period after such date. The VA shall include in the notification to the payee a statement of the right of the payee to submit an application for a waiver under this subsection and a description of the procedures for submitting the application.

CERTAIN BARS TO BENEFITS

The discharge or dismissal due to any of the following shall bar all rights of such person under laws administered by the VA based upon the period of service from which discharged or dismissed, notwithstanding any action subsequent to the date of such discharge by a board established pursuant to Section 1553 of Title 10:

★★

- A sentence by a general court-martial of any person from the Armed Forces; or

- The discharge of any such person on the ground that such person was a conscientious objector who refused to perform military duty, refused to wear the uniform, or otherwise to comply with lawful orders of competent military authority; or

- On the basis of desertion, or;

- On the basis of an absence without authority from active duty for a continuous period of at lease 180 days if such person was discharged under conditions other than honorable; unless such person demonstrates to the satisfaction of the Secretary of the VA that there are compelling circumstances to warrant such prolonged unauthorized absence; or

- The acceptance of an officer's resignation for the good of the service; or

- The discharge of any individual during a period of hostilities as an alien. (This provision shall not apply to any alien whose service was honest and faithful, and who was not discharged on the individual's own application or solicitation as an alien. No individual shall be considered as having been discharged on the individual's own application or solicitation as an alien in the absence of affirmative evidence establishing that the individual was so discharged.)

Notwithstanding the preceding paragraph, if it is established to the VA's satisfaction that, at the time of the commission of an offense leading to a person's court-martial, discharge, or resignation, that person was insane, such person shall not be precluded from benefits under laws administered by the VA based upon the period of service from which such person was separated.

Notwithstanding any other provisions of law, no benefits under laws administered by the VA shall be provided, as a result of a change in or new issuance of a discharge under Section 1553 of Title 10, except upon a case-by-case review by the board of review concerned, subject to review by the Secretary concerned, under such section, of all the evidence and factors in each case under published uniform standards (which shall be historically consistent with criteria for determining honorable service and shall not include any criterion for automatically granting or denying such change or issuance) and procedures generally applicable to all persons administratively discharged or released from active military, naval, or air service under other than honorable conditions.

Any such person described above shall be afforded an opportunity to apply for such review under Section 1553 for a period of time terminating not less than one year after the date on which such uniform standards and procedures are promulgated and published.

PROHIBITION AGAINST DUPLICATION OF BENEFITS

Except to the extent that retirement pay is waived under other provisions of law, not more than one award of pension, compensation, emergency officers', regular, or reserve retirement pay, or initial award of naval pension granted after July 13, 1943, shall be made concurrently to any person based on such

★★★

person's own service, or concurrently to any person based on the service of any other person.

A non-service connected disability pension may be paid to a veteran or surviving spouse concurrently with retired or retirement pay **only** if the annual amount of such retired or retirement pay is counted as annual income when determining the veteran's eligibility for non-service connected disability pension.

The receipt of pension, compensation, or dependency and indemnity compensation by a surviving spouse, child, or parent on account of the death of any person, or receipt by any person of pension or compensation on account of such person's own service, shall not bar the payment of pension, compensation, or dependency and indemnity compensation on account of the death or disability of any other person.

Generally, the receipt of pension, compensation, or dependency and indemnity compensation by a surviving spouse, child, or parent on account of the death of any person, or receipt by any person of pension or compensation on account of such person's own service, shall not bar the payment of pension, compensation, or dependency and indemnity compensation on account of the death or disability of any other person.

However, VA benefits other than insurance may not be paid to any child by reason of the death of more than one parent in the same parental line; although, the child may elect one or more times to receive benefits by reason of the death of any one of such parents.

Additionally, VA benefits other than insurance may not be paid to any person by reason of the death of more than one person to whom such person was married; however, the person may elect one or more times to receive benefits by reason of the death of any one spouse.

Pension, compensation, or retirement pay on account of any person's own service shall not be paid to such person for any period for which such person receives active service pay.

WAIVER OF RETIRED PAY

Any person who is receiving pay pursuant to any provision of law providing retired or retirement pay to person in the Armed Forces, or as a commissioned officer of the National Oceanic and Atmospheric Administration or of the Public Health Service, and who would be eligible to receive pension or compensation under the laws administered by the VA if such person were not receiving such retired or retirement pay, shall be entitled to receive such pension or compensation upon the filing by such person with the department by which such retired or retirement pay is paid of a waiver of so much of such person's retired or retirement pay as is equal in amount to such pension or compensation. To prevent duplication of payments, the department with which any such waiver is filed shall notify the VA of the receipt of such waiver, the amount waived, and the effective date of the reduction in retired or retirement pay.

★★★★★★★★★★★★★★★★★★★★★★★★★★★★★★★★★★★★★★

RENOUNCEMENT OF RIGHT TO BENEFITS

Any person entitled to pension, compensation, or dependency and indemnity compensation under any of the laws administered by the VA may renounce the right of such receipt. The application for such renouncement must be in writing, and must be signed by the individual. Upon the filing of such an application, payment of such benefits shall be terminated, and the person shall be denied any and all rights thereto from such filing.

Renouncement of rights shall not preclude any person from filing a new application for pension, compensation, or dependency and indemnity compensation at a later date, but such new application shall be treated as an original application, and no payments shall be made for any period before the date such new application is filed.

However, if a new application for non-service connected disability pension or for dependency and indemnity compensation for parents is filed within one year after renouncement of that benefit, such application shall not be treated as an original application, and benefits will be payable as if the renouncement had not occurred.

APPORTIONMENT OF BENEFITS

If a veteran is being furnished hospital treatment, institutional, or domiciliary care by the United States, or any political subdivision thereof, all or any part of the compensation, pension, or emergency officers' retirement pay payable may be apportioned on behalf of the veteran's spouse, children, or dependent parents.

Additionally, if a veteran is not living with the veteran's spouse, or if the veteran's children are not in the custody of the veteran, all or any part of the compensation, pension, or emergency officers' retirement pay payable may be apportioned as prescribed by the Secretary of the VA.

If any of the children of a deceased veteran are not in the custody of the veteran's surviving spouse, the pension, compensation, or dependency and indemnity compensation otherwise payable to the surviving spouse may be apportioned as prescribed by the Secretary of the VA.

If a veteran is not living with the veterans' spouse, or if any of the veteran's children are not in the custody of the veteran, any subsistence allowance payable to the veteran under Chapter 31 of Title 38 (Training and Rehabilitation for Veterans with Service-Connected Disabilities), or that portion of the educational assistance allowance4 payable on account of dependents under Chapter 34 of Title 38 (Veterans' Educational Assistance) may be apportioned as prescribed by the Secretary of the VA.

★★

WITHHOLDING BENEFITS OF PERSONS IN TERRITORY OF THE ENEMY

When any alien entitled to gratuitous benefits under laws administered by the VA is located in territory of, or under military control of, an enemy of the United States or any of its allies, any award of such benefits in favor of such alien shall be terminated.

Any alien whose award is terminated shall not be entitled to any further gratuitous benefits, except upon the filing of a new claim, accompanied by evidence satisfactory to the VA showing that such alien was not guilty of mutiny, treason, sabotage, or rendering assistance to such enemy... No gratuitous benefits shall be paid for any period before the date the new claim is filed.

While such alien is located in territory of, or under military control of, an enemy of the United States or any of its allies, the Secretary of the VA may, in his or her discretion, apportion and pay any part of such benefits to the dependents of such alien. No dependent of such alien shall receive benefits by reason of this subsection in excess of the amount to which the dependent would be entitled if such alien were dead.

PAYMENT OF CERTAIN WITHHELD BENEFITS

Any person entitled to benefits under any of the laws administered by the VA, whose award of benefits was terminated due to being an alien located in a territory of, or under military control of, an enemy of the United States or any of its allies, or whose benefits were not paid pursuant to sections 3329 and 3330 of title 31, and who was not guilty of mutiny, treason, sabotage, or rendering assistance to an enemy of the United States or its allies, shall be paid the full amount of any benefits not paid or withheld.

No payments shall be made for any period before the date a claim is filed, to any person whose ward was terminated, or whose benefits were not paid, before July 1, 1954, because such person was a citizen or subject of Germany or Japan residing in Germany or Japan.

PAYMENT OF BENEFITS FOR MONTH OF DEATH

If a surviving spouse is entitled to death benefits from the VA for the month in which a veteran's death occurs, the amount of such death benefits for that month shall be not less than the amount of benefits the veteran would have received for that month, had he or she lived.

If the surviving spouse of a veteran who was in receipt of compensation or pension at the time of death is not entitled to death benefits from the VA for the month in which the veteran's death occurs, that surviving spouse shall be entitled to a benefit for that month in the amount of benefits the veteran would have received for that month, had he or she lived.

If a check or other payment is issued to, and is in the name of the deceased veteran as a benefit payment under chapters 11 or 15 of Title 38 (Pension for Non-Service-Connected Disability or Death) for the month in which death

★★

occurs, that check or other payment shall be treated as being payable to the surviving spouse. If such check or other payment is negotiated or deposited, it shall be considered to be the benefit to which the surviving spouse is entitled. However, if such check or other payment is in an amount less than the amount of the benefit payable to the surviving spouse, the unpaid amount shall be treated as an *accrued benefit.*

INDEBTEDNESS OFFSETS

The VA shall deduct the amount of the indebtedness of any person who has been determined to be indebted to the United States by virtue of such person's participation in a benefits program administered by the VA from future payments made to such person under any law administered by the VA.

Deductions may not be made unless the VA has:

- Made reasonable efforts to notify such person of such person's right to dispute through prescribed administrative processes the existence or amount of such indebtedness and of such person's right to request a waiver of such indebtedness; and

- Made a determination with respect to any such dispute or request or has determined that the time required to make such a determination before making deductions would jeopardize the VA's ability to recover the full amount of such indebtedness through deductions from such payments; and

- Made reasonable efforts to notify such person about the proposed deductions from such payments.

INTEREST AND ADMINISTRATIVE COST CHARGES ON DELINQUENT PAYMENTS OF CERTAIN AMOUNTS DUE THE UNITED STATES

Interest and administrative costs shall be charged, under regulations that the Secretary of the VA shall prescribe, on any amount owed to the United States:

- For an indebtedness resulting from a person's participation in a benefits program administered by the VA other than a loan, loan-guaranty, or loan-insurance program;

- For an indebtedness resulting from the provision of care or services under Chapter 17 of Title 38 (Hospital, Nursing Home, Domiciliary, and Medical Care); or

- To the extent not precluded by the terms of the loan instruments concerned, for an indebtedness resulting from a person's participation in a program of loans, loan guaranties, or loan insurance administered by the Secretary of the VA.

Interest on the amount of any indebtedness shall accrue from the day on which the initial notification of the amount due is mailed to the person who owes such amount (using the most current address of such person that is available to the VA), but interest shall not be charged for any period before October 17, 1980,

★★

or if the amount due is paid within a reasonable period of time. The Secretary of the VA shall determine what constitutes a "reasonable period of time."

The rate of interest to be charged shall be based on the rate of interest paid by the United States for its borrowing, and shall be determined by the Secretary of the VA.

The administrative costs to be charged shall be so much of the costs incurred by the United States in collecting such amount as the Secretary of the VA determines to be reasonable and appropriate.

AUTHORITY TO SUE TO COLLECT CERTAIN DEBTS

The VA shall take appropriate steps to authorize attorneys employed by the VA to exercise the right of the United States to bring suit in any court of competent jurisdiction to recover any indebtedness owed to the United States by a person by virtue of such person's participation in a VA benefit program.

No suit may be filed to recover any indebtedness owed by any person to the United States unless the Secretary of the VA has determined that such person has failed to respond appropriately to reasonable administrative efforts to collect the indebtedness.

The activities of attorneys employed by the VA in bringing suit shall be subject to the discretion and supervision of the Attorney General of the United States, and to such terms and conditions the Attorney General may prescribe.

USE OF INCOME INFORMATION FROM OTHER AGENCIES – NOTICE AND VERIFICATION

The VA shall notify each applicant for:

- Needs-based pension benefits provided under Chapter 15 of Title 38 (Pension for Non-Service Connected Disability or Death), or under any other law administered by the VA.
- Parents' dependency and indemnity compensation
- Health-care services
- Compensation paid under Chapter 11 of Title 38 (Compensation for Service-Connected Disability or Death) at the 100% rate based solely on unemployability and without regard to the fact that the disability or disabilities are not rated as 100% disabling under the rating schedule.

that income information furnished by the applicant may be compared with information obtained by the VA from the Secretary of Health and Human Services or the Secretary of the Treasury. The Secretary of the VA shall periodically transmit to recipients of such benefits and services additional notifications of such matters.

★★★

The VA may not terminate, deny, suspend, or reduce any benefit or service until appropriate steps have been taken to independently verify information relating to the following:

- The amount of the asset or income involved.

- Whether such individual actually has (or had) access to such asset or income for the individual's own use.

- The period or periods when the individual actually had such asset or income.

The VA shall inform the individual of the findings, and shall give the individual an opportunity to contest such findings.

REVIEW OF DEPARTMENT OF HEALTH AND HUMAN SERVICES DEATH INFORMATION

The VA will periodically compare information regarding persons to or for whom compensation or pension is being paid with information in the records of the Department of Health and Human Services relating to persons who have died. This information is used to:

- Determine whether any persons receiving payments are deceased;

- Ensure that such payments to any deceased persons are terminated in a timely manner; and

- Ensure that collection of overpayments of such benefits is initiated in a timely manner.

LIMITATION ON ACCESS TO FINANCIAL RECORDS

The VA may make a request referred to in section 1113(p) of the Right to Financial Privacy Act of 1978 only if the Secretary of the VA determines that the requested information:

1. Is necessary in order for the VA to administer the provisions of law referred to in that section; and

2. Cannot be secured by a reasonable search of records and information of the Department.

Information disclosed may be used solely for the purpose of the administration of benefits programs under laws administered by the VA.

★★★

CHAPTER 42

MINORS, INCOMPETENTS, AND OTHER WARDS

COMMITMENT ACTIONS

The VA may incur necessary court costs and other expenses incident to proceedings for the commitment of mentally incompetent veterans to a VA hospital or domiciliary when necessary for treatment or domiciliary purposes.

Payments To And Supervision Of Fiduciaries

Where it appears to the VA that the interest of the beneficiary would be served thereby, payment of benefits under any law administered by the VA may be made directly to the beneficiary or to a relative or some other person for the use and benefit of the beneficiary, regardless of any legal disability on the part of the beneficiary.

When, in the VA's opinion, any fiduciary receiving funds on behalf of a beneficiary is acting in such a number of cases as to make it impracticable to conserve properly the estates, or to supervise the persons of the beneficiaries, the VA may refuse to make future payments in such cases as the it may deem proper.

In a case in which the VA determines that a commission is necessary in order to obtain the services of a fiduciary in the best interests of a beneficiary, the VA may authorize a fiduciary appointed by the VA to obtain from the beneficiary's estate a reasonable commission for fiduciary services rendered, however, the commission in any year may not exceed 4% of the monetary benefits under laws administered by the Secretary paid on behalf of the beneficiary to the fiduciary during such year. A commission may not be authorized for a fiduciary who receives any other form of remuneration or payment in connection with rendering fiduciary services on behalf of the beneficiary.

Whenever it appears that any guardian, curator, conservator, or other person, in the opinion of the VA, is not properly executing, or has not properly executed the duties of the trust of such guardian, curator, conservator, or other person; or has collected or paid, or is attempting to collect or pay, fees, commission, or allowances that are inequitable or in excess of those allowed by law for the duties performed or expenses incurred, or has failed to make such payments as may be necessary for the benefit of the ward or the dependents of the ward, then the VA's authorized attorney may appear in court to make proper presentation of such matters.

The VA may suspend payments to any such guardian, curator, conservator, or other person who shall neglect or refuse, after reasonable notice, to render an account to the VA from time to time showing the application of such payments for the benefit of such incompetent or minor beneficiary, or who shall neglect or refuse to administer the estate according to law.

The VA may require the fiduciary, as part of such account, to disclose any additional financial information concerning the beneficiary. An authorized VA employee may appear or intervene in any court as an interested party in litigation instituted by the VA or otherwise, directly affecting money paid to such fiduciary.

Payment is authorized of any court or other expenses incident to any investigation or court proceeding for the appointment of any fiduciary or other person for the purpose of payment of benefits, or the removal of such fiduciary and appointment of another.

★★

CHAPTER 43

RECORDS AND INVESTIGATIONS

RECORDS

All files, records, reports and other papers and documents pertaining to any claim under any of the laws administered by the VA, including the names and addresses of present or former members of the Armed Forces, and their dependents, in the possession of the VA shall be confidential and privileged. No disclosure, except as outlined below, shall be made.

The VA shall make disclosure of records, reports, and other papers and documents as follows:

- To a claimant or duly authorized agent or representative of a claimant as to matters concerning the claimant alone when, in the VA's judgment, such disclosure would not be injurious to the physical or mental health of the claimant and to an independent medical expert or experts for an advisory opinion.

- When required by process of a United States court to be produced in any suit or proceeding therein pending.

- When required by any department or other agency of the United States Government.

- In all proceedings in the nature of an inquest into the mental competency of a claimant.

- In any suit or other judicial proceeding when, in the judgment of the VA, such disclosure is deemed necessary and proper.

- In connection with any proceeding for the collection of an amount owed to the United States by virtue of a person's participation in any benefit program administered by the VA, when in the judgment of the VA, such disclosure is deemed necessary and proper.

The amount of any payment made by the VA to any person receiving benefits under a VA program shall be made known to any person who applies for such information.

Any appraisal report or certificate of reasonable value submitted to or prepared by the VA in connection with any loan guaranteed, insured, or made under the VA's Housing or Small Business Loans program shall be made available to any person who applies for such report or certificate.

Subject to the approval of the President of the United States, the VA may publish at any time, and in any manner, any or all information of record pertaining to any claim filed with the VA, if the VA determines that the public interest warrants or requires such publication.

★★★

The Secretary of the VA may, as a matter of discretion, authorize an inspection of Department records by duly authorized representatives of recognized organizations.

The Secretary of the VA may release information, statistics, or reports to individuals or organizations when such release would serve a useful purpose.

The VA may, pursuant to regulations, release the name and/or address of any present or former member of the Armed Forces, or a dependent of a present or former member of the Armed Forces to:

- Any nonprofit organization, if the release is directly connected with the conduct of programs, and the utilization of benefits under this title; or

- Any criminal or civil law enforcement governmental agency or instrumentality charged under applicable law with the protection of the public health or safety, if a qualified representative of such agency has made a written request that such name or address be provided for a purpose authorized by law.

    Any organization or member thereof, or other person who, knowing that the use of any name or address released by the VA pursuant to the preceding paragraph is limited to the purpose specified above, willfully uses such name or address for a purpose other than those so specified, shall be guilty of a misdemeanor, and be fined not more than $5,000 in the case of a first offence, and not more than $20,000 in the case of any subsequent offense.

Subject to the provisions outlined in this chapter, and under regulations prescribed by the Secretary of the VA, the VA may release the name and/or address of any person who is a present or former member of the Armed Forces, or who is a dependent of a present or former member of the Armed Forces, to a consumer reporting agency, if the release of such information is necessary for:

- Locating a person who has been administratively determined to be indebted to the United States by virtue of the person's participation in a benefits program administered by the VA.

- Conducting a study pursuant to evaluation and data collection, and all reasonable steps have been taken to assure that the release of such information will not have an adverse effect on such person.

- Obtaining a consumer report in order to assess the ability of a person to repay his or her indebtedness to the United States. Information may only be released under this clause if the VA determines that such person has failed to respond appropriately to administrative efforts to collect such indebtedness.

A release of information may also be made for the purpose of:

- Determining the creditworthiness, credit capacity, income, or financial resources of a person who has applied for any benefit under the VA's housing or small business loan program, or who has submitted an offer for the purchase of property acquired by the VA.

- Verifying, either before or after the VA has approved a person's application for assistance in the form of a loan guaranty or loan insurance under the VA's housing or small business loan program, information submitted by a lender to the VA regarding the creditworthiness, credit capacity, income, or financial resources of such person.

- Offering for sale or other disposition by the VA, any loan or installment sales contract owned or held by the VA.

- Providing assistance to any applicant for benefits under the VA's housing or small business loan program, or administering such benefits if the VA promptly records the fact of such release in appropriate records pertaining to the person concerning whom such release was made.

Furnishing Of Records

Any person desiring a copy of any record, paper, etc. in the custody of the VA that may be disclosed as outlined in the above section, must submit an application in writing. The application must specifically state:

- The particular record, paper, etc. desired, and whether it must be certified or uncertified; and

- The purpose for which the records are to be used.

The VA may establish a schedule of fees for copies and certification of such records.

Contacting Veterans

The VA cannot release personal information about a veteran without that person's permission. VA can, however, forward a message from an individual to a veteran, providing the veteran has filed a claim with VA, and VA has a current address on record.

Certification Of Records Of District Of Columbia

When a copy of any public record of the District of Columbia is required by the VA to be used in determining the eligibility of any person for benefits under laws administered by the VA, the official custodian of such public record shall, without charge, provide the applicant for such benefits or any person (including any veteran's organization) acting on the veteran's behalf, or the authorized representative of the VA, with a certified copy of such record.

Transcript Of Trial Records

The VA may purchase transcripts of the record, including all evidence, of trial litigated cases.

Confidentiality Of Medical Quality-Assurance Records

Records and documents created by the VA as part of a medical quality-assurance program are confidential and privileged, and may not be disclosed to any person or entity except:

- To a Federal agency or private organization, if such record or document is needed by such agency or organization to perform licensing or accreditation functions related to VA health-care facilities, or to perform monitoring, required by statute, of VA health-care facilities.

- To a Federal executive agency or provider of healthcare services, if such record or document is required by such agency or provider for participation by the Department in a health-care program with such agency or provider.

- To a criminal or civil law enforcement governmental agency or instrumentality charged under applicable law with the protection of the public health or safety, if a qualified representative of such agency or instrumentality makes a written request that such record or document be provided for a purpose authorized by law.

- To health-care personnel, to the extent necessary to meet a medical emergency affecting the health or safety of any individual.

The name and other identifying information regarding any individual patient or employee of the VA, or any other individual associated with the VA for purposes of a medical quality-assurance program, contained in a record or document describe above, shall be deleted from any record or document before any disclosure is made, if disclosure of such name and identifying information would constitute a clearly unwarranted invasion of personal privacy.

No person or entity to whom a record or document has been disclosed shall make further disclosure of such information, except for a purpose provided in this chapter.

Nothing in this chapter shall be construed as authority to withhold any record or document from a committee of either House of Congress or any joint committee of Congress, if such record or document pertains to any matter within the jurisdiction of such committee or joint committee.

Nothing in this chapter shall be construed as authorizing or requiring withholding from any person or entity the disclosure of statistical information regarding VA health-care programs (including such information as aggregate morbidity and mortality rates associated with specific activities at individual VA health-care facilities) that does not implicitly or explicitly identify individual patients or employees of the Department, or individuals who participated in the conduct of a medical quality-assurance review.

Any person, who willfully discloses any record or document in a manner not allowed by the VA, shall be fined not more than $5,000 in the case of a first offense, and not more than $20,000 in the case of a subsequent offense.

★★

INVESTIGATIONS

Authority To Issue Subpoenas

For the purposes of the laws administered by the VA, the VA shall have the power to:

- Issue subpoenas for and compel the attendance of witnesses within a radius of 100 miles from the place of hearing.
- Require the production of books, papers, documents, and other evidence.
- Take affidavits and administer oaths and affirmations.
- Aid claimants in the preparation and presentation of claims.
- Make investigations and examine witnesses upon any matter within the jurisdiction of the VA.

Any person required by such subpoena to attend as a witness, shall be allowed and paid the same fees and mileage as are paid witnesses in the district courts of the United States.

Validity Of Affidavits

Any such oath, affirmation, affidavit or examination, when certified under the hand of any such employee by whom it was administered or taken and authenticated by the seal of the Department, may be offered or used in any court of the United States, and without further proof of the identity or authority of such employee shall have like force and effect as if administered or taken before a clerk of such court.

Disobedience To Subpoena

In case of disobedience to any such subpoena, the aid of any district court of the Untied States may be invoked in requiring the attendance and testimony of witnesses and the production of documentary evidence, and such court within the jurisdiction of which the inquiry is carried on may, in case of contumacy or refusal to obey a subpoena issued to any officer, agent, or employee of any corporation or to any other person, issue an order requiring such corporation or other person to appear or to give evidence touching the matter in question. Any failure to obey such order of the court may be punished by such court as contempt thereof.

CHAPTER 44

AGENTS AND ATTORNEYS

No individual may act as an agent or attorney in the preparation, presentation, or prosecution of any claim under laws administered by the VA unless the VA has recognized such individual for such purposes.

The VA may recognize the following representatives in the preparation, presentation, and prosecution of claims under laws administered by the VA:

- National Red Cross
- American Legion
- Disabled American Veterans
- United Spanish War Veterans
- Veterans of Foreign Wars
- Other organizations as the VA may approve

The VA, in the discretion of the Secretary of the VA, may furnish, if available, space and office facilities for the use of paid full-time representatives of national organizations so recognized.

No individual shall be recognized unless:

- The individual has certified to the VA that no fee or compensation of any nature will be charged any individual for services rendered in connection with any claim; and
- Such individual has filed with the VA a power of attorney, executed in such manner and form as the VA may prescribe.

Unless a claimant specifically indicates in a power of attorney filed with the VA a desire to appoint only a recognized representative of an organization listed in or approved above, the VA may, for any purpose, treat the power of attorney naming such an organization, a specific office of such an organization, or a recognized representative of such an organization as the claimant's representative as an appointment of the entire organization as the claimant's representative.

Whenever the VA is required or permitted to notify a claimant's representative, and the claimant has named in a power of attorney an organization listed in or approved by the VA, a specific office of such an organization, or a recognized representative of such an organization without specifically indicating a desire to appoint only a recognized representative of the organization the VA shall notify the organization at the address designated by the organization for the purpose of receiving the notification concerned.

★★★

Recognition With Respect To Particular Claims

The VA may recognize any individual for the preparation, presentation, and prosecution of any particular claim for benefits under any of the laws administered by the VA if:

- Such individual has certified to the VA that no fee or compensation of any nature will be charged any individual for services rendered in connection with such claim; and
- Such individual has filed with the VA a power of attorney, executed in such a manner and in such form as the VA may prescribe.

Recognition Of Agents And Attorneys Generally

The VA may recognize any individual as an agent or attorney for the preparation, presentation, and prosecution of claims under laws administered by the VA. The VA may require that individuals, before being recognized under this section, show that they are of good moral character and in good repute, are qualified to render claimants valuable service, and otherwise are competent to assist claimants in presenting claims.

The VA, after notice and opportunity for a hearing, may suspend or exclude from further practice before the Department of the VA, any agent or attorney recognized under this section if the VA finds that such agent or attorney:

- Has engaged in any unlawful, unprofessional, or dishonest practice.
- Has been guilty of disreputable conduct.
- Is incompetent.
- Has violated or refused to comply with any of the laws administered by the VA, or with any of the regulations or instructions governing practice before the VA; or
- Has in any manner deceived, misled, or threatened any actual or prospective claimant.

A fee may not be charged, allowed, or paid for services of agents and attorneys with respect to services provided before the date on which the Board of Veterans' Appeals first makes a final decision in the case. Such a fee may be charged, allowed, or paid in the case of services provided after such date only if an agent or attorney is retained with respect to such case before the end of the one-year period beginning on that date. The limitation in the preceding sentence does not apply to services provided with respect to proceedings before a court.

A person who, acting as agent or attorney in a case referred to in the above paragraph, represents a person before the Department or the Board of Veterans' Appeals after the Board first makes a final decision in the case shall file a copy of any fee agreement between them with the Board at such a time as may be specified by the Board. The Board, upon its own motion or the request of either party, may review such a fee agreement and may order a reduction in

★★

the fee called for in the agreement if the Board finds that the fee is excessive or unreasonable. A finding or order of the Board under the preceding sentence may be reviewed by the Court of Appeals for Veterans Claims.

A reasonable fee may be charged or paid in connection with any proceeding before the VA in a case arising out of a loan made, guaranteed, or insured under the VA's home or small business loan program. A person who charges a fee under this paragraph shall enter into a written agreement with the person represented and shall file a copy of the fee agreement with the VA at such time, and in such manner, as may be specified by the VA.

When a claimant and an attorney have entered into a fee agreement described above, the total fee payable to the attorney may not exceed 20% of the total amount of any past-due benefits awarded on the basis of the claim.

A fee agreement referred to in this chapter is one under which the total amount of the fee payable to the attorney:

• Is to be paid to the attorney by the VA directly from any past-due benefits awarded on the basis of the claim; and

• Is contingent on whether or not the matter is resolved in a manner favorable to the claimant.

(A claim shall be considered to have been resolved in a manner favorable to the claimant if all or any part of the relief sought is granted.)

To the extent that past-due benefits are awarded in any proceeding before the VA, the Board of Veterans' Appeals, or the Court of Appeals for Veterans Claims, the VA may direct that payment of any attorneys' fee under a fee arrangement be made out of such past-due benefits. In no event may the VA withhold for the purpose of such payment any portion of benefits payable for a period after the date of the final decision of the Secretary of the VA, the Board of Veterans' Appeals, or Court of Appeals for Veterans Claims making (or ordering the making of) the award.

Penalty For Certain Acts

Whoever directly or indirectly solicits, contracts for, charges, or receives; or attempts to solicit, contract for, charge, or receive any fee or compensation not specifically provided for in this chapter shall be fined as provided in Title 18, or imprisoned not more than one year, or both.

Whoever wrongfully withholds from any claimant or beneficiary any part of a benefit or claim allowed and due to the claimant or beneficiary, shall be fined as provided in Title 18, or imprisoned not more than one year, or both.

CHAPTER 45

PENAL AND FORFEITURE PROVISIONS

The first section of this chapter outlines basic information for veterans with questions concerning the effect of incarceration on VA benefits. The later sections of this chapter provide detailed information regarding misappropriation by fiduciaries, fraudulent acceptance of payments, forfeiture for fraud, forfeiture for treason, and forfeiture for subversive activities.

BASIC INFORMATION

VA benefits are restricted if a veteran, surviving spouse, child, or dependent parent is convicted of a felony and imprisoned for more than 60 days. VA may still pay certain benefits, however, the amount paid depends on the type of benefit and reason for imprisonment. Following is information about the benefits most commonly affected by imprisonment.

Please note that overpayments due to failure to notify VA of a veteran's incarceration results in the loss of all financial benefits until the overpayment is recovered.

VA DISABILITY COMPENSATION

The disability compensation paid to a veteran incarcerated because of a felony is limited to the 10% disability rate, beginning with the 61st day of imprisonment. For a surviving spouse, child, dependent parent or veteran whose disability rating is 10%, the payment is at the 5% rate. (This means that if a veteran was receiving $188 or more prior to incarceration, the new payment amount will be $98. If a veteran was receiving $98 before incarceration, the new payment amount will be $49.)

If a veteran resides in a halfway house, participates in a work release program, or is on parole, compensation payments will not be reduced.

VA DISABILITY PENSION

VA will stop a veteran's pension payments beginning on the 61st day of imprisonment for conviction of either a felony or misdemeanor.

VA MEDICAL CARE

VA policy does permit the treatment of eligible veterans who are in prison. VA medical center directors are responsible for their facilities, and may bar treatment in certain cases. This is particularly true when the presence of armed guards is disruptive to the delivery of quality medical care. If an incarcerated veteran is in need of treatment, he or she should ask prison officials to contact the nearest VA medical facility for further information.

EDUCATIONAL ASSISTANCE / SUBSISTENCE ALLOWANCE

A subsistence allowance may not be paid to an incarcerated veteran convicted of a felony, buy, under certain circumstances, all or part of the veteran's tuition and fees may be paid. Individuals should contact the VA to determine individual eligibility.

CLOTHING ALLOWANCE

In the case of a veteran who is incarcerated in a Federal, State, or local penal institution for a period in excess of 60 days and who is furnished clothing without charge by the institution, the amount of any annual clothing allowance payable to the veteran shall be reduced by an amount equal to 1/365 of the amount of the allowance otherwise payable under that section for each day on which the veteran was so incarcerated during the 12-month period preceding the date on which payment of the allowance would be due.

PAYMENT TO DEPENDENTS

VA may be able to take part of the amount that the incarcerated veteran is not receiving and pay it to his or her dependents, if they can show need. Interested dependents should contact the nearest VA regional office for details on how to apply. They will be asked to provide income information as part of the application process.

RESTORATION OF BENEFITS

When a veteran is released from prison, his or her compensation or pension benefits may be restored. Depending on the type of disability, the VA may schedule a medical examination to see if the veteran's disability has improved or worsened.

MISAPPROPRIATION BY FIDUCIARIES

Whoever, being a guardian, curator, conservator, committee, or person legally vested with the responsibility or care of a claimant or a claimant's estate, or any other person having charge and custody in a fiduciary capacity of money heretofore or hereafter paid under any of the laws administered by the VA for the benefit of any minor, incompetent, or other beneficiary, shall lend, borrow, pledge, hypothecate, use, or exchange for other funds or property, except as authorized by law, or embezzle or in any manner misappropriate any such money or property derived wherefrom in whole or in part, and coming into such fiduciary's control in any matter whatever in the execution of such fiduciary's trust, or under color of such fiduciary's office or service as such fiduciary, shall be fined in accordance with Title 18, or imprisoned not more than 5 ye4ars, or both.

Any willful neglect or refusal to make and file proper accountings or reports concerning such money or property as required by law shall be taken to be sufficient evidence prima facie of such embezzlement or misappropriation.

★★

FRAUDULENT ACCEPTANCE OF PAYMENTS

Any person entitled to monetary benefits under any of the laws administered by the VA whose right to payment ceases upon the happening of any contingency, who thereafter fraudulently accepts any such payment, shall be fined in accordance with Title 18, or imprisoned not more than one year, or both.

Whoever obtains or receives any money or check under any of the laws administered by the VA without being entitled to it, and with intent to defraud the United States or any beneficiary of the United States, shall be fined in accordance with Title 18, or imprisoned not more than one year, or both.

FORFEITURE FOR FRAUD

Whoever knowingly makes or causes to be made or conspires, combines, aids, or assists in, agrees to, arranges for, or in any way procures the making or presentation of a false or fraudulent affidavit, declaration, certificate, statement, voucher, or paper, concerning any claim for benefits under any of the laws administered by the VA (except laws pertaining to insurance benefits) shall forfeit all rights, claims, and benefits under all laws administered by the VA (except laws pertaining to insurance benefits).

Whenever a veteran entitled to disability compensation has forfeited the right to such compensation under this chapter, the compensation payable but for the forfeiture shall thereafter be paid to the veteran's spouse, children, and parents. Payments made to a spouse, children, and parents under the preceding sentence shall not exceed the amounts payable to each if the veteran had died from service-connected disability. No spouse, child, or parent who participated in the fraud for which forfeiture was imposed shall receive any payment by reason of this subsection. Any apportionment award under this subsection may not be made in any case after September 1, 1959.

Forfeiture of benefits by a veteran shall not prohibit payment of the burial allowance, death compensation, dependency and indemnity compensation, or death pension in the event of the veteran's death.

After September 1, 1959, no forfeiture of benefits may be imposed under the rules outlined in this chapter upon any individual who was a resident of, or domiciled in, a State at the time the act or acts occurred on account of which benefits would, but not for this subsection, be forfeited unless such individual ceases to be a resident of, or domiciled in, a State before the expiration of the period during which criminal prosecution could be instituted. The paragraph shall not apply with respect to:

- Any forfeiture occurring before September 1, 1959, or
- An act or acts that occurred in the Philippine Islands before July 4, 1946.

The VA is authorized and directed to review all cases in which, because of a false or fraudulent affidavit, declaration, certificate, statement, voucher, or paper, a forfeiture of gratuitous benefits under laws administered by the VA was imposed, pursuant to this section or prior provisions of the law, on or before

★★★

September 1, 1959. In any such case in which the VA determines that the forfeiture would not have been imposed under the provisions of this section in effect after September 1, 1959, the VA shall remit the forfeiture, effective June 30, 1972. Benefits to which the individual concerned becomes eligible by virtue of any such remission may be awarded, upon application for, and the effective date of any award of compensation, dependency and indemnity compensation, or pension made in such a case shall be fixed in accordance with the facts found, but shall not be earlier than the effective date of the Act or administrative issue. In no event shall such award or increase be retroactive for more than one year from the date of application, or the date of administrative determination of entitlement, whichever is earlier.

FORFEITURE FOR TREASON

Any person shown by evidence satisfactory to the VA to be guilty of mutiny, treason, sabotage, or rendering assistance to an enemy of the United States or its allies shall forfeit all accrued or future gratuitous benefits under laws administered by the VA.

The VA, in its discretion, may apportion and pay any part of benefits forfeited under the preceding paragraph to the dependents of the person forfeiting such benefits. No dependent of any person shall receive benefits by reason of this subsection in excess of the amount to which the dependent would be entitled if such person were dead.

In the case of any forfeiture under this chapter, there shall be no authority after September 1, 1959 to:

- Make an apportionment award pursuant to the preceding paragraph; or

- Make an award to any person of gratuitous benefits based on any period of military, naval, or air service commencing before the date of commission of the offense.

FORFEITURE FOR SUBVERSIVE ACTIVITIES

Any individual who is convicted after September 1, 1959, of any offense listed below shall, from and after the date of commission of such offense, have no right to gratuitous benefits (including the right to burial in a national cemetery) under laws administered by the VA based on periods of military, naval, or air service commencing before the date of commission of such offense, and no other person shall be entitled to such benefits on account of such individual. After receipt of notice of the return of an indictment for such an offense, the VA shall suspend payment of such gratuitous benefits pending disposition of the criminal proceedings. If any individual whose rights to benefits has been terminated pursuant to this section, is granted a pardon of the offense by the President of the United States, the right to such benefits shall be restored as of the date of such pardon.

★★

Chapter 45 - Penal & Forfeiture Provisions

The offenses referred to in the previous paragraph are:

- Sections 894, 904 and 906 of Title 10 (articles 94, 104, and 106 of the Uniform Code of Military Justice)
- Sections 792, 793, 794, 798, 2381, 2382, 2383, 2384, 2385, 2387, 2388, 2389, 2390, and chapter 105 of Title 18
- Sections 222, 223, 224, 225 and 226 of the Atomic Energy Act of 1954 (42 U.S.C. 2272, 2273, 2274, 2275, and 2276)
- Section 4 of the Internal Security Act of 1950 (50 U.S.C. 783)

The Secretary of Defense, the Secretary of Transportation, or the Attorney General, as appropriate, shall notify the VA in each case in which an individual is convicted of an offense mentioned in this chapter.

★★

CHAPTER 46

MILITARY PAY RATES

COMPARATIVE RANKS CHART

The charts below will assist in determining the pay of the Officer, Warrant Officer and Enlisted man.

Pay Grade	Army, Air Force And Marine Corps	Navy, Coast Guard and Coast and Geodetic Survey
O-10	General	Admiral
O-9	Lt. General	Vice Admiral
O-8	Major General	Real Admiral (Upper half)
O-7	Brigadier General	Rear Admiral (Lower half) & Commodore
O-6	Colonel	Captain
O-5	Lt. Colonel	Commander
O-4	Major	Lt. Commander
O-3	Captain	Lieutenant
O-2	First Lieutenant	Lieutenant (Jr. Grade)
O-1	Second Lieutenant	Ensign
W-4	Chief Warrant Officer	Chief Warrant Officer*
W-3	Chief Warrant Officer	Chief Warrant Officer*
W-2	Chief Warrant Officer	Chief Warrant Officer*
W-1	Warrant Officer	Warrant Officer*

(*Not applicable to Coast and Geodetic Survey)

Pay Grade	ARMY
E-9	Sergeant Major Staff Sergeant Major
E-8	First Sergeant – M. Sergeant
E-7	Sergeant 1/c – Specialist – 7
E-6	Staff Sergeant – Specialist - 6
E-5	Sergeant – Specialist - 5
E-4	Corporal – Specialist - 4
E-3	Private 1/c
E-2	Private
E-1	Private

Pay Grade	COAST GUARD
E-9	Master Chief Petty Officer
E-8	Senior Chief Petty Officer
E-7	Chief Petty Officer
E-6	Petty Officer 1/c
E-5	Petty Officer 2/c
E-4	Petty Officer 3/c
E-3	Seaman
E-2	Seaman Apprentice
E-1	Seaman Recruit

★★

Pay Grade	NAVY
E-9	Master Chief Petty Officer
E-8	Senior Chief Petty Officer
E-7	Chief Petty Officer
E-6	Petty Officer 1/c
E-5	Petty Officer 2/c
E-4	Petty Officer 3/c
E-3	Seaman
E-2	Seaman Apprentice
E-1	Seaman Recruit

Pay Grade	MARINE CORPS
E-9	Sergeant Major Master Gunnery Sergeant
E-8	First Sergeant
E-7	Gunnery Sergeant
E-6	Staff Sergeant
E-5	Sergeant
E-4	Corporal
E-3	Lance Corporal
E-2	Private First Class
E-1	Private

Pay Grade	AIR FORCE
E-9	Chief Master Sergeant
E-8	Senior Master Sergeant
E-7	Master Sergeant
E-6	Tech. Sergeant
E-5	Staff Sergeant
E-4	Sergeant
E-3	Airman 1/c
E-2	Airman
E-1	Airman Basic

Special Incentive Pay Rates

Members of the uniformed services are entitled to receive special pay for special kinds of duty, in addition to the incentive rates for aircraft and submarine crews.

ARMED SERVICES PAY ACT OF 2001

Monthly Basic Pay Rates – Active Duty - Effective January 1, 2001

Below are the basic pay rates for active duty, effective January 1, 2001. When a figure is not shown for a given number of completed years of service-for-pay, the amount to the left applies.

COMMISSIONED OFFICERS

Grade	Less Than 2	2	3	4	6
O-10	8518.80	8818.50	8818.50	8818.50	8818.50
O-9	7550.10	7747.80	7912.80	7912.80	7912.80
O-8	6838.20	7062.30	7210.50	7252.20	7437.30
O-7	5682.30	6068.40	6068.40	6112.50	6340.80
O-6	4211.40	4626.60	4930.20	4930.20	4949.10
O-5	3368.70	3954.90	4228.80	4280.40	4450.50
O-4	2839.20	3457.20	3687.90	3739.50	3953.40
O-3	2638.20	2991.00	3228.00	3489.30	3656.40
O-2	2301.00	2620.80	3018.60	3120.30	3184.80
O-1	1997.70	2079.00	2512.80	2512.80	2512.80

★★★

Grade	8	10	12	14	16
O-10	9156.90	9156.90	9664.20	8664.20	10356.00
O-9	8114.10	8114.10	8451.60	8451.60	9156.90
O-8	7747.80	7819.80	8114.10	8198.70	8451.60
O-7	6514.50	6715.50	6915.90	7116.90	7747.80
O-6	5160.90	5189.10	5189.10	5360.70	6005.40
O-5	4450.50	4584.30	4831.80	5155.80	5481.60
O-4	4127.70	4409.70	4629.30	4781.70	4935.00
O-3	3839.70	3992.70	4189.80	4292.10	4292.10
O-2	3184.80	3184.80	3184.80	3184.80	3184.80
O-1	2512.80	2512.80	2512.80	2512.80	2512.80

Grade	18	20	22	24	26
O-10	10356.00	11049.30	11103.90	11334.60	11737.20
O-9	9156.90	9664.20	9803.40	10004.70	10356.00
O-8	8818.50	9156.90	9382.80	9382.80	9382.80
O-7	8280.90	8280.90	8280.90	8280.90	8322.60
O-6	6311.40	6617.40	6791.40	6967.80	7309.80
O-5	5637.00	5790.30	5964.60	5964.60	5964.60
O-4	4986.60	4986.60	4986.60	4986.60	4986.60
O-3	4292.10	4292.10	4292.10	4292.10	4292.10
O-2	3184.80	3184.80	3184.80	3184.80	3184.80
O-1	2512.80	2512.80	2512.80	2512.80	2512.80

**OFFICERS WITH MORE THAN FOUR YEARS ACTIVE-DUTY
AS ENLISTED OR WARRANT OFFICER**

Grade	Less Than 2	2	3	4	6
		Years of Service			
O-3E	00.00	00.00	00.00	3489.30	3656.40
O-2E	00.00	00.00	00.00	3120.30	3184.80
O-1E	00.00	00.00	00.00	2512.80	2684.10

Grade	8	10	12	14	16
		Years of Service			
O-3E	3839.70	3992.70	4189.80	4355.70	4450.50
O-2E	3285.90	3457.20	3589.50	3687.90	3687.90
O-1E	2783.10	2884.20	2984.10	3120.30	3120.30

Grade	18	20	22	24	26
O-3E	4580.40	4580.40	4580.40	4580.40	4580.40
O-2E	3687.90	3687.90	3687.90	3687.90	3687.90
O-1E	3120.30	3120.30	3120.30	3120.30	3120.30

WARRANT OFFICERS (FOR ARMY, NAVY AND MARINE CORPS)

Grade	Less Than 2	2	3	4	6
		Years of Service			
W-5	00.00	00.00	00.00	00.00	00.00
W-4	2688.00	2891.70	2974.80	3056.70	3197.40
W-3	2443.20	2649.90	2649.90	2684.10	2793.90
W-2	2139.60	2315.10	2315.10	2391.00	2512.80
W-1	1782.60	2043.90	2043.90	2214.60	2315.10

Grade	8	10	12	14	16
W-5	00.00	00.00	00.00	00.00	00.00
W-4	3336.30	3477.00	3614.10	3756.30	3892.50
W-3	2919.00	3084.30	3184.80	3294.60	3420.30
W-2	2649.90	2750.70	2851.50	2949.60	3058.20
W-1	2419.20	2523.30	2626.80	2731.50	2835.90

Grade	18	20	22	24	26
W-5	00.00	4640.70	4800.00	4959.90	5120.10
W-4	4032.00	4168.20	4309.50	4448.40	4590.90
W-3	3545.10	3669.90	3794.70	3919.80	4045.20
W-2	3169.50	3280.80	3391.80	3503.40	3503.40
W-1	2940.00	3018.60	3018.60	3018.60	3018.60

ENLISTED MEMBERS

Grade	Less Than 2	2	3	4	6
		Years of Service			
E-9	00.00	00.00	00.00	00.00	00.00
E-8	00.00	00.00	00.00	00.00	00.00
E-7	1831.20	1999.20	2075.10	2149.80	2227.20
E-6	1575.00	1740.30	1817.40	1891.80	1969.50
E-5	1381.80	1549.20	1623.90	1701.00	1777.80
E-4	1288.80	1423.80	1500.60	1576.20	1653.00
E-3	1214.70	1307.10	1383.60	1385.40	1385.40
E-2	1169.10	1169.10	1169.10	1169.10	1169.10
E-1>4	1042.80	1042.80	1042.80	1042.80	1042.80
E-1<4	964.80	00.00	00.00	00.00	00.00

★★★

Grade	8	10	12	14	16
E-9	00.00	3126.90	3197.40	3287.10	3392.40
E-8	2622.00	2697.90	2768.40	2853.30	2945.10
E-7	2303.10	2379.00	2454.90	2529.60	2607.00
E-6	2046.00	2122.80	2196.90	2272.50	2327.70
E-5	1855.80	1930.50	2007.90	2007.90	2007.90
E-4	1653.00	1653.00	1653.00	1653.00	1653.00
E-3	1385.40	1385.40	1385.40	1385.40	1385.40
E-2	1169.10	1169.10	1169.10	1169.10	1169.10
E-1>4	1042.80	1042.80	1042.80	1042.80	1042.80
E-1<4	00.00	00.00	00.00	00.00	00.00

Grade	18	20	22	24	26
E-9	3498.00	3601.80	3742.80	3882.60	4060.80
E-8	3041.10	3138.00	3278.10	3417.30	3612.60
E-7	2683.80	2758.80	2890.80	3034.50	3250.50
E-6	2367.90	2367.90	2370.30	2370.30	2370.30
E-5	2007.90	2007.90	2007.90	2007.90	2007.90
E-4	1653.00	1653.00	1653.00	1653.00	1653.00
E-3	1385.40	1385.40	1385.40	1385.40	1385.40
E-2	1169.10	1169.10	1169.10	1169.10	1169.10
E-1>4	1042.80	1042.80	1042.80	1042.80	1042.80
E-1<4	00.00	00.00	00.00	00.00	00.00

Note: Basic Pay for O-7 – 0-10 is limited to Level III of the Executive Schedule
Note: Basic Pay for 0-6 and below is limited to Level V of the Executive Schedule

Monthly Basic Pay Rates – Reserve Pay - Effective January 1, 2001

Below are the basic pay rates for reserve pay, effective January 1, 2001. When a figure is not shown for a given number of completed years of service-for-pay, the amount to the left applies.

COMMISSIONED OFFICERS

Grade	Less Than 2	2	3	4	6
		Years of Service			
O-10	1135.84	1175.80	1175.80	1175.80	1175.80
O-9	1006.68	1033.04	1055.04	1055.04	1055.04
O-8	911.76	941.64	961.40	966.96	991.64
O-7	757.64	809.12	809.12	815.00	845.44
O-6	561.52	616.88	657.36	657.36	659.88
O-5	449.16	527.32	563.84	570.72	593.40
O-4	378.56	460.96	491.72	498.60	527.12
O-3	351.76	398.80	430.40	465.24	487.52
O-2	306.80	349.44	402.48	416.04	424.64
O-1	266.36	277.20	335.04	335.04	335.04

★★

Grade	8	10	12	14	16
O-10	1220.92	1220.92	1288.56	1288.56	1380.80
O-9	1081.88	1081.88	1126.88	1126.88	1220.92
O-8	1033.04	1042.64	1081.88	1093.16	1126.88
O-7	868.60	895.40	922.12	948.92	1033.04
O-6	688.12	691.88	691.88	714.76	800.72
O-5	593.40	611.24	644.24	687.44	730.88
O-4	550.36	587.96	617.24	637.56	658.00
O-3	511.96	532.36	558.64	572.28	572.28
O-2	424.64	424.64	424.64	424.64	424.64
O-1	335.04	335.04	335.04	335.04	335.04

Grade	18	20	22	24	26
O-10	1380.80	1473.24	1480.52	1511.28	1564.96
O-9	1220.92	1288.56	1307.12	1333.96	1380.80
O-8	1175.80	1220.92	1251.04	1251.04	1251.04
O-7	1104.12	1104.12	1104.12	1104.12	1109.68
O-6	841.52	882.32	905.52	929.04	974.64
O-5	751.60	772.04	795.28	795.28	795.28
O-4	664.88	664.88	664.88	664.88	664.88
O-3	572.28	572.28	572.28	572.28	572.28
O-2	424.64	424.64	424.64	424.64	424.64
O-1	335.04	335.04	335.04	335.04	335.04

**OFFICERS WITH MORE THAN FOUR YEARS ACTIVE-DUTY
AS ENLISTED OR WARRANT OFFICER**

Grade	*Years of Service*				
	Less Than 2	2	3	4	6
O-3E	00.00	00.00	00.00	465.24	487.52
O-2E	00.00	00.00	00.00	416.04	424.64
O-1E	00.00	00.00	00.00	335.04	357.88

Grade	*Years of Service*				
	8	10	12	14	16
O-3E	511.96	532.36	558.64	580.76	593.40
O-2E	438.12	460.96	478.60	491.72	491.72
O-1E	371.08	384.56	397.88	416.04	416.04

Grade	18	20	22	24	26
O-3E	610.72	610.72	610.72	610.72	610.72
O-2E	491.72	491.72	491.72	491.72	491.72
O-1E	416.04	416.04	416.04	416.04	416.04

★★

WARRANT OFFICERS

		Years of Service			
Grade	Less Than 2	2	3	4	6
W-5	00.00	00.00	00.00	00.00	00.00
W-4	358.40	385.56	396.64	407.56	426.32
W-3	325.76	353.32	353.32	357.88	372.52
W-2	285.28	308.68	308.68	318.80	335.04
W-1	237.68	272.52	272.52	295.28	308.68

Grade	8	10	12	14	16
W-5	00.00	00.00	00.00	00.00	00.00
W-4	444.84	463.60	481.88	500.84	519.00
W-3	389.20	411.24	424.64	439.28	456.04
W-2	353.32	366.76	380.20	393.28	407.76
W-1	322.56	336.44	350.24	364.20	378.12

Grade	18	20	22	24	26
W-5	00.00	618.76	640.00	661.32	682.68
W-4	537.60	555.76	574.60	593.12	612.12
W-3	472.68	489.32	505.96	522.64	539.36
W-2	422.60	437.44	452.24	467.12	467.12
W-1	392.00	402.48	402.48	402.48	402.48

ENLISTED MEMBERS

		Years of Service			
Grade	Less Than 2	2	3	4	6
E-9	00.00	00.00	00.00	00.00	00.00
E-8	00.00	00.00	00.00	00.00	00.00
E-7	244.16	266.56	276.68	286.64	296.96
E-6	210.00	232.04	242.32	252.24	262.60
E-5	184.24	206.56	216.52	226.80	237.04
E-4	171.84	189.84	200.08	210.16	220.40
E-3	161.96	174.28	184.48	184.72	184.72
E-2	155.88	155.88	155.88	155.88	155.88
E-1>4	139.04	139.04	139.04	139.04	139.04
E-1<4	128.64	00.00	00.00	00.00	00.00

Grade	8	10	12	14	16
E-9	00.00	416.92	426.32	438.28	452.32
E-8	349.60	359.72	369.12	380.44	392.68
E-7	307.08	317.20	327.32	337.28	347.60
E-6	272.80	283.04	292.92	303.00	310.36
E-5	247.44	257.40	267.72	267.72	267.72
E-4	220.40	220.40	220.40	220.40	220.40
E-3	184.72	184.72	184.72	184.72	184.72
E-2	155.88	155.88	155.88	155.88	155.88
E-1>4	139.04	139.04	139.04	139.04	139.04
E-1<4	00.00	00.00	00.00	00.00	00.00

★★★

Grade	18	20	22	24	26
E-9	466.40	480.24	499.04	517.68	541.44
E-8	405.48	418.40	437.08	455.64	481.68
E-7	357.84	367.84	385.44	404.60	433.40
E-6	315.72	315.72	316.04	316.04	316.04
E-5	267.72	267.72	267.72	267.72	267.72
E-4	220.40	220.40	220.40	220.40	220.40
E-3	184.72	184.72	184.72	184.72	184.72
E-2	155.88	155.88	155.88	155.88	155.88
E-1>4	139.04	139.04	139.04	139.04	139.04
E-1<4	00.00	00.00	00.00	00.00	00.00

Note: Basic Pay for O-7 – 0-10 is limited to$1,485.56; Level III of the Executive Schedule

Note: Basic Pay for 0-6 and below is limited to$1,306.68; Level V of the Executive Schedule

BASIC ALLOWANCE FOR HOUSING

The housing allowance for active-duty personnel combines the basic allowance for quarters and the variable housing allowance into one rate. Separate allowances are calculated for applicable regions, and vary for different regions in the country. For further information, individuals should contact their local military office.

BASIC ALLOWANCE FOR SUBSITENCE

Officers (including commissioned officers, warrants, and aviation cadets):
$153.83 per month

Enlisted Members (when on leave or authorized to mess separately)
Less than 4 months: $7.00 per day
Others: $7.58 per day

Enlisted Members (when rations in-kind are not available):
Less than 4 months: $7.89 per day
Others: $8.54 per day

Enlisted Members (when assigned to duty under emergency conditions where no Government messing is available):
Less than 4 months: $10.46 per day
Others: $11.32 per day

When receiving rations in kind – partial:
$25.50 per month

★★★

SPECIAL AND INCENTIVE PAYS

AVIATION CAREER INCENTIVE PAY	
Years Of Aviation Service	*Amount*
2 or less	$125.00
Over 2	$156.00
Over 3	$188.00
Over 4	$206.00
Over 6	$650.00
Over 14	$840.00
Over 22	$585.00
Over 23	$495.00
Over 24	$385.00
Over 25	$250.00

HAZARDOUS DUTY INCENTIVE PAY (Crew Member) (Non-AWAC)			
Pay Grade	*Amount*	*Pay Grade*	*Amount*
O-10	$ 150.00	W-3	$ 175.00
O-9	150.00	W-2	150.00
O-8	150.00	W-1	150.00
O-7	150.00	E-9	240.00
O-6	250.00	E-8	240.00
O-5	250.00	E-7	240.00
O-4	225.00	E-6	215.00
O-3	175.00	E-5	190.00
O-2	150.00	E-4	165.00
O-1	150.00	E-3	150.00
W-5	250.00	E-2	150.00
W-4	250.00	E-1	150.00

★★

OTHER TYPES OF PAY

Type	Amount
Hazardous Duty Incentive Pay (Non-Crewmember)	$ 150.00
Family Separation Allowance (All Grades)	100.00
Hostile Fire & Imminent Danger Pay (All Grades)	150.00
Hardship Duty Pay - Mission Assignment (All Grades)	150.00
Hardship Duty Pay – Location Assignment:	
E-7 to E-9	22.50
E-6	20.00
E-5	16.00
E-4	13.00
E-3	9.00
E-2 & E-1	8.00
Nurses Incentive Pay - CRNA (All Grades)	6,000.00 (Annual Amount)
Nurses Accession Bonus (All Grades)	5,000.00 (Annual Amount)
Special Pay - Optometry & Veterinary Officers (All Grades)	100.00
Special Pay (Physicians) – Reserve Medical Officers On Active Duty For Less Than 1 Year (All Grades)	450.00

Note: The above charts reflect only some of the types of incentive pay that may be payable. For further information, individuals should contact their local military office.

MILITARY RETIREMENT PAY

The calculation of an individual's military retirement pay is an extremely complicated subject. The amount of an individual's retirement pay depends on many factors, and it is not appropriate in the scope of this book to cover this topic.

Prior to retirement, it is important for individuals to attend any briefings offered by their command concerning the retirement system. The decisions an individual makes at the time of retirement affect the amounts of retirement benefits. Some decisions cannot be changed, so careful consideration of all options is crucial.

★★

CHAPTER 47

OFFICE OF SMALL AND DISADVANTAGED BUSINESS UTILIZATION

The Office of Small and Disadvantaged Business Utilization (OSDBU) serves as the Department of Veterans Affairs (VA) advocate, to assist and support the interests of small businesses. Its purpose is to provide information, counseling, and guidance to small, women-owned, minority-owned and veteran-owned small businesses wishing to do business with VA.

OSDBU also assists VA organizations in locating and working with small businesses.

OSDBU neither awards contracts nor maintains solicitation mailing lists. OSDBU promotes the position of small businesses within the Department, maintains liaison with trade and professional organizations, and serves as the major source of information about VA for small businesses. The office monitors the performance of the Department on these programs.

A related mission of the office is to provide outreach and liaison support to businesses (large and small) and other members of the private sector concerning acquisition related issues. In addition, the office is responsible for monitoring VA implementation and execution of the following socioeconomic procurement programs:

SMALL BUSINESS PROGRAM

The small business program implements the requirements to aid, counsel, assist, and protect the interests of small business concerns to ensure that a fair proportion of total purchases, contracts, and subcontracts for property and services for VA are placed with small businesses. For acquisition purposes, small businesses must be independently owned and operated, not dominant in the field of operation in which they are bidding on Government contracts, and otherwise qualify as small businesses under the criteria and size standards developed by the Small Business Administration (SBA).

SMALL BUSINESS SET-ASIDES

This program requires agencies to limit competition on certain contracts to qualified small businesses so that small firms do not have to compete with large ones for the same contracts. However, because the law requires the Government to buy at competitive prices, contracts are set aside only when two small businesses are expected to submit offers to ensure adequate competition. SBA establishes size standards that determine a firm's eligibility to offer on set-asides. These standards are established on an industry-by-industry basis, using dollar volume of sales or number of employees, to determine eligibility

SMALL DISADVANTAGED BUSINESS PROGRAM

For the purpose of improving and stimulating this small business segment, VA established a realistic Department-wide goal for the award of contracts to small business concerns owned and controlled by socially and economically disadvantaged individuals. OSDBU is also responsible for the Department's program to encourage greater economic opportunity for minority entrepreneurs. To implement these requirements, goals are established for award of contracts to small disadvantaged businesses

If a business is eligible to participate under this program if it is:

- At least 51 percent owned by one or more individuals who are both socially and economically disadvantaged; and

- Managed and controlled by one or more such individuals,

Economically or socially disadvantaged individuals for government procurement purposes include:

- African Americans,

- Hispanic Americans,

- Native Americans, (American Indians, Eskimos, Aleuts, or Native Hawaiians)

- Asian Pacific Americans (persons with origins from Japan, China, the Philippines, Vietnam, Korea, Samoa, Guam, U.S. Trust Territory of the Pacific Islands, Northern Mariana Islands, Laos, Cambodia, or Taiwan),

- Asian Indian Americans (persons with origins from India, Pakistan or Bangladesh); and

- Members of other groups designated from time to time by the SBA under 13 CFR 124.105(d).

8(a) Program

OSDBU promotes increased utilization of small businesses owned and controlled by socially and economically disadvantaged individuals certified under the SBA Section 8(a) Program.

Section 8(a) of the Small Business Act, as amended, authorizes SBA to contract for goods and services with Federal agencies. SBA then subcontracts actual performance of the work to socially and economically disadvantaged small businesses that have been certified by SBA as eligible to receive these contracts. The major advantage of this program is that it provides Government contracts on a noncompetitive basis to socially and economically disadvantaged small businesses. SBA also offers managerial, technical, and financial support to participating firms.

The purpose of the 8(a) Program is to:

- Foster business ownership by individuals who are socially and economically disadvantaged.

- Promote the competitive viability of these firms by providing contract, technical, and management assistance.

- Expand acquisition opportunities for these firms.

To be eligible for the 8(a) Program a concern must qualify as a small businesses (at least 51 percent owned by a U.S. citizen who is determined by SBA to be socially and economically disadvantaged.)

Each SBA 8(a) concern is subject to a fixed program participation term.

WOMEN-OWNED BUSINESS PROGRAM

In response to the need to aid and stimulate women's business enterprises, this advocacy program directs acquisition officials to take appropriate action to facilitate, preserve, and strengthen women's business enterprises and to ensure full participation by women in the free enterprise system.

Appropriate action includes the award of prime contracts and subcontracts and counseling of women-owned businesses. "Women-owned small businesses" means small business concerns that are at least 51 percent owned, controlled, and operated by women who are United States citizens.

OSDBU is responsible for negotiating annual goals with VA acquisition officials to increase Federal prime contracts with women-owned small businesses.

VETERAN-OWNED AND OPERATED SMALL BUSINESS (VOB) PROGRAM

Consistent with its mandate and mission, VA strongly encourages the participation of VOBs in the VA acquisition program. OSDBU is the advocate that monitors the Veteran-owned small business program.

VA is not authorized to set aside contracts for veterans. However, veteran-owned small businesses are identified, targeted, and included in its existing acquisition programs.

SUBCONTRACTING PROGRAM

Recognizing that small firms often do not have the capability to perform as a prime contractor on certain large contracts, VA promotes the involvement of small businesses at the subcontract level. VA requires that any contractor receiving a contract for more than $10,000 shall agree that small business concerns have the maximum practicable opportunity to participate in contracts awarded by the Department.

Furthermore, all prime contracts not awarded to small businesses, in excess of $1,000,000 for construction and $500,000 for all others, which offer subcontracting opportunities must contain a subcontracting plan. Each subcontracting plan must contain percentage goals for the maximum practicable utilization of small business concerns, small disadvantaged business concerns, and women owned small business concerns.

To carry out this program, OSDBU:

- Recommends informational goals for solicitations.
- Reviews subcontracting plans, and offers recommendations.
- Monitors compliance with subcontracting plans.
- Participates in prebid conferences, and conducts small business workshops to provide small, small disadvantaged, women owned and veteran-owned small business firms the opportunity to present their capabilities to prime contractors.
- Publishes a directory of VA prime contractors as a marketing tool to assist small, small disadvantaged, women-owned, and veteran-owned small businesses.

Additional information on these programs may be obtained by contacting:

U.S. Department of Veterans Affairs
Director, Office of Small and Disadvantaged Business Utilization (00SB)
810 Vermont Avenue, N.W.
Washington, DC 20420
Telephone: (202) 565-8124
Toll free: (800) 949-8387
Facsimile: (202) 565-8156

★★

CHAPTER 48

OTHER FEDERAL BENEFITS

There are a variety of benefits for veterans and their dependents that are not administered by the Department of Veterans Affairs. This chapter offers a general overview of the benefits provided by through the Department of Labor, and provides information on who to contact for additional details.

Congress created the Veterans' Employment and Training Service (VETS) as an independent agency within the Department of Labor to:

- Assist veterans making the transition from military to civilian life;
- Train for and find good jobs; and
- Protect the employment and reemployment rights of veterans, Reservists, and National Guard members.

Through cooperative efforts with each State, VETS offers employment and training service to eligible veterans through several programs:

- Disabled Veterans' Outreach Programs (DVOP)
- Local Veterans' Employment Representatives Program (LVER)
- Job Training Partnership Act (JTPA)
- Transition Assistance Program (TAP)
- Uniformed Services Employment and Reemployment Rights Act
- Preference In Hiring
- Federal Contractor Program
- Priority Job Referrals And Special Consideration In Hiring
- State Directors of Veterans' Employment and Training Service (DVETS)

DISABLED VETERANS' OUTREACH PROGRAMS (DVOP)

DVOP specialists develop job and training opportunities for veterans, with special emphasis on veterans with service-connected disabilities. DVOP specialists provide direct services to veterans enabling them to be competitive in the labor market. They provide outreach and offer assistance to disabled and other veterans by promoting community and employer support for employment and training opportunities, including apprenticeship and on-the-job training.

DVOP specialists work with employers, veterans' organizations, the Departments of Veterans Affairs and Defense, and community-based organizations to link veterans with appropriate jobs and training opportunities.

★★

DVOP specialists serve as case managers for veterans enrolled in federally funded job training programs such as the Department of Veterans Affairs' Vocational Rehabilitation program, and other veterans with serious disadvantages in the job market. DVOPs are available to those veterans and their employers to help ensure that necessary follow up services are provided to promote job retention.

The U.S. Department of Labor provides grant funds to each State's employment service to maintain DVOP specialist positions in the State. DVOP specialists are employees of the State and are generally located in State employment service offices.

DVOP specialists may be stationed at regional offices and medical or veterans' outreach centers of the Department of Veterans Affairs, State or county veterans' service offices, Job Training Partnership Act program offices, community-based organizations, and military installations.

To contact a DVOP specialist, call or visit the nearest State Employment Service (sometimes known as Job Service) agency listed in the State Government section of the phone book.

LOCAL VETERANS' EMPLOYMENT REPRESENTATIVES (LVERS)

Local Veterans' Employment Representatives (LVERs) are state employees located in state employment service local offices to provide assistance to veterans by:

- Supervising the provision of all services to veterans furnished by employment service employees, including counseling, testing, and identifying training and employment opportunities;

- Monitoring job listings from Federal contractors to see that eligible veterans get priority in referrals to these jobs;

- Monitoring Federal department and agency vacancies listed at local state employment service offices and preliminary processing of complaints from veterans about the observance of veterans' preference by Federal employers;

- Promoting and monitoring the participation of veterans in Federally-funded employment and training programs;

- Cooperating with the Department of Veterans Affairs to identify and aid veterans who need work-specific prosthetic devices, sensory aids or other special equipment to improve their employability; and

- Contacting community leaders, employers, unions, training programs and veterans' service organizations to be sure eligible veterans get the services to which they are entitled.

JOB TRAINING PARTNERSHIP ACT (JTPA)

The Job Partnership Training Act provides for a national job-training program for disabled, Vietnam Era, and recently separated veterans. Job training programs may be conducted through public agencies and private nonprofit organizations.

★★

Most of the funds of the JTPA are awarded as grants through a competitive solicitation process, and are available to state and local governments, non-profit organizations, and educational institutions. Organizations receiving these grants provide classroom and on-the-job training, remedial education, and other services to enhance the employability of veterans, such as career counseling, aptitude testing, and job placement assistance.

Interested veterans should apply at the nearest state employment office.

TRANSITION ASSISTANCE PROGRAM (TAP)

In cooperation with the Department of Defense and the VA, VETS conducts three-day Transition Assistance Program (TAP) workshops at military installations across the country that provide employment and training information and assistance to armed forces members and their families within 180 days of separation or retirement. Conducted by trained facilitators, the workshops teach participants how to conduct job searches, write resumes, and take job interviews. Participants also receive current labor market information, an assessment of their individual job skills, information about training and retraining opportunities, and other veterans' benefits. Additional hours of individual instruction are available to service members leaving the military with service-connected disabilities.

For information, contact the nearest state employment office or the Transition Office on the nearest military base.

UNIFORMED SERVICES EMPLOYMENT AND REEMPLOYMENT RIGHTS ACT

VETS is also responsible for providing assistance to veterans and members of the National Guard and Reserve called to active duty or training. Protected service members have the right to return to their civilian jobs – in both the private and public sectors – with all the benefits they would have accrued if not for their military service. This means that the person may be entitled to benefits that are based on seniority, such as pensions, pay increases, and promotions. The law also protects a veteran from discharge without just cause for one year from the date of reemployment, and a reservist or National Guard member from discharge without just cause for six months after returning from initial active duty for training. The law also prohibits discrimination in hiring, promotion, or other advantages of employment on the basis of military service.

To qualify for reemployment rights, four requirements must be met:

1. The person must give advance notice of military service to the employer.

2. The cumulative absence from the civilian job shall not exceed five years.

3. The person must submit an application for reemployment.

4. The person must not have been released with a dishonorable or other punitive discharge.

★★★

Applications for reemployment should be given, verbally or in writing, to a person authorized to represent the company for hiring purposes. A record should be kept of the application. If there are problems in attaining reemployment, the employee should contact VETS in the state of the employer concerned.

Employees should contact their agency personnel office about restoring rights. If a job is not restored, or it is restored improperly, the employee has the right to appeal to the Merit Systems Protection Board.

VETS investigates complaints from protected individuals who believe their rights have been violated. When merited, VETS attempts to negotiate voluntary settlements of issues. VETS may recommend legal action in cases where adjudication seems warranted. Technical assistance is provided to employers, veterans' service organizations, and reserve unites to assist them in understanding and complying with the law.

FEDERAL JOBS FOR VETERANS

Certain veterans are accorded preference in hiring for jobs with the federal government. VETS investigates complaints from veterans who believe they have been denied their rights.

FEDERAL CONTRACTOR PROGRAM

Any contractor or subcontractor who receives a contract from the federal government in the amount of $25,000 or more must take affirmative action to hire and promote qualified Vietnam-era and special disabled veterans.

Contractors and subcontractors with openings for jobs, other than executive or top management jobs, must list them with the nearest State Job Service (also known as State Employment Service) office. The requirement applies to vacancies at all locations of a business not otherwise exempt under the company's Federal contract. The job-listing requirement may be satisfied by immediate posting of the job on America's Job Bank.

Qualified Vietnam- era and special disabled veterans receive priority for referral to Federal contractor job openings listed at those offices. The priority for referral is not a guarantee that referred veterans will be hired.

Federal contractors are not required to hire those referred, but must have affirmative action plans when applicable (50 employees and a $50,000 contract). They must be able to show they have followed the plans and that they have not discriminated against veterans or other covered groups. They also must show that they have actively recruited Vietnam-era and special-disabled veterans and disseminated all information internally regarding promotion activities.

Companies must file an annual *VETS-100* report, which shows the number of Vietnam-era and special disabled veterans in their work force by job category, hiring location, and number of new hires, including Vietnam-era and special disabled veterans hired during the reporting period. Instructions, information and follow-up assistance is provided to employers who do not understand the reporting and other legal requirements.

For more information about the *VETS- 100* report contact the VETS-100 Processing Center at (334) 242 2028.

For more information about the Federal Contractor Program, contact the nearest USDOL Veterans' Employment and Training Service representative.

For information about how to list a job opening, contact the nearest State Job Service office listed in the telephone book, or the America's Job Bank.

For copies of *Affirmative Action Obligations of Contractors and Subcontractors for Disabled Veterans and Veterans of the Vietnam Era, Rules and Regulations,* contact:

ESA Office of Federal Contract Compliance Programs
U.S. Department of Labor
200 Constitution Ave., NW
Washington, D.C. 20210

PRIORITY JOB REFERRALS AND SPECIAL CONSIDERATION IN HIRING

VETS is responsible for ensuring that those veterans eligible for priority job referrals or special consideration in hiring are not discriminated against by federal contractors and subcontractors. Federal contractors and subcontractors must list most job openings with the state employment service so that qualified Vietnam-era and special disabled veterans can receive priority referrals for those jobs. These employers must file an annual report with VETS showing the number of Vietnam-era and special disabled veterans in their work forces.

STATE DIRECTORS OF VETERANS' EMPLOYMENT AND TRAINING SERVICE (DVETS)

VETS maintains a network of State Directors of Veterans' Employment and Training Service (DVETS).

For more information about U.S. Department of Labor employment and training programs for veterans, contact the Veterans' Employment and Training Service office nearest you, listed in the phone book in the United States Government under the Labor Department.

★★

CHAPTER 49

MISCELLANEOUS BENEFITS OF INTEREST TO VETERANS

JOB-FINDING ASSISTANCE

State employment offices help veterans find jobs by providing free job counseling, testing, referral and placement services. Veterans are given priority when referring applicants to job openings and training opportunities. Disabled veterans receive the highest priority in referrals.

Employment offices also assist veterans by providing information about unemployment compensation, job markets, and on-job and apprenticeship training opportunities.

Interest veterans should contact the nearest state employment office. If applying in person, veterans should present a copy of their military discharge form DD-214.

UNEMPLOYMENT COMPENSATION

Weekly unemployment compensation may be paid to discharged servicemembers for a limited period of time. Individual state laws govern the amount and duration of payments. To apply for unemployment compensation, veterans should contact their nearest state employment office immediately after leaving military service. If applying in person, veterans should present a copy of their military discharge form DD-214.

OPERATION TRANSITION

The military services provide civilian-transition counseling at least 90 days prior to each service member's discharge in a program called Operation Transition. A Defense Department document (DD Form 2586) is prepared that provides military experience, training history, civilian job equivalent experience and recommended educational credit. The document is delivered to service members 90 to 180 days before the scheduled separation.

The Defense Outplacement Referral System (DORS) refers resumes to potential employers through 350 Transition offices worldwide. Resumes are provided to employers by mail, electronic mail, or facsimile. Employers may place job ads on the electronic Transition Bulletin Board (TBB) kept by Transition offices. Those employers having the proper computer equipment are able to place their ads electronically; others may mail or fax their ads to the TBB. Servicemembers are encouraged to respond directly to employers with their resumes. The electronic bulletin board also contains business opportunities, a calendar of transition seminars and events, and other helpful information.

Two special registries have been developed at Transition offices to help separating servicemembers obtain public community service jobs. The "Registry

★★★

of Public and Community Service Organizations" contains information on organizations desiring to hire servicemembers. The "Personnel Registry" lists servicemembers who desire employment in public and community service occupations. The Defense Department matches people and employers on the two registries, and counsels separating servicemembers on how to apply for positions with public and community service organizations.

SMALL BUSINESS ADMINISTRATION

Although business loans are not available through VA, the Small Business Administration (SBA) has a number of programs designed to help foster and encourage small business enterprises, including financial and management assistance.

Each SBA office has a veteran's affairs officer available to speak with.

Interested veterans should refer to the local telephone directory for the phone number of a local SBA office, or call 1-800-827-5722.

The Veterans Business Outreach Program (VBOP) of the SBA is designed to provide entrepreneurial development services such as business training, counseling and mentoring to eligible veterans owning or considering starting a small business.

Services Provided by VBOP Centers

Pre-Business Plan Workshops
VBOCs conduct entrepreneurial development workshops dealing specifically with the major issues of self-employment. An important segment of these workshops entails the usage of the Internet as a tool for developing and expanding businesses. Each client is afforded the opportunity to work directly with a business counselor to develop an Individual Entrepreneurial Development Plan (IEDP). The IEDP outlines the necessary training and directions required of the entrepreneur.

Concept Assessments
VBOCs assist clients in assessing their entrepreneurial needs and requirements in the implementation of their IEDPs.

Business Plan Preparations
VBOCs assist clients in developing and maintaining a five-year business plan. The business plan includes such elements as the legal form if the business, equipment requirements and cost, organizational structure, a strategic plan, market analysis, and a financial plan. Financial plans include financial projections, budget projections, and funding requirements.

Comprehensive Feasibility Analysis
VBOCs provide assistance in identifying and analyzing the strengths and weaknesses of the business plan to increase the probability of success. The results of the analysis are utilized to revise the strategic planning portion of the business plan.

Entrepreneurial Training and Counseling
VBOCs, working with other SBA resource partners, target entrepreneurial training projects and counseling sessions tailored specifically to address the needs and concerns of the service-disabled veteran entrepreneur.

Mentorship:
VBOCs conduct, as appropriate, on-site visits with clients to ensure adherence to their business plans. Additionally, VBOCs review monthly financial statements to determine whether a revision of the business plan is warranted or that desired results are being attained.

Other Business Developmental Related Services
VBOCs also provide assistance and training in such areas as international trade, franchising, Internet marketing, accounting, etc.

FARM LOANS

VA loan guaranties are not available for farm loans, unless there is a home on the property, which will be personally occupied by the veteran. Non-realty loans for the purchase of equipment, livestock, machinery, etc. are not made.

However, loans and guaranties may be provided by the U.S. Department of Agriculture to buy, improve, or operate farms. Loans and guaranties are available for housing in towns generally up to 20,000 in population. Applications from veterans have preference.

For further information, veterans should contact local Department of Agriculture offices, usually located in county seats. Interested parties may also contact:

Farm Service Agency / Rural Economic and Community Development
U.S. Department of Agriculture
Washington, DC 20250

Other loan programs for farm financing may be available through the Farmers Home Administration, which gives preference to veteran applicants. (Interested veterans should refer to the local telephone directory for the phone number of a local office.)

HUD / FHA LOANS

Veterans are not eligible for VA financing based on service in World War I, Active Duty for Training in the Reserves, or Active Duty for Training in the National Guard (unless "activated" under the authority of Title 10, U.S. Code). However, these veterans may qualify for a HUD / FHA veteran's loan.

The Federal Housing Administration (FHA) is responsible for the Home Mortgage Insurance Program for veterans. These home loans require less down payment than other FHA programs.

★★★

Veterans on **active duty** are eligible if they:

- Enlisted before September 8, 1980; or
- Entered on active duty before October 14, 1982; and
- Were discharged under other than dishonorable conditions with at least 90 days service.

Veterans with enlisted service after September 7, 1980, or who entered on active duty after October 16, 1981, must have served at least 24 months, unless discharged for hardship or disability. (Active duty for training is considered qualifying service.)

The VA's only role in the HUD / FHA program is to determine the eligibility of the veteran, and issue a *Certificate of Veteran Status*, if qualified. Under this program, financing is available for veterans at terms slightly more favorable than those available to non-veterans.

A veteran may request a *Certificate of Veteran Status* by completing VA form 26-8261a. The completed form and required attachments should be submitted to the veteran's regional VA office for a determination of eligibility.

DEATH GRATUITY PAID BY MILITARY COMMAND

Military services provide a death gratuity to a deceased service member's next of kin.

The law fixes $6,000 as the lump-sum payment in the event of death while a member of the Armed Forces is on active duty for training, or inactive duty training. The gratuity is also payable if a member or former member dies of a service-connected cause within 120 days (180 days for service members who die as a result of the Persian Gulf War) after his or her discharge or release from active duty for training.

In the case of inactive duty training, the gratuity is payable if death occurs within 120 days, and is the result of injury received during that training.

The gratuity is paid by the last military command of the deceased. If the beneficiary is not paid automatically, application should be made to the appropriate military service.

COMMISSARY AND EXCHANGE PRIVILEGES

Unlimited exchange and commissary store privileges in the United States are available to:

- Honorably discharged veterans with a service-connected disability rated at 100 %;
- Unremarried surviving spouses of members or retired members of the Armed Forces;
- Recipients of the Medal of Honor, and their dependents and orphans.
- Reservists and their dependents also may be eligible.

Privileges overseas are governed by international law and are available only if agreed upon by the foreign government concerned. VA certifies total disability. VA provides assistance in completing DD Form 1172, *Application for Uniformed Services Identification and Privilege Card.*

ARMED FORCES RETIREMENT HOMES

Veterans may be eligible to live in two retirement homes run by an independent federal agency, the Armed Forces Retirement Home Board.

More than 150 years ago, Congress established a home for destitute Navy officers, sailors and Marines in Philadelphia. Some 20 years later in 1851, with money demanded as booty from the Mexican War, Congress established an asylum for "old and disabled soldiers" in Washington, D.C.

Through the proceeding years, the U.S. Naval Home (USNH), now in Gulfport, Miss., and the U.S. Soldiers' and Airmen's Home (USSAH), still in Washington, D.C., have operated under separate legislation, undergoing many changes. One of the biggest changes came as a result of the Armed Forces Retirement Home Act, Public Law 101-510, which took effect 1991.

This new law established the **Armed Forces Retirement Home** (AFRH), which combined the USSAH and the USNH under the unified management of the Armed Forces Retirement Home Board. Regulations such as resident eligibility, resident fees, operating funds, oversight, etc. now are standardized for both Homes.

The AFRH is an independent federal agency. Each Home has a local advisory board, administered by the AFRH Board appointed by the Secretary of Defense. Funding for the Homes comes from a Congressional trust fund that is fed by monthly, active-duty payroll deductions of 50 cents, fines and forfeitures from military disciplinary actions, interest earned on the trust, and resident fees.

In both Homes, residents can maintain an independent lifestyle in an environment designed for safety, comfort and personal enrichment.

Eligibility Criteria

Veterans are eligible to become a resident of either the U.S. Soldiers' and Airmen's Home or the U.S. Naval Home if their active duty service in the military is at least 50 percent enlisted, warrant officer or limited duty officer and who are:

- Veterans with 20 or more years of active duty service and are at least 60 years old; or
- Veterans unable to earn a livelihood due to a service-connected disability; or
- Veterans unable to earn a livelihood due to non service-connected disability, and who served in a war theater or received hostile fire pay, or;
- Female veterans who served prior to 1948.

Applicants must be free of drug, alcohol, and psychiatric problems, and never have been convicted of a felony.

Married couples are welcome, but both must be eligible in their own right.

At the time of admission applicants must be able to live independently. If increased healthcare is needed after being admitted, assisted living and long term care are available at both Homes.

Resident Fees

Residents pay no entrance deposit, down payment or application fee. Once admitted, they currently pay a monthly fee of 40 percent of all income for independent living. Those residents living in long-term care will pay 65 percent of all income.

This includes:

- Three meals a day;
- A private room with bath;
- Recreational activities, including bowling, golf, fishing, gardening and many trips; and
- Healthcare, including dentistry, optometry, podiatry, etc.

For more information, contact:

Admissions Office 1094
U.S. Soldiers' and Airmen's Home
3700 North Capitol Street NW
Washington, DC 20317
1-800-422-9988

or

U.S. Naval Home
1800 Beach Drive
Gulfport, MS 39507
1-800-332-3527

★★★

CHAPTER 50

SOCIAL SECURITY BENEFITS

There are five major categories of benefits paid for through an individual's Social Security taxes:

- Retirement,
- Disability,
- Family Benefits,
- Survivors, and
- Medicare (highlights of Medicare are discussed on page 392)

(SSI benefits, which are **not** financed by Social Security taxes, are also discussed in this chapter.)

RETIREMENT

Benefits are payable at full retirement age (with reduced benefits available as early as age 62) for anyone with enough Social Security credits. The full retirement age is 65 for persons born before 1938. The age gradually rises until it reaches 67 for persons born in 1960 or later. People who delay retirement beyond full retirement age get special credit for each month they don't receive a benefit until they reach age 70.

DISABILITY

Benefits are payable at any age to people who have enough Social Security credits, and who have a severe physical or mental impairment that is expected to prevent them from doing "substantial" work for a year or more; or who have a condition that is expected to result in death. Generally, earnings of $700 or more per month are considered "substantial". The disability program includes incentives to smooth the transition back into the workforce, including continuation of benefits and healthcare coverage while a person attempts to work.

FAMILY BENEFITS

If an individual is eligible for retirement or disability benefits, other members of his or her family might receive benefits, too. These include:

- The spouse if he or she is at least 62 years old or under 62 but caring for a child under age 16;
- The children if they are unmarried and under age 18, under 19 but still in school or 18 or older but disabled.
- If an individual is divorced, the ex-spouse could be eligible for benefits on the individual's record.

SURVIVORS

When an individual dies, certain members or the family may be eligible for benefits if the individual earned enough Social Security credits while working.

A special one-time payment of $255 may be made to the spouse or minor children when an individual dies. If divorced, the ex-spouse could be eligible for a widow(er)'s benefit on the deceased individual's record.

SUPPLEMENTAL SECURITY INCOME BENEFITS (SSI)

SSI makes monthly payments to people who have a low income and few assets. To receive SSI, an individual must be 65 or older or be disabled.

Children as well as adults qualify for SSI disability payments. As its name implies, Supplemental Security Income "supplements" an individual's income up to various levels--depending on where an individual lives.

The federal government pays a basic rate, and some states add money to that amount. Individuals should check with the local Social Security office for the SSI rates in the appropriate state. Generally, people who get SSI also qualify for Medicaid, food stamps and other assistance.

SSI benefits are **not** paid from Social Security trust funds and are **not** based on past earnings. Instead, SSI benefits are financed by general tax revenues and assure a minimum monthly income for elderly and disabled persons.

EARNING SOCIAL SECURITY "CREDITS"

As an individual works and pays taxes, he or she earns "credits" that count toward eligibility for future Social Security benefits. A maximum of four credits can be earned each year. Most people need 40 credits (10 years of work) to qualify for benefits. Younger people need fewer credits to qualify for disability or survivors' benefits.

ESTIMATING SOCIAL SECURITY BENEFITS

To get a free estimate of the retirement, disability and survivors benefits that would be payable, individuals should call Social Security at **1-800-772-1213**.

WHEN AND HOW TO FILE FOR SOCIAL SECURITY OR SSI

An individual should file for Social Security or SSI disability benefits when he or she becomes too disabled to work and for survivors benefits when a family breadwinner dies. When thinking about retirement, an individual should talk to a Social Security representative in the year before the year he or she plans to retire. It may be to the individual's advantage to start his or her retirement benefits before he or she actually stops working.

To file for benefits, get information or speak to a Social Security representative, individuals should call **1-800-772-1213**.

★★

MILITARY SERVICE AND SOCIAL SECURITY

The earnings of people who serve in military services on active duty or on active duty for training have been covered under Social Security since 1957. Inactive duty service in the armed forces reserves (such as weekend drills) has been covered by Social Security since 1988. However, people who served in the military before 1957 did not pay into Social Security directly, but their records are credited with special earnings for Social Security purposes that count toward any benefits that might be payable. Additional earnings credits are given to military personnel depending on when they served. The following information explains how and when these special earnings are credited, and provides other general information military personnel need to know about the benefits available from Social Security.

Paying Social Security And Medicare Taxes

While in military service (from 1957 on), individuals pay Social Security taxes the same way civilian employees do. Those taxes are deducted from the individual's pay and the U.S. government as the employer pays an equal amount.

When Additional Earnings Are Added To Military Records

The amount an individual gets from Social Security depends on the earnings averaged over much of his or her working lifetime. Generally, the higher the earnings, the higher the Social Security benefit.

Under certain circumstances, special earnings can be credited to an individual's military pay record for Social Security purposes. The extra earnings credits are granted for periods of active duty or active duty for training. These extra earnings may help an individual qualify for Social Security or increase the amount of the Social Security benefit. (Social Security cannot add extra earnings credits to an individual's earnings record until the individual files for Social Security benefits.)

Following is a brief explanation of how the additional earnings are granted:

Service In 1978 And Later:
For every $300 in active duty basic pay, an individual is credited with an additional $100 in earnings, up to a maximum of $1,200 a year. If an individual enlisted after Sept. 7, 1980, and didn't complete at least 24 months of active duty or his or her full tour, he or she may not be able to receive the additional earnings. Check with Social Security for details.

Service In 1957 Through 1977:
An individual is credited with $300 in additional earnings for each calendar quarter in which he or she received active duty basic pay.

Service In 1940 Through 1956:

If an individual was in the military during this period, including attendance at a service academy, he or she did not pay Social Security taxes. However, his or her Social Security record may be credited with $160 a month in earnings for military service from September 16, 1940, through December 31, 1956, under the following circumstances:

- The individual was honorably discharged after 90 or more days of service, or was released because of a disability or injury received in the line of duty; or

- The individual is still on active duty; or

- The widow is applying for survivors' benefits and the veteran died while on active duty.

Individuals cannot receive these special earnings credits if they are already receiving a federal benefit based on the same years of service. There is one exception to this rule: if an individual was on active duty after 1956, he or she can still get the special earnings for 1951 through 1956, even if they are receiving a military retirement based on service during that period.

When applying for Social Security benefits, an individual will be asked for proof of his or her military service (DD Form 214) or information regarding his or her reserves or National Guard service.

Receipt Of Both Social Security And Military Retirement

An individual can get both Social Security benefits and military retirement benefits. Generally, there is no offset of Social Security benefits because of military retirement benefits. The individual will receive his or her full Social Security benefit based on earnings. However, the Social Security benefit may be reduced if he or she also receives a government pension based on a job in which he or she did not pay Social Security taxes.

Social Security survivors' benefits may affect benefits payable under the optional Department of Defense Survivors Benefit Plan. Individuals should check with the Department of Defense or their military retirement advisor for more information.

IF A CHILD RECEIVES SSI

If an individual has a child who receives SSI, those payments may continue if the individual is stationed outside the United States (including Puerto Rico and U.S. territories and possessions) while in military service and the child lives with the individual. The child must have received SSI the month before the individual reported for duty.

★★★

SPECIAL BENEFITS FOR CERTAIN WORLD WAR II VETERANS

Public Law (P.L.) 106-169, enacted on December 14, 1999, provides special benefits to certain World War II veterans. The law applies to veterans who served in the active military, naval or air services of the United States. It also includes Filipino veterans of World War II who served in the organized military forces of the Philippines while those forces were in the service of the U.S. Armed Forces.

What The Law Says

Under P.L. 106-169, veterans who served in the U.S. military during the period beginning September 16, 1940, and through July 24, 1947, or who served in the organized military of the Philippines during the period beginning July 26, 1941, and through December 30, 1946, **and** who also meet the other qualifications may be entitled to receive a special benefit for each month after September 2000 if they subsequently reside outside the U.S.

Who May Qualify

Under the new law, an individual must meet all of the following requirements to be eligible for the special benefits:

- Be age 65 or older on December 14, 1999, the date P.L. 106-169 was enacted;
- Be a World War II veteran as described above;
- File an application for the special veterans benefits;
- Be eligible for Supplemental Security Income (SSI) for December 1999;
- Be eligible for SSI for the month he or she applies for the special benefits; and
- Have other benefit income that is **less than** 75 percent of the current SSI federal benefit rate.

A veteran who meets all the requirements described above is entitled to these special benefits for each month after September 2000 in which he or she is residing outside the United States starting on the first day of the month.

The Special Benefit Amount

Qualified veterans will receive a monthly benefit equal to 75 percent of the current SSI federal benefit rate **less** the amount of their benefit income for the month. There is no provision for the payment of benefits to dependents or survivors.

For More Information

Contact the local Social Security office for more information about applying for these special benefits.

★★★

CHAPTER 51

RAILROAD RETIREMENT & SURVIVOR BENEFITS

OVERVIEW

The Railroad Retirement Act is a Federal law that provides retirement and disability annuities for qualified railroad employees, spouse annuities for their wives or husbands, and survivor benefits for the families of deceased employees who were insured under the Act. These benefit programs are administered by the U.S. Railroad Retirement Board. It also administers the Railroad Unemployment Insurance Act, and has administrative responsibilities under the Social Security Act for certain benefit payments and railroad workers' Medicare coverage. *The information provided in this chapter is intended as a brief summary of Medicare only.*

A toll-free help line is available at 1-800-808-0772, which can be used to obtain the addresses and telephone numbers of the Board's field offices. Employees can use the Help Line to obtain statements of creditable service and compensation, and beneficiaries on the rolls can use it to verify their current monthly benefit rate or secure a replacement Medicare card. Information on unemployment-sickness benefits can also be obtained by using the Help Line, which is available 24 hours a day, 7 days a week.

BASIC SERVICE REQUIREMENT

The basic requirement for a regular employee annuity is 120 months (10 years) of creditable railroad service. Service months need not be consecutive, and in some cases military service may be counted as railroad service.

Credit for a month of railroad service is given for every month in which an employee had some compensated service for an employer covered by the Railroad Retirement Act, even if only one day's service is performed in the month. (However, local lodge compensation earned after 1974 is disregarded for any calendar month in which it is less than $25.) Under certain circumstances, additional months of service may be deemed.
Covered employers include railroads engaged in interstate commerce and certain of their subsidiaries, railroad associations and national railway labor organizations.

Railroad retirement benefits are based on months of service and earnings credits. Earnings are creditable up to certain annual maximums on the amount of compensation subject to railroad retirement taxes.

★★★

WHEN MILITARY SERVICE IS CREDITABLE TOWARD BENEFITS UNDER THE RAILROAD RETIREMENT ACT

Credit may be allowed for active service in the Armed Forces if, before entering such service, the employee performed creditable railroad service in the same year the military service began or in the preceding year, and he or she:

- Entered such service voluntarily or involuntarily during one of the following periods:

    o April 6, 1917 through November 11, 1918 (World War I)

    o September 8, 1939 through June 14, 1948 (state of national emergency including World War II)

    o December 16, 1950 through September 14, 1978 (state of national emergency); or

- Was required to enter and continue in military service during the period May 9, 1916 to February 5, 1917 (Mexican Border Disturbances); or

- Entered military service involuntarily or was ordered to active duty during the period June 15, 1948 through December 15, 1950; or

- Entered military service voluntarily during the period June 15, 1948 through December 15, 1950, and upon release from such service returned to railroad service in the same year, or the year immediately following such year, without any non-railroad employment of any duration occurring after the military service and before the return to railroad service; or

- Was required to enter military service involuntarily and continue in military service during any other period, by call of the President, or by an Act of Congress or regulation, order or proclamation pursuant thereto.

When an individual entered military service in any of the above-stated periods and otherwise meets the requirements set forth above, he is entitled to credit for all military service performed prior to his discharge or reenlistment unless:

- The individual voluntarily entered military service during the period January 1, 1947 through June 14, 1948, and upon release from such service did not return to railroad service in the same year or the year immediately following, or did return, but had non-railroad employment of any duration occurring after the military service and before the return to railroad service. In this event, the individual is entitled to credit for military service only through June 14, 1948, or the date of discharge, whichever is earlier; or

- The individual voluntarily entered military service after December 15, 1950, and before September 15, 1978. In this event, the individual is entitled to credit for military service only through September 14, 1978, or the date of discharge, whichever is earlier.

★★

EMPLOYEES WITH RAILROAD RETIREMENT AND SOCIAL SECURITY BENEFITS

Since 1975, if a retired or disabled railroad retirement annuitant is also awarded social security benefits, the Social Security Administration determines the amount due, but a combined monthly dual benefit payment is issued by the Railroad Retirement Board.

APPLYING FOR AN ANNUITY

Applications for railroad retirement or survivor benefits are generally filed at one of the Board's field offices, or with a traveling Board representative at an itinerant point, or by telephone and mail. The Board accepts applications up to three months in advance of an annuity beginning date. However, applications for employee disability annuities may not be filed until an employee is no longer in compensated service. Compensated service includes the receipt of pay for time lost, some wage continuation payments, or any other employer compensation preventing the payment of railroad retirement benefits.

CHAPTER 52

MEDICARE & MEDICAID

MEDICARE

The Healthcare Financing Administration (HCFA) administers Medicare, the nation's largest health insurance program, which covers 39 million Americans. *The information provided in this chapter is intended as a brief summary of Medicare only.*

Medicare is a Health Insurance Program for:

- People 65 years of age and older.
- Some people with disabilities, under 65 years of age.
- People with End-Stage Renal Disease (permanent kidney failure requiring dialysis or a transplant).

Medicare has Two Parts:

- Part A (Hospital Insurance)
- Most people do not have to pay for Part A.
- Part B (Medical Insurance)
  Most people pay monthly for Part B.

Individuals must call the Social Security Administration at 1-800-772-1213 or contact the local Social Security Office to verify Medicare Part A and Part B coverage. This information can also be found on the red, white, and blue Medicare card.

Eligibility For Medicare

Generally, an individual is eligible for Medicare if the individual and his or her spouse worked for at least 10 years in Medicare-covered employment and the individual is 65 years old and a citizen or permanent resident of the United States. Younger individuals may also qualify for coverage if they have a disability or chronic kidney disease.

Individuals may qualify for Part A at age 65 without having to pay premiums if they:

- Are already receiving retirement benefits from Social Security or the Railroad Retirement Board.
- Are eligible to receive Social Security or Railroad benefits but have not yet filed for them.
- Had Medicare-covered government employment (or spouse had Medicare-covered government employment).

★★

Individuals under age 65 may qualify for Part A without having to pay premiums if they:

- Have received Social Security or Railroad Retirement Board disability benefit for 24 months.
- Are kidney dialysis or kidney transplant patients.

While individuals do not have to pay a premium for Part A if they meet one of the above conditions, they must pay for Part B if they want it. The Part B monthly premium in 2001 is $50.00. It is deducted from the individual's Social Security, Railroad Retirement, or Civil Service Retirement check.

If an individual has healthcare protection from VA or under the CHAMPUS or CHAMPVA program, his or her health benefits may change or end when he or she becomes eligible for Medicare. These individuals should contact the VA, the Department of Defense or a military health benefits advisor for more information.

Individuals with questions about eligibility for Medicare Part A or Part B, or who want to apply for Medicare, should call the Social Security Administration. The toll-free telephone number is: 1-800-772-1213. The TTY-TDD number for the hearing and speech impaired is 1-800-325-0778.

Enrollment In Medicare

Enrollment in Medicare is handled in two ways – an individual is either enrolled automatically or has to apply.

Those who are not yet 65 and already getting Social Security or Railroad Retirement Board benefits do not have to apply for Medicare. They will be enrolled automatically in both Part A and Part B effective the month they are 65. A Medicare card will be mailed about 3 months before the 65th birthday. If an individual does not want Part B, he or she must follow the instructions that come with the card.

MEDICAID

Medicaid is a federal program for low-income, financially needy people, set up by the federal government and administered differently in each state. This program is called Medi-Cal in California.

Medicaid rules differ in each state. Medicaid information is available at local county social services, welfare or Department of Human Services offices.

★★

CHAPTER 53

LIST OF COMMON FORMS USED BY VA

While the following list is not exhaustive, following are some of the forms frequently used by VA.

GENERAL ADMINISTRATION FORMS

Form #	Purpose
20-572	Request For Change Of Address / Cancellation Of Direct Deposit
20-5655	Financial Status Report

COMPENSATION AND PENSION FORMS

Form #	Purpose
21-22	Appointment Of Veterans Service Organization As Claimant's Representative
21-0304	Application For Spina Bifida Benefits
21-0510	Eligibility Verification Report Instructions
21-0514-1	Parent's DIC Eligibility Verification Report
21-526	Veteran's Application For Compensation Or Pension
21-527	Income-Net Worth And Employment Statement
21-530	Application For Burial Benefits
21-534	Application For DIC, Death Pension, And Accrued Benefits By A Surviving Spouse Or Child
21-535	Application For DIC By Parents
21-601	Application For Reimbursement From Accrued Amounts Due A Deceased Beneficiary
21-674	Request For Approval Of School Attendance
21-686c	Declaration Of Status Of Dependents
21-2008	Application For United States Flag For Burial Purposes
21-4138	Statement In Support Of Claim
21-4142	Authorization And Consent To Release Information To The Department Of Veterans Affairs
21-4502	Application For Automobile Or Other Conveyance And Adaptive Equipment
21-4703	Fiduciary Agreement
21-6753	Original Or Amended DIC Award
21-8416	Medical Expense Report
21-8678	Application For Annual Clothing Allowance
21-8940	Veteran's Application For Increased Compensation Based On Unemployability
21-8951-2	Notice Of Waiver Of VA Compensation Or Pension To Receive Military Pay And Allowances

★★

Education Forms

Form #	*Purpose*
22-1990	Application For VA Education Benefits
22-1990t	Application And Enrollment Certification For Individualized Tutorial Assistance
22-1995	Request For Change Of Program Or Place Of Training
22-5490	Application For Survivors' And Dependents' Educational Assistance
22-5495	Request For Change Of Program Or Place Of Training – Survivors' And Dependents' Educational Assistance
22-6553c	Monthly Certification Of Flight Training
22-8690	Time Record (Work-Study Program)
22-8691	Application For Work-Study Allowance
22-8873	Supplemental Information For Change Of Program Or Reenrollment After Unsatisfactory Attendance, Conduct Or Progress

Home Loan Guaranty Forms

Form #	*Purpose*
26-0826	VA Loan Summary Sheet
26-0503	Federal Collection Policy Notice
26-0592	Counseling Checklist For Military Homebuyers
26-1802a	HUD / VA Addendum To Uniform Residential Loan Application
26-1814	Batch Transmittal – Loan Code Sheet
26-1817	Request For Determination Of Loan Guaranty Eligibility – Unremarried Surviving Spouses
26-1820	Report And Certification Of Loan Disbursement
26-1839	Compliance Inspection Report
26-1847	Request For Postponement Of Offsite Or Exterior Onsite Improvements – Home Loan
26-1852	Description Of Materials
26-1880	Request For A Certificate Of Eligibility For VA Home Loan Benefits
26-6382	Statement Of Purchaser Or Owner Assuming Seller's Loan
26-6393	Loan Analysis
26-6684	Statement Of Fee Appraisers Or Compliance Inspectors
26-6705	Offer To Purchase And Contract Of Sale
26-6705b	Credit Statement Of Prospective Purchaser
26-6807	Financial Statement
26-8630	Manufactured Home Loan Claim Under Loan Guaranty
26-8712	Manufactured Home Appraisal Report
26-8736a	Non-Supervised Lender's Nomination And Recommendation Of Credit Underwriter
26-8791	VA Affirmative Marketing Certification
26-8812	VA Equal Opportunity Lender Certification
26-8937	Verification Of VA Benefit-Related Indebtedness

★★

Vocational Rehabilitation and Employment Forms

Form #	Purpose
28-1900	Disabled Veterans Application For Vocational Rehabilitation
28-1902	Counseling Record – Personal Information
28-1902n	Counseling Record – Narrative Report
28-8872	Rehabilitation Plan
28-8872a	Rehabilitation Plan – Continuation Sheet
28-8890	Important Information About Rehabilitation

VA Insurance Forms

Form #	Purpose
29-336	Designation Of Beneficiary – Government Life Insurance
29-1546	Application For Cash Surrender Value / Application For Policy Loan
29-4125	Claim For One Sum Payment
29-4364	Application For Service-Disabled Insurance

Finance and Budget Forms

Form #	Purpose
24-0296	Direct Deposit Enrollment
24-5281	Application For Refund Of Education Contributions - VEAP

Miscellaneous Forms

Form #	Purpose
DD 149	Application For Correction Of Military Record
DD 214	Report of Separation From Active Duty
DD 293	Application For The Review Of Discharge OR Dismissal From The Armed Forces Of The United States
SF 15	Application For 10-Point Veteran's Preference
SF 180	Request Pertaining To Military Records
SGLV8283	Claim For Death Benefits – Form Returned To Office Of Servicemembers' Group Life Insurance
SGLV8285	Request For Insurance (Servicemembers' Group Life Insurance)
SGLV8286	Servicemembers' Group Life Insurance Election And Certificate
SGLV8714	Application For Veterans' Group Life Insurance
SGLF8721	Beneficiary Designation for Veterans Group Life Insurance
VAF 8	Certification To Appeal
VAF 9	Appeal To Board Of Veterans' Appeals
VAF 10 – 10ez	Instructions For Completing Application For Health Benefits
VAF 3288	Request For And Consent To Release Of Information From Claimant's Records
VAF 4107	Notice Of Procedural And Appellate Rights
VAF 4107b	Notice Of Procedural And Appellate Rights (Spanish Version)
40-1330	Application For Standard Government Headstone Or Marker For Installation In A Private Or State Veterans' Cemetery

★★

CHAPTER 54

IMPORTANT PHONE NUMBERS

GENERAL BENEFITS

Disability, Compensation, Pension, Education & Training, Vocational Rehabilitation, Home Loans	1-800-827-1000
Burial, Headstones & Markers	1-800-697-6947
Life Insurance	1-800-669-8477
Education Programs	1-888-GI-BILL

HEALTHCARE BENEFITS

Veterans Healthcare	1-800-827-1000
Veterans Healthcare in Canada	1-800-296-6379
Veterans Healthcare in Philippines	011-632-833-4566
Veterans Healthcare in all other Countries	1-303-331-7590
National Mammography Helpline	1-888-492-7844
CHAMPVA	1-800-733-8387
Spina Bifida	1-800-827-1000
Emergency Medical Preparedness	1-304-263-0811

MISCELLANEOUS BENEFITS

Debt Management Center	1-800-827-0648
Persian Gulf Hotline	1-800-PGW-VETS
Telecommunication Device for the Deaf (TDD)	1-800-829-4833
Persian Gulf TDD	1-800-829-4833
Sexual Trauma Hotline	1-800-827-1000
Income Verification Center	1-800-949-1008 or 404-235-1300

VAONLINE Bulletin Board Service – via data line 1-800-US1-VETS up to 28.8KBPS at 8-N-1 modem setting

★★

INDEX

A

B

C

D

E

F

G

★★

H

I

J

K

★★★

L

M

N

★★★

O

P

R

S

★★★

T

★★★

U

V

★★

W

★★★

Would You Like Additional Copies Of
"What Every Veteran Should Know"?

Simply tear out this form, and:

Phone or Fax Orders: 309-757-7760

Mail To: VETERANS INFORMATION SERVICE
P.O. Box 111
East Moline, IL 61244-0111

☐ Yes! Send me _____ copies of *"What Every Veteran Should Know"*, at $15.00 each (shipping & handling included).

☐ Yes! I would like to subscribe to *"What Every Veteran Should Know"* monthly supplement (an 8-page newsletter which keeps your book up-to-date), and receive _____ copies of all 12 monthly issues (1 year) for $27.00 per subscription (shipping & handling included).

☐ Yes! I want to save money, and receive both the book and the monthly supplement. I would like _____ sets, at $40 per set (shipping & handling included).

Name

Address

City / State / Zip Code

Telephone Number   E-mail Address

Amount Enclosed   Daytime Phone # (including area code)

Method of Payment:

☐ Check   ☐ Visa   ☐ MasterCard   ☐ Money Order

Credit Card #   Expiration Date (Month/Year)

Signature

Thank you for your order!
If you have any questions, contact us at:
(309) 757-7760
Email: vis111@home.com

Would You Like Additional Copies Of
"What Every Veteran Should Know"?

Simply tear out this form, and:

Phone or Fax Orders: 309-757-7760

Mail To: VETERANS INFORMATION SERVICE
P.O. Box 111
East Moline, IL 61244-0111

☐ Yes! Send me _____ copies of *"What Every Veteran Should Know"*, at $15.00 each (shipping & handling included).

☐ Yes! I would like to subscribe to *"What Every Veteran Should Know"* monthly supplement (an 8-page newsletter which keeps your book up-to-date), and receive _____ copies of all 12 monthly issues (1 year) for $27.00 per subscription (shipping & handling included).

☐ Yes! I want to save money, and receive both the book and the monthly supplement. I would like _____ sets, at $40 per set (shipping & handling included).

Name

Address

City / State / Zip Code

Telephone Number   E-mail Address

Amount Enclosed   Daytime Phone # (including area code)

Method of Payment:

☐ Check   ☐ Visa   ☐ MasterCard   ☐ Money Order

Credit Card #   Expiration Date (Month/Year)

Signature

Thank you for your order!
If you have any questions, contact us at:
(309) 757-7760
Email: vis111@home.com

**Would You Like Additional Copies Of
"What Every Veteran Should Know"?**

Simply tear out this form, and:

Phone or Fax Orders: 309-757-7760

**Mail To: VETERANS INFORMATION SERVICE
P.O. Box 111
East Moline, IL 61244-0111**

☐ Yes! Send me _____ copies of "What Every Veteran Should Know", at $15.00 each (shipping & handling included).

☐ Yes! I would like to subscribe to "What Every Veteran Should Know" monthly supplement (an 8-page newsletter which keeps your book up-to-date), and receive _____ copies of all 12 monthly issues (1 year) for $27.00 per subscription (shipping & handling included).

☐ Yes! I want to save money, and receive both the book and the monthly supplement. I would like _____ sets, at $40 per set (shipping & handling included).

Name

Address

City / State / Zip Code

Telephone Number   E-mail Address

Amount Enclosed   Daytime Phone # (including area code)

Method of Payment:

☐ Check   ☐ Visa   ☐ MasterCard   ☐ Money Order

Credit Card #   Expiration Date (Month/Year)

Signature

**Thank you for your order!
If you have any questions, contact us at:
(309) 757-7760
Email: vis111@home.com**

Would You Like Additional Copies Of
"What Every Veteran Should Know"?

Simply tear out this form, and:

Phone or Fax Orders: 309-757-7760

Mail To: VETERANS INFORMATION SERVICE
P.O. Box 111
East Moline, IL 61244-0111

☐ Yes! Send me _____ copies of *"What Every Veteran Should Know"*, at $15.00 each (shipping & handling included).

☐ Yes! I would like to subscribe to *"What Every Veteran Should Know"* monthly supplement (an 8-page newsletter which keeps your book up-to-date), and receive _____ copies of all 12 monthly issues (1 year) for $27.00 per subscription (shipping & handling included).

☐ Yes! I want to save money, and receive both the book and the monthly supplement. I would like _____ sets, at $40 per set (shipping & handling included).

_____

Name

_____

Address

_____

City / State / Zip Code

_____

Telephone Number   E-mail Address

_____

Amount Enclosed   Daytime Phone # (including area code)

Method of Payment:

☐ Check   ☐ Visa   ☐ MasterCard   ☐ Money Order

_____

Credit Card #   Expiration Date (Month/Year)

_____

Signature

Thank you for your order!
If you have any questions, contact us at:
(309) 757-7760
Email: vis111@home.com